The Old Farmer's Almanac

CALCULATED ON A NEW AND IMPROVED PLAN FOR THE YEAR OF OUR LORD

2014

BEING 2ND AFTER LEAP YEAR AND (UNTIL JULY 4) 238TH YEAR OF AMERICAN INDEPENDENCE

Fitted for Boston and the New England states, with special corrections and calculations to answer for all the United States.

Containing, besides the large number of Astronomical Calculations and the Farmer's Calendar for every month in the year, a variety of

NEW, USEFUL, & ENTERTAINING MATTER.

Established in 1792 by Robert B. Thomas (1766–1846)

Each day the world is born anew
For him who takes it rightly.

–James Russell Lowell, American poet (1819–91)

Cover T.M. registered in U.S. Patent Office

Copyright © 2013 by Yankee Publishing Incorporated
ISSN 0078-4516

Library of Congress Card No. 56-29681

Original wood engraving by Randy Miller

THE OLD FARMER'S ALMANAC • DUBLIN, NH 03444 • 603-563-8111 • ALMANAC.COM

Outdoor Hands Skin Therapy Cream:

- Alleviates Cracked Skin Anywhere You Have It!
- Pharmacist Formulated
- Unique Blend of Botanical Extracts and Organic Oils
- Non-Greasy / Light Scent
- Helps Other Common Skin Problems Like Eczema and Psoriasis

Li'l Pucker's Lip Cream:

- Designed to Moisturize and Heal Cracked, Chapped and Dry Lips
- Contains Lanolin and Vitamin E
- Refreshing Mint Flavor

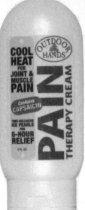

Also Available:
Fast-Acting Pain Therapy Cream
and
Gentle, Exfoliating Poison Ivy Scrub

Ask for Outdoor Hands at your local pharmacy, farm, hardware or garden store.
Or visit **www.outdoorhands.com**
to find a retailer near you.

Find us on Facebook

Contents

The Old Farmer's Almanac • 2014

(continued on page 6)

Contents

(continued from page 4)

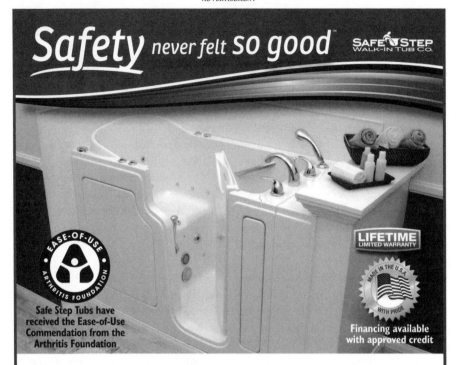

Once (a Year) Is Not Enough

An "almanac," according to *Merriam–Webster's Collegiate Dictionary,* is "a publication containing astronomical and meteorological data for a given year, and often including a miscellany of other information."

Certainly that describes this Almanac: Astronomical data? Absolutely. Meteorological data? Daily. For a given year? Precisely—and then some. Miscellany? More than most.

Indeed, we who labor to maintain this Almanac's place in our time and its purpose in modern life, as our predecessors did in their day, understand this genre's components and its span. Each year, we aim to execute and so meet (or, perchance, exceed) readers' expectations around the clock, in any weather, on any matter.

It was management's new idea, presented in a meeting last year, that we could not predict or, initially, fathom: a *monthly* Almanac. For an instant, time stopped. Then, as if on a ship in a storm, we, the editors, pitched and yawed against these winds of change, sensing to the depths of our beings that our anchor in tradition was irretrievably lost. (Dear reader, if you, too, are railing right now, we sympathize and urge restraint as you read on.)

Finally, sinking spirits paused to gasp for air. In that moment, management's second lightning bolt struck our masthead: "The *Almanac Monthly* will be an e-book—and unique in the genre."

As details were unfurled, color returned to ashen faces. This much-loved annual would continue in this print form, with Calendar Pages intact, weather forecasts in full, miscellany unmatched, and more pages than ever.

The *Almanac Monthly* contains timely, seasonal, typical Almanac articles in full color about astronomy and calendar events, gardening, outdoors, food and cooking, home and home remedies, history, how-to, and more, plus (a first!) weather forecast updates. What's more, the technology of the electronic magazine's "pages" allows reading matter to be enriched with audio recordings as well as how-to and other videos. (See for yourself at Almanac.com/Monthly.)

While with the *Almanac Monthly* we may be bending the definition of the genre, we are also setting the course for our future and continuing the legacy of our founder, Robert B. Thomas. Be assured, however, that our goal and obligation in all of our endeavors remains the same: to make Almanacs that you, our loyal users, find consistently and unfailingly "useful, with a pleasant degree of humor."

–J. S., June 2013

However, it is by our works and not our words that we would be judged. These, we hope, will sustain us in the humble though proud station we have so long held in the name of

Your obedient servant,

Robt. B. Thomas.

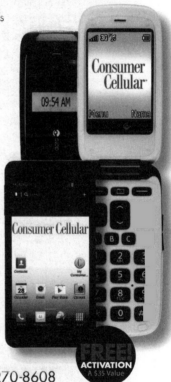

A GIFT FOR YOU

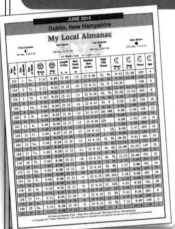

2014 Trends

On the Farm

Look for more of our cities and suburban areas to adopt codes that allow residents to keep chickens, goats, and other livestock more commonly found "down on the farm."

–Kirsten Conrad Buhls,
extension agent,
Fairlington Community Center,
Arlington, Virginia

NOW GROWING

■ **peacotum:** a reddish-yellow fruit that is part peach, apricot, and plum

■ **new varieties:** crispier romaine lettuce, sweeter seedless watermelons, milder onions, and antioxidant-rich broccoli

Managing invasive exotic plants, protecting streams from sediment runoff, and maintaining wildlife connectivity are providing benefits to the health of the land, livestock, and crops.

–Thomas Woltz, principal,
Nelson Byrd Woltz Landscape
Architects, New York City

■ **heirloom flours** of ancient grains: einkorn, sorghum, millet, and teff

■ **corn** that requires less water

■ **perennial grains,** making annual plowing unnecessary

■ **seaweed** on farms in the ocean, for use as food and biofuel

COMING SOON

■ **automated tractors** that operate without a person behind the wheel

■ **robots** with foam-padded hands that pick strawberries without bruising the fruit

■ **trucks** with cameras to locate oranges and hydraulic arms to knock the fruit loose from the trees

■ **small, helicopter-like drones** to fly over crops and transmit pictures that show farmers whether plants are healthy

URBAN UNDERTAKINGS

■ **vertical farms** in abandoned factories, with vegetables grown on small rafts floating on water, nourished by waste produced by fish (aka aquaponics).

Forecasts, facts, and trends that define our life and times

BY THE NUMBERS

$28 billion: cost of damage by wildlife to crops, landscaping, and infrastructure

63 percent: portion of acreage farmed using conservation tillage, which reduces erosion on cropland while using less energy

7,800+: number of U.S. farmers' markets (top three states: California, New York, Massachusetts)

600+: farmers' markets in Canada

$2 billion: spent annually at North American farmers' markets

In the Garden

People are using gardening to create a sense of neighborhood unity and as a social and recreational focal point. —*Kirsten Conrad Buhls*

BY THE NUMBERS

$1.6 billion: spent by gardeners on vegetable seeds, plants, fertilizer, and tools

■ **community orchards** kept year-round by members who get to harvest the fruit for themselves

■ **community vegetable gardens** on land occupied by apartment buildings, churches, fire stations, and businesses

RURAL RENAISSANCE

■ More and more **young people and fed-up employees** are leaving cities and suburbs to start farms.

■ **Farmers** are taking a more active role in managing the unculti-vated land surrounding their fields.

WE'RE PREOCCUPIED WITH POLLINATION

■ **Researchers are breeding roses with fragrance to restore strong aroma and ultimately the "scent trail" used by pollinating insects.**

■ **People are mounting beehives on windows and then watching the bees work, eventually harvesting the honey indoors through a connected opening.**

■ **Beehives are being added to gardens so that bees can pollinate flowers and people can harvest honey.**

—Gardenpix/SuperStock

Gardeners are coming to terms with how hardiness zones have shifted northward. . . . The palette of plants used by many will be altered toward adaptable, low-maintenance plants that can tolerate heat, drought, flooding, and unexpected freezes.

—Casey Sclar, executive director, American Public Gardens Association, Kennett Square, Pennsylvania

NATIVES WITH LOOKS TO LOVE

■ **'Standing Ovation'** bluestem grass that stays upright (doesn't flop over)

■ **'Prairie Moon'** rattlesnake master with steely-blue foliage that provides eye-catching accents to cut flower arrangements

■ **'Guava Ice'** coneflower, a fully double echinacea with thick stems

WE'RE MAKING ENDS MEET BY . . .

■ **pairing drought-tolerant plantings with found objects, e.g., a wall made of recycled bottles with native grasses**

■ **using soil-moisture sensors to reduce water use**

■ **allowing lawns to turn into meadows, mown once a year in late winter**

■ **using scythes to cut our lawns**

GOOD PLANTS IN SMALL PACKAGES

■ small-space blueberries such as **'Jelly Bean'** and **'Peach Sorbet'** *(right)*

—Fall Creek Farm

■ repeat-blooming **'Short and Sassy'** sneezeweed

■ compact **'Pardon My Pink'** bee balm and **'Rosita'** coneflower

■ **'Raspberry Shortcake'**, a thornless dwarf raspberry that produces sweet fruit in midsummer *(right)*

—Sonia Uyterhoeven, Gardener for Public Education, The New York Botanical Garden

—Fall Creek Farm

HOW WE'RE ADAPTING TO CLIMATE CHANGE

By region, we're planting more . . .

■ **Northeast:** flood-tolerant maples

■ **Southeast:** succulents, e.g., yucca, in a variety of showy colors and forms

■ **Midwest:** chokeberries, hollies, and maples

■ **West:** coyote mint, sedges, and soap weed

■ **Eastern Canada:** birches, pines, and spruces; pearly everlasting

■ **Western Canada:** piggyback plant and pines

Our Animal Friends

We will see more travel-related pet services, as pet-friendly hotels, pet frequent flyer points, and boarding and grooming facilities in airports become more prevalent.

–Laura Bennett, CEO, Embrace Pet Insurance

BY THE NUMBERS

90: minutes that pet owners spend in cleaning up after their dogs and cats each week

$43: amount spent by a dog owner on toys, on average, each year

PEOPLE ARE TALKING ABOUT . . .

■ owners of mixed-breed dogs getting a DNA test to learn what kind of ancestors the dog has

■ **spending more on veterinary care, especially wellness care and elective procedures,** as pet parents catch up on their pets' health

OUR FIT FURRY FRIENDS

■ Dogs are taking swimming classes, while owners watch through underwater viewing windows.

■ Pets are chasing or swatting at feeders that release morsels of food.

■ Cats earn treats for winning at play with puzzle toys.

Collectors' Corner

Collectors with money want the best of the best and are willing to pay for it. It doesn't appear that middle-class collectors have significant disposable income to invest beyond making token purchases.

–Leila Dunbar, appraiser, New York City

GOING ONCE, GOING TWICE, SOLD!

$4.4 million: price of a uniform worn by Babe Ruth

$357,000: cost of the Liberty Cap, a rare U.S. half-cent coin from 1796

$26,450: amount paid for a ridable 1892 American Telegram bicycle

MORE

2014 Trends

ITEMS ATTRACTING INTERE$T

■ technology "firsts," e.g., the first handheld calculator, the first personal computer

■ black-and-white and color snapshots of anonymous yet interesting subjects

■ Vietnam War–era combat knives

■ Space Race–era artifacts

■ early maps of China made in the West for tourists   —*Gary Piattoni, appraiser, Evanston, Illinois*

Health & Wellness

We will move from today's sick-care system to a true health care system that encourages wellness.

—Adam Perlman, M.D., M.P.H., associate vice president, Duke Health & Wellness, Durham, North Carolina

HAPPINESS RESEARCH RESULTS

■ People with a sense of purpose live longer than those who dwell on how happy they are.

■ Happier people earn more money than unhappy folks.

BY THE NUMBERS

75 percent: portion of health spending used to treat chronic diseases

45 million: number of people who start a diet each year

40 percent: portion of rural residents who are obese

33 percent: portion of urban residents who are obese

83 percent: portion of adults who say that they are "pretty happy" or "very happy"

PEOPLE ARE TALKING ABOUT . . .

■ getting DNA samples analyzed to prevent chronic conditions for which they are at risk

■ gym-goers choosing towels made from recycled coconut shells for fewer odor-causing bacteria

GOOD-HEALTH GADGETS

■ **vibrating forks** that tell us to eat more slowly

■ **bracelets** that track and measure our deep sleep

MORE

■ **alarms** that wake us during the lightest part of our sleep cycle

■ **tools** that diagnose our health problems using exhaled breath

■ **wristbands** that scold us when we sit still for too long

■ **microchip-size implantable devices** that dispense medications so that we don't need to remember to swallow them

The major trend for 2014 will be the increasing use of the smart phone as the hub for medicine and health. This is not DIY medicine, but one in which the consumer is truly empowered and creates a new partnership model with the physician, still needing the knowledge, empathy, communication, and experience of the doctor.

–*Dr. Eric Topol,*
chief academic officer,
Scripps Health, San Diego

Good Eats

Farmers are leading a revival of a range of products that recall another era. The return of small-batch whiskeys, relishes, pickles, and meats is meeting the public appetite for locally made products.

–Thomas Woltz

FLAVORS WE'RE CRAVING

■ **omelets** filled with fruit or dusted with powdered sugar

■ **pumpkin seed, cherry pit, or chile seed oils** drizzled on salads, meats, and ice cream

■ **beer-flavor jelly** spread over pancakes

■ **hard cider** produced in Virginia and New York

■ **whey supplements** made by organic dairies in Wisconsin

PEOPLE ARE TALKING ABOUT . . .

■ **home cooks re-creating lost family recipes, aided by vintage cookware and cookbooks from the era**

■ **metric devotees repro-gramming their ovens to display degrees in Celsius**

■ **eating Korean, Ethiopian, or other uncommon ethnic foods**

■ **chefs burning vegetables or hay and using the ash to flavor food**

COMING SOON

■ **natural compounds** that sweeten foods and drinks without added sugar

■ **grapefruit hybrids** that don't interact with medications

MORE

WE'RE BECOMING PICKY EATERS

■ **reading labels** and **selecting foods** based on taste, ingredients, and nutritional composition

■ **seeking snacks with low saturated fats,** such as gluten-free chips made from legumes (e.g., lentils and chickpeas) and fruit chips made from apple slices

■ **substituting** nuts, seeds, legumes, eggs, and tofu for meat-based protein

Around the House

The line between utility and beauty will blur further, as we continue to demand good design from even the most workaday items like mops and trash cans.

–Sarah Gray Miller, editor in chief, Country Living

> Anything that combines homespun and high-tech motifs will be big.
> *–Sarah Gray Miller*

SOLUTIONS FOR SEVERE WEATHER

■ **foot-thick concrete walls wrapped in rubberized material to withstand strong winds**

■ **precast, patterned, concrete roofs that surround a layer of insulation to hold up during hurricanes**

BY THE NUMBERS

60 percent: portion of custom-built homes with two master bedrooms so that couples can sleep separately

150 sq. ft.: living space in microapartments with pop-up tables and pullout beds

■ **kitchens and living rooms on the second floor, in case of floods**

BRIGHT IDEAS

■ **lowering the capacity of circuit breakers** so that we use less electricity as we launder with washboards, clean with a broom, and cool with handheld fans

DIY DELIGHTS

■ **Homeowners are designing fabrics and wallpapers.**

■ **People will be using 3-D printers to create replacement parts for broken furnishings and kitchen hardware.**

■ **wind turbines** for the home

■ **concrete made with living, inactive bacterial spores** that become active when wet, converting the calcium of their nutrients into limestone to fill in any small cracks that form

■ **robot plant carriers** that water houseplants and move them to sunny spots

MORE

■ **houseplants that reduce dust particles and airborne contaminants**—peace lily, asparagus fern, weeping fig, English ivy—aided by electric fans to trap pollutants around plant roots

■ **aromatic firewood**—applewood, cherry, hickory, piñon pine, and white birch—mixed with cedar shavings, orange peel, or cinnamon sticks for even more fragrance

DECORATORS ARE USING . . .

■ **pixelated patterns** combined with floral cross-stitch

■ **several chandeliers** in a single room

■ **copper faucets and fixtures**

■ **muted greens** that are easy on eyes that spend hours on screens

Tech Talk

Adults will seek to balance . . . myriad organized and tech-based activities with more unstructured time and recreational pursuits, and inject play into everyday life.

–*Ann Mack, director of trendspotting, JWT, New York City*

WE'RE GETTING THERE . . .

■ on **hoverbikes** with fans that keep us up to 15 feet off the ground

■ in **amphibious sports cars** that avoid traffic jams at bridges and tunnels by driving across water

■ with **freight trucks** powered by overhead electric wires

Culture Cues

PEOPLE ARE TALKING ABOUT . . .

■ **retirees eliminating home ownership** to live at short-term rentals and travel

■ by pushing a button in a **driverless car**

With technology allowing for more people to work wherever they can get a good Internet connection, there will be more families, and singles, and retirees moving to places that are small, rural, even close-to-ghost towns.

–*Reba Kennedy, blog author, Everyday Simplicity, San Antonio, Texas*

■ **massage chairs with hidden wheels** that feel like human thumbs

IN PURSUIT OF SILLINESS, WE'LL SEE . . .

■ **grown-ups racing** on adult-size tricycles

■ "horseless horse" shows, with youngsters on foot "galloping" and jumping small fences

■ bikes with seating for more than a dozen pedaling passengers

MORE

Haunting Sounds , Magic Memories®

NORTH COUNTRY

WIND BELLS®

Wind bells playing the mystique of bell buoys and the sea! Perfect for gifts year round!

Call for free catalog!

(877) 930-5435
www.northcountrywindbells.com

LOG HOME Preservation Products
www.iwoodc.com

Log Home Care for All Seasons

- Log Cleaners
- Wood Strippers
- Sanding & Blasting Materials
- Mildewcide
- Insect Control Products
- Preservatives
- Log Repair/ Wood Fillers
- Caulk Guns & Equipment

- Paint Brushes
- Application Tools
- Fasteners & Log Gasket
- Exterior Stains
- Caulking & Chinking Products
- Interior Wood Finishes
- Bar Top & Hobby Coatings

We carry products by: Sashco • Sikkens • ABR-X100
• Continental-Weatherseal • Lifetime • And More!

sashco · **Conceal** · **LogJam**

Contact us at 1-800-721-7715
E: info@iwoodc.com • www.iwoodc.com

FREE:THE ESSIAC HANDBOOK

Learn about the Famous Ojibway Herbal Healing Remedy

Write for a Free Copy:
P.O. Box 1182
Crestone, CO 81131

Or Call Toll-Free:
1-888-568-3036

WE'RE MAKING HISTORY . . .

- **sending genealogical companies our DNA** to learn the migration paths of ancient ancestors and then connect with living relatives who share our DNA

- **digitizing old photographs** and handwritten letters to preserve them

- **becoming rare mileage collectors** by striving to ride as much of the U.S. rail system as possible

and even chartering special trains to traverse freight routes that are usually off-limits to passengers

- **paying to participate as a passenger or pilot** in acrobatic maneuvers performed in WWII airplanes

---

BY THE NUMBERS

2.6 weeks: median amount of vacation time earned by full-time U.S. workers

1 percent: portion of employers that offer unlimited paid vacation time

50 percent: portion of workers polled who take work to bed

60 percent: portion of home owners 60 and older who say that they have more possessions than they need

200,000: book titles self-published each year

MORE

Fitting Fashions

PEOPLE ARE TALKING ABOUT . . .

- shopping for clothing in boutiques located in repurposed bank vaults
- taking online classes to make a copy of favorite jeans at home
- jackets in fabric made by bacteria in a sugary tea solution, which is dried, cut, sewn, and dyed

> ### BY THE NUMBERS
> **$2 million:** how much Americans spend annually to stretch tight-fitting shoes

MENSWEAR

Men are realizing that they have to up their game in terms of personal style. Guys are now expected to look well put together, even in a casual setting.

–Mark-Evan Blackman, assistant professor of menswear at Fashion Institute of Technology, New York City

CLOTHES THAT MAKE THE MAN

- **wider, boxier coats** and sweaters

- **comfortable blazers** with lavish pants: slim-cut gray flannel trousers, finely crafted khakis, or designer denim jeans
- **black leather pullover shirts**
- **suede and silk baseball jackets**
- **luxury pants** made from fibers such as cashmere or wool

FORMAL WEAR

- pocket squares and bow ties
- shirts with sleeves in contrasting colors
- suede wing-tip shoes with colored soles

GARB THAT GETS A SECOND LOOK

- slim-fitting safari jackets
- cardigan sweaters with leather buttons
- galoshes in bright colors, with a lining that shines your shoes as you walk

> It will be a very tailored year. A sense of formality is in the air.
>
> *–Steven Faerm, director of fashion design, Parsons The New School for Design, New York City*

GUYS, YOUR COLORS . . .

- deep maroons and clarets
- midtone blue suits
- charcoal gray for evening, light gray for daytime, both with brown shoes

MORE

You know where you want to go...
...how are you going to get there?

THE TEARDROP ADVANTAGE
◇ Lightweight & Easy to Tow
◇ Minimal Effect on Gas Mileage
◇ Sleek, Aerodynamic & Practical
◇ Roomier than You Think
◇ Throwback to Simpler Times

www.golittleguy.com ◇ 1-877-545-4897

MARTIN METAL
YOUR SOURCE FOR QUALITY BUILDINGS & SUPPLIES
Working Hard for Your Success

Metal Roofing & Siding
Overhead Garage Doors
Walk-in Doors • Windows
Lumber Products
Wood Trusses
Complete Post & Stud
Frame Building Packages

Your One Stop Shop

Your 1-Stop Shop for any
Post, Stud, or Steel Frame
Building Project

New Truss Plant

Versailles, MO - Phone: (866) 378-4050
www.MartinMetalllc.com

Trust the Original.®
Natural Rodent Repellent
Protecting Farms & Families Since 1995

FRESH CAB
Botanical
RODENT REPELLENT
KEEP OUT OF REACH OF CHILDREN

FRESH CAB
Botanical
RODENT REPELLENT
KEEPS MICE OUT

NO POISONS • PET SAFE
100% GUARANTEED
EPA CERTIFIED • U.S. MADE
Learn more at Earth-Kind.com/ofa

THE LATEST FOR LADIES

The fashion-forward have turned to bright colors and complex, often clashing, print patterns—the more diverse in ethnic origin and style, the better.

–Brent Luvaas, author,
DIY Style

WHAT WOMEN WANT

■ **matching denim,** head to toes

■ **bright-color flats** that are part shoe, part boot

■ **longer hems** and tent dresses

■ **plain-white collared shirts,** worn fully buttoned

■ **knapsacks** that match clothing

■ prints depicting mountains and forests, in **rustic cotton fabrics**

GALS, YOUR COLORS . . .

■ green in every shade, from muted to kelly green to deep emerald

■ sandy and sun-bleached

■ whites with a slight "drop" of color in them

On ladies, we'll see stretchy, easy-to-wear fabrics and flat shoes.
–Sheila Dicks,
fashion expert, Nova Scotia

- -

Money Matters

We are entering the age of the Meaningful Economy. Families are looking to purchase goods and experiences based on [the product's or service's] ability to help us be better people.

–Daniel Levine, executive director,
Avant-Guide Institute, NYC

BY THE NUMBERS

$2.3 billion: amount spent on genealogy products and services

58 percent: portion of people who believe that it's okay to regift an item

PEOPLE ARE TALKING ABOUT . . .

■ summer camps, Web sites, schools, and other pre-K–to–high school services offering investment classes for children

■ apps that not only allow you to order in restaurants, but also compile your ordering history for future reference and reorders

■ hiring helpers online to do time-consuming personal errands, e.g., clean cars, bake cupcakes, wait in lines, wrap gifts

MORE

Thanks to BetterWOMAN, I'm winning the battle for
Bladder Control.

All Natural
Clinically-Tested
Herbal Supplement

- Reduces Bladder Leaks
- Reduces Urinary Frequency
- Safe and Effective –
  No Known Side Effects
- Costs Less than Traditional
  Bladder Control Options
- Sleep Better All Night
- **Live Free of Worry,
  Embarrassment, and
  Inconvenience**

You don't have to let
bladder control problems
control you.
Call now!

Frequent nighttime trips to the bathroom, embarrassing leaks and the inconvenience of constantly searching for rest rooms in public – for years, I struggled with bladder control problems. After trying expensive medications with horrible side effects, ineffective exercises and undignified pads and diapers, I was ready to resign myself to a life of bladder leaks, isolation and depression. But then I tried **BetterWOMAN**.

When I first saw the ad for BetterWOMAN, I was skeptical. So many products claim they can set you free from leaks, frequency and worry, only to deliver disappointment. When I finally tried BetterWOMAN, I found that it actually works! It changed my life. Even my friends have noticed that I'm a new person. And because it's all natural, I can enjoy the results without the worry of dangerous side effects. Thanks to BetterWOMAN, I finally fought bladder control problems and I won!

Also Available: **BetterMAN**®
The 3-in-1 Formula Every Man Needs –
Better **BLADDER**, Better **PROSTATE**, and Better **STAMINA!**
Order online at www.BetterMANnow.com.

Limited Time Offer

Call Now & Ask How To Get A
FREE BONUS BOTTLE
CALL TOLL-FREE 1-888-812-3286
or order online: www.BetterWOMANnow.com

These statements have not been evaluated by the FDA. This product is not intended to diagnose, treat, cure or prevent any disease.
Use as directed. Individual results may vary.
BetterMAN and BetterWOMAN are the trademarks of Interceuticals, Inc. ©2012 Interceuticals, Inc.

> More consumers will opt to do without paid TV and cobble together their content from a variety of sources.
>
> *–Kelli B. Grant, senior consumer reporter, MarketWatch*

WE'RE MAKING ENDS MEET BY . . .

■ **using small spatulas** to scoop beauty products from the bottom of their containers and tube flatteners to squeeze out every bit of toothpaste

■ **buying subscriptions to electronic editions** of magazines because "e" is cheaper than paper

Words for the Wise: THE SHARE ECONOMY

We're sharing, renting, and borrowing tools, cars, sports gear, musical instruments, wedding gowns, home electronics, and more to reduce personal expense and responsibility.

Home cooks are serving relatively inexpensive meals in their kitchens to strangers that they connect with online, all for a small fee and help in washing dishes.

□□

Stacey Kusterbeck, a frequent contributor to *The Old Farmer's Almanac,* writes about popular culture from New York State.

ATHENA PHEROM♥NES™ INCREASE AFFECTION YOU GET FROM OTHERS

Dr. Winnifred Cutler co-discovered human pheromones in 1986
(TIME 12/1/86; NEWSWEEK 1/12/87)

Add to your fragrance. These odorless additives contain synthesized human pheromones. A vial of 1/6 oz., added to 2 to 4 ounces of fragrance, **should be a 4 to 6 months supply,** or use straight. Athena Pheromones increase your attractiveness.

unscented

♥ **Cynthia (MN)** "I never told my husband I bought the Athena pheromones. **And they really DO work! I put it on 3 days in a row and his whole behavior toward me changed.** My girlfriend watched him around me and said it was amazing how well 10:13 worked. It worked exactly like that tv show where they tested the Athena products in a bar how it attracted the opposite sex."

♥ **Robert (FL)** 4th order "My wife had been uninterested in our marriage and I did not know what else to do. **I was trying everything I could and then I decided to try the Athena Pheromones. I was skeptical. But It's all reversed now. She's now all over me.** I am not interested in anyone else. Although it is working everywhere. We had been having a lot of problems. **Those problems are gone. I am very happy with my 10X. You are creating a great benefit, helping my marriage."**

Not in stores. Not guaranteed to work for <u>everyone</u>; will work for <u>most.</u> Not aphrodisiacs.

To order, call: (610) 827-2200   click: athenainstitute.com
Or mail to: **Athena Institute, Dept FA, 1211 Braefield Rd., Chester Spgs, PA 19425**

PLEASE SEND ME_____ 10:13 VIALS @ US$98.50 and/or _____ 10X Vials @ US$99.50
and___ empty blue bottle (2oz screw cap) @$5.00   for a *total price of US$_____
Enclosed is a ❏ USCheck ❏ Money Order payable to "Athena Institute"
Charge my ❏ Visa/MC/Disc# _____-_____-_____-_____ Exp_____CVV:_____
Name_____ Phone: (   ) _____-_____
Address_____ City/State_____ Zip _____
email _____ Signature:_____
  *PA add 6% tax. Canada add US $10 shipping surcharge per vial Other countries call.   FA

ATHENA PHEROM♥NES: The Gold Standard since 1993™

–finished food photography, Becky Luigart-Stayner; food styling, Ana Kelly; prop styling, Jan Gautro

A Life of PIE

Celebrate the ultimate one-pot dish.

BY KEN HAEDRICH

(recipes begin on next page)

S ome people could eat pie morning, noon, and night: meat pies, sweet pies, "kitchen sink" pies—any dish with a melt-in-the-mouth crust and a satisfying filling.

As "dean" of **ThePieAcademy .com** and a lifelong pie baker with more than 600 pie recipes under my belt (so to speak!), I'm passionate about pies. Naming my favorite pie is next to impossible. Choosing a pie-day menu—a pie recipe for every meal on **National Pie Day, January 23, 2014**—is no easy task either, but here is mine:

BREAKFAST
──────────
Mexican-Style Quiche

LUNCH
─────
Chicken or Turkey Potpie, or Maryland Crab Potpie

DINNER
──────
Meat Pie, My Way

DESSERT
───────
Chocolate Chess Pie
(because chocolate is good for you)

All of these use my Dad's Pie Pastry. Go to **Almanac.com/ Cooking** for other crust recipes or use your favorite packaged crust.

Of course, you don't have to wait for January 23 to make any of these pies. Any day is a good day for pie!

Eat enough piecrust and it will make you wise.
                                    –proverb

DAD'S PIE PASTRY
Double for a double-crust pie.

1½ cups all-purpose flour
1 tablespoon sugar (reduce to 1 teaspoon or eliminate for savory pies)
½ teaspoon salt
¼ cup (½ stick) cold, unsalted butter, cut into ¼-inch pieces
¼ cup (¼ stick) cold vegetable shortening, in about 8 pieces
¼ cup ice-cold water

To make the pastry with a food processor: Combine the flour, sugar, and salt in a food processor. Pulse several times to mix. Scatter the butter over the dry mixture. Pulse three or four times.

Scatter the shortening over the mixture. Pulse four or five times, until all of the fat is broken into small pieces. Sprinkle the water evenly over the mixture. Pulse again, in very short bursts, just until the dough forms clumpy little crumbs.

To make the pastry by hand: Mix the flour, sugar, and salt in a large bowl. Add the butter and cut it into the dry ingredients with a pastry blender until the butter forms pea-size pieces. Add the shortening and continue to cut, until the mixture resembles coarse crumbs and the butter is in very small pieces. Sprinkle the water over the mixture and mix quickly with a fork until the dough starts to form.

To make the pie shell: Dump the crumbs onto your counter or into a large bowl. Pack the dough together as you would a snowball, but don't overdo it. Place the ball on a piece of plastic wrap. Flatten into a ¾-inch-thick disk. Wrap tightly in the plastic and refrigerate for 1½ to 2 hours before rolling. Roll out your dough on a piece of wax paper sprinkled with flour to about 13 inches in diameter. Pick up the wax paper and invert it over the pie plate. Starting at one of the edges, gently peel the paper away from the dough. Carefully tuck the dough down into the plate. Trim the overhanging dough to about 1 inch wide. Then, pinch the dough back and under to form an upstanding rim. **Makes enough dough for a 9½-inch deep-dish pie shell.**

How to Partially Prebake Dad's Pie Shell

Place the pie shell in the freezer for 15 to 20 minutes to firm, and preheat the oven to 400°F. When the pie shell is firm, tear off a 16-inch-long sheet of aluminum foil and press it into the shell so that it fits like a glove; you should be able to clearly make out the crease where the pan bottom meets the side.

To prevent the crust from puffing up during baking, fill the foil-lined pie shell three-quarters full with dried beans, banking them up the side so that they push against the entire crust. Gently fold the edge of the foil over the rim of the dough. Don't flatten it against the dough rim; just bend it down a little to deflect heat away from the edge of the pastry. The beans can be exposed to the heat of the oven.

Bake on the center oven rack for 15 minutes. Lower the heat to 350°F. Remove the pie shell from the oven, loosen the foil at the rim, and lift out the foil and beans. (Save these beans. I've been using the same ones for my pies for years.) With a fork, prick the bottom of the crust six or seven times, here and there, twisting the fork slightly as you do to enlarge the holes a little. The holes will prevent the crust from "ballooning" off the bottom of the pan. Return the pie shell to the oven and bake for 10 more minutes. Look for light golden browning. Cool on a rack.

Always plug the holes you made with the fork so that none of the filling leaks under the crust and causes trouble during baking. Dab a bit of cream cheese in each hole, as though you're filling a tiny nail hole in the wall. If you're making the quiche, cover the holes instead with shavings of cheese as soon as the shell comes out of the oven; the cheese melts over the holes.

(continued)

35

breakfast

Mexican-Style Quiche

FILLING:

4 slices bacon
1 medium onion, thinly sliced
1 small green pepper, thinly sliced
1 teaspoon mild chili powder
½ cup salsa
2 cups diced new potatoes (peeled, if desired), cooked until just tender
3 large eggs
1 cup light cream or half-and-half
1 teaspoon dried oregano
¼ teaspoon salt
1½ cups grated pepper jack or sharp cheddar cheese, divided

For crust: Prepare Dad's Pie Pastry as directed and partially prebake *(see page 34).* Cool before filling.

For filling: Preheat the oven to 375°F. Crisp-cook the bacon in a skillet. Transfer the bacon to a paper towel–lined plate. Discard all but about 2 tablespoons of bacon fat from the pan. Add the onion and pepper and sauté over medium heat for about 8 minutes, until the vegetables are soft. Stir in the chili powder and continuously stir for 30 seconds. Add the salsa and potatoes. Stir until evenly mixed, then remove from the heat and set aside.

In a bowl, whisk the eggs, light cream, oregano, and salt. Set aside. Spread the vegetables evenly in the pie shell. Sprinkle with half of the cheese, then the bacon, crumbling it with your fingers. Pour the egg mixture on top. Sprinkle with the remaining cheese.

Bake on the center oven rack for about 40 minutes, until the custard is set and the top is golden brown. Transfer the quiche to a rack to cool. **Makes 8 or more servings.**

(continued)

Chicken or Turkey Potpie

Use any combination of cooked vegetables or fowl that you have.

FILLING:

**4 tablespoons (½ stick) unsalted butter,
plus more for buttering the baking dish**
1 medium onion, chopped
2 stalks celery, chopped
5 tablespoons all-purpose flour
1¼ cups chicken or turkey stock
1¼ cups milk, half-and-half, or light cream
1 teaspoon crumbled or powdered sage
¾ teaspoon dried thyme
salt and freshly ground pepper, to taste
**2 to 2½ cups diced, cooked chicken or
turkey**
**2½ cups (total) cooked corn, green beans,
peas, and/or other vegetables**

For crust: Prepare Dad's Pie Pastry as directed on page 34. (Do not prebake it.)

For filling: Butter a 2-quart casserole. Melt the 4 tablespoons of butter in a large sauté pan over moderate heat. Stir in the onion and celery. Cover and sweat the vegetables for about 8 minutes, stirring occasionally. Stir in the flour. Increase the heat and cook for 1 minute, stirring. Add the stock, whisking well. As the mixture starts to thicken, whisk in the milk, sage, thyme, salt, and pepper. Add the chicken or turkey. Continue to heat for 5 minutes, stirring. Taste and adjust seasonings, if necessary. Add the cooked vegetables. Remove from the heat. Transfer the filling to the casserole. Set aside for 15 minutes.

Preheat the oven to 400°F. As the oven heats, roll the dough on a sheet of lightly floured wax paper to a size that is slightly larger than the casserole. Invert the dough over the filling and peel off the paper. Tuck the edge of the dough down the sides of the casserole. Make several steam vents in the dough with a paring knife. Bake on the center oven rack for 35 to 40 minutes, until bubbly and golden brown. (If the filling sits high in the casserole, before baking, put the casserole on an aluminum foil–lined baking sheet to catch spillovers.) **Makes 6 servings.**

Maryland Crab Potpie

If you wish, substitute shrimp or scallops for some of the crab in the filling. This recipe makes five single portions but can easily be made as one large pie.

FILLING:

1 cup peeled, finely diced new potatoes
1 cup fresh cut or frozen corn kernels
**4 tablespoons (½ stick) unsalted butter,
divided, plus more for buttering the
baking dishes**
1 cup finely chopped onion
1 cup finely chopped celery
½ cup finely chopped green bell pepper
¼ cup all-purpose flour
**2¼ teaspoons Old Bay or other seafood
seasoning**
2 bottles (8 ounces each) clam juice

(continued)

⅓ cup light cream or half-and-half
12 to 16 ounces crabmeat
salt and freshly ground pepper, to taste

For crust: Prepare Dad's Pie Pastry on page 34. To make five individual servings, turn the dough out onto your counter when it starts to form large, clumpy crumbs and shape it into five equal-size balls. On a floured surface, flatten the balls into disks about ½-inch thick. Wrap the disks individually in plastic wrap and refrigerate for 45 to 60 minutes.

For filling: Combine the diced potatoes and corn in a saucepan and add enough water to cover, lightly salt, and bring to a boil. Simmer for 5 to 6 minutes, until the potatoes are barely tender. Drain and set aside.

Melt 2 tablespoons of butter in a saucepan. Add the onion, celery, and green pepper. Sauté gently for about 8 minutes, stirring often. Add the remaining 2 tablespoons of butter, let it melt, then stir in the flour and Old Bay seasoning. Cook over medium heat, stirring, for 1 minute. Add the clam juice and light cream. Continue to cook over medium heat, stirring, for 5 to 7 minutes, until it is somewhat thick. Add the crab and reserved vegetables. Heat for 2 to 3 minutes, stirring. Season with salt and pepper, to taste. Set aside to cool.

Preheat the oven to 400°F. Butter five small baking dishes, such as gratin dishes or pie plates. Divide the filling evenly into them; do not fill to the top. Place the dishes on a large, foil-lined baking sheet. Working with one portion at a time on a lightly floured sheet of wax paper, roll

the dough until it is about ½-inch larger than the dish. Invert the dough over the filling and peel off the paper. Tuck the edge of the dough down the sides of the dish. Cut several steam vents into the dough with a paring knife. Repeat for the remaining potpies.

Bake, on the baking sheet, for 20 minutes. Reduce the heat to 375°F and bake for 20 minutes more, until the pastry is golden brown and pies are bubbly. Cool the pies on a rack for 10 to 15 minutes before serving. **Makes 5 servings.**

(continued)

2014

Meat Pie, My Way

dinner

FILLING:

- 1 tablespoon unsalted butter
- 1 cup finely chopped onion
- 2 stalks celery, finely chopped
- 2 cloves garlic, minced
- 1½ pounds ground pork or ¾ pound each ground pork and ground beef
- 1 cup chicken stock
- 1 large baking potato, peeled and cut into ¼-inch dice
- ¾ cup finely diced carrots
- ¾ teaspoon salt
- ½ teaspoon dried thyme
- ½ teaspoon cinnamon
- ¼ teaspoon ground cloves
- ¼ teaspoon black pepper
- 2 tablespoons chili sauce
- 1½ teaspoons Worcestershire sauce
- 1 egg yolk beaten with 1 tablespoon water, for glaze

For crust: Prepare a double batch of Dad's Pie Pastry on page 34. Roll one portion of the dough into a 13-inch circle and line a 9½-inch deep-dish pie pan with it, letting the excess dough drape over the edge of the pan. Refrigerate it and the other batch of dough.

For filling: Melt the butter in a Dutch oven over medium heat. Add the onion and celery and sauté, stirring, for 5 minutes. Add the garlic and meat. Brown the meat, stirring often. Spoon off some of the fat, then add the chicken stock, potato, carrots, salt, thyme, cinnamon, cloves, and pepper. Bring the mixture to a simmer, cover, and simmer for 10 minutes. Uncover and simmer until most of the liquid evaporates, about 20 to 30 minutes. Stir in the chili sauce and Worcestershire sauce. When the meat mixture is slightly thick, remove from the heat.

Preheat the oven to 400°F. Spoon the filling into the refrigerated pie shell. On a sheet of floured wax paper, roll the remaining dough into an 11-inch circle. Moisten the rim of the pie shell, then invert it over the pie. Center it and peel off the wax paper. Press the dough edges together to seal. Using a paring knife, trim the edge of the dough flush with the side of the pan. Crimp the edge with a fork. Brush the top of the pie with the egg glaze, then make several steam vents in the top with the knife. Bake on the center oven rack for 20 minutes, then reduce the temperature to 375°F and bake for 30 minutes more. Transfer the pie to a rack and cool for about 15 minutes before slicing and serving. **Makes 10 servings.**

(continued)

dessert

Chocolate Chess Pie

Why is it called "chess" pie? One story explains that a Southern gentleman came home one evening and asked his wife, an accomplished yet modest cook, what smelled so good. "It's jes' pie," she replied.

FILLING:

- ½ cup (1 stick) unsalted butter, coarsely chopped
- 4 ounces bittersweet chocolate, coarsely chopped
- 1¼ cups sugar
- 1 tablespoon fine cornmeal
- ¼ teaspoon salt
- 1 teaspoon instant coffee granules
- 3 large eggs plus 1 egg yolk, at room temperature
- ¼ cup milk
- 1½ teaspoons vanilla extract or
  1¼ teaspoons vanilla extract plus
  ¼ teaspoon almond extract

For crust: Prepare Dad's Pie Pastry as directed and partially prebake *(see page 34)*. Cool before filling.

For filling: Preheat the oven to 350°F. Put the butter into the top of a double boiler over not-quite-simmering water. Add the chocolate. When it is melted, whisk to smooth. Remove the pan insert from the heat and set aside. Mix the sugar, cornmeal, salt, and instant coffee in a large bowl. Add the eggs and yolk, milk, and vanilla. Whisk to blend. Add the chocolate and whisk until smooth. Pour the filling into the pie shell.

Bake on the center oven rack for about 50 minutes. When done, the pie will puff up like a squat top hat. Cool on a rack for at least 1 hour before slicing

and serving. Serve warm, chilled, or at room temperature. Refrigerate, if not serving within a couple of hours. **Makes 8 servings.**

□□

Ken Haedrich is the author of many cookbooks (most recently, of *The Old Farmer's Almanac Everyday Baking*) and "dean" of ThePieAcademy.com.

WINNERS

in the 2013 Beet Recipe Contest

We were deliciously amazed at all of the different ways that Almanac readers cook beets—and hope that you are, too!

FIRST PRIZE: $250

Beets and Potatoes Au Gratin

2 cups half-and-half

2 cloves garlic, minced

1 teaspoon salt

½ teaspoon freshly ground black pepper

½ teaspoon dried thyme

½ teaspoon dried oregano

1 pinch nutmeg

3 medium potatoes

3 medium red beets

1½ cups grated mozzarella cheese

1 cup grated Parmesan cheese

1 egg

In a small saucepan, bring the half-and-half to a simmer. Add the garlic, salt, pepper, thyme, oregano, and nutmeg, then set the pan aside to cool. Generously butter a 1½-quart round casserole and preheat the oven to 375°F. Wash and peel the potatoes and beets. Slice them into ⅛-inch-thick rounds. Arrange the potatoes in one layer, in the bottom of the casserole. Combine the cheeses and sprinkle ⅓ cup over the potatoes. Add a layer of beets, overlapping as needed, and sprinkle with another ⅓ cup of cheese. Alternate the layers of potatoes and beets, with ⅓ cup of cheese between each, until they reach the rim of the casserole. Press the layers down to compact them and top with the remaining cheese. When the half-and-half mixture has reached room temperature, add the egg, whisking vigorously, and pour the mixture over the potatoes and beets. Cover the casserole loosely with foil and set it on a large baking sheet. Bake for 1 hour, or until the vegetables feel tender when pierced. Remove the foil and turn the oven to broil. Broil for 3 to 5 minutes, or until the cheese is lightly browned. Remove from the oven and let stand for 15 to 20 minutes. Cut into wedges and serve. **Makes 8 servings.**

–Brandi Morang, Seattle, Washington

–Aimee Seavey

(continued)

Raspberry Roasted Beets and Chèvre Over Shallot, Walnut, and Beet Greens Couscous

- 10 baby beets, multicolor if available, with 4 cups greens
- ¾ cup raspberry walnut vinaigrette dressing, divided
- ½ teaspoon freshly ground black pepper, divided
- ⅓ cup roughly chopped walnuts
- 3 tablespoons walnut oil or light olive oil, divided
- ¾ cup thinly sliced shallot or mild onion
- ½ teaspoon kosher salt
- 4 cups couscous (prepared according to package directions, preferably using chicken broth)
- ½ cup goat cheese (chèvre), herbed if available, crumbled
- 2 tablespoons lightly chopped fresh tarragon leaves (optional)

Remove the greens from the beet roots. Wash and peel the beet roots. Wash, then roughly chop the greens. Slice the beet roots lengthwise. In a shallow ovenproof dish, toss the beet roots with ½ cup of dressing; allow to marinate for at least 30 minutes; if longer—up to overnight—refrigerate. Preheat the oven to 350°F. Drain the beet roots, discarding the marinade; season them with half of the pepper, and roast on the center rack for 45 minutes, or until tender. In a large, nonstick pan over medium heat, toast the nuts for about 5 minutes, shaking the pan to prevent burning. Remove the nuts from the pan and set them aside to cool. Return the pan to the heat, warm 2 tablespoons of oil, and then add the shallots and sauté until they begin to caramelize. Add the beet greens and cook for another 3 minutes, or until tender. Add the remaining oil, the salt, the remaining pepper, and the cooked couscous. Stir to blend and heat through. Remove from the heat. Serve the couscous mixture topped with roasted beets, crumbled cheese, and nuts. Drizzle with the remaining dressing and scatter tarragon on top, if using. **Makes 4 servings.**

—Susan Scarborough, Fernandina Beach, Florida

(continued)

Sweet Cherry Tomato and Beet Crostini

1 cup finely chopped cherry tomatoes

½ cup coarsely chopped beet greens

¼ cup golden raisins

2 tablespoons finely chopped shallot

4 teaspoons olive oil, divided

1 teaspoon balsamic vinegar

¼ teaspoon sea salt

¼ teaspoon freshly ground black pepper

¼ cup crumbled feta cheese

½ cup finely chopped cooked beets

½ cup ricotta cheese

¾ teaspoon finely grated lemon zest

32 slices baguette bread, cut ¼-inch thick

2 tablespoons finely chopped fresh basil

In a medium bowl, stir together the tomatoes, beet greens, raisins, shallot, 1 teaspoon of olive oil, vinegar, sea salt, and pepper until well combined. Stir in the feta and beets until just combined, then set aside. In a small bowl, stir together the ricotta and lemon zest until combined. Preheat the oven broiler on a low setting. Place the baguette slices on a large cookie sheet coated with nonstick cooking spray or parchment paper. Lightly brush the bread slices with the remaining 3 teaspoons of olive oil. Broil the bread for 1 to 2 minutes, or until golden brown. Evenly spread the ricotta mixture over the bread slices. Top with even amounts of the tomato–beet mixture. Evenly sprinkle basil over the bread slices and serve. **Makes 8 servings.**

–Emily Hobbs, Chicago, Illinois

–Lou Eastman

For More Unbeatable Beets

Go to **Almanac.com/RecipeContest** for other beet recipes submitted by readers and tested in our kitchens.

➡ **ENTER THE 2014 RECIPE CONTEST: CARROTS**

What is your favorite recipe using carrots? Enter it to win! The recipe must be yours, original, and unpublished. Amateur cooks only, please. See contest rules on page 229.

Beautiful to Look At, *Delicious* to Eat

Decorative vegetables can transform a landscape.

BY SHERYL NORMANDEAU

Are you among the rising number of homeowners who are replacing the front lawn with an edible vegetable garden? Whether you want to transform your yard into a productive plot or simply add edibles among your ornamentals in pots, consider these tasty and eye-pleasing plants.

BASIC GROUND RULES

→ Most edibles require at least 6 hours of sunlight per day.

→ Vegetables generally can not tolerate excessive heat. Plant different sizes and types of vegetables to help shade plants that might become heat-stressed, such as salad greens.

→ Be prepared to water your edible garden deeply and consistently. Most vegetables are not drought tolerant.

→ Most edible plants require well-drained garden soil amended with plenty of compost or well-rotted manure.

(continued)

Opposite: *The bright-pink stems of 'Pink Passion' chard add shape and dimension to a mixed planting of petunias, rudbeckia, and delphinium.*

Other edible charmers include 'Trionfo Violetto' pole bean (right, top), *the black and white blooms of fava beans* (right), *and lettuce varieties* (left) *such as red leaf lettuce that can be grown in containers or in a border.*

–top, W. Atlee Burpee & Co.; above, www.LoveAppleFarms.com; opposite, Elke Borkowski/GAP Photos

Take It Up a Notch

In floral or ornamental gardens, arborvitae and other evergreens add height and provide privacy. You can achieve that effect, or create a focal point, by going vertical with these vegetables.

'Trionfo Violetto' pole bean *(Phaseolus vulgaris)* climbs on a support to a height of 9 feet, with a spread of 18 inches. This variety has lavender flowers, purple-vein leaves, and 10-inch-long purple pods (which are best when harvested at 6 inches). Avoid fertilizers that are high in nitrogen; they will slow the setting of pods. Instead, use an inoculant that contains nitrogen-fixing bacteria. Pick pods regularly, to stimulate the production of more beans. Cook the beans before eating.

–Christa Brand/GAP Photos

Deep purple 'Redbor' kale sets off a border of miscanthus and verbena.

–Pam Steeley

Malabar spinach

'Red Express' cabbage

–Johnny's Selected Seeds

Fava (fah-vah) beans *(Vicia faba),* with showy white and black blooms, will reach a height of 5 feet. They tolerate most soil types, including saline, and are very cold hardy. Harvest fava beans when they are plump in their pods and cook before eating. Beans may also be dried on the stalks.

Malabar spinach *(Basella alba)* is not related to spinach, but its heart-shape, semisucculent leaves taste like Popeye's favorite veggie! Its vines will reach lengths of 8 to 10 feet and require support. (Try it beside or intertwined with pole beans.) This plant performs best in high heat and humidity and in sandy soil rich in organic matter. Prolonged cool weather (below 80°F) slows growth and lowers yields. Water regularly, or the plants will flower and the leaves will become bitter-tasting.

(continued)

Fill With Foliage

Quick-growing annual greens or lettuce can add character to a plain spot or line a border like annual flowers often do. Peruse a seed catalog for heading and

leafing lettuces, noting shapes, textures, and colors, and then choose a few. For example, 'Strela Green' lettuce has a distinct star shape while small; left to bolt, it can top out at about 4 feet in height and produce small yellow flowers. Compact heirloom cultivar 'Speckles' lives up to its name in red and green.

Mixed greens and herbs will add an interesting texture to a border garden.

Looseleaf and oakleaf lettuce tend to hold up best in the heat of summer. In very hot weather, many salad greens will bolt, or go to seed (not necessarily an unattractive stage). For best results, grow greens and lettuces in the shadow of larger plants, try bolt-resistant cultivars, or plant in spring and/or fall.

Packaged mesclun seed mixes may include lettuce, spinach, arugula, Swiss chard, mustard greens, mâche, and radicchio and produce a riot of vibrant color and mouth-pleasing tastes and chew. These seeds usually germinate and grow at approximately the same rate, enabling you to harvest the crops together.

Think beyond typical "salad greens": Use carrot tops, dill, and the parsleys (both flat and curly) to add texture.

Create Drama

Cabbages with decorative, small heads add whimsy. Romanesque broccoli types lend texture.

Sturdy vegetables, such as the cruciferous family of cabbages, kale, and other brassicas that have weight, height, and longer growing seasons, anchor a bed similar to small bushes or large flowering plants. Be aware that although the kale and cabbage cultivars labeled "ornamental" or "flowering" are perfectly edible, they are not nearly as flavorful as these, which are grown for eating.

'Lacinato' kale (*Brassica oleracea,* Acephala group), a cool-weather crop, makes a statement with dark blue-green, crinkled, straplike leaves, while 'Red Russian' matures with bright red stems and gray-green leaves. Treat kale as a cut-and-come-again crop by periodically snipping off the outer leaves with a pair of sharp scissors. Plants will continue to grow from the center. (continued)

Mt. Caesar
Alpacas

Maker of The Best Socks on Earth!
Call for our Catalog

AMERICAN DESIGNERS & PRODUCERS OF
Luxurious, Natural
Alpaca Clothing
www.mtcaesaralpacas.com
603-355-3555

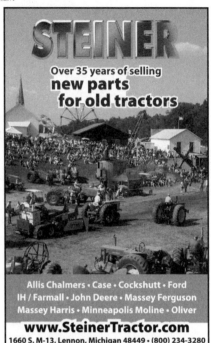

STEINER

Over 35 years of selling
new parts
for old tractors

Allis Chalmers • Case • Cockshutt • Ford
IH / Farmall • John Deere • Massey Ferguson
Massey Harris • Minneapolis Moline • Oliver

www.SteinerTractor.com
1660 S. M-13, Lennon, Michigan 48449 • (800) 234-3280
Call or click for a FREE catalog!

Sandwich Lantern

Handmade on Cape Cod!

» Onion Lights
» Anchor Lights
» Chandeliers
» Sconces

Available in:
Solid Copper or Solid Brass

17 Jan Sebastian Drive, Unit #1
Sandwich, MA 02563

888-741-0714
508-833-0515
Since 1988
sandwichlantern.com

made in
USA

Casperita F1 ~ *Stays White!* ~
This 1 lb. personal size pumpkin is just the
right size for cooking and excellent for display. 77 days.

Recipe Online!

A NO GMO SEED COMPANY

neseed
New England Seed Company

Vegetable, Flower, Herb & Organic Seeds for
Home Gardeners & Fresh Market Growers

www.**neseed**.com

'Celio' broccoli, a Romanesque type, adds texture with its bright-green head.

Go heavy on the compost when planting brassicas, as they are all heavy feeders. Additional weekly feedings of liquid kelp are also beneficial. Rotate brassica crops annually in the garden bed, to prevent the spread of pests and diseases.

Cabbages (*B. oleracea,* Capitata group) with decorative, small heads add whimsy. Marbled purple and white cultivar 'Red Express' produces 2-pound heads within 2 months of germination. 'Savoy Express' is another fast-maturing type, with exceptionally wrinkled medium-green leaves. You will need to lift entire plants when harvesting, so be ready to fill in the empty space with other fast-growing veggies, or use plants in succession to stagger harvest times.

Color adds vibrancy, so experiment—and eat any mistakes.

Romanesque broccoli types (*B. oleracea,* Botrytis group) lend texture with twisting, spiral-shape heads. 'Natalino' also brings striking pale green color. To prevent crown rot, harvest mature broccoli heads with a diagonal cut. Promote the growth of a second crown by maintaining an active feeding and watering schedule.

Brussels sprouts (*B. oleracea* var. *gemmifera*) may take a long time to mature—up to 120 days for most varieties—but if climate permits, you benefit from their unusual form and size: They can grow up to 3 feet tall, so position them near the back or center of the bed. If the green cultivars are not of interest, try 'Falstaff', with attractive, purplish-red leaves and sprouts. Harvest only a few sprouts at a time from each plant.

Play With Color

Color adds vibrancy, so experiment—and eat any mistakes.

'Bull's Blood' beetroot *(Beta vulgaris)* has gorgeous, deep red tops; allow a few to mature to harvest the

'Vulkan' beetroot provides a bold background for alliums along a paved walk.

roots. Sow seeds directly in the garden; beets don't transplant well. Beet seeds are actually clusters. Each one can produce up to six plants, so thin to about 3 inches apart for best root growth.

'Bright Lights' Swiss chard (*B. vulgaris* ssp. *cicla*) produces edible stems in hues of red, pink, yellow, and white. Harvest either as baby greens or when mature. Devein and then prepare like spinach.

Red-leaf chicories, aka radicchio (*Cichorium intybus*), add drama. Slightly bitter-tasting 'Treviso' radicchio, with its elongated shape, resembles Belgian endive; 'Palla Rossa' radicchio produces a compact, round head. Can't wait? Harvest the emerging foliage before the head forms. Red-leaf types are green in summer and turn red with the cool temperatures of autumn.

—Manuela Goehner/GAP Photos

Red-leaf orache complements cosmos and dahlias along a rustic fence.

Orache *(Atriplex hortensis)* is often called "mountain" spinach because its taste and culinary usage are similar to those of its leafy green namesake. Harvest its leaves like other cut-and-come-again plants. Try cultivar 'Red Flash': It can reach up to 3 feet in height and has deep burgundy leaves with magenta undersides.

Don't forget edible flowers and beneficial plants.

Most peppers (*Capsicum* spp.) require a long hot season to set fruit, but the reward is a brilliant flash of color. Try 'Thai Dragon', a fiery-red elongated pepper that grows in upward-facing clusters, or serrano chile peppers, which begin green and turn red, orange, or yellow at maturity. To keep these heavy feeders going, establish a regular watering schedule and give them liquid kelp weekly.

Grow brightly colored nasturtiums to perk up a salad.

Don't forget edible flowers and beneficial plants. Nasturtiums produce bright yellow, orange, and red blooms that add peppery dash to salads. Fragrant bee balm and borage attract butterflies and bees; use the leaves and flowers in refreshing beverages.

(continued)

TRACTOR OWNERS:
Get hitched to a DR® Chipper!

Just load a DR® RAPID-FEED™ CHIPPER, step back, and watch it chip branches up to 5½" thick!

SELF-FEEDING saves time and energy. Most branches can be dropped into the hopper and will self-feed, instead of having to force-feed them.

HARNESS YOUR TRACTOR'S POWER! The 3-Point Hitch DR® CHIPPER transforms up to 65 HP of tractor power into raw chipping power!

 NO TRACTOR? NO PROBLEM! *Self-Powered Models with engines up to 18 HP available!*

79591X © 2013

Call for a FREE DVD and Catalog!
TOLL FREE **800-731-0493**
DRchipper.com

Leaves Nothing In Its Path.
Except The Competition.

Put an end to fall cleanup hassle with a DR® LEAF and LAWN VACUUM. No other is built stronger or lasts longer.

UNSTOPPABLE POWER Collect and shred acres of leaves, pine cones, pine needles, grass clippings, nuts.

HUGE CAPACITY Exclusive shredding action reduces debris, for more vacuuming and less unloading.

BUILT TO LAST Beefy steel frame, large hoses, hard shell collector, commercial engine options.

WALK-BEHIND MODELS AVAILABLE!

DR® LEAF and LAWN VACUUM

79592X © 2013

Call for a FREE DVD and Catalog!
TOLL FREE **800-731-0493**
DRleafvac.com

Add Continuity

Perennial edibles are a welcome sight each season.

Vining oca *(Oxalis tuberosa)* is finicky: It requires a partly shady location, well-draining soil, and moderate temperatures all season. (It tolerates neither drought nor heat.) Harvest its small, nubby tubers, shamrocklike leaves, and yellow flowers. Use the tubers dried, raw, or cooked in a variety of dishes; add the fresh leaves and flowers to salads. Oca is daylight-sensitive and will set tubers only where and/or when there is less than 12 hours of daylight per day. Protect plants from frost if tubers are to be harvested.

Vining oca (background) with 'Perpetual Spinach' leaf beet
–Thomas Alamy/GAP Photos

The walking onion *(Allium cepa var. proliferum)* gets its name from its method of self-propagation: If it is left unharvested, a second stalk with bulbils (small onion bulbs, which are edible) emerges from the first set. The bulbils' weight causes the stem to bend and make contact with the soil, where they root. In this way, walking onions can actually creep across the garden! Eat the young leaves as you would chives or spring onions.

The spiky hollow leaves and bright purple flowers (both edible) of chives *(A. schoenoprasum)* add texture. This fast-growing member of the onion family likes full sun, well-drained soil, and regular watering. Garlic chives *(A. tuberosum)* have white flowers and a strong garlicky taste.

'Purple Passion' asparagus
–Johnny's Selected Seeds

We typically eat green asparagus *(Asparagus officinalis);* for a change, try 'Purple Passion', a purple cultivar. Set the crowns in deep, composted beds (roots can exceed 6 feet in length). The spears are more tender and have a higher sugar content than that of green asparagus, appealing even to young palates.

'Valentine' rhubarb *(Rheum* x *hybridum)* matures with large (poisonous) green leaves and thick, edible, green-and-red stalks. If left untouched, tall stalks of flowers will emerge. (Grow two: one for food, one for blooms.) This cold-hardy plant performs best where summer temperatures are below 75°F, on average. Use the stalks in pies and preserves and spread the leaves as mulch in the garden.

These are only a few of numerous choices. Select plants that you love to eat and admire: It's your yard, your bounty! ◻◻

Sheryl Normandeau is an avid gardener, writer, and blogger from Calgary, Alberta.

STEPHEN BRIDGER

HOW TO
HOOK 'EM

One expert's secrets to catching seven tricky fish

R ecently, while mulling my modest life list of fish landed in more than 60 years of fishing, I recalled how catching each species often taught lessons leading to the landing of others.

My first fish, landed when I was 12, was a 7-pound **northern pike,** taken on a classic Eppinger Dardevle spoon cast into a school of panicky baitfish. The Dardevle (central white stripe on a red background) and the Len Thompson (central red stripe on a white background) became my preferred pike spoons, with the occasional change-up pitch of a jointed red and white Pikie Minnow. Later, caught up in the trendy frenzy of fly-fishing for pike, I found that any big streamer fly would do, as long as it, too, was red and white. *(continued)*

BY BOB SCAMMELL

Walleye
often sip the
jig as it is
sinking to
the bottom;
developing
the sixth
sense to
know when
to strike is
important . . .

Whatever the lure for pike, it has to keep moving. Often I'd see a huge pike following my lure, so I'd freeze and stop reeling—and the monster would turn away. One day, while fishing with my friend Griz in our leaky old scow, I kept on reeling. Then he compounded that "gaffe" by heaving a "green" pike of about 25 pounds aboard in our bedraggled old landing net.

Then the fight started! The big tail slapped our tackle box into orbit and anything else aboard into flotsam and maybe even jetsam. We abandoned ship just before the pike heaved itself up over the gunn'l and away. The important lesson was that pike and many fish are relentless predators that hunt down fugitives and take no prisoners.

For the popular and delicious **walleye,** erroneously aka "pickerel" to Canadians, we learned to fish deep and slow, often at night, with green and yellow plugs—until the discovery that saltwater jigs also worked in fresh water. A dealer sold me a card of jigs with green heads and yellow feathers. Near dark one evening, the big pickerel weren't playing with plugs, so I tied on one of my new jigs, heaved it out there, and retrieved slowly, bouncing it up and down off the bottom, as the dealer had prescribed.

A big walleye took the first cast, followed by eight others on the next eight. After I had strung my ninth big walleye, my rod disappeared. Griz made one cast with it, jigged, and landed a big walleye.

Handing my rod back, he explained: "I just wanted to see if it was the fool on one end or the sick canary on the other."

I have never succumbed to the tedious high technology of modern walleye fishing. If my stock of sick canaries holds out, I am set for life.

Walleye often sip the jig as it is sinking to the bottom on a slack line; developing the sixth sense to know when to strike and hook genteel feeders is important with many species. I have never needed to use strike indicators to tell me when, down deep, a trout has inhaled my drifting nymph.

Goldeyes are optimistic, underrated sport fish; always looking up, they will see and take your lure in shallower, muddier water than any other fish I know. They are perfect dry-fly quarry on any fly at all as long as it looks like a grasshopper

–Victor Young/NH Fish and Game

w a l l e y e

LeafCat®

www.leafcat.com

Turn your lawn tractor into a Leaf Eating Machine

Large Capacity | Open Mesh Design | Collapsible Design
Quick Disconnect | Drop Doors for Quick & Easy Unload
Universal Design Works with Most Lawn Tractors

CASE IH

ShopCaseIH.com

ALL RED MERCHANDISE, ALL IN ONE PLACE.

© Case IH and International Harvester are
registered trademarks of CNH America LLC.

There's more of everything at Almanac.com.

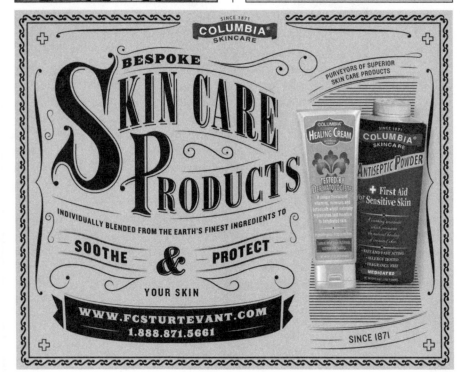

SINCE 1871
COLUMBIA® SKINCARE

BESPOKE

SKIN CARE PRODUCTS

PURVEYORS OF SUPERIOR SKIN CARE PRODUCTS

INDIVIDUALLY BLENDED FROM THE EARTH'S FINEST INGREDIENTS TO

SOOTHE & PROTECT

YOUR SKIN

WWW.FCSTURTEVANT.COM
1.888.871.5661

COLUMBIA® HEALING CREAM

COLUMBIA® SKINCARE
ANTISEPTIC POWDER
+ First Aid for Sensitive Skin

SINCE 1871

goldeye

brown
trout

Your reel
will suddenly
start
screaming
as a silvery
missile hauls
all of your
line behind,
leaping its
way back to
the salt.

and provided that you are not too skilled a caster. Flawless casters with textbook drag-free floats generally get skunked on goldeye, while beginners clean up with casts swinging around downstream and dragging sufficiently to leave a wake.

Fly-fishing for goldeye was an education for a career move into **brown trout** country. The brown is said to be the Ph.D. of troutdom, catchable only on minuscule dry flies, always cast upstream, without any drag, on leaders wispy as angel hair. Even though most of my casts, even with dry flies, were in the ol' wet-fly style, downstream and across, and even if dreaded drag set in, so much the better, I found: The effete brown trout is also a dedicated predator, unable to resist chasing down flies presented in virtually any way.

My favorite floating streamer is the Jekyll-Hyde fly, resembling a Stimulator but with gaudy, flashy material in its wing and tail. It's deadly when floated downstream on a slack line to the end and then pulled under and stripped back in. Big browns that have ignored the floating Dr. Jekyll insect imitation often smash it just as it transforms into the underwater Mr. Hyde persona of a fleeing baitfish.

Atlantic salmon, "the fish of 1,000 casts," are anadromous, commuters between saltwater and their natal freshwater rivers, where you generally fly-fish for them. You do a counting two-step: Cast downstream and across, let the fly swing, take two steps downstream, repeat. Without any noticeable sip or nibble, somewhere in your cast-count to 1,000, your reel will suddenly start screaming as a silvery missile hauls all of your line behind, leaping its way back to the salt.

Many modern freshwater anglers eventually migrate to the salt, particularly for the purpose of "sight fishing" for **bonefish,** permit, and sometimes tarpon on shallow Caribbean tidal flats. *You* will sight nothing: You must know how to tell time and rely totally on the osprey eyes of your generally superb Floridian or Caribbean guide. Most fishermen speak Anglish; here it often helps to also understand Spanglish.

As he poles the skiff from an elevated platform, the guide will announce that a school of macabi, or "bones," is incoming

–fish illustrations: goldeye, Joseph Tomelleri; brown trout, Duane Raver/USFWS

"Our time in the bedroom has never been better!"

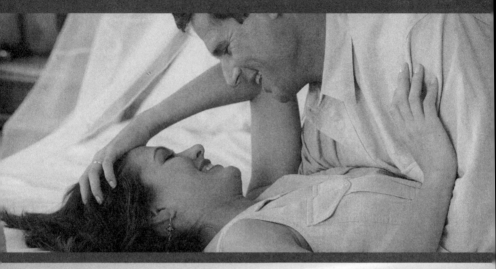

"My wife is so excited about our amazing new sex life, it has rejuvenated our relationship." –Adam, North Carolina

Performance when you need it!

When it's time for sex, you don't want delays and you certainly don't want any misfortune. Now thanks to **bravado™**, you can be confident that you'll be ready when the situation presents itself!

The only male enhancement formula with F.O.R.T.™

Bravado™ is the only male enhancement product on the market with **F.O.R.T.™**, **Flow Oral Release Technology**. F.O.R.T.™ is a patented pharmaceutical delivery system that allows key nutrients to flow into your body in various stages as your body needs it so you can perform at your best. **bravado™**, with its revolutionary technology is the only male enhancement product available that ensures 100% of the active ingredients will be absorbed into your bloodstream quickly and efficiently for the best results possible. Ordinary pills or capsules end up sitting in your stomach waiting to be slowly dissolved. With **bravado™**, rather than hitting your system all at once, the ingredients become available to your system quickly and continue to work over time as needed.

What are you waiting for? Call today for your risk-free trial!

If you're ready to improve your sex life, call now, **1-800-605-5786** and get your risk free trial of **bravado™** rushed right out to you! Your satisfaction is guaranteed and **bravado™** is now available to the general public confidentially without a prescription. So there's no embarrassment, doctor's appointments, or risk!

Thanks to **bravado™** thousands of couples are enjoying more pleasurable sexual experiences, and now you can too! Call today, **1-800-605-5786**, mention offer **#901** for your risk-free trial. Your partner will thank you!

bravado™

1-800-605-5786
Offer #901

69

Outdoors

at 40 feet at 12 o'clock, straight ahead of the skiff, or maybe even at *tres,* to starboard, or *nuevo,* to the port side. Make a cast that leads and doesn't spook the incomers. Your guide will advise, "Streep . . . streep . . . streep"—and then, sometimes, "Strike!" Provided that you remember not to execute a straight-up freshwater strike and instead perform a sidewinder "strip strike," simultaneously hauling with the line hand, you'll experience the legendary electrifying long run of a hooked bonefish or permit.

If you're after **tarpon,** a repeated command by the guide to "Strike!" means that he is urging you to sink the hook hard into the fish's mouth. Tarpon have a mouth like the inside of a cinder block, so hard that an unsunk hook often drops out during typical tarpon high jumps. But the fun ends anyway when the jumps are over; landing a solidly hooked tarpon is utter agony, like playing—and landing—an aquatic grand piano with your fly rod. Many anglers learn to ignore the repeated strike orders and just enjoy "jumping" a tarpon, flying it like a kite, until the hook, mercifully, drops out.

Inevitably on the salt flats, you will see on your line alongside the skiff an evil caricature of a pike on steroids with a baleful grin—a barracuda, whose name means "overlapping teeth." Flash back to that early pike mayhem: Never bring a live one aboard.   □□

Bob Scammell is an outdoors sportswriter from Alberta. His columns and articles have won many national awards, and he was recently inducted into the Alberta Sports Hall of Fame and Museum. He is the author of *The Phenological Fly* (Johnson Gorman Publishers, 1995).

Choose Life
Grow Young with HGH

From the landmark book Grow Young with HGH comes the most powerful, over-the-counter health supplement in the history of man. Human growth hormone was first discovered in 1920 and has long been thought by the medical community to be necessary only to stimulate the body to full adult size and therefore unnecessary past the age of 20. Recent studies, however, have overturned this notion completely, discovering instead that the natural decline of Human Growth Hormone (HGH), from ages 21 to 61 (the average age at which there is only a trace left in the body) and is the main reason why the body ages and fails to regenerate itself to its 25 year-old biological age.

Like a picked flower cut from the source,

we gradually wilt physically and mentally and become vulnerable to a host of degenerative diseases, that we simply weren't susceptible to in our early adult years.

Modern medical science now regards aging as a disease that is treatable and preventable and that "aging", the disease, is actually a compilation of various diseases and pathologies, from everything, like a rise in blood glucose and pressure to diabetes, skin wrinkling and so on. All of these aging symptoms can be stopped and rolled back by maintaining Growth Hormone levels in the blood at the same levels HGH existed in the blood when we were 25 years old.

There is a receptor site in almost every

Astronomy

T

he aurora borealis, aka northern lights, has long been known by far-northern peoples as the most magical of celestial illuminations. Those in arctic lands watch the dazzling display—gossamer arcs of color and vertical rays that undulate like curtains dancing gently in a cosmic breeze—against a backdrop of glistening stars.

The greatest light show over Earth

At their most awesome and awe-inspiring, the lights drift overhead and morph into the rarest and most glorious of all sights, a wildly boiling crown of color known as an auroral corona.

For millennia, this remarkable "sky fire" has fascinated and mystified observers. Ancient civilizations, lacking the cosmic perspective and the technology to grasp what played out in the skies, invented stories. Eskimos believed the light to be playful spirits of the departed.

by Dennis Mammana

Right: *A dazzling display of aurora lights hovers over Grøtfiorden, Troms Fylke, Norway, on April 27, 2012.*

—Thorbjoern Haagensen/www.haagensenfoto.no

CONTINUED

The Norse believed it to be light glinting off the armor of Valkyrie warriors. The Chinese imagined its twisting, snakelike forms as celestial serpents.

Today, we know that the source of auroras is the Sun—specifically, the bursts of electrically charged particles that it emits during coronal mass ejections (CMEs). Some of the particles are captured in Earth's protective magnetosphere, causing a geomagnetic storm over the North and South magnetic poles. In our planet's rarefied upper atmosphere, the particles slam into atoms and molecules of oxygen and nitrogen, causing them to glow in colors ranging from green, the most common color, to red, blue, pink, and purple. Invisible and unknown to many observers is the amount of energy produced by even the most modest display: more than 100 million kilowatts, equivalent to the capacity of

–Thorbjoern Haagensen/www.haagensenfoto.no

Mysteries and Misconceptions

Many mysteries about auroras elude scientists: Why do the lights form patterns and movements? Do the lights make sound, as many observers have reported? How can we predict more accurately when auroras will appear and how they will look? (You can find aurora predictions at SpaceWeatherLive.com.)

Then there are the common misconceptions held by the public. Based on your knowledge, are these statements true or false? *(Answers follow on page 78.)*

1. Auroras appear best in bitter-cold temperatures.

2. Auroras extend to, or touch, the ground.

CONTINUED

Astronomy

Answers to
Mysteries and Misconceptions:

1. False: The lights are visible only when the night sky is clear. At these times, and at high latitudes, which tend to be colder, heat from Earth can escape into the atmosphere, making the air feel more frigid.

2. False: This illusion results from the curvature of Earth. Most auroras occur about 50 to 200 miles above Earth but look close enough to touch.

all of the world's power plants combined.

Space satellites reveal two auroral ovals that circle Earth's magnetic poles at between 64 and 70 degrees of latitude: one in the north (the aurora borealis) and one in the south (the aurora australis). Astronomers have found auroral ovals over Jupiter and its largest moon, Ganymede, as well as around Saturn, Uranus, and Neptune.

Auroral science is still in its infancy, even though Galileo Galilei coined the term "aurora borealis" (after the Roman goddess of morning, Aurora) in 1619. Norwegian physicist Kristian Birkeland (1867–1917) was the first to seek an explanation in a scientific way when, after monitoring the real thing from his home, he created an artificial aurora with terrellas, magnetized spheres meant to represent Earth, and discharged gas in a vacuum chamber. (Line art of his apparatus appears on Norway's 200 kroner banknote.)

Modern scientists study auroral properties by peering down on them from

80

Astronomy

Earth-orbiting satellites and launching rockets into them from Alaska's Poker Flat Research Range and other high-latitude sites.

Some of the best places in the Northern Hemisphere to view auroras' lights are Alaska, much of Canada, Iceland, and Norway. However, during the current phase in the Sun's 11-years-on-average sunspot cycle, when magnetic storms tend to intensify, it is often not necessary to leave home. In recent years, auroras have painted the heavens as far south as Florida, Texas, Arizona, and Southern California—and the show is likely to occur again in 2014.

LIGHTS? CAMERA!

To photograph the lights, you need a camera that can be set and focused manually and a solid tripod. If you're in a dark, rural area, start with settings such as 15 seconds at f/2.8 and ISO 800. Focus on infinity (∞), and remove all filters from your lens. Review your photos on the camera's LCD screen, and change the settings to get the best possible image. Experiment to ensure that you get a good shot. □□

Dennis Mammana is an astronomer and the author of "Stargazers," the only nationally syndicated newspaper column about astronomy. For more information, visit www.dennismammana.com.

Travel With Us to See the Aurora!

For details on our first-ever customized *Old Farmer's Almanac* tour to Alaska to see the aurora borealis, turn to page 91.

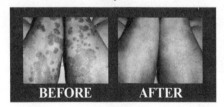
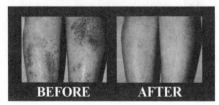

A Strange Ri

Lucy O'Keefe Hancock once asked her father if she should worry about other people stealing her ideas. He said, "If you have a truly new idea, you don't have to worry about people stealing it. You will have to pound it into their heads!"

John A. O'Keefe was not only Lucy's father, but also one of the fathers of the American space program. As assistant chief of the Theoretical Division at NASA's Goddard Space Flight Center from 1958 to 1974, he played an important role in the Golden Age of manned space flight and lunar exploration.

In 1980, he conceived a truly new idea, and he spent the rest of his life (until 2000, when he died) trying to pound it into other people's heads. He failed, but his daughter is determined that his idea gets a fair hearing.

O'Keefe had a long-standing interest in a mysterious form of naturally occurring glass called tektites (from the Greek *tektos,* molten), pieces of dark-color glass *(example below)* that resemble obsidian, rock that forms when lava cools. Tektites, concentrated in certain broad bands of Earth's surface and in deep-sea drilling cores, range in size from microscopic beads to one 53-pound sample from Southeast Asia.

(continued)

–NOAA

–Triff/shutterstock.com

–Zoe Bentley/NASA/JPL

ing Sensation

**Does Earth
have rings,
like Saturn's,
that influence
our weather?**

BY TIM CLARK

O'Keefe

believed

that volcanoes

on the Moon

hurled tektites

into the grip

of Earth's

gravity.

Nobody is absolutely sure where tektites came from; there are two competing theories about their origin. Most scientists now think that meteorites or comets crashed into Earth, which splashed molten rocks back into space, and it's those pieces that eventually fell back to Earth. (Everyone agrees that at some point tektites fell through Earth's atmosphere.)

O'Keefe believed that volcanoes on the Moon hurled tektites out of the low lunar gravitational field and into the grip of Earth's gravity. Some of this material fell to Earth into the broad bands called "strewn fields" that cover an estimated 60 percent of Earth's surface.

In 1980, as rings were being discovered around more planets of the solar system, O'Keefe began to wonder about our own planet. In a letter to *Nature,* he first proposed that the lunar debris that did not fall to Earth formed a ring around our planet, similar to the rings around Saturn. What's more, he suggested, the ring could have brought on the Ice Ages—such as what

John A. O'Keefe

Saturn's rings in visible light

Volcanic craters on
the Moon's surface

biologists describe as the Terminal Eocene Event, a sudden drastic cooling of Earth about 34 million years ago. Winter temperatures dropped about 20 degrees F, ending a greenhouse-like warm period, producing the Antarctic ice cap, and causing an ecological catastrophe.

Hancock recalls, "Father mainly talked about how the shadow covers the winter hemisphere, making winter deeper. Then [as Earth rotates on its tilted axis and revolves around the Sun] the shadow 'moves' to the *other* hemisphere's winter."

Hancock long believed that her father's theory had a measure

A Most Unusual Gift of Love

THE POEM READS:

"Across the years I will walk with you—
in deep, green forests; on shores of sand:
and when our time on earth is through,
in heaven, too, you will have my hand."

Dear Reader,

The drawing you see above is called *The Promise*. It is completely composed of dots of ink. After writing the poem, I worked with a quill pen and placed thousands of these dots, one at a time, to create this gift in honor of my youngest brother and his wife.

Now, I have decided to offer *The Promise* to those who share and value its sentiment. Each litho is numbered and signed by hand and precisely captures the detail of the drawing. As a wedding, anniversary or Christmas gift or simply as a standard for your own home, I believe you will find it most appropriate.

Measuring 14" by 16", it is available either fully framed in a subtle copper tone with hand-cut mats of pewter and rust at $135, or in the mats alone at $95. Please add $14.50 for insured shipping and packaging. Your satisfaction is completely guaranteed.

My best wishes are with you.

The Art of Robert Sexton, 491 Greenwich St. (at Grant), San Francisco, CA 94133

MASTERCARD and VISA orders welcome. Please send card name, card number, address and expiration date, or phone (415) 989-1630 between noon-8 P.M. EST. Checks are also accepted. *Please allow 3 weeks for delivery.*

The Promise is featured with many other recent works in my book, *Journeys of the Human Heart.*
It, too, is available from the address above at $12.95 per copy postpaid. Please visit my Web site at

www.robertsexton.com

The rings change

through the

years . . .

becoming

denser or less

dense, dustier

or less dusty.

This image of Jupiter, taken by *Voyager 1*, shows early evidence of a ring around the planet.

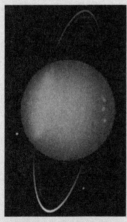

A Hubble Telescope view shows Uranus surrounded by its four major rings.

—images above, NASA

of credibility, but until recently, she had failed to grasp one key aspect. "I did not understand for a few years that [Father] meant an equatorial ring. I thought from the beginning about a ring in the plane of the lunar orbit."

The mental block was not for lack of knowledge: Hancock has an undergraduate degree in astronomy and a Ph.D. in physics. Her work at the World Bank has to do with the economic impact of weather, and she has access to the vast data banks of the National Oceanic and Atmospheric Administration (NOAA) on global weather conditions.

She just couldn't get her head around the Earth equatorial ring.

The Breakthrough

In the summer of 2010, Hancock went on vacation. "I was holidaying on the Isle of Man with my husband. I went to visit the observatory there, talked to some of the members of the Isle of Man Astronomical Society, and learned that a ring had been discovered [in 2009] around Saturn in the plane of its moon Phoebe. It is tenuous but it is there. This encouraged me because this ring seems to originate at a moon—Saturn's moon Phoebe. Father would have loved it, and this is the type of ring that I had always thought he was talking about."

With this clarity, Hancock has, in recent years, expanded on her father's theory and posited a few of her own.

She now believes that her proposed Earth equatorial ring is not smooth but has gaps like Saturn's. The rings cast bands of shadows on Earth, cooling the atmosphere; the gaps allow sunlight through, warming it. The variations in air temperatures alter air pressure, causing variable weather: winds, fronts, precipitation, and other turbulence.

She also now believes that there is a second ring—a Moon ring. (In 1856, U.S. Navy chaplain and astronomer Rev. George Jones proposed the existence of "a nebulous ring around the Earth." Hancock believes that the Moon ring is it.) "This second one," she explains, "is located in the plane of the Moon's orbit, like Saturn's Phoebe ring, and it circulates, or oscillates, through the seasons and thus can warm or cool either hemisphere." It also has gaps.

(continued)

Weather

—Randy Montoya

Materials of the type that may create rings around Earth are on display at the University of New Mexico Meteorite Museum.

"Remember the Joplin [Missouri] tornadoes in May 2011? Remember the tornadoes in New England in June 2011?" asks Hancock. "Those, among some other events, seem to me to have occurred when the Moon ring gaps were swinging overhead."

The rings, she says, change through the years, centuries, millennia, and eons, becoming denser or less dense, dustier or less dusty. The dust density would be due primarily to the YORP effect (named for scientists Ivan Osipovich Yarkovsky, John A. O'Keefe, V. V. Radzievskii, and Stephen Paddack), which states that over time—say, 10,000 years—sunlight on a rock in space slowly sets the rock to spinning. Rocky material might spin faster and faster until the rock bursts into several pieces. Then the smaller particles spin and burst. Eventually, fine dust is produced.

The dust would be perturbed by momentum from solar radiation pressure and solar wind, the influence of planets

in various conjunctions, and other influences of the inner solar system and ultimately be swept out of the rings. "Stuff must fall, most likely to Earth and sometimes as sandstorms," she says.

"The practical effect is that the rings would fade, diminishing their cooling effect, and there would be a gradual warming of Earth's climate, especially in winter. It is the dust—not the rock—that makes the rings effective in causing shade."

This might put the theory to rest, if the rings were not replenished. Hancock believes that they are, in two different time frames:

"First, I think that lunar volcanism may still eject material into space from time to time. After all, there are many tektite strewn fields dated to times later than the Eocene. Big events would be expected to happen erratically, occasionally, infrequently. In each case, some material would fall directly to Earth, and other material would be caught in orbit.

"Second, material caught in orbit would be constantly ground up into dust by the YORP effect. Thus the dust in the ring would be replenished continually, not erratically and occasionally, but all the time."

Rings Cast a Shadow on Global Warming?

"During the Maunder Minimum, or Little Ice Age [1645 to 1715]," says Hancock, "the Sun was quiet and rock dust accumulated in the ring. Then solar activity increased, and since then, the ring has been fading. This is what has heated up the climate of the 20th century." (continued)

"Curtains of white and green light draped over us. It seemed like we could reach up and touch the folds."

—Nancy V., Ventura, CA, about a Bob Berman trip

See the Northern Lights With *The Old Farmer's Almanac!*

Join us in Alaska to see the aurora borealis from February 24 to March 1, 2014.
Led by the Almanac's astronomy editor, Bob Berman,
this 6-day, 5-night adventure promises to be the trip of a lifetime.

By night, we'll behold the blazing and magical curtains of light. By day, we'll tour Alaska!

The trip includes
- first-class suite accommodations
- most meals
- all ground travel and transfers in Alaska
- a visit to the Museum of the North
- a visit to the International Ice Sculpting Competition
- dog sledding
- a flight-tour of Mount McKinley
- and much, much more!

Space is limited! For details and reservations, visit SpecialInterestTours.net.

Top photo: Senior Airman Joshua Strang, USAF; Ice Sculpture photo: FairbanksMike

This, she says, is both the point of the theory and the point of difference from conventional thought: "The 20th-century greenhouse gas warming theory does not predict more winter warming than summer warming. It is about year-round warming. However, 20th-century global warming has been more important in winter than summer."

She believes that 20th-century warming was a result of the effects of the period's strong solar cycles and solar activity on the rings:

"In the last few years, the Sun has become more quiet than it was. With little solar activity, very little dust was dislodged from the rings, and Earth's atmosphere began to cool a bit. Solar Cycle 24 started up in September 2009 or so, but its activity is below average. A low in solar activity sometimes is accompanied by big solar outbursts. These should be followed, in my theory, by sandstorms and by brief warming—of weeks, not years—while the dust in the rings resettles and replenishes.

Corroboration or Coincidence?

■ To test her ring theories, Lucy O'Keefe Hancock created a computer model that visualizes the two bands of shadow as they would fall on Earth for any date during the past thousand years or so and on into the next few hundred. To see videos explaining her ring theory and check her weather predictions based on the ring shadows, visit her Web site: http://naturesverdict.net.

"In May 2012, and ever since, there have been large outbursts from the Sun's corona, following which [came] huge sandstorms on Earth and a very hot June, followed by cooling a bit again. This fits the [ring] theory of weather. As to the future, I suppose that the dust is already beginning to regather. I don't know how fast this happens, but if climate is sensitive to the 11-year sunspot cycle, recovery of the dust cloud must happen pretty fast."

Shadows of Doubt

Dr. Linda Spilker, an authority on planetary rings with the Jet Propulsion Lab at Caltech—she was part of the *Cassini* team, which sent a satellite into orbit around Saturn—is skeptical. Asked to comment on how rings might affect Earth's weather, she wrote, "Any rings orbiting our planet would need to be dense enough to block some of the incoming sunlight. . . . To the best of my knowledge, no ring shadows or Earth rings have been detected that would be dense enough to impact Earth's weather.

"Another problem is that dusty rings would be easily visible under certain conditions. When the Sun is just behind the dusty ring, something you might see from the space station, for instance, even a small amount of dust—much, much less than would cast a shadow—would become very bright."

Spilker is not the lone skeptic, and Hancock has a ready response.

Hancock believes that a ring in the plane of Earth's orbit (the one her father theorized) would appear as a glow low on the southern horizon in the early evening for observers in the Northern Hemisphere and might be mistaken for urban light pollution. The ring would be invisible at

Weather

–Yuri Beletsky/ESO Paranal

around midnight (it would be shaded by Earth) and visible again before dawn.

A second ring, in the plane of the Moon's orbit, she says, would be located where the zodiacal light and Gegenschein are found. The zodiacal light *(example above)*, a pyramid-shape glow in eastern skies just before dawn and in western skies just after sunset, has been observed for thousands of years. The Gegenschein is a fainter glow that arches in the night sky between the two positions of zodiacal light.

Hancock agrees with Spilker that, from space, dust should be observable when lit from behind, brightening as described. Looking at the Sun might be dangerous to eyes but, says Hancock, the Moon also should show such an effect to Earth-based observers when the geometry is right—such as near the totality of a total solar eclipse, when you might see a brightening of the Moon.

Hancock plans to continue to promote her father's theory. "I am not determined to prove him right, just determined to do what I can to get him a fair hearing to make sure that his ideas aren't forgotten simply because they are a minority opinion," she says. □□

Tim Clark, long a contributor to this Almanac, says that after working on this topic, his head was spinning.

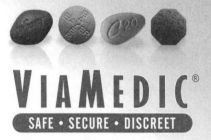

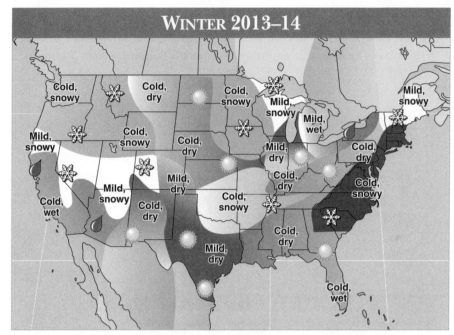

WINTER 2013–14

These weather maps correspond to the winter (November through March) and summer (June through August) predictions in the General Weather Forecast (opposite). Forecast terms here represent deviations from the normals; learn more on page 202.

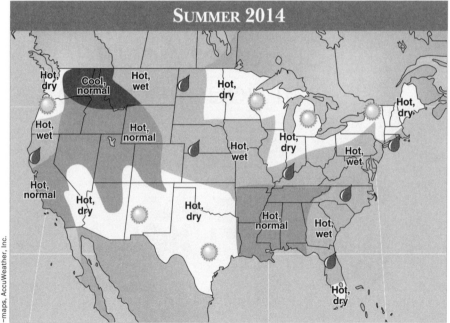

SUMMER 2014

–maps, AccuWeather, Inc.

The General Weather Forecast and Report

For regional forecasts, see pages 204–219.

As solar activity declines from the low peak of Solar Cycle 24, we expect much of the nation to have below-normal winter temperatures and above-normal snowfall. Other key factors include a neutral-to-weak El Niño Southern Oscillation (ENSO) and a cool phase of the Pacific Decadal Oscillation (PDO), as well as a warm phase in the Atlantic Multidecadal Oscillation (AMO) and a cold phase in the North Atlantic Oscillation (NAO), during most of the winter. We also expect low ice coverage and thickness in the Arctic. (Oscillations are linked ocean–atmosphere patterns that influence the weather over periods of weeks to years.)

Spring and summer 2014 will bring above-normal temperatures nearly everywhere. Spring will be drier than normal across most of the nation, and summer drought may be a problem on the southern tip of Florida; from New England westward through the Lower Lakes and Upper Midwest; from Texas and Oklahoma westward through the Desert Southwest; and in the upper Pacific Northwest. In most other areas, rainfall will be near or above normal. Expect an active hurricane season overall, with a major hurricane making landfall on the central Gulf coast in July and several hurricanes and tropical storms threatening Florida and the Atlantic seaboard in September.

November through March temperatures will be below normal, on average, in most of the nation. The only exceptions will be in northern New England, the area from northeastern Minnesota into central Illinois and Indiana, and the area from northern California and southern Oregon to central Colorado and down through southern Texas. Precipitation will be above normal in the Northeast, southern Florida, the Upper Midwest, the area from northeast Texas into southern Missouri and western Tennessee, and the western quarter of the nation; it will be below normal elsewhere. Snowfall will be above normal from Boston to Atlanta, from Upper Michigan to northeast Nebraska, from the Dallas–Fort Worth Metroplex northward to southeast Kansas and eastward to western Tennessee, in the Intermountain Region, in the Pacific Northwest, and in the higher elevations of the Desert Southwest and Pacific Southwest; it will be near or below normal elsewhere.

April and May will be warmer than normal, on average, everywhere except in the Northeast. Rainfall will be above normal in Georgia and Florida, in the Lower Lakes, and from Houston westward through the Desert Southwest; it will be near or below normal elsewhere.

June through August temperatures will be above normal, on average, in nearly the entire nation, with the northern Intermountain Region the only exception. Rainfall will be below normal from northern New England into the eastern Dakotas, from Texas and Oklahoma through the Desert Southwest, in southern Florida, and in the northern Pacific Northwest; it will be at or above normal elsewhere.

September and October will be cooler than normal in the Southeast, from southwest Pennsylvania to central Illinois, in eastern Oklahoma, the Intermountain Region, and from Las Vegas to San Diego, and near or above normal elsewhere. Rainfall will be above normal in Maine and Florida, from Indianapolis to Denver, and from San Francisco through the Pacific Northwest, and near or below normal elsewhere.

To learn how we make our weather predictions and to get a summary of the results of our forecast for last winter, turn to page 202.

The Old Farmer's Almanac

Established in 1792 and published every year thereafter

ROBERT B. THOMAS, *founder* (1766–1846)

YANKEE PUBLISHING INC.

EDITORIAL AND PUBLISHING OFFICES

P.O. Box 520, 1121 Main Street, Dublin, NH 03444
Phone: 603-563-8111 • Fax: 603-563-8252

EDITOR *(13th since 1792):* Janice Stillman
ART DIRECTOR: Margo Letourneau
COPY EDITOR: Jack Burnett
SENIOR RESEARCH EDITOR: Mare-Anne Jarvela
SENIOR EDITOR: Heidi Stonehill
SENIOR ASSOCIATE EDITOR: Sarah Perreault
EDITORIAL ASSISTANCE: Tim Clark
INTERN: Sarah Drory
WEATHER GRAPHICS AND CONSULTATION:
AccuWeather, Inc.

V.P., NEW MEDIA AND PRODUCTION:
Paul Belliveau
PRODUCTION DIRECTORS:
Susan Gross, David Ziarnowski
SENIOR PRODUCTION ARTISTS:
Lucille Rines, Rachel Kipka

WEB SITE: ALMANAC.COM

NEW MEDIA EDITOR: Catherine Boeckmann
WEB DESIGNERS: Lou S. Eastman, Amy O'Brien
E-COMMERCE MANAGER: Alan Henning
PROGRAMMING: Reinvented, Inc.

CONTACT US

We welcome your questions and comments about articles in and topics for this Almanac. Mail all editorial correspondence to Editor, The Old Farmer's Almanac, P.O. Box 520, Dublin, NH 03444-0520; fax us at 603-563-8252; or contact us through Almanac.com/Feedback. *The Old Farmer's Almanac* can not accept responsibility for unsolicited manuscripts and will not acknowledge any hard-copy queries or manuscripts that do not include a stamped and addressed return envelope.

OUR CONTRIBUTORS

Bob Berman, our astronomy editor, is the director of Overlook Observatory in Woodstock and Storm King Observatory in Cornwall, both in New York. In 1976, he founded the Catskill Astronomical Society. Bob has led many aurora and eclipse expeditions, venturing as far as the Arctic and Antarctic.

Tim Clark, a retired high school English teacher from New Hampshire, has composed the weather doggerel on the Calendar pages since 1980.

Bethany E. Cobb, our astronomer, earned a Ph.D. in astronomy at Yale University and is an Assistant Professor of Honors and Physics at George Washington University. She also conducts research on gamma-ray bursts and follows numerous astronomy pursuits, including teaching astronomy to adults at the Osher Lifelong Learning Institute at UC Berkeley. When she is not scanning the sky, she enjoys playing the violin, figure skating, and reading science fiction.

George Lohmiller, author of the Farmer's Calendar essays, owns Our Town Landscaping in Hancock, New Hampshire. He has been writing for Almanac publications for more than 15 years, including the essays that formerly appeared in our Gardening Calendar and are now available at Almanac.com/GardeningCalEssays.

Celeste Longacre, our astrologer, often refers to astrology as "a study of timing, and timing is everything." A New Hampshire native, she has been a practicing astrologer for more than 25 years. Her book, *Love Signs* (Sweet Fern Publications, 1999), is available for sale on her Web site, www.yourlovesigns.com.

Michael Steinberg, our meteorologist, has been forecasting weather for the Almanac since 1996. In addition to college degrees in atmospheric science and meteorology, he brings a lifetime of experience to the task: He began predicting weather when he attended the only high school in the world with weather Teletypes and radar.

"Food Canning Secrets!"

By Mike Walters
Staff Writer, Off The Grid News

Did you know canning was pioneered in the 1790s by a French confectioner named Nicolas Appert... and then... successfully tested by the French Navy around 1806?

It's true!

They successfully canned fruit, vegetables, milk, and even meat well over 200 years ago!

And to this day, canning is one of the very best ways to save money by preserving and storing your own food. It's also a great way to become more self-sufficient and ensure a safe, nutritious, and abundant food supply for your family should there be some kind of crisis situation.

Makes Canning Foods Easy!

There's a new set of instructional DVD's titled, Food Storage Secrets. Combined, they contain 20-years-worth of old time canning secrets.

These DVD's take you by the hand, step-by-step, through the entire process of "putting away" almost any food you can think of.

There are no special skills required... and... there's no need to spend a lot of money to get started. These DVD's reveal the easiest, quickest and absolutely best food canning secrets available, such as,

• **How to cut your learning time in half and be up and running overnight**

• How to make your canned foods taste five times better than grocery store food

• **Why advice many "old time" canners give is dead wrong**

• Where to buy the best produce for canning

• **How to produce potent "canned medicines"... and... a simple ingredient that turns each jar of prepared food into canned "Super Food"**

• An easy way to determine which foods can be canned and which ones cannot

• **How to create your own basement or pantry supermarket**

• The best ways to keep food fresh for a year at a time and protect against food poisoning

• **How to get more vitamins, minerals and trace elements into your canned food**

• And much, much more

I don't have space here to mention even 1/10th of what you'll discover on the Food Storage Secrets DVD's... so... I'm going to make you a 100% Risk-Free, Half-Price Offer and let you see everything for yourself.

90 Day Unconditional Money Back Guarantee!

Food Storage Secrets normally sells for $39.95. Order the DVD's for **$19.97** and test drive them for 90 Days. Then, if you're not satisfied for any reason, or no reason at all, send them back for a full, no questions asked refund

Fair enough? If so...

It's Easy To Order!

For Fastest Service go online (and enter coupon code OFA103 during checkout) at:

www.FoodShortageUSA.com

For Fast Service call toll-free: 1-877-327-0365 Dept. OFA103

To order by Check or Money Order: Send $24.97 ($19.97 + $5 S&H) to:

**Solutions From Science
Food Storage Secrets
Dept. OFA103
2200 IL Rte. 84 P.O. Box 518
Thomson, IL 61285**

Two Free Gifts Valued At $29.95!

Order now and you'll receive two free gifts that are yours to keep even if you return Food Storage Secrets for a refund: **1. Food Dehydrating Secrets DVD**... and... **2.** A 63-page Food Storage Secrets eBook. Supplies are limited so you must hurry!

Eclipses

■ There will be four eclipses in 2014, two of the Sun and two of the Moon. Solar eclipses are visible only in certain areas and require eye protection to be viewed safely. Lunar eclipses are technically visible from the entire night side of Earth, but during a penumbral eclipse, the dimming of the Moon's illumination is slight.

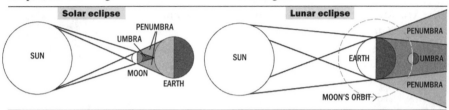

April 15: Total eclipse of the Moon. This eclipse will be visible from North America. The Moon will enter the penumbra at 12:52 A.M. EDT. Totality begins at 3:06 A.M. The Moon will leave the penumbra at 6:39 A.M.

April 29: Annular eclipse of the Sun. This annular eclipse will not be visible from North America but will be visible from Antarctica and Australia.

October 8: Total eclipse of the Moon. This eclipse will be fully visible from Hawaii and western North America (including Alaska). Observers in the eastern areas will see only part of the eclipse before the Moon sets below the horizon. The Moon will enter the penumbra at 4:14 A.M., EDT. Totality begins at 6:25 A.M., and the Moon will leave the penumbra at 9:35 A.M.

October 23: Partial eclipse of the Sun. This partial solar eclipse will be visible from most of North America. Western parts will see the full extent of the eclipse, while eastern areas will see only the very beginning before the Sun sets below the horizon. The eclipse will begin at 3:38 P.M. EDT and will end at 7:52 P.M. The times during which the eclipse is visible from any specific location will vary significantly, typically starting between 4:00 and 6:00 P.M.

Full-Moon Dates (Eastern Time)					
	2014	2015	2016	2017	2018
Jan.	15	4	23	12	1 & 31
Feb.	14	3	22	10	–
Mar.	16	5	23	12	1 & 31
Apr.	15	4	22	11	29
May	14	3	21	10	29
June	13	2	20	9	28
July	12	1 & 31	19	9	27
Aug.	10	29	18	7	26
Sept.	8	27	16	6	24
Oct.	8	27	16	5	24
Nov.	6	25	14	4	23
Dec.	6	25	13	3	22

and ending 2 to 3 hours later (or when the Sun sets). For example, in Detroit, Michigan, the eclipse will be visible from 5:40 P.M. to 6:36 P.M., when the Sun sets.

The Moon's Path

The Moon's path across the sky changes with the seasons. Full Moons are very high in the sky (at midnight) between November and February and very low in the sky between May and July.

Next Total Eclipse of the Sun

March 20, 2015: visible from northern Africa, northern Asia, and Europe.

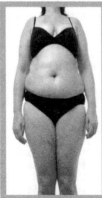
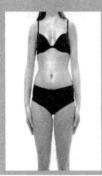

Bright Stars

Transit Times

■ This table shows the time (EST or EDT) and altitude of a star as it transits the meridian (i.e., reaches its highest elevation while passing over the horizon's south point) at Boston on the dates shown. The transit time on any other date differs from that of the nearest date listed by approximately 4 minutes per day. To find the time of a star's transit for your location, convert its time at Boston using Key letter C **(see Time Corrections, page 252).**

–Beth Krommes

| Star | Constellation | Magnitude | Time of Transit (EST/EDT) Bold = P.M. Light = A.M. | | | | | | Altitude (degrees) |
			Jan. 1	Mar. 1	May 1	July 1	Sept. 1	Nov. 1	
Altair	Aquila	0.8	**12:50**	8:58	5:59	1:59	**9:51**	**5:51**	56.3
Deneb	Cygnus	1.3	**1:41**	9:49	6:49	2:49	**10:41**	**6:42**	92.8
Fomalhaut	Psc. Aus.	1.2	**3:57**	**12:05**	9:05	5:05	1:02	**8:58**	17.8
Algol	Perseus	2.2	**8:07**	**4:15**	**1:15**	9:15	5:12	1:12	88.5
Aldebaran	Taurus	0.9	**9:34**	**5:42**	**2:42**	10:43	6:39	2:39	64.1
Rigel	Orion	0.1	**10:13**	**6:21**	**3:21**	11:21	7:17	3:17	39.4
Capella	Auriga	0.1	**10:15**	**6:23**	**3:23**	11:24	7:20	3:20	93.6
Bellatrix	Orion	1.6	**10:23**	**6:31**	**3:32**	11:32	7:28	3:28	54.0
Betelgeuse	Orion	var. 0.4	**10:53**	**7:01**	**4:01**	**12:02**	7:58	3:58	55.0
Sirius	Can. Maj.	−1.4	**11:43**	**7:51**	**4:51**	**12:51**	8:48	4:48	31.0
Procyon	Can. Min.	0.4	12:41	**8:45**	**5:45**	**1:45**	9:42	5:42	52.9
Pollux	Gemini	1.2	12:47	**8:51**	**5:51**	**1:52**	9:48	5:48	75.7
Regulus	Leo	1.4	3:10	**11:14**	**8:14**	**4:14**	**12:10**	8:11	59.7
Spica	Virgo	var. 1.0	6:26	2:34	**11:30**	**7:30**	**3:27**	11:27	36.6
Arcturus	Boötes	−0.1	7:16	3:24	12:24	**8:21**	**4:17**	**12:17**	66.9
Antares	Scorpius	var. 0.9	9:30	5:38	2:38	**10:34**	**6:30**	**2:31**	21.3
Vega	Lyra	0	11:37	7:45	4:45	12:45	**8:37**	**4:37**	86.4

Rise and Set Times

■ To find the time of a star's rising at Boston on any date, subtract the interval shown at right from the star's transit time on that date; add the interval to find the star's setting time. To find the rising and setting times for your city, convert the Boston transit times above using the Key letter shown at right before applying the interval **(see Time Corrections, page 252).** The directions in which the stars rise and set, shown for Boston, are generally useful throughout the United States. Deneb, Algol, Capella, and Vega are circumpolar stars—they never set but appear to circle the celestial north pole.

Star	Interval (h. m.)	Rising Key	Rising Dir.*	Setting Key	Setting Dir.*
Altair	6 36	B	EbN	E	WbN
Fomalhaut	3 59	E	SE	D	SW
Aldebaran	7 06	B	ENE	D	WNW
Rigel	5 33	D	EbS	B	WbS
Bellatrix	6 27	B	EbN	D	WbN
Betelgeuse	6 31	B	EbN	D	WbN
Sirius	5 00	D	ESE	B	WSW
Procyon	6 23	B	EbN	D	WbN
Pollux	8 01	A	NE	E	NW
Regulus	6 49	B	EbN	D	WbN
Spica	5 23	D	EbS	B	WbS
Arcturus	7 19	A	ENE	E	WNW
Antares	4 17	E	SEbE	A	SWbW

*b = "by"

"I just couldn't understand what people were saying – now I CAN!"

SAVE 80%

"I was surprised how easy it was."

I had known for years I wasn't understanding everything I heard, but if only others would stop mumbling it would be okay. Is it really such a big deal if I turn up the TV? Then my family got me this catalog and I thought, "Why not give it a try?"

> "It's great. I can now hear all of my church service, TV, friends, conversations and the telephone. It's a miracle."
>
> **Dr. Rex Bullington – Utah**

I wasn't convinced but I ordered my first pair of hearing aids. They were shipped to my home (free shipping) and I didn't have to go anywhere or make an appointment. I even had 45 days to try them at home – no risk, no pressure. And my price was far less than what my friends paid!

> "This hearing aid has allowed me to keep working. I was ready to retire."
>
> **Dr. Daniel Keller – Tennessee**

Well, I didn't need 45 days to decide to keep them. They are small, fit great in my ears, and they couldn't be easier to set. Just what I needed! Those folks at Hearing Help Express® really know their business. I'm glad I gave them a try. You'll be glad too!

FREE Hearing Aid Catalog

NEW

© Hearing Help Express®, Inc.

TRIED HEARING AIDS BEFORE BUT THEY DIDN'T WORK? TRY THESE!

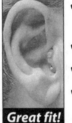

Great fit!

✓ Up to 80% less than you'd pay locally

✓ 45-day home trial

✓ No restocking fees

✓ Extra protection – 1 year warranty, no extra charge

✓ 100% money-back guarantee

Call For Your FREE Catalog

1-800-782-6316

ext. 15-427

ACCREDITED BUSINESS
BBB
BBB Rating: A+

Satisfaction 100% Guarantee

SEND NO MONEY! Clip and mail or go online:
www.HearingHelpExpress.com/15427

☑ **YES!** I want to save 80%. Rush me my FREE Hearing Aid Catalog.

Dr./Mr./Mrs./Ms._____

Address_____

City/State/Zip_____

Mail to:
Hearing Help Express
105 North First St., Dept 15-427
DeKalb, IL 60115-0586

The Twilight Zone

Twilight is the time when the sky is partially illuminated preceding sunrise and again following sunset. The ranges of twilight are defined according to the Sun's position below the horizon. **Civil twilight** occurs when the Sun's center is between the horizon and 6 degrees below the horizon (visually, the horizon is clearly defined). **Nautical twilight** occurs when the center is between 6 and 12 degrees below the horizon (the horizon is indistinct). **Astronomical twilight** occurs when the center is between 12 and 18 degrees below the horizon (sky illumination is imperceptible). When the center is at 18 degrees (**dawn** or **dark**) or below, there is no illumination.

Length of Astronomical Twilight (hours and minutes)

LATITUDE	Jan. 1 to Apr. 10	Apr. 11 to May 2	May 3 to May 14	May 15 to May 25	May 26 to July 22	July 23 to Aug. 3	Aug. 4 to Aug. 14	Aug. 15 to Sept. 5	Sept. 6 to Dec. 31
25°N to 30°N	1 20	1 23	1 26	1 29	1 32	1 29	1 26	1 23	1 20
31°N to 36°N	1 26	1 28	1 34	1 38	1 43	1 38	1 34	1 28	1 26
37°N to 42°N	1 33	1 39	1 47	1 52	1 59	1 52	1 47	1 39	1 33
43°N to 47°N	1 42	1 51	2 02	2 13	2 27	2 13	2 02	1 51	1 42
48°N to 49°N	1 50	2 04	2 22	2 42	—	2 42	2 22	2 04	1 50

TO DETERMINE THE LENGTH OF TWILIGHT: The length of twilight changes with latitude and the time of year. Use the **Time Corrections** table, **page 252**, to find the latitude of your city or the city nearest you. Use that figure in the chart above with the appropriate date to calculate the length of twilight in your area.

TO DETERMINE WHEN DAWN OR DARK WILL OCCUR: Calculate the sunrise/sunset times for your locality using the instructions in **How to Use This Almanac, page 116.** Subtract the length of twilight from the time of sunrise to determine when dawn breaks. Add the length of twilight to the time of sunset to determine when dark descends.

EXAMPLE:

Boston, Mass. (latitude 42°22')

Sunrise, August 1	5:36 A.M. EDT
Length of twilight	− 1 52
Dawn breaks	3:44 A.M.
Sunset, August 1	8:03 P.M. EDT
Length of twilight	+ 1 52
Dark descends	9:55 P.M.

Principal Meteor Showers

SHOWER	BEST VIEWING	POINT OF ORIGIN	DATE OF MAXIMUM*	NO. PER HOUR**	ASSOCIATED COMET
Quadrantid . . . .**Predawn**		N	**Jan. 4**	25	—
Lyrid . . . . .Predawn		S	Apr. 22	10	Thatcher
Eta Aquarid . . . . .Predawn		SE	May 4	10	Halley
Delta Aquarid . . . . . . .Predawn		S	July 30	10	—
Perseid . . . .**Predawn**		NE	**Aug. 11–13**	50	**Swift-Tuttle**
Draconid . . . . .Late evening		NW	Oct. 9	6	Giacobini-Zinner
Orionid . . . . .Predawn		S	Oct. 21–22	15	Halley
Taurid . . . . .Late evening		S	Nov. 9	3	Encke
Leonid . . . . .Predawn		S	Nov. 17–18	10	Tempel-Tuttle
Andromedid . . . . .Late evening		S	Nov. 25–27	5	Biela
Geminid . . . .**All night**		NE	**Dec. 13–14**	75	—
Ursid . . . . .Predawn		N	Dec. 22	5	Tuttle

*May vary by one or two days   **Moonless, rural sky   **Bold** = most prominent

The Visible Planets

■ Listed here for Boston are viewing suggestions for and the rise and set times (EST/EDT) of Venus, Mars, Jupiter, and Saturn on specific days each month, as well as when it is best to view Mercury. Approximate rise and set times for other days can be found by interpolation. Use the Key letters at the right of each listing to convert the times for other localities **(see pages 116 and 252).** *For all planet rise and set times by zip code, visit* **Almanac.com/Astronomy.**

Venus

♀ This is not a great year for Venus; it never gets higher than 15 degrees at the end of civil twilight. Venus starts January as an evening star, too close to the Sun to be readily seen. It passes inferior conjunction on January 11 and soon materializes as a morning star. Venus shines at its greatest brilliancy on Valentine's Day. It's still dazzling but low in March. Venus gets progressively dimmer and stays low through spring and summer and into early autumn, the tedium somewhat broken by a few meetings with the crescent Moon and a close conjunction with Jupiter on August 18. Venus disappears into the solar glare in late September. It returns as an evening star in late December, low in the west after sunset.

Jan. 1 .... **set**	**5:44**	B	Apr. 1.......rise	4:37	D	July 1.......rise	3:15	A	Oct. 1.......rise	6:08	C
Jan. 11 .....rise	6:49	D	Apr. 11.....rise	4:28	D	July 11 .....rise	3:19	A	Oct. 11.....rise	6:33	D
Jan. 21.....rise	5:43	D	Apr. 21.....rise	4:18	D	July 21.....rise	3:29	A	Oct. 21..... **set**	**5:55**	B
Feb. 1.....rise	4:51	D	May 1 .....rise	4:06	C	Aug. 1......rise	3:45	A	Nov. 1..... **set**	**5:45**	B
Feb. 11.....rise	4:22	D	May 11 ....rise	3:54	C	Aug. 11.....rise	4:05	A	Nov. 11 ..... **set**	**4:40**	B
Feb. 21.....rise	4:06	D	May 21 ....rise	3:43	B	Aug. 21.....rise	4:28	B	Nov. 21..... **set**	**4:39**	A
Mar. 1 ......rise	3:58	D	June 1 ......rise	3:31	B	Sept. 1 .....rise	4:54	B	Dec. 1 .... **set**	**4:44**	A
Mar. 11 ...rise	4:51	D	June 11 ....rise	3:22	B	Sept. 11....rise	5:19	B	Dec. 11 ..... **set**	**4:56**	A
Mar. 21 ....rise	4:45	D	June 21 ....rise	3:17	B	Sept. 21 ...rise	5:44	C	Dec. 21 ..... **set**	**5:13**	A
									Dec. 31 ..... **set**	**5:35**	A

Mars

♂ Mars starts out in Virgo, rising at midnight, and rapidly brightens. It rises at around 10:00 P.M. in February and 9:00 P.M. in March; it appears at sunset during its opposition on April 8, when it is out all night. At magnitude –1.5, it matches the brilliance of the sky's brightest star, Sirius. Mars remains very bright in late spring, falls to magnitude 0 in early July, passes below Saturn from August 22 to 27, and then gets dimmer in the autumn as its eastward motion takes it into Sagittarius in November. The Moon conspicuously meets Mars on May 10, June 7, July 5, August 3 and 31, and September 29.

Jan. 1 .... **rise**	**11:53**	D	Apr. 1....... **rise**	**7:45**	D	July 1 .... **set**	12:50	C	Oct. 1........ **set**	**9:13**	A
Jan. 11 ..... **rise**	**11:34**	D	Apr. 11......set	6:21	C	July 11 ......set	12:19	C	Oct. 11...... **set**	**9:01**	A
Jan. 21 ..... **rise**	**11:14**	D	Apr. 21.....set	5:32	C	July 21...... **set**	**11:48**	B	Oct. 21...... **set**	**8:52**	A
Feb. 1..... **rise**	**10:48**	D	May 1 .....set	4:44	C	Aug. 1..... **set**	**11:18**	B	Nov. 1...... **set**	**8:45**	A
Feb. 11..... **rise**	**10:20**	D	May 11 ....set	3:58	C	Aug. 11..... **set**	**10:53**	B	Nov. 11..... **set**	**7:41**	A
Feb. 21..... **rise**	**9:47**	D	May 21 .....set	3:16	C	Aug. 21..... **set**	**10:29**	B	Nov. 21..... **set**	**7:39**	A
Mar. 1 ...... **rise**	**9:17**	D	June 1 ......set	2:32	C	Sept. 1 ...... **set**	**10:05**	B	Dec. 1 .... **set**	**7:39**	A
Mar. 11 .... **rise**	**9:35**	D	June 11 .....set	1:56	C	Sept. 11..... **set**	**9:45**	A	Dec. 11 ..... **set**	**7:39**	B
Mar. 21 .... **rise**	**8:46**	D	June 21 .....set	1:22	C	Sept. 21 .... **set**	**9:28**	A	Dec. 21 ..... **set**	**7:41**	B
									Dec. 31 ..... **set**	**7:43**	B

☞ **Bold = P.M.** ☞ Light = A.M.

–illustrations, Beth Krommes

Jupiter

♃ Jupiter's opposition occurs on January 5, when it is at its brightest and largest of the year, at a dazzling magnitude –2.7. It is out all night in January and most of the night throughout the winter and early spring. Jupiter never loses its luster this year. It slowly becomes an evening star and by May occupies the western sky a few hours after dusk. Jupiter vanishes behind the Sun in a conjunction on July 24. It appears as a morning star low in the east in August and closely meets Venus on August 18. By November, it rises before midnight; it returns in full force by late December, when it's up by 8:30 P.M.

Jan. 1 ...... **rise**	**4:35**	A	Apr. 1........ set	2:32	E	July 1........ **set**	**9:26**	E	Oct. 1........rise	2:13	B
Jan. 11 ...... set	6:58	E	Apr. 11...... set	1:56	E	July 11 ...... **set**	**8:54**	E	Oct. 11 .....rise	1:42	B
Jan. 21 ...... set	6:14	E	Apr. 21...... set	1:21	E	July 21 ...... **set**	**8:22**	E	Oct. 21.....rise	1:10	B
Feb. 1........ set	5:26	E	May 1 .... set	12:48	E	Aug. 1......rise	5:08	B	Nov. 1.......rise	12:34	B
Feb. 11...... set	4:44	E	May 11 ..... set	12:14	E	Aug. 11....rise	4:40	B	Nov. 11 .... **rise**	**10:56**	B
Feb. 21...... set	4:02	E	May 21 .... **set**	**11:38**	E	Aug. 21....rise	4:12	B	Nov. 21.... **rise**	**10:20**	B
Mar. 1 .... set	3:30	E	June 1 ...... **set**	**11:02**	E	Sept. 1 .....rise	3:41	B	Dec. 1...... **rise**	**9:43**	B
Mar. 11 .... set	3:50	E	June 11 .... **set**	**10:30**	E	Sept. 11....rise	3:12	B	Dec. 11 .... **rise**	**9:04**	B
Mar. 21 .... set	3:12	E	June 21 .... **set**	**9:58**	E	Sept. 21 ...rise	2:43	B	Dec. 21.... **rise**	**8:23**	B
									Dec. 31 .... **rise**	**7:40**	B

Saturn

♄ Saturn varies its appearance depending on the orientation of its famous rings. They were edge-wise to Earth in 2009, which made Saturn half as bright as usual. This year, the rings are particularly beautiful because they are virtually "wide open." Saturn spends 2014 in Libra. In early January, it doesn't rise until 3:00 A.M., but it clears the horizon before midnight in March and by 10:00 P.M. in April. The planet attains a bright magnitude of 0.1 during its opposition on May 10. Saturn is visible most of the night in June and July, remaining well placed through August, when it is an evening object. It becomes low in September and goes behind the Sun on November 18. By late December, it appears low in the east before dawn.

Jan. 1 ....rise	3:11	D	Apr. 1....... **rise**	**10:23**	D	July 1........ set	2:16	B	Oct. 1........ **set**	**8:19**	B
Jan. 11 .....rise	2:36	D	Apr. 11..... **rise**	**9:41**	D	July 11 ...... set	1:36	B	Oct. 11 ...... **set**	**7:43**	B
Jan. 21 .....rise	2:00	D	Apr. 21..... **rise**	**8:59**	D	July 21...... set	1:00	B	Oct. 21...... **set**	**7:07**	B
Feb. 1........rise	1:20	D	May 1 .... **rise**	**8:16**	D	Aug. 1...... set	12:13	B	Nov. 1....... **set**	**6:27**	B
Feb. 11......rise	12:43	D	May 11 ..... set	5:46	B	Aug. 11.... **set**	**11:30**	B	Nov. 11 .... set	4:51	B
Feb. 21......rise	12:05	D	May 21 ..... set	5:04	B	Aug. 21.... **set**	**10:52**	B	Nov. 21....rise	6:24	E
Mar. 1 ...... **rise**	**11:29**	D	June 1 .... set	4:19	B	Sept. 1 .... **set**	**10:10**	B	Dec. 1.......rise	5:50	E
Mar. 11 .... **rise**	**11:50**	D	June 11 .... set	3:38	B	Sept. 11.... **set**	**9:33**	B	Dec. 11 ....rise	5:17	E
Mar. 21 .... **rise**	**11:09**	D	June 21 ..... set	2:57	B	Sept. 21 ... **set**	**8:56**	B	Dec. 21....rise	4:43	E
									Dec. 31 ....rise	4:09	E

Mercury

☿ Mercury alternately darts above the eastern and western skylines, switching off every 2 months or so. This year, the planet offers two excellent evening star apparitions, both 40 minutes after sunset, in which its brightness is at magnitude 0 or better and it is at least 10 degrees above the horizon. These occur from January 21 to February 4 and between May 10 and May 23. Mercury offers its best morning star view in the predawn eastern sky from October 28 to November 9.

DO NOT CONFUSE ■ *Mars and Spica, July 4–20. Mars is brighter; Spica is blue.* ■ *Venus and Jupiter, August 18–25. Venus is six times brighter.* ■ *Mars and Saturn, close together in Libra from August 22–27. They are the same brightness, but Mars is orange.* ■ *Uranus and any star right below the Moon on December 1. Uranus is green.*

Astronomical Glossary

Aphelion (Aph.): The point in a planet's orbit that is farthest from the Sun.

Apogee (Apo.): The point in the Moon's orbit that is farthest from Earth.

Celestial Equator (Eq.): The imaginary circle around the celestial sphere that can be thought of as the plane of Earth's equator projected out onto the sphere.

Celestial Sphere: An imaginary sphere projected into space that represents the entire sky, with an observer on Earth at its center. All celestial bodies other than Earth are imagined as being on its inside surface.

Circumpolar: Always visible above the horizon, such as a circumpolar star.

Conjunction: The time at which two or more celestial bodies appear closest in the sky. **Inferior (Inf.):** Mercury or Venus is between the Sun and Earth. **Superior (Sup.):** The Sun is between a planet and Earth. Actual dates for conjunctions are given on the **Right-Hand Calendar Pages, 121–147;** the best times for viewing the closely aligned bodies are given in **Sky Watch** on the **Left-Hand Calendar Pages, 120–146.**

Declination: The celestial latitude of an object in the sky, measured in degrees north or south of the celestial equator; analogous to latitude on Earth. This Almanac gives the Sun's declination at noon.

Eclipse, Lunar: The full Moon enters the shadow of Earth, which cuts off all or part of the sunlight reflected off the Moon. **Total:** The Moon passes completely through the **umbra** (central dark part) of Earth's shadow. **Partial:** Only part of the Moon passes through the umbra. **Penumbral:** The Moon passes through only the **penumbra** (area of partial darkness surrounding the umbra). **See page 102** for more information about eclipses.

Eclipse, Solar: Earth enters the shadow of the new Moon, which cuts off all or part of the Sun's light. **Total:** Earth passes through the umbra (central dark part) of the Moon's shadow, resulting in totality for observers within a narrow band on Earth. **Annular:** The

Moon appears silhouetted against the Sun, with a ring of sunlight showing around it. **Partial:** The Moon blocks only part of the Sun.

Ecliptic: The apparent annual path of the Sun around the celestial sphere. The plane of the ecliptic is tipped 23½° from the celestial equator.

Elongation: The difference in degrees between the celestial longitudes of a planet and the Sun. **Greatest Elongation (Gr. Elong.):** The greatest apparent distance of a planet from the Sun, as seen from Earth.

Epact: A number from 1 to 30 that indicates the Moon's age on January 1 at Greenwich, England; used in calculations for determining the date of Easter.

Equinox: When the Sun crosses the celestial equator. This event occurs two times each year: **Vernal** is around March 20 and **Autumnal** is around September 22.

Evening Star: A planet that is above the western horizon at sunset and less than 180° east of the Sun in right ascension.

Golden Number: A number in the 19-year cycle of the Moon, used in calculations for determining the date of Easter. (Approximately every 19 years, the Moon's phases occur on the same dates.) Add 1 to any given year and divide by 19; the remainder is the Golden Number. If there is no remainder, use 19.

Greatest Illuminated Extent (Gr. Illum. Ext.): When the maximum surface area of a planet is illuminated as seen from Earth.

Magnitude: A measure of a celestial object's brightness. **Apparent** magnitude measures the brightness of an object as seen from Earth.

(continued)

Embarrassed By
THIN HAIR?

My mother's hair was extremely thin. She was terribly embarrassed by it. You could look right through the hair and see large spots of exposed scalp; and she had split ends. She tried everything available but nothing worked, until we found Neutrolox™. Today, my mother's hair looks thick and gorgeous; she looks years younger and she was able to donate her wigs for use by cancer patients.

Neutrolox™ is not just a hair thickening cream; its effective ingredients are the answer to the embarrassing problem of thinning hair and it lets your hair grow fast and naturally. My name is John Peters and I was balding at an extreme rate. After using Neutrolox™ we both are getting compliments on our hair for the first time in our lives. It is great for men and women and can be used on color-treated, permed or processed hair. There is nothing like Neutrolox™ and it is not yet available in stores. Neurolox™ is in a class of its own.

We honestly believe in Neutrolox™ and know you will too! Try Neutrolox™, if you don't agree you get every penny of your money back—no one can beat a 100% no-risk money-back guarantee. To order send $16.95 (plus $4.00 S&H) for a medium, or the most SAVINGS come with the large (you save $9.95), send only $26.95, plus $4.00 S&H for each order to:

NEUTROLOX™, Dept. FA-N2014, BOX 366, Taylor, MI 48180

RINGING in the EARS?
GREAT NEWS for YOU!

If you ever experience ringing in the ears, buzzing, hissing or any other annoying sounds that may be interfering with your life, you should know about Dr. John's Special Ear Drops™. The drops are truly remarkable; for example: 79-year-old Gloria Gains of Richmond, VA writes: "I tried everything available and my doctor told me I would have to live with my trouble. I had trouble sleeping at night and the sounds were driving me out of my mind. Thank God, I saw your ad. I hardly notice anything at all anymore and I'm sleeping like a baby. Your drops have been a God-Send." Thousands of users like Gloria have written to us regarding Dr. John's Special Ear Drops™. If your doctor has not been able to help you, I strongly urge you to give Dr. John's Special Ear Drops™ a try. You won't be sorry!

The drops are guaranteed to be better for you than anything you have tried or you will get every cent of your money back, no questions asked. You can't beat that!

Send $16.95 plus $4.00 S&H (that's only $20.95) for 1 bottle. Or better yet save $10.00 by ordering 2 bottles for only $26.95 plus $4.00 S&H (a total of $30.95). Send payment with your name and address to:

Dr. John's Research, Dept. FA-DJ2014, Box 637, Taylor, MI 48180

Dr. John's Research is celebrating its 35th anniversary this year providing only the best products. Results may vary. A testimonial reflects the opinion of that person. The FDA does not review claims made on herbal products and the drops are not intended to diagnose, treat, cure or prevent any disease. You should see a doctor if you think you have a disease. If you suffer from ringing in the ears, don't wait a minute longer. Order Today!

Objects with an apparent magnitude of 6 or less are observable to the naked eye. The lower the magnitude, the greater the brightness. An object with a magnitude of –1, for example, is brighter than an object with a magnitude of +1. **Absolute** magnitude expresses how bright objects would appear if they were all the same distance (about 33 light-years) from Earth.

Midnight: Astronomically, the time when the Sun is opposite its highest point in the sky. Both 12 hours before and after noon (so, technically, both A.M. and P.M.), midnight in civil time is usually treated as the beginning of the day, rather than the end. It is typically displayed as 12:00 A.M. on 12-hour digital clocks. On a 24-hour time cycle, 00:00, rather than 24:00, usually indicates midnight.

Moon on Equator: The Moon is on the celestial equator.

Moon Rides High/Runs Low: The Moon is highest above or farthest below the celestial equator.

Moonrise/Moonset: When the Moon rises above or sets below the horizon.

Moon's Phases: The changing appearance of the Moon, caused by the different angles at which it is illuminated by the Sun. **First Quarter:** Right half of the Moon is illuminated. **Full:** The Sun and the Moon are in opposition; the entire disk of the Moon is illuminated. **Last Quarter:** Left half of the Moon is illuminated. **New:** The Sun and the Moon are in conjunction; the Moon is darkened because it lines up between Earth and the Sun.

Moon's Place, Astronomical: The position of the Moon within the constellations on the celestial sphere. **Astrological:** The position of the Moon within the tropical zodiac, whose twelve 30° segments (signs) along the ecliptic were named more than 2,000 years ago after constellations within each area. Because of precession and other factors, the zodiac signs no longer match actual constellation positions.

Morning Star: A planet that is above the eastern horizon at sunrise and less than 180° west of the Sun in right ascension.

Node: Either of the two points where a celestial body's orbit intersects the ecliptic. **Ascending:** When the body is moving from south to north of the ecliptic. **Descending:** When the body is moving from north to south of the ecliptic.

Opposition: The Moon or a planet appears on the opposite side of the sky from the Sun (elongation 180°).

Perigee (Perig.): The point in the Moon's orbit that is closest to Earth.

Perihelion (Perih.): The point in a planet's orbit that is closest to the Sun.

Precession: The slowly changing position of the stars and equinoxes in the sky caused by a slight wobble as Earth rotates around its axis.

Right Ascension (R.A.): The celestial longitude of an object in the sky, measured eastward along the celestial equator in hours of time from the vernal equinox; analogous to longitude on Earth.

Solar Cycle: In the Julian calendar, a period of 28 years, at the end of which the days of the month return to the same days of the week.

Solstice, Summer: When the Sun reaches its greatest declination (23½°) north of the celestial equator, around June 21. **Winter:** When the Sun reaches its greatest declination (23½°) south of the celestial equator, around December 21.

Stationary (Stat.): The brief period of apparent halted movement of a planet against the background of the stars shortly before it appears to move backward/westward (retrograde motion) or forward/eastward (direct motion).

Sun Fast/Slow: When a sundial reading is ahead of (fast) or behind (slow) clock time.

Sunrise/Sunset: The visible rising and setting of the upper edge of the Sun's disk across the unobstructed horizon of an observer whose eyes are 15 feet above ground level.

Twilight: For definitions of civil, nautical, and astronomical twilight, see page 106. □□

An Ounce of Hydrogen Peroxide is Worth a Pound of Cure

(SPECIAL) - Hydrogen peroxide is trusted by every hospital and emergency room in the country for its remarkable ability to kill deadly germs like E. coli. In fact, it has attracted so much interest from doctors that over 6000 articles about it have appeared in scientific publications around the world.

Research has discovered that hydrogen peroxide enables your immune system to function properly and fight infection and disease. Doctors have found it can shrink tumors and treat **allergies, Alzheimer's, asthma, clogged arteries, diabetes, digestive problems and migraine headaches**.

Smart consumers nationwide are also discovering there are hundreds of health cures and home remedy uses for hydrogen peroxide. A new book called *The Magic of Hydrogen Peroxide* is now available that tells you exactly how to use hydrogen peroxide by itself... and mixed with simple everyday kitchen items... to make liniments, rubs, lotions, soaks and tonics that treat a wide variety of ailments.

It contains tested and proven health cures that do everything from relieving **chronic pain** to making **age spots** go away. You'll be amazed to see how a little hydrogen peroxide mixed with a pinch of this or that from your cupboard can:

• Relieve arthritis, rheumatism & fibromyalgia
• Treat athlete's foot, foot and nail fungus
• Clear up allergies and sinus problems
• Soothe sore throats, fight colds and flu
• Help heal boils and skin infections
• Whiten teeth without spending a fortune
• Destroy dental bacteria and heal gingivitis
• Help heal cold sores, canker sores
• Relieve insect bites and stings
• Soothe sore feet, soothe muscle aches
• Help minor wounds and cuts heal faster
• Clear up acne, rashes and age spots
• Help heal yeast infections

Besides killing E. coli, hydrogen peroxide also destroys botulism, salmonella and other harmful organisms. It works by making viruses and bacteria self-destruct on the cellular level. Amazingly, for something so powerful, hydrogen peroxide is <u>safe</u>. That's because after it makes germs self-destruct, hydrogen peroxide turns into harmless water.

The Magic of Hydrogen Peroxide book is a valuable health improvement treasure that also shows you how to make tons of household cleaners that work better and more economically than expensive store-bought products. Discover formulas that:

• **Kill germs on kitchen surfaces and utensils**
• **Make a powerful scouring powder that works wonders on sinks, refrigerators and ovens**
• **Disinfect coffee makers, tea pots and blenders**
• **Sanitize wood cutting boards and spoons**
• **Clean out and disinfect clogged drains**
• **Make wood floors, grout and linoleum gleam**
• **Get rid of harmful bacteria on fruits, vegetables and meats with this safe and effective food rinse**
• **Clean toilet bowls, bath tubs and showers**
• **Sterilize dentures**
• **Clean and disinfect pet stains**
• **Remove mold and mildew**
• **Remove wine, ink and blood stains**
• **Boost laundry detergent power**
• **Streak-free-clean windows & mirrors**
• **Rid pets of parasites and bacteria**
• **Make plants flourish**

The Magic of Hydrogen Peroxide also gives you a list of qualified physicians who use hydrogen peroxide in their practices to treat serious ailments. Also included FREE are home remedy formulas using vinegar, garlic baking soda and teas.

To get your copy of *The Magic of Hydrogen Peroxide* direct from the publisher at the special introductory price of $19.95 plus $3.98 shipping and handling (total of $23.93, OH residents please add 6.25% sales tax) simply do this:

Write "Hydrogen Peroxide" on a piece of paper and mail it along with your check or money order payable to: James Direct, Inc., Dept HP387, 500 S. Prospect Ave., Box 980, Hartville, Ohio 44632.

Credit card orders send card number, expiration date and signature.

Save even more and get two books for only $30 postpaid. 90 day money back guarantee.

FREE GIFT! You will also receive a copy of the handy booklet *"How To Grow, Dry, Use & Prepare Herbs"* as our gift to you. Even if you return the book, it is yours to keep with no obligation.

Supplies are limited. Act now.

©2013 JDI HP113S02

http://www.jamesdirect.com

2013

January
S	M	T	W	T	F	S
		1	2	3	4	5
6	7	8	9	10	11	12
13	14	15	16	17	18	19
20	21	22	23	24	25	26
27	28	29	30	31		

February
S	M	T	W	T	F	S
					1	2
3	4	5	6	7	8	9
10	11	12	13	14	15	16
17	18	19	20	21	22	23
24	25	26	27	28		

March
S	M	T	W	T	F	S
					1	2
3	4	5	6	7	8	9
10	11	12	13	14	15	16
17	18	19	20	21	22	23
24	25	26	27	28	29	30
31						

April
S	M	T	W	T	F	S
	1	2	3	4	5	6
7	8	9	10	11	12	13
14	15	16	17	18	19	20
21	22	23	24	25	26	27
28	29	30				

May
S	M	T	W	T	F	S
			1	2	3	4
5	6	7	8	9	10	11
12	13	14	15	16	17	18
19	20	21	22	23	24	25
26	27	28	29	30	31	

June
S	M	T	W	T	F	S
						1
2	3	4	5	6	7	8
9	10	11	12	13	14	15
16	17	18	19	20	21	22
23	24	25	26	27	28	29
30						

July
S	M	T	W	T	F	S
	1	2	3	4	5	6
7	8	9	10	11	12	13
14	15	16	17	18	19	20
21	22	23	24	25	26	27
28	29	30	31			

August
S	M	T	W	T	F	S
				1	2	3
4	5	6	7	8	9	10
11	12	13	14	15	16	17
18	19	20	21	22	23	24
25	26	27	28	29	30	31

September
S	M	T	W	T	F	S
1	2	3	4	5	6	7
8	9	10	11	12	13	14
15	16	17	18	19	20	21
22	23	24	25	26	27	28
29	30					

October
S	M	T	W	T	F	S
		1	2	3	4	5
6	7	8	9	10	11	12
13	14	15	16	17	18	19
20	21	22	23	24	25	26
27	28	29	30	31		

November
S	M	T	W	T	F	S
					1	2
3	4	5	6	7	8	9
10	11	12	13	14	15	16
17	18	19	20	21	22	23
24	25	26	27	28	29	30

December
S	M	T	W	T	F	S
1	2	3	4	5	6	7
8	9	10	11	12	13	14
15	16	17	18	19	20	21
22	23	24	25	26	27	28
29	30	31				

2014

January
S	M	T	W	T	F	S
			1	2	3	4
5	6	7	8	9	10	11
12	13	14	15	16	17	18
19	20	21	22	23	24	25
26	27	28	29	30	31	

February
S	M	T	W	T	F	S
						1
2	3	4	5	6	7	8
9	10	11	12	13	14	15
16	17	18	19	20	21	22
23	24	25	26	27	28	

March
S	M	T	W	T	F	S
						1
2	3	4	5	6	7	8
9	10	11	12	13	14	15
16	17	18	19	20	21	22
23	24	25	26	27	28	29
30	31					

April
S	M	T	W	T	F	S
		1	2	3	4	5
6	7	8	9	10	11	12
13	14	15	16	17	18	19
20	21	22	23	24	25	26
27	28	29	30			

May
S	M	T	W	T	F	S
				1	2	3
4	5	6	7	8	9	10
11	12	13	14	15	16	17
18	19	20	21	22	23	24
25	26	27	28	29	30	31

June
S	M	T	W	T	F	S
1	2	3	4	5	6	7
8	9	10	11	12	13	14
15	16	17	18	19	20	21
22	23	24	25	26	27	28
29	30					

July
S	M	T	W	T	F	S
		1	2	3	4	5
6	7	8	9	10	11	12
13	14	15	16	17	18	19
20	21	22	23	24	25	26
27	28	29	30	31		

August
S	M	T	W	T	F	S
					1	2
3	4	5	6	7	8	9
10	11	12	13	14	15	16
17	18	19	20	21	22	23
24	25	26	27	28	29	30
31						

September
S	M	T	W	T	F	S
	1	2	3	4	5	6
7	8	9	10	11	12	13
14	15	16	17	18	19	20
21	22	23	24	25	26	27
28	29	30				

October
S	M	T	W	T	F	S
			1	2	3	4
5	6	7	8	9	10	11
12	13	14	15	16	17	18
19	20	21	22	23	24	25
26	27	28	29	30	31	

November
S	M	T	W	T	F	S
						1
2	3	4	5	6	7	8
9	10	11	12	13	14	15
16	17	18	19	20	21	22
23	24	25	26	27	28	29
30						

December
S	M	T	W	T	F	S
	1	2	3	4	5	6
7	8	9	10	11	12	13
14	15	16	17	18	19	20
21	22	23	24	25	26	27
28	29	30	31			

2015

January
S	M	T	W	T	F	S
				1	2	3
4	5	6	7	8	9	10
11	12	13	14	15	16	17
18	19	20	21	22	23	24
25	26	27	28	29	30	31

February
S	M	T	W	T	F	S
1	2	3	4	5	6	7
8	9	10	11	12	13	14
15	16	17	18	19	20	21
22	23	24	25	26	27	28

March
S	M	T	W	T	F	S
1	2	3	4	5	6	7
8	9	10	11	12	13	14
15	16	17	18	19	20	21
22	23	24	25	26	27	28
29	30	31				

April
S	M	T	W	T	F	S
			1	2	3	4
5	6	7	8	9	10	11
12	13	14	15	16	17	18
19	20	21	22	23	24	25
26	27	28	29	30		

May
S	M	T	W	T	F	S
					1	2
3	4	5	6	7	8	9
10	11	12	13	14	15	16
17	18	19	20	21	22	23
24	25	26	27	28	29	30
31						

June
S	M	T	W	T	F	S
	1	2	3	4	5	6
7	8	9	10	11	12	13
14	15	16	17	18	19	20
21	22	23	24	25	26	27
28	29	30				

July
S	M	T	W	T	F	S
			1	2	3	4
5	6	7	8	9	10	11
12	13	14	15	16	17	18
19	20	21	22	23	24	25
26	27	28	29	30	31	

August
S	M	T	W	T	F	S
						1
2	3	4	5	6	7	8
9	10	11	12	13	14	15
16	17	18	19	20	21	22
23	24	25	26	27	28	29
30	31					

September
S	M	T	W	T	F	S
		1	2	3	4	5
6	7	8	9	10	11	12
13	14	15	16	17	18	19
20	21	22	23	24	25	26
27	28	29	30			

October
S	M	T	W	T	F	S
				1	2	3
4	5	6	7	8	9	10
11	12	13	14	15	16	17
18	19	20	21	22	23	24
25	26	27	28	29	30	31

November
S	M	T	W	T	F	S
1	2	3	4	5	6	7
8	9	10	11	12	13	14
15	16	17	18	19	20	21
22	23	24	25	26	27	28
29	30					

December
S	M	T	W	T	F	S
		1	2	3	4	5
6	7	8	9	10	11	12
13	14	15	16	17	18	19
20	21	22	23	24	25	26
27	28	29	30	31		

How to Use This Almanac

The Calendar Pages (120–147) are the heart of *The Old Farmer's Almanac*. They present sky sightings and astronomical data for the entire year and are what make this book a true almanac, a "calendar of the heavens." In essence, these pages are unchanged since 1792, when Robert B. Thomas published his first edition. The long columns of numbers and symbols reveal all of nature's precision, rhythm, and glory, providing an astronomical look at the year 2014.

–Beth Krommes

Why We Have Seasons

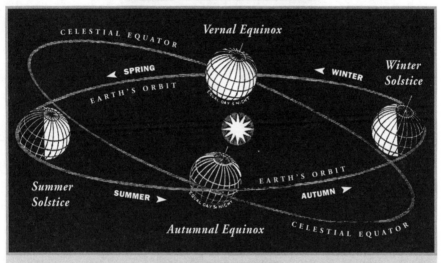

THE SEASONS OF 2014

Vernal equinox .. March 20, 12:57 P.M. EDT	Autumnal equinox Sept. 22, 10:29 P.M. EDT
Summer solstice ... June 21, 6:51 A.M. EDT	Winter solstice ..... Dec. 21, 6:03 P.M. EST

■ The seasons occur because as Earth revolves around the Sun, its axis remains tilted at 23.5 degrees from the perpendicular. This tilt causes different latitudes on Earth to receive varying amounts of sunlight throughout the year.

In the Northern Hemisphere, the summer solstice marks the beginning of summer and occurs when the North Pole is tilted toward the Sun. The winter solstice marks the beginning of winter and occurs when the North Pole is tilted away from the Sun.

The equinoxes occur when the hemispheres equally face the Sun. At this time, the Sun rises due east and sets due west. The vernal equinox marks the beginning of spring; the autumnal equinox marks the beginning of autumn.

In the Southern Hemisphere, the seasons are the reverse of those in the Northern Hemisphere. **(continued)**

How to Use

The Left-Hand Calendar Pages • 120–146

The **Left-Hand Calendar Pages** contain sky highlights, daily Sun and Moon rise and set times, the length of day, high tide times, the Moon's astronomical place and age, and more for Boston. Examples of how to calculate astronomical times for your location are shown below.

A S A M P L E M O N T H

SKY WATCH ☆ *The box at the top of each Left-Hand Calendar Page describes the best times to view celestial highlights, including conjunctions, meteor showers, and planets. The dates on which select astronomical events occur appear on the Right-Hand Calendar Pages.*

① ② ③ ④ ⑤ ⑥ ⑦ ⑧

Get these pages with times set to your zip code at Almanac.com/Access.

Day of Year	Day of Month	Day of Week	☀ Rises h. m.	Rise Key	☀ Sets h. m.	Set Key	Length of Day h. m.	Sun Fast m.	Declination of Sun ° '	High Tide Times Boston	☽ Rises h. m.	Rise Key	☽ Sets h. m.	Set Key	☽ Place	☽ Age
1	1	W.	7:13	E	4:22	A	9 09	12	22 s.57	10½ 11¾	6:59	E	5:05	C	SAG	0
2	2	Th.	7:13	E	4:23	A	9 10	12	22 52	11¼ —	7:50	E	6:19	C	SAG	1
3	3	Fr.	7:13	E	4:24	A	9 11	11	22 46	12 12¾	8:33	E	7:34	C	CAP	2

① To calculate the sunrise time for your locale: Note the Sun Rise Key letter on the chosen day. In the **Time Corrections** table on **page 252**, find your city or the city nearest you. Add or subtract the minutes that correspond to the Sun Rise Key letter to/from the sunrise time given for Boston.

E X A M P L E :

■ To calculate the time of sunrise in Denver, Colorado, on the first day of the month:

Sunrise, Boston, with Key letter E (above)	7:13 A.M. EST
Value of Key letter E for Denver (p. 252)	+ 7 minutes
Sunrise, Denver	7:20 A.M. MST

Use the same procedure with Boston's sunset time and the Sun Set Key letter value to calculate the time of sunset in your locale.

② To calculate the length of day for your locale: Note the Sun Rise and Sun Set Key letters on the chosen day. In the **Time Corrections** table on **page 252**, find your city. Add or subtract the minutes that correspond to the Sun Set Key letter to/from Boston's length of day. *Reverse* the sign (minus to plus, or plus to

minus) of the Sun Rise Key letter minutes. Add or subtract it to/from the first result.

E X A M P L E :

■ To calculate the length of day in Richmond, Virginia, on the first day of the month:

Length of day, Boston (above)	9h. 09m.
Sunset Key letter A for Richmond (p. 256)	+ 41m.
	9h. 50m.
Reverse sunrise Key letter E for Richmond (p. 256, +11 to –11)	– 11m.
Length of day, Richmond	9h. 39m.

③ Use the Sun Fast column to change sundial time to clock time. A sundial reads natural, or Sun, time, which is neither Standard nor Daylight time. To calculate clock time on a sundial in Boston, subtract the minutes given in this column; add the minutes when preceded by an asterisk [*]. To convert the time to your city, use Key letter C in the table on **page 252**.

ATTENTION, READERS: *All times given in this edition of the Almanac are for Boston, Massachusetts, and are in Eastern Standard Time (EST), except from 2:00 A.M., March 9, until 2:00 A.M., November 2, when Eastern Daylight Time (EDT) is given.*

E X A M P L E :

■ To change sundial time to clock time in Boston, or, for example, in Salem, Oregon:

Sundial reading (Boston or Salem)	12:00 noon
Subtract Sun Fast (p. 116)	– 12 minutes
Clock time, Boston	11:48 A.M. EST
Use Key letter C for Salem (p. 255)	+ 27 minutes
Clock time, Salem	12:15 P.M. PST

4 This column gives the degrees and minutes of the Sun from the celestial equator at noon EST or EDT.

5 This column gives the approximate times of high tides in Boston. For example, the first high tide occurs at 10:30 A.M. and the second occurs at 11:15 P.M. the same day. (A dash indicates that high tide occurs on or after midnight and is recorded on the next day.) Figures for calculating high tide times and heights for localities other than Boston are given in the **Tide Corrections** table on **page 250**.

6 To calculate the moonrise time for your locale: Note the Moon Rise Key letter on the chosen day. Find your city on **page 252**. Add or subtract the minutes that correspond to the Moon Rise Key letter to/from the moonrise time given for Boston. (A dash indicates that the moonrise occurs on or after midnight and is recorded on the next day.) Find the longitude of your city on **page 252**. Add a correction in minutes for your city's longitude (see table, above right).

➡ Get the Left-Hand Calendar Pages with times set to your zip code at **Almanac.com/Access.**

–Beth Krommes

Longitude of city	Correction minutes
58°–76°	0
77°–89°	+1
90°–102°	+2
103°–115°	+3
116°–127°	+4
128°–141°	+5
142°–155°	+6

E X A M P L E :

■ To calculate the time of moonrise in Lansing, Michigan, on the first day of the month:

Moonrise, Boston, with Key letter E (p. 116)	6:59 A.M. EST
Value of Key letter E for Lansing (p. 254)	+ 54 minutes
Correction for Lansing longitude, 84° 33'	+ 1 minute
Moonrise, Lansing	7:54 A.M. EST

Use the same procedure with Boston's moonset time and the Moon Set Key letter value to calculate the time of moonset in your locale.

7 The Moon's Place is its *astronomical* placement in the heavens at midnight. Do not confuse this with the Moon's *astrological* place in the zodiac. All calculations in this Almanac are based on astronomy, not astrology, except for those on **pages 246–248**.

In addition to the 12 constellations of the zodiac, this column may indicate these: Auriga **(AUR)**, a northern constellation between Perseus and Gemini; Cetus **(CET)**, which lies south of the zodiac, just south of Pisces and Aries; Ophiuchus **(OPH)**, a constellation primarily north of the zodiac but with a small corner between Scorpius and Sagittarius; Orion **(ORI)**, a constellation whose northern limit first reaches the zodiac between Taurus and Gemini; and Sextans **(SEX)**, which lies south of the zodiac except for a corner that just touches it near Leo.

8 The last column gives the Moon's Age, which is the number of days since the previous new Moon. (The average length of the lunar month is 29.53 days.) **(continued)**

The Right-Hand Calendar Pages • 121–147

A SAMPLE MONTH

- Weather prediction rhyme.
- Symbols for notable celestial events. (See opposite page for explanations.)
- Proverbs, poems, and adages generally appear in this font.
- Sundays and special holy days generally appear in this font.
- The bold letter is the Dominical Letter (from A to G), a traditional ecclesiastical designation for Sunday determined by the date on which the first Sunday falls. For 2014, the Dominical Letter is **E**.
- Noteworthy historical events, folklore, and legends appear in this font.
- High tide heights, in feet, at Boston, Massachusetts.
- Civil holidays and astronomical events appear in this font.
- Religious feasts generally appear in this font. A T indicates a major feast that the church has this year temporarily transferred to a date other than its usual one.

Day of Month	Day of Week	Dates, Feasts, Fasts, Aspects, Tide Heights	Weather
1	W.	New Year's Day • Holy Name • New ● • ☾ AT PERIG. • ☌☿☾ • ☌♇☉	*No*
2	Th.	☌♀☾ • USSR's *Luna 1*, first spacecraft to reach Moon's vicinity, launched, 1959	*worries:*
3	Fr.	*As the days grow longer, / The storms grow stronger.* • {10.9 / 12.2	*It's*
4	Sa.	St. Elizabeth Ann Seton • ⊕ AT PERIHELION • ☌♆☾ • {11.0 / 11.9	*only*
5	**E**	Twelfth Night • ♃ AT ☍ • Educator George Washington Carver died, 1943	*flurries.*
6	M.	Epiphany • ☾ ON EQ. • Global Television Network began programming, Ontario, 1974	*Mild*
7	Tu.	Distaff Day • ☌☿♀ • ☌♅☾ • D. Landreth Seed Co. established, Philadelphia, 1784	*and*
8	W.	–50°F, San Jacinto, Nev., 1937 • Tides {10.2 / 9.5	*beamy,*
9	Th.	☾ AT ☋ • 6.5-magnitude earthquake struck offshore, Ferndale, Calif., 2010 • {10.0 / 9.0	*then the*
10	Fr.	*A lie can go around the world while the truth is getting its britches on.* • Tides {9.8 / 8.7	*opposite.*
11	Sa.	♀ IN INF. ☌ • U.S. Surgeon General released report "Smoking and Health," 1964 • {9.8 / 8.6	*A*
12	**E**	1st S. af. Ep. • Boeing 747 completed first transatlantic proving flight, N.Y. to London, 1970	*thaw*
13	M.	St. Hilary • Plough Monday • ☾ RIDES HIGH • {9.9 / 8.8	*feels*
14	Tu.	"The Fundamental Orders of Connecticut" adopted, 1639	*dreamy.*
15	W.	**Full Wolf** ○ • ☾ AT APO. • ☌♃☾ • Tides {10.1 / 9.0	*Rain*
16	Th.	*At a great pennyworth, pause a while.* • Tides {10.1 / 9.1	*(just*
17	Fr.	U.S. statesman Benjamin Franklin born, 1706 • Tides {10.1 / —	*a*
18	Sa.	Two lights formed a manlike shape and arose out of water, Boston, 1644 • Tides {9.2 / 10.1	*drop of it).*
19	**E**	2nd S. af. Ep. • Painter Paul Cézanne born, 1839 • {9.3 / 9.9	*Snow*
20	M.	**Martin Luther King Jr.'s Birthday (observed)** • ☾ ON EQ. • Tides {9.3 / 9.7	*bursts,*
21	Tu.	Confederate general "Stonewall" Jackson born, 1824 • {9.4 / 9.4	*at*
22	W.	St. Vincent • *If St. Vincent's has sunshine, One hopes much rye and wine.* • Tides {9.4 / 9.2	*worst.*
23	Th.	☾ AT ☊ • ☌♂☾ • Fire devastated Regina's streetcar barns, Sask., 1949 • {9.5 / 8.9	*Drip,*
24	Fr.	4" snow fell near Lake Jocassee, S.C., 1991 • Tides {9.6 / 8.7	*drip,*
25	Sa.	**Conversion of Paul** • ☌♄☾ • 44-lb. 10-oz. cod caught, Five Fathom Bank, Del., 1975	*mixed*
26	**E**	3rd S. af. Ep. • Raiders first to play in four separate decades of Super Bowls, 2003	*precip.*

☞ **For explanations of Almanac terms, see the glossaries on pages 110, 149, and 150.**

Predicting Earthquakes

■ Note the dates in the **Right-Hand Calendar Pages** when the Moon rides high or runs low. The date of the high begins the most likely 5-day period of earthquakes in the Northern Hemisphere; the date of the low indicates a similar 5-day period in the Southern Hemisphere. Also noted are the 2 days each month when the Moon is on the celestial equator, indicating the most likely time for earthquakes in either hemisphere.

–Beth Krommes

■ Throughout the **Right-Hand Calendar Pages** are groups of symbols that represent notable celestial events. The symbols and names of the principal planets and aspects are:

☉	**Sun**	♆	**Neptune**
○●☽	**Moon**	♇	**Pluto**
☿	**Mercury**	☌	**Conjunction (on the**
♀	**Venus**		**same celestial**
⊕	**Earth**		**longitude)**
♂	**Mars**	☊	**Ascending node**
♃	**Jupiter**	☋	**Descending node**
♄	**Saturn**	☍	**Opposition (180**
♅	**Uranus**		**degrees from Sun)**

EXAMPLE:

☌♀☽ on the 2nd day of the month (see opposite page) means that on that date a conjunction (☌) of Venus (♀) and the Moon (☽) occurs: They are aligned along the same celestial longitude and appear to be closest together in the sky.

EARTH AT PERIHELION AND APHELION

■ Perihelion: January 4, 2014. Earth will be 91,406,752 miles from the Sun. Aphelion: July 3, 2014. Earth will be 94,506,543 miles from the Sun.

2014 Calendar Highlights

MOVABLE RELIGIOUS OBSERVANCES

Septuagesima Sunday.	**February 16**
Shrove Tuesday.	**March 4**
Ash Wednesday.	**March 5**
Palm Sunday	**April 13**
First day of Passover	**April 15**
Good Friday.	**April 18**
Easter	**April 20**
Orthodox Easter.	**April 20**
Rogation Sunday.	**May 25**
Ascension Day.	**May 29**
Whitsunday–Pentecost.	**June 8**
Trinity Sunday.	**June 15**
Corpus Christi	**June 22**
First day of Ramadan.	**June 29**
Rosh Hashanah	**September 25**
Yom Kippur	**October 4**
First Sunday of Advent	**November 30**
First day of Chanukah	**December 17**

CHRONOLOGICAL CYCLES

Dominical Letter.	**E**
Epact.	**29**
Golden Number (Lunar Cycle).	**1**
Roman Indiction	**7**
Solar Cycle	**7**
Year of Julian Period	**6727**

−Beth Krommes

ERAS

Era	Year	Begins
Byzantine	**7523**	September 14
Jewish (A.M.)*	**5775**	September 25
Chinese (Lunar) [Year of the Horse]	**4712**	January 31
Roman (A.U.C.)	**2767**	January 14
Nabonassar	**2763**	April 20
Japanese	**2674**	January 1
Grecian (Seleucidae)	**2326**	September 14 (or October 14)
Indian (Saka)	**1936**	March 22
Diocletian	**1731**	September 11
Islamic (Hegira)*	**1436**	October 25

Year begins at sunset the evening before.

SKY WATCH ☆ *The year's only total eclipse, of the Sun, occurs on the 3rd and is visible from the equatorial Atlantic Ocean and west central Africa. Saturn is gone, but Venus starts to show some elevation gain as it noticeably brightens to magnitude –4.8. The Moon, dangling below invisible Pluto, stands above Venus on the 6th. The Moon hovers just above Uranus on the 13th, to the lower right of Jupiter on the 21st, and to the right of faint Mars on the 27th. Orange Mars is now rising at 1:00 A.M. Mercury, at magnitude –0.7, appears low in the east at about 40 minutes before sunrise, where it closely meets returning planet Saturn, which shines at a bright magnitude 0.6, on the 25th and 26th.*

●	**New Moon**	3rd day	7th hour	50th minute
◐	**First Quarter**	10th day	0 hour	57th minute
○	**Full Moon**	17th day	10th hour	16th minute
◑	**Last Quarter**	25th day	14th hour	28th minute

After 2:00 A.M. on November 3, Eastern Standard Time is given.

Get these pages with times set to your zip code at Almanac.com/Access.

305	1	Fr.	7:17	D	**5:37**	B	10 20	32	14 s. 38	10	**10½**	5:04	E	**4:29**	C	}
306	2	Sa.	7:18	D	**5:35**	B	10 17	32	14 56	10¾	**11¼**	6:12	E	**5:05**	B	)
307	3	**F**	6:20	D	**4:34**	B	10 14	32	15 15	10½	**11**	6:21	E	**4:46**	B	)
308	4	M.	6:21	D	**4:33**	B	10 12	32	15 34	11¼	**11¾**	7:30	E	**5:34**	B	1
309	5	Tu.	6:22	D	**4:32**	B	10 10	32	15 52	**12**	—	8:36	E	**6:29**	B	2
310	6	W.	6:23	E	**4:31**	B	10 08	32	16 10	12½	**12¾**	9:38	E	**7:31**	B	3
311	7	Th.	6:25	E	**4:30**	B	10 05	32	16 27	1½	**1¾**	10:32	E	**8:37**	B	4
312	8	Fr.	6:26	E	**4:28**	B	10 02	32	16 45	2¼	**2½**	11:20	E	**9:46**	C	5
313	9	Sa.	6:27	E	**4:27**	B	10 00	32	17 02	3¼	**3½**	**12:01**	E	**10:56**	C	6
314	10	**F**	6:29	E	**4:26**	B	9 57	32	17 19	4¼	**4¾**	**12:37**	D	—	–	7
315	11	M.	6:30	E	**4:25**	B	9 55	32	17 35	5¼	**5¾**	**1:10**	D	12:04	D	8
316	12	Tu.	6:31	E	**4:24**	B	9 53	32	17 51	6½	**6¾**	**1:42**	D	1:11	D	9
317	13	W.	6:32	E	**4:23**	B	9 51	31	18 07	7½	**7¾**	**2:13**	C	2:17	D	10
318	14	Th.	6:33	E	**4:22**	B	9 49	31	18 23	8¼	**8¾**	**2:44**	C	3:22	E	11
319	15	Fr.	6:35	E	**4:22**	B	9 47	31	18 38	9	**9¾**	**3:18**	B	4:26	E	12
320	16	Sa.	6:36	E	**4:21**	B	9 45	31	18 53	10	**10½**	**3:54**	B	5:28	E	13
321	17	**F**	6:37	E	**4:20**	B	9 43	31	19 08	10½	**11¼**	**4:34**	B	6:28	E	14
322	18	M.	6:38	E	**4:19**	B	9 41	31	19 22	11¼	**11¾**	**5:18**	B	7:25	E	15
323	19	Tu.	6:40	E	**4:18**	B	9 38	30	19 36	**12**	—	**6:06**	B	8:17	E	16
324	20	W.	6:41	E	**4:18**	B	9 37	30	19 49	12½	**12½**	**6:58**	B	9:04	E	17
325	21	Th.	6:42	E	**4:17**	B	9 35	30	20 03	1¼	**1¼**	**7:51**	B	9:46	E	18
326	22	Fr.	6:43	E	**4:16**	B	9 33	30	20 15	2	**2**	**8:47**	C	10:24	E	19
327	23	Sa.	6:44	E	**4:16**	B	9 32	29	20 28	2¾	**2¾**	**9:44**	C	10:57	E	20
328	24	**F**	6:46	E	**4:15**	B	9 29	29	20 40	3½	**3½**	**10:42**	C	11:28	D	21
329	25	M.	6:47	E	**4:14**	A	9 27	29	20 52	4¼	**4½**	**11:41**	D	11:57	D	22
330	26	Tu.	6:48	E	**4:14**	A	9 26	28	21 03	5	**5¼**	—	–	**12:26**	D	23
331	27	W.	6:49	E	**4:14**	A	9 25	28	21 14	6	**6¼**	12:42	D	**12:55**	C	24
332	28	Th.	6:50	E	**4:13**	A	9 23	28	21 24	6¾	**7¼**	1:44	D	**1:25**	C	25
333	29	Fr.	6:51	E	**4:13**	A	9 22	27	21 34	7½	**8**	2:49	E	**1:58**	C	26
334	30	Sa.	6:52	E	**4:12**	A	9 20	27	21 s. 44	8¼	**9**	3:57	E	**2:36**	B	27

The hoar-frost gathered, o'er each leaf and spray
Weaving its filmy network; thin and bright. –Sarah Helen Whitman

Day of Month	Day of Week	Weather
1		
2		
3		
4		
5		
6		
7		
8		
9		
10		
11		
12		
13		
14		
15		
16		
17		
18		
19		
20		
21		
22		
23		
24		
25		
26		
27		
28		
29		
30		

Humor is mankind's greatest blessing. –Mark Twain

Farmer's Calendar

■ After a treacherous voyage and brutal first winter spent along the shore of Cape Cod Bay, the Pilgrims of Plymouth Colony had a stroke of good fortune. Members of the Wampanoag Nation offered to teach them how to gather food from the wild and cultivate native crops such as corn. The first harvest, in 1621, proved so successful that Governor William Bradford ordered a feast to celebrate. We now call this the Pilgrims' first Thanksgiving, although they considered it simply a harvest festival. The event, however, was a far cry from today's observance.

The thankful colonists, soon joined by their generous Native American friends, took part in a 3-day party that included singing, dancing, musket and bow-and-arrow competitions, and footraces.

Historians can document with certainty only two items on the menu for that day: fowl provided by the Pilgrims and venison brought by the Wampanoag. Seafood such as bass, cod, eels, clams, and mussels may have been on the table, possibly along with game such as harbor seal, waterfowl, rabbit, and gray squirrel. Roots, fruit, and nuts were also common fare of the day. We don't know for sure whether turkey was served, but it has somehow become a tradition—and that's another reason to celebrate.

SKY WATCH ☆ *Venus continues to climb higher in the west after sunset as it brightens to magnitude –4.9, its most dazzling display of the year. An easy 25 degrees high, it dangles beneath the crescent Moon on the 5th. The Moon floats above green Uranus on the 10th and is to the left of Taurus's orange star Aldebaran on the 15th. In its fat gibbous phase, the Moon diminishes the normally reliable Geminid meteors on the 13th and stands to the right of Jupiter on the 18th. Jupiter, in Gemini, conveniently rises by 7:00 P.M. and shines at a brilliant magnitude –2.7; the Giant Planet is now a telescopic showpiece in advance of its imminent opposition on January 5. Winter begins with the solstice at 12:11 P.M. on the 21st.*

● New Moon	2nd day	19th hour	22nd minute
◐ First Quarter	9th day	10th hour	12th minute
○ Full Moon	17th day	4th hour	28th minute
◑ Last Quarter	25th day	8th hour	48th minute

All times are given in Eastern Standard Time.

Get these pages with times set to your zip code at Almanac.com/Access.

Day of Year	Day of Month	Day of Week	☼ Rises	Key	☼ Sets	Key	Length of Days	Sun Fast	Declination of Sun	High Tide Boston		☾ Rises	Key	☾ Sets	Key	☾ Place	☾ Age
335	1	F	6:53	E	**4:12**	A	9 19	27	21 s. 53	9¼	9¾	5:06	E	**3:21**	B	LIB	28
336	2	M.	6:54	E	**4:12**	A	9 18	26	22 02	10	10½	6:15	E	**4:13**	B	LIB	0
337	3	Tu.	6:55	E	**4:12**	A	9 17	26	22 11	10¾	11½	7:21	E	**5:13**	B	OPH	1
338	4	W.	6:56	E	**4:11**	A	9 15	25	22 19	11½	—	8:21	E	**6:20**	B	SAG	2
339	5	Th.	6:57	E	**4:11**	A	9 14	25	22 26	12¼	12½	9:14	E	**7:31**	C	SAG	3
340	6	Fr.	6:58	E	**4:11**	A	9 13	25	22 33	1¼	1½	9:59	E	**8:43**	C	SAG	4
341	7	Sa.	6:59	E	**4:11**	A	9 12	24	22 40	2	2¼	10:38	E	**9:54**	D	AQU	5
342	8	F	7:00	E	**4:11**	A	9 11	24	22 46	3	3¼	**11:13**	D	**11:03**	D	AQU	6
343	9	M.	7:01	E	**4:11**	A	9 10	23	22 52	4	4¼	**11:45**	D	—	–	AQU	7
344	10	Tu.	7:02	E	**4:11**	A	9 09	23	22 57	5	5½	**12:16**	C	12:10	D	PSC	8
345	11	W.	7:03	E	**4:11**	A	9 08	22	23 02	6	6½	**12:48**	C	1:15	E	PSC	9
346	12	Th.	7:04	E	**4:11**	A	9 07	22	23 07	7	7½	**1:20**	C	2:19	E	PSC	10
347	13	Fr.	7:05	E	**4:12**	A	9 07	21	23 11	8	8½	**1:55**	B	3:21	E	ARI	11
348	14	Sa.	7:05	E	**4:12**	A	9 07	21	23 14	8¾	9¼	**2:33**	B	4:21	E	ARI	12
349	15	F	7:06	E	**4:12**	A	9 06	20	23 17	9½	10¼	**3:15**	B	5:18	E	TAU	13
350	16	M.	7:07	E	**4:12**	A	9 05	20	23 20	10¼	10¾	**4:01**	B	6:11	E	TAU	14
351	17	Tu.	7:08	E	**4:13**	A	9 05	19	23 22	11	11½	**4:51**	B	7:00	E	TAU	15
352	18	W.	7:08	E	**4:13**	A	9 05	19	23 23	11½	—	**5:44**	B	7:44	E	GEM	16
353	19	Th.	7:09	E	**4:13**	A	9 04	19	23 25	12¼	12¼	**6:39**	C	8:24	E	GEM	17
354	20	Fr.	7:09	E	**4:13**	A	9 04	18	23 25	12¾	12¾	**7:35**	C	8:59	E	CAN	18
355	21	Sa.	7:10	E	**4:14**	A	9 04	18	23 26	1½	1½	**8:33**	C	9:31	E	CAN	19
356	22	F	7:10	E	**4:15**	A	9 05	17	23 25	2	2¼	**9:31**	D	10:00	D	LEO	20
357	23	M.	7:11	E	**4:16**	A	9 05	17	23 25	2¾	3	**10:29**	D	10:28	D	SEX	21
358	24	Tu.	7:11	E	**4:16**	A	9 05	16	23 24	3½	3¾	**11:29**	D	10:56	C	LEO	22
359	25	W.	7:11	E	**4:17**	A	9 06	16	23 22	4¼	4½	—	–	11:25	C	VIR	23
360	26	Th.	7:12	E	**4:18**	A	9 06	15	23 20	5	5½	12:31	E	11:55	C	VIR	24
361	27	Fr.	7:12	E	**4:18**	A	9 06	15	23 17	6	6½	1:36	E	**12:30**	C	VIR	25
362	28	Sa.	7:12	E	**4:19**	A	9 07	14	23 14	6¾	7½	2:42	E	**1:09**	B	LIB	26
363	29	F	7:12	E	**4:19**	A	9 07	14	23 11	7¾	8½	3:50	E	**1:56**	B	LIB	27
364	30	M.	7:13	E	**4:20**	A	9 07	13	23 07	8¾	9¼	4:57	E	**2:51**	B	SCO	28
365	31	Tu.	7:13	E	**4:21**	A	9 08	13	23 s. 02	9½	10¼	6:01	E	**3:55**	B	OPH	29

Then came the merry maskers in,
And carols roar'd with blithesome din. –Sir Walter Scott

Day of Month	Day of Week		Weather
1			
2			
3			
4			
5			
6			
7			
8			
9			
10			
11			
12			
13			
14			
15			
16			
17			
18			
19			
20			
21			
22			
23			
24			
25			
26			
27			
28			
29			
30			
31			

Farmer's Calendar

■ If you are like most gardeners, you probably put your tools away at the end of the growing season and don't think very much about them until they are needed in the spring. But if you take a bit of time during the off-season to maintain and repair your tools, they will be safer and easier to use.

Wooden handles on tools such as shovels and iron rakes may become rough and splintery with weather, use, and age. Often, you can restore them by sanding the surface until it becomes smooth again and then applying linseed oil to protect the wood. Handles with deep cracks are a hazard and should be replaced.

Repair rusted metal tools by cleaning them with steel wool or a wire brush and then wiping on 30-weight motor oil to prevent further rusting.

Chances are, the blades on your pruners, loppers, and hedge shears could use sharpening. Use a fine flat file to touch them up. Be careful to keep the original angle of the blade's cutting edge. While you're at it, sharpen the metal edges of shovels and hoes to make digging easier.

Well-maintained, quality garden tools will last for years and can even be passed down from one generation to the next. Perhaps you can pass down the wisdom of how to take care of them, too.

SKY WATCH ☆ *Earth reaches perihelion early in the morning on the 4th. Venus starts the year too low in the solar glare to be readily seen and is in conjunction on the 11th. It will appear as a low morning star most of this year. The real brilliancy belongs to Jupiter in Gemini, which reaches opposition on the 5th; the Giant Planet, at magnitude –2.7, rises at dusk and is out all night. Mars rises at midnight at magnitude 1.0; it forms a lovely orange contrast with the blue star Spica below it. Saturn, at magnitude 0.6, is a morning object, rising at 3:00 A.M. Uranus, in the evening sky, will spend the year in Pisces.*

● New Moon	1st day	6th hour	14th minute
◑ First Quarter	7th day	22nd hour	39th minute
○ Full Moon	15th day	23rd hour	52nd minute
◐ Last Quarter	24th day	0 hour	19th minute
● New Moon	30th day	16th hour	39th minute

All times are given in Eastern Standard Time.

Get these pages with times set to your zip code at Almanac.com/Access.

1	1	W.	7:13	E	**4:22**	A	9 09	12	22 s.57	10½	**11¼**	6:59	E	**5:05**	C	SAG	
2	2	Th.	7:13	E	**4:23**	A	9 10	12	22 52	11¼	—	7:50	E	**6:19**	C	SAG	
3	3	Fr.	7:13	E	**4:24**	A	9 11	11	22 46	12	**12¼**	8:33	E	**7:34**	C	CAP	
4	4	Sa.	7:13	E	**4:25**	A	9 12	11	22 40	1	**1¼**	9:12	D	**8:47**	D	CAP	
5	5	**E**	7:13	E	**4:26**	A	9 13	10	22 33	1¾	**2**	9:47	D	**9:57**	D	AQU	
6	6	M.	7:13	E	**4:27**	A	9 14	10	22 26	2¾	**3**	10:19	C	**11:05**	D	PSC	
7	7	Tu.	7:13	E	**4:28**	A	9 15	10	22 18	3½	**4**	10:51	C	—	-	PSC	
8	8	W.	7:13	E	**4:29**	A	9 16	9	22 10	4½	**5**	11:23	C	12:11	E	PSC	
9	9	Th.	7:12	E	**4:30**	A	9 18	9	22 02	5½	**6**	11:57	B	1:14	E	ARI	
10	10	Fr.	7:12	E	**4:31**	A	9 19	8	21 53	6½	**7**	**12:34**	B	2:14	E	ARI	
11	11	Sa.	7:12	E	**4:32**	A	9 20	8	21 44	7½	**8**	**1:14**	B	3:12	E	TAU	）
12	12	**E**	7:11	E	**4:33**	A	9 22	7	21 34	8¼	**9**	**1:59**	B	4:07	E	TAU	1
13	13	M.	7:11	E	**4:34**	A	9 23	7	21 24	9¼	**9¾**	**2:47**	B	4:57	E	TAU	2
14	14	Tu.	7:11	E	**4:35**	A	9 24	7	21 13	10	**10½**	**3:38**	B	5:43	E	ORI	3
15	15	W.	7:10	E	**4:36**	A	9 26	6	21 02	10½	**11¼**	**4:33**	B	6:24	E	GEM	4
16	16	Th.	7:10	E	**4:38**	A	9 28	6	20 51	11¼	**11¾**	**5:29**	C	7:00	E	GEM	5
17	17	Fr.	7:09	E	**4:39**	B	9 30	6	20 39	11¾	—	**6:26**	C	7:34	E	CAN	6
18	18	Sa.	7:09	E	**4:40**	B	9 31	5	20 27	12¼	**12½**	**7:24**	C	8:04	D	LEO	7
19	19	**E**	7:08	E	**4:41**	B	9 33	5	20 14	1	**1**	**8:22**	D	8:33	D	LEO	8
20	20	M.	7:07	E	**4:42**	B	9 35	5	20 01	1½	**1¾**	**9:21**	D	9:01	D	LEO	9
21	21	Tu.	7:07	E	**4:44**	B	9 37	5	19 48	2¼	**2½**	**10:21**	D	9:29	C	VIR	20
22	22	W.	7:06	E	**4:45**	B	9 39	4	19 34	3	**3¼**	**11:23**	E	9:58	C	VIR	21
23	23	Th.	7:05	E	**4:46**	B	9 41	4	19 20	3¾	**4**	—	-	10:30	C	VIR	22
24	24	Fr.	7:05	E	**4:47**	B	9 42	4	19 06	4½	**5**	12:26	E	11:05	B	VIR	23
25	25	Sa.	7:04	E	**4:49**	B	9 45	4	18 51	5½	**6**	1:31	E	11:47	B	LIB	24
26	26	**E**	7:03	E	**4:50**	B	9 47	3	18 36	6¼	**7**	2:36	E	**12:36**	B	LIB	25
27	27	M.	7:02	E	**4:51**	B	9 49	3	18 20	7¼	**8**	3:40	E	**1:33**	B	OPH	26
28	28	Tu.	7:01	E	**4:53**	B	9 52	3	18 05	8¼	**9**	4:40	E	**2:38**	B	SAG	27
29	29	W.	7:00	E	**4:54**	B	9 54	3	17 48	9¼	**10**	5:34	E	**3:49**	C	SAG	28
30	30	Th.	6:59	E	**4:55**	B	9 56	3	17 32	10¼	**10¾**	6:22	E	**5:04**	C	CAP	0
31	31	Fr.	6:58	E	**4:57**	B	9 59	2	17 s.15	11	**11¾**	7:04	E	**6:20**	D	AQU	1

Only a night from old to new!
Only a night, and so much wrought! –Helen Hunt Jackson

Day of Month	Day of Week	Dates, Feasts, Fasts, Aspects, Tide Heights	Weather
1	W.	New Year's Day • Holy Name • New ● • ☾ AT PERIG. • ☌☿☽ • ☌♄☉	*No*
2	Th.	☌☿☾ • USSR's *Luna 1*, first spacecraft to reach Moon's vicinity, launched, 1959	*worries:*
3	Fr.	*As the days grow longer, / The storms grow stronger.* • Tides {10.9 / 12.2}	*It's*
4	Sa.	St. Elizabeth Ann Seton • ⊕ AT PERIHELION • ☌♅☾ • Tides {11.0 / 11.9}	*only*
5	E	Twelfth Night • ♃ AT ♄ • Educator George Washington Carver died, 1943	*flurries.*
6	M.	𝕰piphany • ☾ ON EQ. • Global Television Network began programming, Ontario, 1974	*Mild*
7	Tu.	Distaff Day • ☌♂♀ • ☌♄☾ • D. Landreth Seed Co. established, Philadelphia, 1784	*and*
8	W.	–50°F, San Jacinto, Nev., 1937 • Tides {10.2 / 9.5}	*beamy,*
9	Th.	☾ AT ☋ • 6.5-magnitude earthquake struck offshore, Ferndale, Calif., 2010 • Tides {10.0 / 9.0}	*then the*
10	Fr.	*A lie can go around the world while the truth is getting its britches on.* • Tides {9.8 / 8.7}	*opposite.*
11	Sa.	♀ IN INF. ☌ • U.S. Surgeon General released report "Smoking and Health," 1964 • Tides {9.8 / 8.6}	*A*
12	E	1st ☉. af. 𝕰p. • Boeing 747 completed first transatlantic proving flight, N.Y.C. to London, 1970	*thaw*
13	M.	St. Hilary • Plough Monday • ☾ RIDES HIGH • Tides {9.9 / 8.8}	*feels*
14	Tu.	"The Fundamental Orders of Connecticut" adopted, 1639	*dreamy.*
15	W.	Full Wolf ○ • ☾ AT APO. • ☌♃☾ • Tides {10.1 / 9.0}	*Rain*
16	Th.	*At a great pennyworth, pause a while.* • Tides {10.1 / 9.1}	*(just*
17	Fr.	U.S. statesman Benjamin Franklin born, 1706 • Tides {10.1 / —}	*a*
18	Sa.	Two lights formed a manlike shape and arose out of water, Boston, 1644 • Tides {9.2 / 10.1}	*drop of it).*
19	E	2nd ☉. af. 𝕰p. • Painter Paul Cézanne born, 1839 • Tides {9.3 / 9.9}	*Snow*
20	M.	Martin Luther King Jr.'s Birthday (observed) • ☾ ON EQ. • Tides {9.3 / 9.7}	*bursts,*
21	Tu.	Confederate general "Stonewall" Jackson born, 1824 • Tides {9.4 / 9.4}	*at*
22	W.	St. Vincent • *If St. Vincent's has sunshine, / One hopes much rye and wine.* • Tides {9.4 / 9.2}	*worst.*
23	Th.	☾ AT ☋ • ☌♂☾ • Fire devastated Regina's streetcar barns, Sask., 1949 • Tides {9.5 / 8.9}	*Drip,*
24	Fr.	4" snow fell near Lake Jocassee, S.C., 1991 • Tides {9.6 / 8.7}	*drip,*
25	Sa.	Conversion of Paul • ☌♄☾ • 44-lb. 10-oz. cod caught, Five Fathom Bank, Del., 1975	*mixed*
26	E	3rd ☉. af. 𝕰p. • Raiders first to play in four separate decades of Super Bowls, 2003	*precip.*
27	M.	☾ RUNS LOW • Carl Lewis made long jump of 28 ft. 10.06 in., N.Y.C., 1984 • Tides {10.5 / 9.3}	*Bright,*
28	Tu.	St. Thomas Aquinas • ☌☿☾ • ☌♂☉ • {11.0 / 9.8}	*bracing*
29	W.	Carl Taylor's ice cream cone– rolling machine patented, 1924 • 62°F, Nampa, Idaho, 1954	*for*
30	Th.	New ● • ☾ AT PERIG. • Raccoons mate now. • {11.9 / 10.8}	*toboggan*
31	Fr.	Chinese New Year • ☿ GR. ELONG. (18° EAST) • ♀ STAT. • {12.1 / 11.1}	*racing.*

Farmer's Calendar

■ It's easy for those of us who live in northern climates to envy gardeners in the Deep South, who enjoy colorful gardens, green leaves, and songbirds year-round. Still, we too can grow a number of plants that attract a wide range of winter birds and create beautiful, off-season interest.

Evergreens are the star performers of the winter garden. Conical, rich green Canadian hemlock; compact globe blue spruce; pyramidal golden Hinoki cypress; and countless other selections give the garden a variety of colors, textures, and shapes while sheltering birds from weather and predators.

Fruit that persist well into the season become the flowers of winter. Those of cranberry viburnums, blue hollies, and flowering crab apples attract flocks of hungry songbirds.

Striking characteristics of many deciduous plants may go unnoticed when they are in leaf. The exfoliating cinnamon brown bark of river birch and the deeply fissured bark of black cherry now become dominant features in the landscape. Bright-color barks of flame willow and red- and yellow-twig dogwoods make bold statements against newly fallen snow.

All in all, the special look of a well-planned winter garden may just make a few southern gardeners a little envious.

SKY WATCH ☆ *On the 1st in evening twilight, a skinny crescent Moon hovers above low Mercury, which at a bright magnitude –0.5 can be glimpsed the next night as well. At midmonth, Venus, in Sagittarius, attains its greatest brilliancy of the year, at a shadow-casting –4.9 magnitude in the eastern morning twilight. Mars brightens greatly to magnitude 0 as Earth approaches it. The Moon floats below Jupiter on the 10th and then helps to create a wonderful conjunction on the 19th, when it stands to the upper right of blue star Spica and orange Mars. The Moon dangles below Saturn on the 22nd, when the pair rises at around 1:00 A.M.; the Ringed World now appears high in the south, just as morning twilight begins.*

◐	**First Quarter**	6th day	14th hour	22nd minute
○	**Full Moon**	14th day	18th hour	53rd minute
◑	**Last Quarter**	22nd day	12th hour	15th minute

All times are given in Eastern Standard Time.

Get these pages with times set to your zip code at Almanac.com/Access.

32	1	Sa.	6:57	E	**4:58**	B	10 01	2	16 s. 58	**12**	—	7:42	D	**7:34**	D	AQU	
33	2	**E**	6:56	E	**4:59**	B	10 03	2	16 41	12½	**12¾**	8:17	D	**8:46**	D	PSC	
34	3	M.	6:55	D	**5:00**	B	10 05	2	16 23	1½	**1¾**	8:50	C	**9:55**	E	PSC	
35	4	Tu.	6:54	D	**5:02**	B	10 08	2	16 05	2¼	**2½**	9:24	C	**11:01**	E	PSC	
36	5	W.	6:53	D	**5:03**	B	10 10	2	15 47	3	**3½**	9:58	C	—	–	PSC	
37	6	Th.	6:52	D	**5:04**	B	10 12	2	15 29	4	**4½**	10:35	B	12:04	E	ARI	
38	7	Fr.	6:51	D	**5:06**	B	10 15	2	15 10	5	**5½**	11:14	B	1:04	E	TAU	
39	8	Sa.	6:49	D	**5:07**	B	10 18	2	14 51	6	**6½**	11:57	B	2:01	E	TAU	
40	9	**E**	6:48	D	**5:08**	B	10 20	2	14 32	7	**7½**	**12:44**	B	2:53	E	TAU	)
41	10	M.	6:47	D	**5:10**	B	10 23	2	14 12	7¾	**8½**	**1:34**	B	3:40	E	ORI	1
42	11	Tu.	6:45	D	**5:11**	B	10 26	2	13 53	8¾	**9¼**	**2:27**	B	4:22	E	GEM	2
43	12	W.	6:44	D	**5:12**	B	10 28	2	13 33	9½	**10**	**3:22**	C	5:01	E	GEM	3
44	13	Th.	6:43	D	**5:13**	B	10 30	2	13 12	10¼	**10¾**	**4:19**	C	5:35	E	CAN	4
45	14	Fr.	6:42	D	**5:15**	B	10 33	2	12 52	10¾	**11¼**	**5:17**	C	6:07	E	CAN	5
46	15	Sa.	6:40	D	**5:16**	B	10 36	2	12 32	11½	12	**6:15**	D	6:36	D	LEO	6
47	16	**E**	6:39	D	**5:17**	B	10 38	2	12 11	**12**	—	**7:15**	D	7:05	D	SEX	17
48	17	M.	6:37	D	**5:19**	B	10 42	2	11 50	12½	**12¾**	**8:15**	D	7:33	C	LEO	18
49	18	Tu.	6:36	D	**5:20**	B	10 44	2	11 29	1	**1¼**	**9:16**	E	8:02	C	VIR	19
50	19	W.	6:34	D	**5:21**	B	10 47	2	11 07	1¾	**2**	**10:18**	E	8:33	C	VIR	20
51	20	Th.	6:33	D	**5:22**	B	10 49	2	10 46	2¼	**2¾**	**11:21**	E	9:07	B	VIR	21
52	21	Fr.	6:31	D	**5:24**	B	10 53	2	10 24	3	**3½**	—	–	9:46	B	LIB	22
53	22	Sa.	6:30	D	**5:25**	B	10 55	2	10 02	4	**4½**	12:24	E	10:30	B	LIB	23
54	23	**E**	6:28	D	**5:26**	B	10 58	3	9 40	5	**5½**	1:27	E	11:22	B	OPH	24
55	24	M.	6:27	D	**5:27**	B	11 00	3	9 18	6	**6½**	2:26	E	**12:21**	B	OPH	25
56	25	Tu.	6:25	D	**5:29**	B	11 04	3	8 56	7	**7¾**	3:21	E	**1:27**	C	SAG	26
57	26	W.	6:24	D	**5:30**	B	11 06	3	8 33	8	**8¾**	4:10	E	**2:38**	C	SAG	27
58	27	Th.	6:22	D	**5:31**	B	11 09	3	8 11	9	**9½**	4:54	E	**3:52**	C	AQU	28
59	28	Fr.	6:21	D	**5:32**	C	11 11	3	7 s. 48	10	**10½**	5:34	D	**5:06**	D	CAP	29

 To use this page, see p. 116; for Key letters, see p. 252. ☞ **Bold = P.M.** ☞ Light = A.M.

And now the feathery snowflakes slowly fly
In many a mazy circle round and round. –Charles Turner Dazey

Day of Month	Day of Week	Dates, Feasts, Fasts, Aspects, Tide Heights	Weather
1			
2			
3			
4			
5			
6			
7			
8			
9			
10			
11			
12			
13			
14			
15			
16			
17			
18			
19			
20			
21			
22			
23			
24			
25			
26			
27			
28			

Many are the stars I see,
Yet in my eye, no star like thee.
–18th-century English verse

Farmer's Calendar

■ **February 2.** All of a sudden, it's February and Groundhog Day is upon us. According to legend, if a groundhog sees its shadow on this day, there will be six more weeks of winter; if it doesn't, then spring is right around the corner.

The groundhog, or woodchuck, typically makes its home in the brambles and thickets that grow where forests meet fields. There, it digs burrows between 4 and 6 feet deep and up to 40 feet long—removing as much as 700 pounds of dirt in the process.

Like its squirrel relatives, the groundhog eats leaves, grass, flowers, bark, and twigs and climbs trees to reach tender buds or fruit. The pesky animal will also go after just about any crop, favoring beans, peas, and carrot tops. It may even take a bite out of every squash or pumpkin in a row, instead of consuming just one.

But the mischief-maker is not all nuisance. Its burrows allow air and water to penetrate the soil and, when abandoned, they become homes for opossums and other small animals. The groundhog itself serves as food for larger creatures, such as bobcats, foxes, and wolves.

With hungry predators on the prowl, it takes courage for a groundhog to emerge from its hole every February to make its forecast. It must take its job *very* seriously.

SKY WATCH ☆ *Mars rises at around 9:00 P.M. early in the month. It continues to brighten explosively, to magnitude –0.9 at midmonth. Brilliant Jupiter forms a pair with the Moon below on the 9th, parading above Orion and at its highest between 7:00 and 8:00 P.M. The Moon forms a lovely triangle with blue star Spica and Mars on the 18th, best seen after 11:00 P.M., and then meets Saturn on the 20th; the pair rises just before midnight and gets progressively higher through the wee hours. Spring begins with the vernal equinox at 12:57 P.M. on the 20th. Look for a brilliant conjunction between Venus and the Moon low in the eastern sky before sunrise on the 27th.*

●	New Moon	1st day	3rd hour	0 minute
◐	First Quarter	8th day	8th hour	27th minute
○	Full Moon	16th day	13th hour	8th minute
◑	Last Quarter	23rd day	21st hour	46th minute
●	New Moon	30th day	14th hour	45th minute

After 2:00 A.M. on March 9, Eastern Daylight Time is given.

Get these pages with times set to your zip code at Almanac.com/Access.

☾ Age

			☀ Rises	K.	☀ Sets	K.	Length of Days	Sun Fast	Declination of Sun	High Tide Boston		☾ Rises	K.	☾ Sets	K.	☾ Place	☾ Age
60	1	Sa.	6:19	D	**5:34**	C	11 15	4	7 s.25	10¾	**11¼**	6:10	D	**6:19**	D	AQU	0
61	2	E	6:17	D	**5:35**	C	11 18	4	7 02	11¾	—	6:45	C	**7:31**	E	PSC	1
62	3	M.	6:16	D	**5:36**	C	11 20	4	6 39	12¼	**12½**	7:20	C	**8:40**	E	PSC	2
63	4	Tu.	6:14	D	**5:37**	C	11 23	4	6 16	1	**1½**	7:55	C	**9:47**	E	PSC	3
64	5	W.	6:13	D	**5:38**	C	11 25	4	5 53	1¾	**2¾**	8:31	B	**10:51**	E	ARI	4
65	6	Th.	6:11	D	**5:40**	C	11 29	5	5 30	2½	**3**	9:11	B	**11:50**	E	ARI	5
66	7	Fr.	6:09	C	**5:41**	C	11 32	5	5 06	3½	**4**	9:53	B	—	-	TAU	6
67	8	Sa.	6:08	C	**5:42**	C	11 34	5	4 43	4¼	**5**	10:39	B	12:45	E	TAU	7
68	9	E	7:06	C	**6:43**	C	11 37	5	4 20	6¼	**7**	**12:29**	B	1:34	E	TAU	8
69	10	M.	7:04	C	**6:44**	C	11 40	6	3 56	7¼	**8**	**1:21**	B	3:19	E	GEM	9
70	11	Tu.	7:02	C	**6:46**	C	11 44	6	3 33	8¼	**9**	**2:15**	B	3:59	E	GEM	10
71	12	W.	7:01	C	**6:47**	C	11 46	6	3 09	9¼	**9¾**	**3:11**	C	4:35	E	CAN	11
72	13	Th.	6:59	C	**6:48**	C	11 49	6	2 45	10	**10½**	**4:09**	C	5:08	E	CAN	12
73	14	Fr.	6:57	C	**6:49**	C	11 52	7	2 22	10¾	**11**	**5:07**	D	5:38	D	LEO	13
74	15	Sa.	6:56	C	**6:50**	C	11 54	7	1 58	11¼	**11¾**	**6:06**	D	6:07	D	SEX	14
75	16	E	6:54	C	**6:51**	C	11 57	7	1 34	**12**	—	**7:06**	D	6:36	D	LEO	15
76	17	M.	6:52	C	**6:53**	C	12 01	8	1 11	12¼	**12¾**	**8:08**	E	7:05	C	VIR	16
77	18	Tu.	6:50	C	**6:54**	C	12 04	8	0 47	1	**1¾**	**9:11**	E	7:36	C	VIR	17
78	19	W.	6:49	C	**6:55**	C	12 06	8	0 s.23	1½	**2**	**10:14**	E	8:10	C	VIR	18
79	20	Th.	6:47	C	**6:56**	C	12 09	8	0 N.00	2¼	**2¾**	**11:18**	E	8:47	B	LIB	19
80	21	Fr.	6:45	C	**6:57**	C	12 12	9	0 23	3	**3½**	—	-	9:30	B	LIB	20
81	22	Sa.	6:44	C	**6:58**	C	12 14	9	0 47	3¾	**4¼**	12:20	E	10:18	B	OPH	21
82	23	E	6:42	C	**6:59**	C	12 17	9	1 11	4½	**5¼**	1:19	E	11:14	B	OPH	22
83	24	M.	6:40	C	**7:01**	C	12 21	10	1 34	5½	**6¼**	2:14	E	**12:16**	B	SAG	23
84	25	Tu.	6:38	C	**7:02**	C	12 24	10	1 58	6½	**7¼**	3:04	E	**1:23**	C	SAG	24
85	26	W.	6:37	C	**7:03**	C	12 26	10	2 21	7¾	**8¼**	3:48	E	**2:33**	C	CAP	25
86	27	Th.	6:35	C	**7:04**	C	12 29	11	2 45	8¾	**9¼**	4:28	E	**3:44**	C	AQU	26
87	28	Fr.	6:33	C	**7:05**	C	12 32	11	3 08	9¾	**10¼**	5:05	D	**4:56**	D	AQU	27
88	29	Sa.	6:31	C	**7:06**	C	12 35	11	3 32	10¾	**11¼**	5:40	D	**6:07**	D	PSC	28
89	30	E	6:30	C	**7:07**	D	12 37	11	3 55	11½	**12**	6:14	C	**7:17**	E	PSC	0
90	31	M.	6:28	C	**7:08**	D	12 40	12	4 N.18	**12½**	—	6:49	C	**8:26**	E	PSC	1

Spanning the winter's cold gulf with an arch,
Over it, rampant, rides in the wild March. –Constance Fenimore Woolson

Day of Month	Day of Week		Weather
1			
2			
3			
4			
5			
6			
7			
8			
9			
10			
11			
12			
13			
14			
15			
16			
17			
18			
19			
20			
21			
22			
23			
24			
25			
26			
27			
28			
29			
30			
31			

Farmer's Calendar

■ In America's early days, fresh vegetables were scarce or nonexistent during the late winter months. Colonists referred to the period from January through March as the "starving time" because stored crops had often run out and, in northern climates, the ground was too frozen to start new ones. By raising some of their crops in cold frames and hot beds, families could extend the growing season by a month or more on either end; in some southern locations, they could garden right through the winter.

A cold frame is a glass-topped, bottomless box that is often built into the ground or bermed with earth to retain heat. Inside it, colonists planted cool-season vegetables such as carrots, lettuce, and peas for an early crop. Later in the season, they replanted for a fall and early winter harvest.

Beans, cucumbers, squashes, and other warm-season plants were started in hot beds, a cold frame in which at least 2 feet of manure was buried under the soil. As the manure decomposed, it gave off heat to the plants' root zone.

These structures also served as a protected place to store the harvest, harden off new seedlings, force spring bulbs, and incubate eggs—which shows that despite the "starving time," the colonists weren't starving for new ideas.

APRIL

THE FOURTH MONTH • 2014

SKY WATCH ☆ *The Moon glides below Jupiter on the 6th. Mars reaches opposition on the 8th and is closest to Earth on the 14th. Orange Mars, now at magnitude –1.5, matches the brilliance of the Dog Star, Sirius. Mars is slightly larger at 15 arcseconds than at its last opposition in 2012. Vesta, the brightest asteroid at magnitude 5.8, reaches opposition on the 13th in Virgo. It can be seen by the naked eye as a dim object centered between the stars Spica and Arcturus. The Moon comes close to Spica and Mars on the 14th. A total lunar eclipse is visible throughout the United States and Canada on the 15th. The partial phase begins at 1:58* A.M.*; totality starts at 3:06* A.M. *Only the western states will see the end of the event.*

◐ **First Quarter**	7th day	4th hour	31st minute
○ **Full Moon**	15th day	3rd hour	42nd minute
◑ **Last Quarter**	22nd day	3rd hour	52nd minute
● **New Moon**	29th day	2nd hour	14th minute

All times are given in Eastern Daylight Time.

Get these pages with times set to your zip code at Almanac.com/Access.

																	☾ Age
91	1	Tu.	6:26	C	**7:10**	D	12 44	12	4 N. 41	12¾	**1¼**	7:25	C	**9:32**	E	ARI	2
92	2	W.	6:24	C	**7:11**	D	12 47	12	5 05	1½	**2**	8:04	B	**10:34**	E	ARI	3
93	3	Th.	6:23	C	**7:12**	D	12 49	13	5 27	2¼	**2¾**	8:46	B	**11:33**	E	TAU	4
94	4	Fr.	6:21	C	**7:13**	D	12 52	13	5 50	3	**3½**	9:32	B	—	–	TAU	5
95	5	Sa.	6:19	C	**7:14**	D	12 55	13	6 13	3¾	**4½**	10:21	B	12:26	E	TAU	6
96	6	**E**	6:18	C	**7:15**	D	12 57	13	6 36	4¾	**5¼**	11:12	B	1:13	E	ORI	7
97	7	M.	6:16	B	**7:16**	D	13 00	14	6 58	5½	**6¼**	**12:06**	B	1:55	E	GEM	8
98	8	Tu.	6:14	B	**7:17**	D	13 03	14	7 21	6½	**7¼**	**1:02**	C	2:33	E	CAN	9
99	9	W.	6:13	B	**7:19**	D	13 06	14	7 43	7½	**8¼**	**1:58**	C	3:07	E	CAN	10
100	10	Th.	6:11	B	**7:20**	D	13 09	15	8 05	8½	**9**	**2:56**	C	3:38	D	LEO	11
101	11	Fr.	6:09	B	**7:21**	D	13 12	15	8 27	9¼	**9¾**	**3:55**	D	4:08	D	SEX	12
102	12	Sa.	6:08	B	**7:22**	D	13 14	15	8 49	10	**10½**	**4:54**	D	4:36	D	LEO	13
103	13	**E**	6:06	B	**7:23**	D	13 17	15	9 11	10¾	**11**	**5:56**	E	5:06	C	VIR	14
104	14	M.	6:04	B	**7:24**	D	13 20	16	9 33	11½	**11¾**	**6:59**	E	5:36	C	VIR	15
105	15	Tu.	6:03	B	**7:25**	D	13 22	16	9 54	**12¼**	—	**8:03**	E	6:09	C	VIR	16
106	16	W.	6:01	B	**7:26**	D	13 25	16	10 15	12½	**1**	**9:08**	E	6:46	B	LIB	17
107	17	Th.	6:00	B	**7:28**	D	13 28	16	10 37	1	**1½**	**10:12**	E	7:27	B	LIB	18
108	18	Fr.	5:58	B	**7:29**	D	13 31	16	10 58	1¾	**2¼**	**11:14**	E	8:15	B	SCO	19
109	19	Sa.	5:56	B	**7:30**	D	13 34	17	11 18	2½	**3¼**	—	–	9:09	B	OPH	20
110	20	**E**	5:55	B	**7:31**	D	13 36	17	11 39	3¼	**4**	12:10	E	10:10	B	SAG	21
111	21	M.	5:53	B	**7:32**	D	13 39	17	11 59	4¼	**5**	1:02	E	11:15	C	SAG	22
112	22	Tu.	5:52	B	**7:33**	D	13 41	17	12 19	5¼	**6**	1:47	E	**12:23**	C	CAP	23
113	23	W.	5:50	B	**7:34**	D	13 44	17	12 39	6¼	**7**	2:28	E	**1:32**	C	AQU	24
114	24	Th.	5:49	B	**7:35**	D	13 46	18	12 59	7½	**8**	3:04	D	**2:42**	D	AQU	25
115	25	Fr.	5:47	B	**7:37**	D	13 50	18	13 19	8½	**9**	3:39	D	**3:51**	D	PSC	26
116	26	Sa.	5:46	B	**7:38**	D	13 52	18	13 38	9½	**10**	4:12	C	**5:00**	D	PSC	27
117	27	**E**	5:44	B	**7:39**	E	13 55	18	13 57	10½	**10¾**	4:46	C	**6:08**	E	PSC	28
118	28	M.	5:43	B	**7:40**	E	13 57	18	14 16	11¼	**11½**	5:21	C	**7:14**	E	PSC	29
119	29	Tu.	5:42	B	**7:41**	E	13 59	18	14 35	**12¼**	—	5:58	B	**8:18**	E	ARI	0
120	30	W.	5:40	B	**7:42**	E	14 02	19	14 N. 53	12¼	**1**	6:39	B	**9:19**	E	ARI	1

 To use this page, see p. 116; for Key letters, see p. 252. ☞ **Bold = P.M.** ☞ Light = A.M.

The bluebird knows it is April,
and soars toward the Sun and sings. –Eben Eugene Rexford

Day of Month	Day of Week		Weather
1			
2			
3			
4			
5			
6			
7			
8			
9			
10			
11			
12			
13			
14			
15			
16			
17			
18			
19			
20			
21			
22			
23			
24			
25			
26			
27			
28			
29			
30			

Pen and ink is wit's plough. –John Clarke

Farmer's Calendar

■ *He who plants trees loves others besides himself.* This old English proverb may explain why it is so meaningful to plant a tree to celebrate a birthday or anniversary or to honor the life of a loved one who has passed away. A tree planted today will be enjoyed by generations to come, serving as a living memorial that also benefits the environment.

An appropriate tree could be one that blooms on the anniversary date. Or, it might be a favorite of the person whom you are honoring. Consider also a tree that symbolizes cherished characteristics of your loved one, feelings about your relationship, a statement about the future, or similar. In the language of flowers, for example, an acacia signifies friendship; birch, grace; lilac, memory; linden, marriage; and mountain ash, "I watch over you."

As you select a site, keep in mind the tree's mature height and spread—you don't want it to outgrow the spot that you've chosen. When planting a tree in memory of a relative, think about the person's favorite place in the yard or a garden that he or she had enjoyed tending.

If you lack the space to plant a memorial tree, consider donating one to a school, cemetery, park, or the National Arbor Day Foundation. You will truly be loving many others besides yourself.

SKY WATCH ☆ *Saturn reaches opposition on the 10th. This is its brightest and best opposition since 2005, because the rings are now very "open," their edges virtually encircling the entire planet. The rings can be seen through any telescope magnification above 30×. On the 3rd and again on the 31st, Jupiter is above the Moon, but the Giant Planet is getting lower each evening and will soon be gone. The Moon forms an all-night pair with Mars to its left on the 10th, before passing to the right of Saturn on the 13th. On the 25th, the Moon stands to the right of Venus, which, at magnitude –4.0, has now lost more than half of its light since February and remains low at dawn.*

◐ **First Quarter**	6th day	23rd hour	15th minute
○ **Full Moon**	14th day	15th hour	16th minute
◑ **Last Quarter**	21st day	8th hour	59th minute
● **New Moon**	28th day	14th hour	40th minute

All times are given in Eastern Daylight Time.

Get these pages with times set to your zip code at Almanac.com/Access.

			☼ Rises		☼ Sets		Length	Sun Fast	Declination	High Tide		☽ Rises		☽ Sets		☽ Place	☽ Age
121	1	Th.	5:39	B	7:43	E	14 04	19	15 N.11	1	1¾	7:23	B	10:15	E	TAU	2
122	2	Fr.	5:38	B	7:44	E	14 06	19	15 29	1¾	2½	8:11	B	11:05	E	TAU	3
123	3	Sa.	5:36	B	7:46	E	14 10	19	15 47	2½	3¾	9:02	B	11:50	E	ORI	4
124	4	E	5:35	B	7:47	E	14 12	19	16 04	3¼	4	9:55	B	—	–	GEM	5
125	5	M.	5:34	B	7:48	E	14 14	19	16 22	4	4¾	10:51	C	12:30	E	GEM	6
126	6	Tu.	5:32	B	7:49	E	14 17	19	16 38	5	5½	11:47	C	1:06	E	CAN	7
127	7	W.	5:31	B	7:50	E	14 19	19	16 55	5¾	6½	12:44	C	1:38	E	CAN	8
128	8	Th.	5:30	B	7:51	E	14 21	19	17 11	6¾	7¼	1:42	D	2:08	D	LEO	9
129	9	Fr.	5:29	B	7:52	E	14 23	19	17 27	7¾	8¼	2:40	D	2:36	D	SEX	10
130	10	Sa.	5:28	B	7:53	E	14 25	19	17 43	8½	9	3:41	D	3:05	D	LEO	11
131	11	E	5:27	B	7:54	E	14 27	19	17 59	9½	9¾	4:43	E	3:34	C	VIR	12
132	12	M.	5:25	B	7:55	E	14 30	19	18 14	10¼	10½	5:47	E	4:06	C	VIR	13
133	13	Tu.	5:24	B	7:56	E	14 32	19	18 28	11	11¾	6:52	E	4:41	B	VIR	14
134	14	W.	5:23	B	7:57	E	14 34	19	18 43	11¾	12	7:58	E	5:21	B	LIB	15
135	15	Th.	5:22	A	7:58	E	14 36	19	18 57	12½	—	9:03	E	6:07	B	LIB	16
136	16	Fr.	5:21	A	7:59	E	14 38	19	19 11	12¾	1¼	10:03	E	7:00	B	OPH	17
137	17	Sa.	5:20	A	8:00	E	14 40	19	19 25	1½	2	10:58	E	8:00	B	SAG	18
138	18	E	5:19	A	8:02	E	14 43	19	19 38	2¼	3	11:46	E	9:05	C	SAG	19
139	19	M.	5:18	A	8:02	E	14 44	19	19 51	3	3½	—	–	10:14	C	SAG	20
140	20	Tu.	5:18	A	8:03	E	14 45	19	20 03	4	4¾	12:29	E	11:24	C	AQU	21
141	21	W.	5:17	A	8:04	E	14 47	19	20 15	5	5¾	1:07	D	12:34	E	CAP	22
142	22	Th.	5:16	A	8:05	E	14 49	19	20 27	6	6¾	1:42	D	1:42	D	AQU	23
143	23	Fr.	5:15	A	8:06	E	14 51	19	20 39	7¼	7¾	2:15	D	2:50	D	PSC	24
144	24	Sa.	5:14	A	8:07	E	14 53	19	20 50	8¼	8¾	2:47	C	3:57	E	PSC	25
145	25	E	5:14	A	8:08	E	14 54	19	21 01	9¼	9½	3:21	C	5:02	E	PSC	26
146	26	M.	5:13	A	8:09	E	14 56	19	21 11	10¼	10½	3:56	B	6:06	E	ARI	27
147	27	Tu.	5:12	A	8:10	E	14 58	18	21 21	11	11¾	4:35	B	7:07	E	ARI	28
148	28	W.	5:12	A	8:11	E	14 59	18	21 31	11¾	12	5:17	B	8:05	E	TAU	0
149	29	Th.	5:11	A	8:12	E	15 01	18	21 40	12½	—	6:03	B	8:58	E	TAU	1
150	30	Fr.	5:10	A	8:12	E	15 02	18	21 49	12¾	1¼	6:53	B	9:45	E	TAU	2
151	31	Sa.	5:10	A	8:13	E	15 03	18	21 N.58	1½	2	7:45	B	10:27	E	GEM	3

May hath 31 days • 2014

Would that thou couldst last for aye,
Merry, ever-merry May! –William D. Gallagher

Day of Month	Day of Week		Weather
1	Th.	Sts. Philip & James • **May Day** • Architect Benjamin Latrobe born, 1764	*Maypole*
2	Fr.	St. Athanasius • ☾ RIDES HIGH • Tides {10.8 / 9.7	*dancing*
3	Sa.	*All the flowers of tomorrow are in the seeds of yesterday.*	*calls*
4	**E**	3rd S. of Easter • ☌♃☾ • *Magellan* spacecraft launched from Space Shuttle *Atlantis,* 1989	*for*
5	M.	**Cinco de Mayo** • Journalist Nellie Bly born, 1864 • Tides {9.6 / 8.8	*rain*
6	Tu.	☾ AT APO. • Successful flight of Samuel Langley's model Aerodrome No. 5 aircraft, 1896 • {9.3 / 8.7	*boots;*
7	W.	Glenn Miller recorded "Chattanooga Choo Choo," 1941	*trade*
8	Th.	St. Julian of Norwich • First Catholic mass in an airship *(Hindenburg)* over ocean, 1936	*them*
9	Fr.	St. Gregory of Nazianzus • ☾ ON EQ. • Hairstylist Vidal Sassoon died, 2012 • {8.9 / 9.1	*in*
10	Sa.	♄ AT ☍ • Sonic boom possibly due to meteor, Virginia Beach, Va., 2011 • Tides {9.0 / 9.5	*for*
11	**E**	**4th S. of Easter** • **Mother's Day** • ☌♂☾ • **Three**	*skimpy*
12	M.	☾ AT ☊ • *Shear your sheep in May, and shear them all away.* • **Chilly**	*swimsuits!*
13	Tu.	Boxer Joe Louis born, 1914 • **Saints** • {9.7 / 10.8	*Lightning*
14	W.	Vesak • **Full Flower** ○ • ☌♄☾ • Tides {10.0 / 11.2	*warns*
15	Th.	☌♀⛢ • Cranberries in bud now. • Fish fell from sky, Olneyville, R.I., 1900 • {10.2 / —	*us,*
16	Fr.	☾ RUNS LOW • Mill River flood, western Mass., 1874 • Tides {11.4 / 10.3	*thunder*
17	Sa.	District of Alaska created, 1884 • Tides {11.5 / 10.3	*thrills,*
18	**E**	**5th S. of Easter** • ☾ AT PERIG. • ☌♇☾ • {11.5 / 10.3	*sunshine*
19	M.	St. Dunstan • **Victoria Day (Canada)** • 7.1-magnitude earthquake, Imperial Valley, Calif., 1940	*warms*
20	Tu.	Rare Madagascar teal duck born, Louisville Zoo, Ky., 2009	*us,*
21	W.	♂ STAT. • *If thou injurest conscience, it will have its revenge upon thee.* • {10.7 / 10.2	*drizzle*
22	Th.	☾ ON EQ. • ☌♆☾ • Space Needle's revolving restaurant dedicated, Seattle, Wash., 1961	*chills,*
23	Fr.	Actor Errol Flynn on *LIFE* magazine's cover, 1938	*meadows*
24	Sa.	☌⛢☾ • First major league baseball night game, Cincinnati, Ohio, 1935 • Tides {10.0 / 10.7	*teem*
25	**E**	**Rogation S.** • ☾ AT ☋ • ☌♀☾ • ☿ GR. ELONG. (23° EAST)	*with*
26	M.	**Memorial Day (observed)** • Canada and U.S. sign Pacific Albacore Tuna Treaty, 1981 • {9.9 / 11.0	*daffodils.*
27	Tu.	*Where there is sugar, there are bound to be ants.*	*Summerlike:*
28	W.	**New** ● • Patent application for John B. Gruelle's Raggedy Ann doll filed, 1915	*rain*
29	Th.	**Ascension** • Orthodox Ascension • ☾ RIDES HIGH • {9.8 / —	*pounds*
30	Fr.	☌☿☾ • U.S. brigadier general Norman Cota born, 1893 • Tides {10.8 / 9.6	*down,*
31	Sa.	Visit. of Mary • 98°F, Chicago, Ill. 1934 • {10.6 / 9.5	*drummerlike.*

Farmer's Calendar

■ Almost everyone who has eaten fiddlehead ferns agrees that this wild vegetable is delicious, but many can not agree on what it tastes like. Some detect a hint of artichoke, while others compare the flavor to that of asparagus, green beans, spinach, or a combination.

Foraging the forest floor for fiddleheads has long been a springtime tradition across much of North America. Early settlers learned about them from Native Americans, who used the early-season vegetable not only as food, but also as a restorative medicine after a long winter with no greenery.

Fiddleheads, named for their resemblance to a violin's scroll, are young fern fronds that have not yet opened. While all ferns have fiddleheads, many are inedible or even poisonous. The ostrich fern *(Matteuccia struthiopteris)* is the safest to eat. Have a plant expert show you how to identify it in the wild.

When gathering, choose bright green fiddleheads with tightly coiled tops that are no more than 1 to 1½ inches in diameter. Snap them off at the ground, taking only a few from each clump. Remove the brown husks and wash the fiddleheads thoroughly in cold water. Steam them for 10 to 12 minutes or boil them for 15 minutes. Even if you can't figure out what they taste like, you might find the flavor most agreeable.

THE SIXTH MONTH • 2014

SKY WATCH ☆ *The Moon performs several beautiful close conjunctions this month during the short hours of the night. It passes just below Mars in Virgo on the 7th. Although orange Mars now fades to magnitude –0.3, it still outshines spring's brightest star, Arcturus, which has the same color, albeit a paler version. On the 10th, the Moon passes closely to the left of Saturn in Libra; Saturn's magnitude of 0.2 is just half the brightness of Mars. The full Moon stands very close to invisible Pluto in Sagittarius on the 13th; on the 24th, the Moon appears to the right of fading Venus, now low in dawn's brightening twilight. Summer begins with the solstice on the 21st, at 6:51* A.M.

◐	**First Quarter**	5th day	16th hour	39th minute
○	**Full Moon**	13th day	0 hour	11th minute
◑	**Last Quarter**	19th day	14th hour	39th minute
●	**New Moon**	27th day	4th hour	8th minute

All times are given in Eastern Daylight Time.

Get these pages with times set to your zip code at Almanac.com/Access.

1	**E**	5:09	A	**8:14**	E	15	05	18	22 N.	06	2	**2¾**	8:40	B	**11:05**	E	GEM	
2	M.	5:09	A	**8:15**	E	15	06	18	22	14	2¾	**3½**	9:36	C	**11:38**	E	CAN	
3	Tu.	5:09	A	**8:16**	E	15	07	17	22	21	3½	**4¼**	10:33	C	—	–	CAN	
4	W.	5:08	A	**8:16**	E	15	08	17	22	28	4¼	**5**	11:30	C	12:09	D	LEO	
5	Th.	5:08	A	**8:17**	E	15	09	17	22	35	5¼	**5¾**	**12:28**	D	12:38	D	SEX	
6	Fr.	5:07	A	**8:18**	E	15	11	17	22	41	6	**6½**	**1:26**	D	1:06	D	LEO	
7	Sa.	5:07	A	**8:18**	E	15	11	17	22	47	7	**7½**	**2:27**	E	1:34	C	VIR	
8	**E**	5:07	A	**8:19**	E	15	12	17	22	52	7¾	**8¼**	**3:29**	E	2:04	C	VIR	
9	M.	5:07	A	**8:19**	E	15	12	16	22	57	8¾	**9**	**4:33**	E	2:37	C	VIR	2
10	Tu.	5:07	A	**8:20**	E	15	13	16	23	02	9½	**9¾**	**5:39**	E	3:14	B	LIB	3
11	W.	5:06	A	**8:21**	E	15	15	16	23	06	10½	**10½**	**6:45**	E	3:56	B	LIB	4
12	Th.	5:06	A	**8:21**	E	15	15	16	23	10	11¼	**11½**	**7:48**	E	4:46	B	OPH	5
13	Fr.	5:06	A	**8:22**	E	15	16	16	23	13	**12**	—	**8:47**	E	5:44	B	OPH	6
14	Sa.	5:06	A	**8:22**	E	15	16	15	23	16	12¼	**1**	**9:40**	E	6:49	C	SAG	7
15	**E**	5:06	A	**8:22**	E	15	16	15	23	19	1	**1¾**	**10:27**	E	7:59	C	SAG	8
16	M.	5:06	A	**8:23**	E	15	17	15	23	21	2	**2¾**	**11:08**	E	9:11	C	CAP	9
17	Tu.	5:06	A	**8:23**	E	15	17	15	23	23	3	**3½**	**11:44**	D	10:22	D	CAP	0
18	W.	5:06	A	**8:23**	E	15	17	15	23	24	3¾	**4½**	—	–	11:33	D	AQU	21
19	Th.	5:07	A	**8:24**	E	15	17	14	23	25	4¾	**5½**	12:18	D	**12:42**	D	PSC	22
20	Fr.	5:07	A	**8:24**	E	15	17	14	23	25	5¾	**6½**	12:51	C	**1:49**	E	PSC	23
21	Sa.	5:07	A	**8:24**	E	15	17	14	23	26	7	**7½**	1:24	C	**2:55**	E	PSC	24
22	**E**	5:07	A	**8:24**	E	15	17	14	23	25	8	**8¼**	1:58	C	**3:59**	E	ARI	25
23	M.	5:07	A	**8:24**	E	15	17	13	23	25	9	**9¼**	2:35	B	**5:00**	E	ARI	26
24	Tu.	5:08	A	**8:25**	E	15	17	13	23	23	10	**10**	3:15	B	**5:58**	E	TAU	27
25	W.	5:08	A	**8:25**	E	15	17	13	23	22	10¾	**11**	3:59	B	**6:52**	E	TAU	28
26	Th.	5:08	A	**8:25**	E	15	17	13	23	20	11½	**11¾**	4:47	B	**7:41**	E	TAU	29
27	Fr.	5:09	A	**8:25**	E	15	16	13	23	18	**12¼**	—	5:38	B	**8:25**	E	ORI	0
28	Sa.	5:09	A	**8:25**	E	15	16	12	23	15	12¼	**1**	6:32	B	**9:04**	E	GEM	1
29	**E**	5:10	A	**8:25**	E	15	15	12	23	12	1	**1½**	7:28	C	**9:39**	E	CAN	2
30	M.	5:10	A	**8:25**	E	15	15	12	23 N.	08	1¾	**2¼**	8:24	C	**10:11**	D	CAN	3

The world turns softly
Not to spill its lakes and rivers. –Hilda Conkling

Day of Month	Day of Week		Weather
1			
2			
3			
4			
5			
6			
7			
8			
9			
10			
11			
12			
13			
14			
15			
16			
17			
18			
19			
20			
21			
22			
23			
24			
25			
26			
27			
28			
29			
30			

The heart has its summer and its winter. –Turkish proverb

Farmer's Calendar

■ *Married in the month of roses, June, / Life will be one long honeymoon.*

June is traditionally the most popular month to have a wedding. The custom dates back more than 2,000 years to when the ancient Romans named the month after their goddess of marriage and childbirth, Juno. It was thought that happiness and prosperity would come to those who wed during her month.

Romans also preferred June weddings for more practical reasons. By this time, the local wet season had ended in most places, so celebrants could usually rely on dry, comfortable weather—a fact for which the bride, whose intricate nuptial hairdo featured six locks wreathed in blossoms, must have been especially thankful.

Getting married in June meant that the first child would most likely be born during the following spring, instead of in the dead of winter when times were lean. Plus, a spring childbirth wouldn't interfere with the busy fall harvest.

Today, couples often do as the Romans did and choose a June wedding. Not only is the weather fairly predictable, but also the days are long, the festive aroma of flowers fills the air, and many schools and colleges are out of session, making it easier for families to attend the event—which are all practical reasons, too.

SKY WATCH ☆ *Demoted ex-planet Pluto reaches opposition at a hopeless magnitude 14.1 on the 4th. The Moon displays two superbly tight conjunctions this month. First, it floats just below zero-magnitude Mars on the 5th, with blue Spica close by on the left; the grouping is best seen at nightfall. Then, on the 7th, it's very close to Saturn, with the pair highest at nightfall in the south. Mercury hovers below Venus low in the eastern morning sky on the 17th; the innermost planet is at magnitude 0 but struggles against the twilight glow. Venus, fading further to –3.8, stands to the left of the Moon low in eastern twilight on the 24th. Jupiter finally vanishes into solar glare as it crosses into Cancer and passes the Sun in a conjunction on the 24th.*

◐	First Quarter	5th day	7th hour	59th minute
○	Full Moon	12th day	7th hour	25th minute
◑	Last Quarter	18th day	22nd hour	8th minute
●	New Moon	26th day	18th hour	42nd minute

All times are given in Eastern Daylight Time.

Get these pages with times set to your zip code at Almanac.com/Access.

Day	Wk	Rise	Set	Length		Dec.			Rise	Set	Place	
1	Tu.	5:11 A	8:24 E	15 13	12	23 N.04	2¼	3	9:21 C	10:41 D	LEO	
2	W.	5:11 A	8:24 E	15 13	12	23 00	3	3½	10:18 D	11:09 D	LEO	
3	Th.	5:12 A	8:24 E	15 12	11	22 55	3¾	4¼	11:16 D	11:36 C	LEO	
4	Fr.	5:12 A	8:24 E	15 12	11	22 50	4½	5	12:14 D	—	VIR	
5	Sa.	5:13 A	8:23 E	15 10	11	22 44	5¼	5¾	1:14 E	12:05 C	VIR	
6	**E**	5:14 A	8:23 E	15 09	11	22 38	6¼	6¾	2:16 E	12:35 C	VIR	
7	M.	5:14 A	8:23 E	15 09	11	22 32	7¼	7½	3:19 E	1:09 C	VIR	
8	Tu.	5:15 A	8:22 E	15 07	11	22 25	8	8¼	4:24 E	1:48 B	LIB	
9	W.	5:16 A	8:22 E	15 06	10	22 18	9	9¼	5:28 E	2:33 B	SCO	
10	Th.	5:16 A	8:22 E	15 06	10	22 10	10	10¼	6:30 E	3:26 B	OPH	
11	Fr.	5:17 A	8:21 E	15 04	10	22 02	10¾	11	7:27 E	4:27 B	SAG	
12	Sa.	5:18 A	8:21 E	15 03	10	21 54	11¾	12	8:18 E	5:35 C	SAG	5
13	**E**	5:19 A	8:20 E	15 01	10	21 45	12½	—	9:03 E	6:48 C	CAP	6
14	M.	5:19 A	8:19 E	15 00	10	21 36	12¾	1½	9:42 D	8:03 C	AQU	7
15	Tu.	5:20 A	8:19 E	14 59	10	21 27	1¾	2¼	10:19 D	9:17 D	AQU	8
16	W.	5:21 A	8:18 E	14 57	10	21 17	2½	3¼	10:53 C	10:29 D	PSC	9
17	Th.	5:22 A	8:17 E	14 55	10	21 07	3½	4	11:27 C	11:39 E	PSC	10
18	Fr.	5:23 A	8:17 E	14 54	10	20 56	4½	5	—	12:46 E	PSC	11
19	Sa.	5:24 A	8:16 E	14 52	9	20 45	5½	6	12:01 C	1:51 E	PSC	12
20	**E**	5:25 A	8:15 E	14 50	9	20 34	6½	7	12:37 B	2:54 E	ARI	13
21	M.	5:25 A	8:14 E	14 49	9	20 23	7½	8	1:16 B	3:53 E	TAU	14
22	Tu.	5:26 A	8:13 E	14 47	9	20 11	8½	9	1:58 B	4:48 E	TAU	15
23	W.	5:27 A	8:13 E	14 46	9	19 58	9½	9¾	2:44 B	5:38 E	TAU	26
24	Th.	5:28 A	8:12 E	14 44	9	19 46	10½	10½	3:34 B	6:24 E	ORI	27
25	Fr.	5:29 A	8:11 E	14 42	9	19 33	11¼	11¼	4:27 B	7:05 E	GEM	28
26	Sa.	5:30 A	8:10 E	14 40	9	19 20	11¾	12	5:21 C	7:41 E	GEM	0
27	**E**	5:31 A	8:09 E	14 38	9	19 06	12½	—	6:17 C	8:14 E	CAN	1
28	M.	5:32 A	8:08 E	14 36	9	18 52	12½	1¼	7:14 C	8:44 D	LEO	2
29	Tu.	5:33 B	8:07 E	14 34	9	18 38	1¼	1¾	8:11 C	9:13 D	LEO	3
30	W.	5:34 B	8:06 E	14 32	9	18 24	2	2¼	9:08 D	9:41 D	LEO	4
31	Th.	5:35 B	8:04 E	14 29	9	18 N.09	2½	3	10:06 D	10:09 C	VIR	5

Beautiful cloud! with folds so soft and fair,
Swimming in the pure quiet air! –William Cullen Bryant

Day of Month	Day of Week	Weather
1		
2		
3		
4		
5		
6		
7		
8		
9		
10		
11		
12		
13		
14		
15		
16		
17		
18		
19		
20		
21		
22		
23		
24		
25		
26		
27		
28		
29		
30		
31		

Farmer's Calendar

■ For years, farmers have depended on dowsing to find the best location to dig a well or pond. The dowser would hold a forked stick in front of him with both hands and then slowly walk over a piece of ground. When the stick "dowsed," or dipped, toward the earth, the presence of water was indicated.

No one is certain when dowsing began, but artwork from ancient China and Egypt depicts men using what appear to be dowsing (divining) rods. In the Middle Ages, the technique was used not only to find water, but also to locate underground deposits of coal and ore.

During the 15th and 16th centuries, dowsing fell into disfavor, especially after German Protestant leader Martin Luther denounced it as the work of the devil. The practice then became known as water-witching.

Even though religious leaders still opposed it, dowsing became popular once again in the late 1600s, when Frenchman Jacques Aymar found a murder victim by chance while dowsing for water and then used the rod to find the murderer. The police later hired him to help with other criminal cases.

Dowsing came to North America with the European colonists and has always had its skeptics. On the other hand, to this day its many adherents believe that the practice holds water.

SKY WATCH ☆ *The Moon floats between blue Spica and orange Mars on the 3rd. The next night, it sits between Mars and Saturn. The 10th brings the year's closest Moon, just 221,765 miles away. It is full in the hour of its closest approach, creating a large rising Moon at sunset and higher-than-normal tides the next day. The Perseid meteor shower will be ruined by the light of this Moon on the 11th. Venus spectacularly meets Jupiter low in the east just before dawn on the 18th. Mars, in Libra, passes dramatically below Saturn at nightfall from the 22nd to the 27th in the southwestern sky. Neptune, in Aquarius, reaches opposition on the 29th. The Moon plops between orange Mars and pale Saturn on the 31st; both planets have the same magnitude 0.6 brightness.*

◑ **First Quarter**	3rd day	20th hour	50th minute
○ **Full Moon**	10th day	14th hour	9th minute
◐ **Last Quarter**	17th day	8th hour	26th minute
● **New Moon**	25th day	10th hour	13th minute

All times are given in Eastern Daylight Time.

Get these pages with times set to your zip code at Almanac.com/Access.

((
Age

			Rise		Set		Length	Sun Fast	Declination	High Tide		Rise		Set		Place	Age
213	1	Fr.	5:36	B	8:03	E	14 27	9	17 N.54	3¼	3¾	11:04	E	10:38	C	VIR	6
214	2	Sa.	5:37	B	8:02	E	14 25	10	17 38	4	4½	12:04	E	11:10	C	VIR	7
215	3	**E**	5:38	B	8:01	E	14 23	10	17 23	4¾	5¼	1:05	E	11:45	C	VIR	8
216	4	M.	5:39	B	8:00	E	14 21	10	17 07	5¾	6	2:08	E	—	–	LIB	9
217	5	Tu.	5:40	B	7:58	E	14 18	10	16 51	6½	7	3:10	E	12:26	B	LIB	10
218	6	W.	5:41	B	7:57	E	14 16	10	16 34	7½	7¾	4:12	E	1:13	B	OPH	11
219	7	Th.	5:42	B	7:56	E	14 14	10	16 17	8½	8¾	5:10	E	2:09	B	OPH	12
220	8	Fr.	5:43	B	7:55	E	14 12	10	16 00	9½	9¾	6:03	E	3:12	C	SAG	13
221	9	Sa.	5:44	B	7:53	E	14 09	10	15 43	10½	10¾	6:52	E	4:22	C	SAG	14
222	10	**E**	5:46	B	7:52	E	14 06	10	15 26	11¼	11½	7:35	E	5:36	C	AQU	15
223	11	M.	5:47	B	7:50	E	14 03	11	15 08	12¼	—	8:14	D	6:51	D	CAP	16
224	12	Tu.	5:48	B	7:49	D	14 01	11	14 50	12½	1	8:50	D	8:06	D	AQU	17
225	13	W.	5:49	B	7:48	D	13 59	11	14 32	1½	2	9:26	C	9:19	D	PSC	18
226	14	Th.	5:50	B	7:46	D	13 56	11	14 13	2¼	2¾	10:01	C	10:30	C	PSC	19
227	15	Fr.	5:51	B	7:45	D	13 54	11	13 54	3¼	3¾	10:38	C	11:39	C	PSC	20
228	16	Sa.	5:52	B	7:43	D	13 51	12	13 36	4¼	4½	11:16	B	12:44	E	ARI	21
229	17	**E**	5:53	B	7:42	D	13 49	12	13 16	5	5½	11:58	B	1:45	E	ARI	22
230	18	M.	5:54	B	7:40	D	13 46	12	12 57	6¼	6½	—	–	2:43	E	TAU	23
231	19	Tu.	5:55	B	7:39	D	13 44	12	12 37	7¼	7½	12:43	B	3:35	E	TAU	24
232	20	W.	5:56	B	7:37	D	13 41	12	12 18	8¼	8½	1:31	B	4:22	E	ORI	25
233	21	Th.	5:57	B	7:36	D	13 39	13	11 58	9¼	9¼	2:23	B	5:04	E	GEM	26
234	22	Fr.	5:58	B	7:34	D	13 36	13	11 38	10	10¼	3:17	C	5:42	E	GEM	27
235	23	Sa.	5:59	B	7:33	D	13 34	13	11 17	10¾	11	4:12	C	6:16	E	CAN	28
236	24	**E**	6:00	B	7:31	D	13 31	14	10 57	11½	11½	5:08	C	6:47	D	CAN	29
237	25	M.	6:01	B	7:29	D	13 28	14	10 36	12	—	6:05	C	7:17	D	LEO	0
238	26	Tu.	6:02	B	7:28	D	13 26	14	10 15	12¼	12½	7:02	D	7:45	D	SEX	1
239	27	W.	6:04	B	7:26	D	13 22	14	9 54	12¾	1¼	8:00	D	8:13	C	LEO	2
240	28	Th.	6:05	B	7:24	D	13 19	15	9 33	1½	1¾	8:58	D	8:42	C	VIR	3
241	29	Fr.	6:06	B	7:23	D	13 17	15	9 12	2	2½	9:57	E	9:13	C	VIR	4
242	30	Sa.	6:07	B	7:21	D	13 14	15	8 50	2¾	3	10:57	E	9:46	B	VIR	5
243	31	**E**	6:08	B	7:19	D	13 11	16	8 N.29	3½	3¾	11:58	E	10:24	B	LIB	6

The asters twinkle in clusters bright,
While the corn grows ripe and the apples mellow. – Celia Thaxter

Day of Month	Day of Week	Weather
1		
2		
3		
4		
5		
6		
7		
8		
9		
10		
11		
12		
13		
14		
15		
16		
17		
18		
19		
20		
21		
22		
23		
24		
25		
26		
27		
28		
29		
30		
31		

Farmer's Calendar

■ Without a doubt, a leisurely walk in the woods lifts our spirits and makes us feel good. In Japan, this has developed into a new form of therapy and preventative medicine known as *shinrin-yoku,* or "forest bathing," which involves taking a relaxing stroll among the trees, breathing it all in.

A woodland walk affects all of our senses. The soft feel of moss or pine needles underfoot; the welcoming fragrance of forest air; the peaceful sounds of a flowing brook and tweeting birds; and the shapes, textures, and colors of leaves and bark all contribute to our enjoyment.

And to our health. Even a short walk in the forest will lower blood pressure and pulse rate, decrease fatigue and tension, increase the number of anticancer proteins, and encourage the growth and activity of disease-fighting white blood cells. Some of these effects occur after we inhale chemical compounds from plants, fungi, and bacteria. These include phytoncides, which trees and other plants emit to protect themselves against insect attacks and rotting.

Increasingly recognized by the medical community, the Japanese practice is catching on in North America. But it is still unfamiliar to many—so be ready to explain what you have in mind before asking someone to join you in "forest bathing."

SKY WATCH ☆ *The full Harvest Moon comes quite early this year on the night of the 8th. The Moon and Uranus are very close together on the 10th; use binoculars to see the Green Planet in Pisces. Optimally from dark rural sites, observe the Milky Way, splitting the sky from north to south, at nightfall between the 15th and the 26th. Watch for three fine late-month lunar conjunctions: On the 20th, the Moon meets returning Jupiter at 5:00 A.M.; on the 27th, it accompanies departing Saturn, just 10 degrees above the western horizon; and on the 29th, it visits esoteric constellation Ophiuchus to hover right above magnitude 0.8 Mars at nightfall. The equinox brings autumn on the 22nd at 10:29 P.M.*

◐ **First Quarter**	2nd day	7th hour	11th minute
○ **Full Moon**	8th day	21st hour	38th minute
◑ **Last Quarter**	15th day	22nd hour	5th minute
● **New Moon**	24th day	2nd hour	14th minute

All times are given in Eastern Daylight Time.

Get these pages with times set to your zip code at Almanac.com/Access.

℃
Age

244	1	M.	6:09	B	7:18	D	13 09	16	8 N.07	4¼	4½	12:59	E	11:08	B	LIB	7
245	2	Tu.	6:10	C	7:16	D	13 06	16	7 45	5¼	5½	1:59	E	11:58	B	OPH	8
246	3	W.	6:11	C	7:14	D	13 03	17	7 23	6	6½	2:57	E	—	-	OPH	9
247	4	Th.	6:12	C	7:13	D	13 01	17	7 01	7	7½	3:50	E	12:56	B	SAG	10
248	5	Fr.	6:13	C	7:11	D	12 58	17	6 39	8¼	8½	4:40	E	2:00	C	SAG	11
249	6	Sa.	6:14	C	7:09	D	12 55	18	6 16	9	9½	5:25	E	3:10	C	CAP	12
250	7	**E**	6:15	C	7:07	D	12 52	18	5 54	10	10½	6:05	D	4:24	C	AQU	13
251	8	M.	6:16	C	7:06	D	12 50	18	5 31	11	11¼	6:43	D	5:38	D	AQU	14
252	9	Tu.	6:17	C	7:04	D	12 47	19	5 09	11¾	—	7:20	D	6:53	D	PSC	15
253	10	W.	6:18	C	7:02	D	12 44	19	4 46	12¼	12¾	7:56	C	8:07	E	PSC	16
254	11	Th.	6:19	C	7:00	D	12 41	19	4 23	1	1½	8:33	C	9:18	E	PSC	17
255	12	Fr.	6:20	C	6:59	D	12 39	20	4 00	2	2¼	9:12	B	10:27	E	ARI	18
256	13	Sa.	6:21	C	6:57	D	12 36	20	3 38	2¾	3¼	9:54	B	11:32	E	ARI	19
257	14	**E**	6:22	C	6:55	C	12 33	20	3 15	3¾	4	10:39	B	12:33	E	TAU	20
258	15	M.	6:24	C	6:53	C	12 29	21	2 51	4¾	5	11:27	B	1:28	E	TAU	21
259	16	Tu.	6:25	C	6:52	C	12 27	21	2 28	5¾	6	—	-	2:18	E	TAU	22
260	17	W.	6:26	C	6:50	C	12 24	21	2 05	6¾	7	12:18	B	3:02	E	GEM	23
261	18	Th.	6:27	C	6:48	C	12 21	22	1 42	7¾	8	1:11	B	3:42	E	GEM	24
262	19	Fr.	6:28	C	6:46	C	12 18	22	1 19	8½	8¾	2:06	C	4:17	E	CAN	25
263	20	Sa.	6:29	C	6:45	C	12 16	22	0 55	9½	9¾	3:02	C	4:49	D	CAN	26
264	21	**E**	6:30	C	6:43	C	12 13	23	0 32	10¼	10½	3:59	C	5:19	D	LEO	27
265	22	M.	6:31	C	6:41	C	12 10	23	0 N.09	10¾	11	4:56	D	5:48	D	SEX	28
266	23	Tu.	6:32	C	6:39	C	12 07	23	0 S.14	11½	11¾	5:53	D	6:16	C	LEO	29
267	24	W.	6:33	C	6:38	C	12 05	24	0 37	**12**	—	6:52	D	6:45	C	VIR	0
268	25	Th.	6:34	C	6:36	C	12 02	24	1 00	12½	12¾	7:51	E	7:16	C	VIR	1
269	26	Fr.	6:35	C	6:34	C	11 59	25	1 24	1	1¼	8:51	E	7:49	C	VIR	2
270	27	Sa.	6:36	C	6:32	C	11 56	25	1 47	1¾	2	9:52	E	8:26	B	LIB	3
271	28	**E**	6:37	C	6:30	C	11 53	25	2 10	2¼	2½	10:53	E	9:07	B	LIB	4
272	29	M.	6:39	C	6:29	C	11 50	26	2 34	3	3¼	11:53	E	9:55	B	SCO	5
273	30	Tu.	6:40	C	6:27	C	11 47	26	2 S.57	4	4¼	12:50	E	10:48	B	OPH	6

When the air is white with the down o' the thistle,
And the sky is red with the Harvest Moon. –Richard Watson Gilder

Day of Month	Day of Week		Weather
1			
2			
3			
4			
5			
6			
7			
8			
9			
10			
11			
12			
13			
14			
15			
16			
17			
18			
19			
20			
21			
22			
23			
24			
25			
26			
27			
28			
29			
30			

Autumn is a second spring where every leaf is a flower. –Albert Camus

Farmer's Calendar

■ Long before the advent of calendars, many people used the twelve full Moons of a year to keep track of time. The Harvest Moon, occurring in September or early October, is the full Moon closest to the autumnal equinox, which gives it a unique quality: In midnorthern latitudes, the Moon rises an average of 50 minutes later each day. But for a number of days near the start of autumn, it rises only 30 minutes later. This meant that for several evenings surrounding the Harvest Moon, farmers of old could gather their crops well into the night, without the usual dark period between sunset and moonrise.

The Harvest Moon, like other full Moons, often appears red or orange when close to the horizon. Here, moonlight encounters more atmospheric particles than when it shines from overhead, causing more of the light's bluish components, which have short wavelengths, to scatter. The longer-wave reddish components are better able to pass directly to our eyes.

The full Moon also appears to be larger when near the horizon, but this is a trick of the brain known as the Moon illusion that, to this day, has no accepted explanation.

Folks still enjoy watching full Moons, but unlike our ancestors who used full Moons as calendars, we use calendars to keep track of full Moons.

SKY WATCH ☆ *Mercury starts as a low, poor evening star, then vanishes and emerges as a morning star, low in the east before sunrise at month's end. Venus does the opposite, ending its low morning star apparition to reach superior conjunction on the 25th. On the 7th, Uranus has its opposition in Pisces at magnitude 5.8. The 8th brings the year's second total lunar eclipse visible from the United States and Canada, with the West Coast again favored. The partial phase starts at 5:14 A.M.; totality starts at 6:25 A.M. On the 23rd, most of North America can see a partial solar eclipse just before sunset. Be sure to use eye protection.*

◐	**First Quarter**	1st day	15th hour	33rd minute
○	**Full Moon**	8th day	6th hour	51st minute
◑	**Last Quarter**	15th day	15th hour	12th minute
●	**New Moon**	23rd day	17th hour	57th minute
◐	**First Quarter**	30th day	22nd hour	48th minute

All times are given in Eastern Daylight Time.

Get these pages with times set to your zip code at Almanac.com/Access.

☾
Age

274	1	W.	6:41	C	**6:25**	C	11 44	26	3 s. 20	4¾	**5**	**1:44**	E	**11:49**	B	SAG	7
275	2	Th.	6:42	C	**6:24**	C	11 42	27	3 44	5¾	**6**	**2:33**	E	—	–	SAG	8
276	3	Fr.	6:43	C	**6:22**	C	11 39	27	4 07	6¾	**7**	**3:18**	E	12:54	C	SAG	9
277	4	Sa.	6:44	C	**6:20**	C	11 36	27	4 30	7¾	**8¼**	**3:59**	E	2:03	C	AQU	10
278	5	**E**	6:45	C	**6:18**	C	11 33	27	4 53	8¾	**9¼**	**4:37**	D	3:15	D	CAP	11
279	6	M.	6:46	D	**6:17**	C	11 31	28	5 16	9¾	**10¼**	**5:13**	D	4:28	D	AQU	12
280	7	Tu.	6:47	D	**6:15**	C	11 28	28	5 39	10½	**11**	**5:49**	C	5:41	D	PSC	13
281	8	W.	6:48	D	**6:13**	C	11 25	28	6 02	11½	**12**	**6:26**	C	6:53	E	PSC	14
282	9	Th.	6:50	D	**6:12**	C	11 22	29	6 25	12¼	—	**7:04**	C	8:04	E	PSC	15
283	10	Fr.	6:51	D	**6:10**	C	11 19	29	6 47	12¾	**1**	**7:46**	B	9:12	E	ARI	16
284	11	Sa.	6:52	D	**6:08**	C	11 16	29	7 10	1½	**1¾**	**8:30**	B	10:17	E	TAU	17
285	12	**E**	6:53	D	**6:07**	C	11 14	29	7 32	2½	**2¾**	**9:18**	B	11:16	E	TAU	18
286	13	M.	6:54	D	**6:05**	C	11 11	30	7 55	3¼	**3½**	**10:09**	B	**12:10**	E	TAU	19
287	14	Tu.	6:55	D	**6:03**	B	11 08	30	8 17	4¼	**4½**	**11:03**	B	**12:57**	E	ORI	20
288	15	W.	6:56	D	**6:02**	B	11 06	30	8 39	5	**5¼**	**11:58**	C	**1:39**	E	GEM	21
289	16	Th.	6:58	D	**6:00**	B	11 02	30	9 01	6	**6¼**	—	–	**2:16**	E	CAN	22
290	17	Fr.	6:59	D	**5:59**	B	11 00	30	9 23	7	**7¼**	12:53	C	**2:50**	E	CAN	23
291	18	Sa.	7:00	D	**5:57**	B	10 57	31	9 45	8	**8¼**	1:50	C	**3:20**	D	LEO	24
292	19	**E**	7:01	D	**5:56**	B	10 55	31	10 07	8¾	**9**	2:46	C	**3:49**	D	LEO	25
293	20	M.	7:02	D	**5:54**	B	10 52	31	10 28	9½	**9¾**	3:44	D	**4:18**	D	LEO	26
294	21	Tu.	7:04	D	**5:52**	B	10 48	31	10 50	10¼	**10½**	4:42	D	**4:47**	C	VIR	27
295	22	W.	7:05	D	**5:51**	B	10 46	31	11 11	10¾	**11¼**	5:41	E	**5:17**	C	VIR	28
296	23	Th.	7:06	D	**5:49**	B	10 43	32	11 32	11½	**12**	6:42	E	**5:49**	C	VIR	0
297	24	Fr.	7:07	D	**5:48**	B	10 41	32	11 53	**12**	—	7:44	E	**6:25**	B	VIR	1
298	25	Sa.	7:08	D	**5:47**	B	10 39	32	12 14	12½	**12¾**	8:46	E	**7:06**	B	LIB	2
299	26	**E**	7:10	D	**5:45**	B	10 35	32	12 34	1¼	**1½**	9:47	E	**7:52**	B	LIB	3
300	27	M.	7:11	D	**5:44**	B	10 33	32	12 54	2	**2¼**	10:46	E	**8:44**	B	OPH	4
301	28	Tu.	7:12	D	**5:42**	B	10 30	32	13 15	2¾	**3**	11:41	E	**9:42**	B	SAG	5
302	29	W.	7:13	D	**5:41**	B	10 28	32	13 34	3½	**3¾**	**12:31**	E	**10:46**	C	SAG	6
303	30	Th.	7:14	D	**5:40**	B	10 26	32	13 54	4½	**4¾**	**1:16**	E	**11:53**	C	SAG	7
304	31	Fr.	7:16	D	**5:38**	B	10 22	32	14 s. 14	5½	**5¾**	**1:57**	E	—	–	AQU	8

Winds! are they winds?
—or myriad ghosts, that shriek? –Paul Hamilton Hayne

Day of Month	Day of Week	Dates, Feasts, Fasts, Aspects, Tide Heights	Weather
1			
2			
3			
4			
5			
6			
7			
8			
9			
10			
11			
12			
13			
14			
15			
16			
17			
18			
19			
20			
21			
22			
23			
24			
25			
26			
27			
28			
29			
30			
31			

Farmer's Calendar

■ During the growing season, ladybugs are garden heroes, eating many species of aphids, as well as mites and a variety of other small insects. They are a joy to watch and are thought to bring good luck if they land on you. But as temperatures tumble in the fall, ladybugs change their status from heroes to pests by entering cracks and crevices in houses and barns as they look for a place to overwinter.

Ladybugs do not bite, sting, or eat fabric or our food. When threatened, however, they secrete a bit of their orange-yellow blood, which has a strong, unpleasant odor and may permanently stain curtains, walls, and carpeting. The secretions can also cause skin irritations or inhalant allergies. In addition, ladybugs release pheromones, "perfumes" that will attract others of their kind from up to a quarter-mile away. The long-lasting scents can lure swarms of these insects year after year.

The best way to deal with ladybugs in the house is to keep them out in the first place. Caulk or seal any cracks where they can enter. Pay close attention to areas around doors, windows, and water pipes.

Use a handheld vacuum to collect any intruders and release them outdoors, far away from your home. Giving these important creatures a second chance is sure to bring good luck to you— and especially to your garden.

SKY WATCH ☆ *Mercury has its best morning star apparition during the first 10 days of the month, 10 degrees above the eastern horizon 40 minutes before sunrise. With Venus and Saturn gone and Mars dim and low in Sagittarius, the action shifts to reappearing, brightening Jupiter, now in Leo, which rises at around 11:00 P.M. in midmonth and is visible for more than half the night. The Moon is to its right on the 13th. Also at midmonth, Orion rises by 9:00 P.M., with Sirius, the Dog Star, up an hour later, introducing the brilliant stars of the cold season. A crowd surrounds the Sun on the 22nd: the Moon, Saturn, Mercury, and Venus, all tightly clustered but unseen in the solar glare.*

○	**Full Moon**	6th day	17th hour	23rd minute
◑	**Last Quarter**	14th day	10th hour	15th minute
●	**New Moon**	22nd day	7th hour	32nd minute
◐	**First Quarter**	29th day	5th hour	6th minute

After 2:00 A.M. on November 2, Eastern Standard Time is given.

Get these pages with times set to your zip code at Almanac.com/Access.

305	1	Sa.	7:17	D	5:37	B	10 20	32	14 s. 33	$6\frac{1}{4}$	$6\frac{3}{4}$	2:35	D	1:01	CAP	—
306	2	**E**	6:18	D	4:36	B	10 18	32	14 52	$6\frac{1}{2}$	7	2:11	D	1:11	AQU	)
307	3	M.	6:19	D	4:35	B	10 16	32	15 11	$7\frac{1}{2}$	8	2:45	C	2:22	PSC	1
308	4	Tu.	6:21	E	4:33	B	10 12	32	15 29	$8\frac{1}{2}$	9	3:21	C	3:32	PSC	2
309	5	W.	6:22	E	4:32	B	10 10	32	15 47	$9\frac{1}{4}$	$9\frac{3}{4}$	3:57	C	4:42	PSC	13
310	6	Th.	6:23	E	4:31	B	10 08	32	16 05	10	$10\frac{3}{4}$	4:37	C	5:51	ARI	14
311	7	Fr.	6:24	E	4:30	B	10 06	32	16 23	11	$11\frac{1}{2}$	5:20	B	6:58	ARI	15
312	8	Sa.	6:26	E	4:29	B	10 03	32	16 41	$11\frac{3}{4}$	—	6:07	B	8:00	TAU	16
313	9	**E**	6:27	E	4:28	B	10 01	32	16 58	$12\frac{1}{4}$	$12\frac{1}{2}$	6:57	B	8:57	TAU	17
314	10	M.	6:28	E	4:27	B	9 59	32	17 15	1	$1\frac{1}{4}$	7:51	B	9:49	ORI	18
315	11	Tu.	6:29	E	4:26	B	9 57	32	17 31	$1\frac{3}{4}$	2	8:46	C	10:34	GEM	19
316	12	W.	6:31	E	4:25	B	9 54	32	17 47	$2\frac{3}{4}$	$2\frac{3}{4}$	9:42	C	11:14	GEM	20
317	13	Th.	6:32	E	4:24	B	9 52	31	18 03	$3\frac{1}{2}$	$3\frac{3}{4}$	10:39	C	11:49	CAN	21
318	14	Fr.	6:33	E	4:23	B	9 50	31	18 19	$4\frac{1}{4}$	$4\frac{1}{2}$	11:35	C	12:21	CAN	22
319	15	Sa.	6:34	E	4:22	B	9 48	31	18 34	$5\frac{1}{4}$	$5\frac{1}{2}$	—	–	12:50	LEO	23
320	16	**E**	6:36	E	4:21	B	9 45	31	18 49	6	$6\frac{1}{2}$	12:32	D	1:19	SEX	24
321	17	M.	6:37	E	4:20	B	9 43	31	19 04	7	$7\frac{1}{4}$	1:30	D	1:47	LEO	25
322	18	Tu.	6:38	E	4:19	B	9 41	31	19 18	$7\frac{3}{4}$	$8\frac{1}{4}$	2:28	D	2:16	VIR	26
323	19	W.	6:39	E	4:18	B	9 39	30	19 32	$8\frac{1}{2}$	9	3:28	E	2:47	VIR	27
324	20	Th.	6:41	E	4:18	B	9 37	30	19 46	$9\frac{1}{4}$	$9\frac{3}{4}$	4:30	E	3:22	VIR	28
325	21	Fr.	6:42	E	4:17	A	9 35	30	19 59	10	$10\frac{1}{2}$	5:32	E	4:01	LIB	29
326	22	Sa.	6:43	E	4:16	A	9 33	30	20 12	$10\frac{1}{2}$	$11\frac{1}{4}$	6:35	E	4:45	LIB	0
327	23	**E**	6:44	E	4:16	A	9 32	29	20 25	$11\frac{1}{4}$	12	7:37	E	5:37	OPH	1
328	24	M.	6:45	E	4:15	A	9 30	29	20 37	**12**	—	8:35	E	6:34	OPH	2
329	25	Tu.	6:46	E	4:15	A	9 29	29	20 49	$12\frac{3}{4}$	$12\frac{3}{4}$	9:28	E	7:37	SAG	3
330	26	W.	6:48	E	4:14	A	9 26	28	21 00	$1\frac{1}{2}$	$1\frac{3}{4}$	10:16	E	8:44	SAG	4
331	27	Th.	6:49	E	4:14	A	9 25	28	21 11	$2\frac{1}{4}$	$2\frac{1}{2}$	10:59	E	9:53	CAP	5
332	28	Fr.	6:50	E	4:13	A	9 23	28	21 22	$3\frac{1}{4}$	$3\frac{1}{2}$	11:37	D	11:02	AQU	6
333	29	Sa.	6:51	E	4:13	A	9 22	27	21 32	$4\frac{1}{4}$	$4\frac{1}{2}$	12:13	D	—	AQU	7
334	30	**E**	6:52	E	4:12	A	9 20	27	21 s. 42	$5\frac{1}{4}$	$5\frac{1}{2}$	12:47	D	12:12	PSC	8

November, month of mornings misty-bright
With golden light. –Mortimer Collins

Day of Month	Day of Week	Dates, Feasts, Fasts, Aspects, Tide Heights	Weather
1	Sa.	All Saints' • Sadie Hawkins Day • ♂♀☽ • ☿ GR. ELONG. (19° WEST)	Mild
2	E	21st ⬒. af. ℗. • Daylight Saving Time ends, 2:00 A.M. • ☾ PERIG.	retreat
3	M.	All Souls'ᵀ • ☾ ON EQ. • Mary Jacob received patent for a brassiere, 1914 • Tides {10.6 10.5	means
4	Tu.	Election Day • ☾ AT ☊ • ♂☽☾ • Tides {11.0 10.6	muddy
5	W.	U.S. president Franklin D. Roosevelt reelected to third term in office, 1940 • Tides {11.4 10.7	feet.
6	Th.	Full Beaver ◯ • Black bears head to winter dens now. • Tides {11.6 10.7	Enjoy
7	Fr.	98-mph winds, Block Island, R.I., 1953 • Tides {11.7 10.5	the
8	Sa.	Royal Canadian Mint ordered to change 12-sided nickel back to round shape, 1962 • Tides {11.5 —	sunshine
9	E	22nd ⬒. af. ℗. • ☾ RIDES HIGH • Abolitionist Elijah Parish Lovejoy born, 1802	while
10	M.	♂♂♇ • Jeweler Harry Winston donated Hope Diamond to Smithsonian, D.C., 1958 • {9.9 10.8	it
11	Tu.	St. Martin of Tours • Veterans Day • Oklahoma City, Okla., 1911	lasts:
12	W.	Indian Summer • Lobsters move to offshore waters. • {9.2 9.8	piles of
13	Th.	♂♀♄ • Thousands of meteors fell per hour, eastern U.S., 1833 • Tides {8.9 9.4	snow
14	Fr.	☾ AT APO. • ♂♃☾ • Jean Drapeau became mayor of Montreal for 8th time, 1982	and
15	Sa.	When wild geese soar overhead, even terrapins stamp their feet on the ground. • Tides {8.7 8.8	blustery
16	E	23rd ⬒. af. ℗. • ♆ STAT. • Crab apples are ripe now.	blasts!
17	M.	St. Hugh of Lincoln • ☾ ON EQ. • Baseball player Roger Peckinpaugh died, 1977	Don't
18	Tu.	♂♄☉ • Comic strip Calvin and Hobbes debuted, 1985 • Tides {9.4 9.0	be
19	W.	☾ AT ☊ • Columbus first sighted Puerto Rico, 1493 • Tides {9.8 9.2	ungrateful;
20	Th.	Astronomer Edwin P. Hubble born, 1889 • {10.1 9.4	give
21	Fr.	♂♀☾ • 3.8 earthquake near Northglenn, Colo., 1965 • Tides {10.5 9.6	thanks
22	Sa.	New ● • ♂♀☾ • ♂♄☾ • Pirate Blackbeard died, 1718 • {10.8 9.8	for
23	E	24th ⬒. af. ℗. • U.S. Coast Guard Women's Reserve (SPARs) authorized, 1942	every
24	M.	☾ RUNS LOW • Cape Breton Railway opened, N.S., 1890 • Tides {11.2 —	plateful.
25	Tu.	♂♇☾ • The sun at home warms better than the sun elsewhere. • Tides {9.9 11.2	Snow's
26	W.	♂♀♄ • ♂♂☾ • Comedian Milton Berle married Lorna Adams, 1991	hateful,
27	Th.	Thanksgiving Day • ☾ AT PERIG. • Tides {10.0 10.9	but
28	Fr.	Tennis player Dwight Davis died, 1945 • Tides {10.0 10.6	removal
29	Sa.	♂♆☾ • Fire destroyed much of Maryland Agricultural College, College Park, Md., 1912	wins
30	E	1st ⬒. of Advent • ☾ ON EQ. • Tides {10.1 10.0	approval.

He travels best that knows when to return. –Thomas Middleton

Farmer's Calendar

■ The old New England saying, "Chop your own wood and it will warm you twice," is definitely an understatement. As anyone who has processed their own firewood knows, the activity warms you many more times than that: Once the tree is felled, it must be cut to length, split, stacked, covered, and then carried into the house daily. Certainly with chainsaws and power splitters, today's wood-cutters have it easier than their ancestors, but they still work hard.

Putting up your own firewood saves money, but as most wood enthusiasts will tell you, it is rewarding in other ways, too. Many folks enjoy cutting wood for the exercise and the chance to spend time outdoors. Some do it to help the environment: Not only is wood a renewable energy source, but also burning it responsibly may contribute less to global warming than using oil, coal, or natural gas. Woody plants take in carbon dioxide from the air, thereby recycling the gas that was released from decaying or burning logs.

Of course, wood supplies a soothing warmth that no other fuel can provide, encouraging family and friends to gather around a roaring fire for pleasant conversation. Many romances have blossomed in front of a flickering fireplace–just one more wonderful way that wood warms you.

SKY WATCH ☆ *The Moon hovers just above greenish Uranus at nightfall on the 1st. Use binoculars. The Moon visits the Hyades star cluster in Taurus on the 5th. The 13th brings the year's best meteor shower, the Geminids. A meteor every minute or two should appear in dark rural skies between 8:00 and 11:00 P.M. After 11:30, the unwelcome Moon will rise to brighten the heavens. Winter begins with the solstice on the 21st, at 6:03 P.M. After that date, Jupiter starts rising by 8:30 P.M. and is nicely high after 10:00 P.M. Venus might be glimpsed low in the west at dusk by month's end—a harbinger of its superb evening star apparition this coming spring. Saturn can be seen low in the east before dawn.*

○ **Full Moon**	6th day	7th hour	27th minute
◐ **Last Quarter**	14th day	7th hour	51st minute
● **New Moon**	21st day	20th hour	36th minute
◑ **First Quarter**	28th day	13th hour	31st minute

All times are given in Eastern Standard Time.

Get these pages with times set to your zip code at Almanac.com/Access.

☾ Age

			Rises		Sets				Sun Decl.			Rises		Sets		Place	Age
335	1	M.	6:53	E	4:12	A	9 19	27	21 s. 51	6¼	6¾	1:21	C	1:20	D	PSC	9
336	2	Tu.	6:54	E	4:12	A	9 18	26	22 00	7¼	7¾	1:56	C	2:29	E	PSC	10
337	3	W.	6:55	E	4:12	A	9 17	26	22 09	8	8¼	2:33	C	3:36	E	PSC	11
338	4	Th.	6:56	E	4:11	A	9 15	25	22 17	9	9½	3:13	B	4:42	E	ARI	12
339	5	Fr.	6:57	E	4:11	A	9 14	25	22 24	9¾	10½	3:57	B	5:45	E	TAU	13
340	6	Sa.	6:58	E	4:11	A	9 13	25	22 32	10½	11¼	4:46	B	6:45	E	TAU	14
341	7	**E**	6:59	E	4:11	A	9 12	24	22 38	11¼	12	5:38	B	7:39	E	TAU	15
342	8	M.	7:00	E	4:11	A	9 11	24	22 45	12	—	6:33	B	8:27	E	GEM	16
343	9	Tu.	7:01	E	4:11	A	9 10	23	22 51	12¾	12¾	7:29	C	9:10	E	GEM	17
344	10	W.	7:02	E	4:11	A	9 09	23	22 56	1½	1½	8:26	C	9:47	E	CAN	18
345	11	Th.	7:03	E	4:11	A	9 08	22	23 01	2¼	2¾	9:23	C	10:21	E	CAN	19
346	12	Fr.	7:04	E	4:11	A	9 07	22	23 06	3	3	10:20	C	10:51	D	LEO	20
347	13	Sa.	7:04	E	4:11	A	9 07	22	23 10	3¾	3¾	11:17	D	11:20	D	SEX	21
348	14	**E**	7:05	E	4:12	A	9 07	21	23 13	4½	4¾	—	–	11:48	C	LEO	22
349	15	M.	7:06	E	4:12	A	9 06	21	23 16	5¼	5¾	12:15	D	12:16	C	VIR	23
350	16	Tu.	7:06	E	4:12	A	9 06	20	23 19	6¼	6½	1:13	E	12:46	C	VIR	24
351	17	W.	7:07	E	4:12	A	9 05	20	23 21	7	7½	2:13	E	1:18	C	VIR	25
352	18	Th.	7:08	E	4:13	A	9 05	19	23 23	7¾	8¼	3:14	E	1:54	B	LIB	26
353	19	Fr.	7:08	E	4:13	A	9 05	19	23 24	8½	9¼	4:17	E	2:36	B	LIB	27
354	20	Sa.	7:09	E	4:14	A	9 05	18	23 25	9¼	10	5:20	E	3:24	B	SCO	28
355	21	**E**	7:09	E	4:14	A	9 05	18	23 26	10	10¾	6:21	E	4:19	B	OPH	0
356	22	M.	7:10	E	4:15	A	9 05	17	23 25	11	11½	7:18	E	5:22	C	SAG	1
357	23	Tu.	7:10	E	4:15	A	9 05	17	23 25	11¾	—	8:11	E	6:30	C	SAG	2
358	24	W.	7:11	E	4:16	A	9 05	16	23 24	12¼	12½	8:57	E	7:40	C	CAP	3
359	25	Th.	7:11	E	4:16	A	9 05	16	23 22	1¼	1½	9:38	E	8:52	C	AQU	4
360	26	Fr.	7:12	E	4:17	A	9 05	15	23 20	2	2¼	10:16	D	10:02	D	AQU	5
361	27	Sa.	7:12	E	4:18	A	9 06	15	23 18	3	3¼	10:51	D	11:12	D	AQU	6
362	28	**E**	7:12	E	4:19	A	9 07	14	23 15	3¾	4¼	11:25	C	—	–	PSC	7
363	29	M.	7:12	E	4:19	A	9 07	14	23 11	4¾	5¼	11:59	C	12:21	E	PSC	8
364	30	Tu.	7:13	E	4:20	A	9 07	13	23 08	5¾	6¼	12:34	C	1:28	E	PSC	9
365	31	W.	7:13	E	4:21	A	9 08	13	23 s. 03	6¾	7½	1:13	B	2:33	E	ARI	10

There he stands in the foul weather,
The foolish, fond Old Year. –Henry Wadsworth Longfellow

Day of Month	Day of Week		Weather
1			
2			
3			
4			
5			
6			
7			
8			
9			
10			
11			
12			
13			
14			
15			
16			
17			
18			
19			
20			
21			
22			
23			
24			
25			
26			
27			
28			
29			
30			
31			

Farmer's Calendar

■ The year went by in the blink of an eye. Soon, the holidays will be over and a new year will be upon us. Now is the time to look back and reflect on the past months to see what we have accomplished—or tried to accomplish. There are some who say, "Take off the rearview mirror and drive on," but reviewing the past is a valuable learning tool that keeps us from repeating mistakes and reminds us of the things that worked, helping us to make better choices now and in the future.

Journaling is a wonderful way to keep track of the past. Write in your journal every day, even if it is just a sentence, and date your entries. This will allow you to revisit the progression of your thoughts and actions over the past year.

A journal is a practical way of keeping track of things like weather events and planting dates, but, more important, it allows you to think about your life. Did you do something that you came to regret? What things did you do that made you proud? Could you have done something differently that may have resulted in a different outcome? Do you have any habits or behaviors that you'd like to improve? In what ways have you become a better person?

Moving forward into the new year should be easier if we remember to keep the rearview mirror in adjustment.

Holidays and Observances

For Movable Religious Observances, see page 119. Federal holidays are listed in bold.

Jan. 1	New Year's Day		**July 4**	**Independence Day**
Jan. 19	Robert E. Lee Day *(Fla., Ky., La.)*		**July 24**	Pioneer Day *(Utah)*
			Aug. 1	Colorado Day
Jan. 20	**Martin Luther King Jr.'s Birthday *(observed)***		**Aug. 4**	Civic Holiday *(Canada)*
Feb. 2	Groundhog Day		**Aug. 16**	Bennington Battle Day (traditional, *Vt.*)
Feb. 12	Abraham Lincoln's Birthday			
Feb. 14	Valentine's Day		**Aug. 19**	National Aviation Day
Feb. 15	Susan B. Anthony's Birthday *(Fla., Wis.)*		**Aug. 26**	Women's Equality Day
			Sept. 1	**Labor Day**
Feb. 17	**Washington's Birthday *(observed)***		**Sept. 7**	Grandparents Day
Mar. 2	Texas Independence Day		**Sept. 9**	Admission Day *(Calif.)*
Mar. 4	Mardi Gras *(Baldwin & Mobile counties, Ala.; La.)* Town Meeting Day *(Vt.)*		**Sept. 11**	Patriot Day
			Sept. 17	Constitution Day
			Sept. 21	International Day of Peace
Mar. 15	Andrew Jackson Day *(Tenn.)*		**Oct. 6**	Child Health Day
Mar. 17	St. Patrick's Day Evacuation Day, *(Suffolk Co., Mass.)*		**Oct. 9**	Leif Eriksson Day
			Oct. 13	**Columbus Day *(observed)*** Native Americans' Day *(S.Dak.)* Thanksgiving Day *(Canada)*
Mar. 31	Seward's Day *(Alaska)*			
Apr. 2	Pascua Florida Day			
Apr. 21	Patriots Day *(Maine, Mass.)* San Jacinto Day *(Tex.)*		**Oct. 18**	Alaska Day (traditional)
			Oct. 24	United Nations Day
Apr. 22	Earth Day		**Oct. 31**	Halloween Nevada Day
Apr. 25	National Arbor Day			
May 5	Cinco de Mayo		**Nov. 4**	Election Day Will Rogers Day *(Okla.)*
May 8	Truman Day *(Mo.)*			
May 11	Mother's Day		**Nov. 11**	**Veterans Day** Remembrance Day *(Canada)*
May 17	Armed Forces Day			
May 19	Victoria Day *(Canada)*		**Nov. 19**	Discovery Day *(Puerto Rico)*
May 22	National Maritime Day		**Nov. 27**	**Thanksgiving Day**
May 26	**Memorial Day *(observed)***		**Nov. 28**	Acadian Day *(La.)*
June 5	World Environment Day		**Dec. 7**	National Pearl Harbor Remembrance Day
June 11	King Kamehameha I Day *(Hawaii)*			
June 14	Flag Day		**Dec. 15**	Bill of Rights Day
June 15	Father's Day		**Dec. 17**	Wright Brothers Day
June 17	Bunker Hill Day *(Suffolk Co., Mass.)*		**Dec. 25**	**Christmas Day**
June 19	Emancipation Day *(Tex.)*		**Dec. 26**	Boxing Day *(Canada)* First day of Kwanzaa
June 20	West Virginia Day			
July 1	Canada Day			

Tidal Glossary

Apogean Tide: A monthly tide of decreased range that occurs when the Moon is at apogee (farthest from Earth).

Diurnal Tide: A tide with one high water and one low water in a tidal day of approximately 24 hours.

Mean Lower Low Water: The arithmetic mean of the lesser of a daily pair of low waters, observed over a specific 19-year cycle called the National Tidal Datum Epoch.

Neap Tide: A tide of decreased range that occurs twice a month, when the Moon is in quadrature (during its first and last quarters, when the Sun and the Moon are at right angles to each other relative to Earth).

Perigean Tide: A monthly tide of increased range that occurs when the Moon is at perigee (closest to Earth).

Semidiurnal Tide: A tide with one high water and one low water every half day. East Coast tides, for example, are semidiurnal, with two highs and two lows during a tidal day of approximately 24 hours.

Spring Tide: A tide of increased range that occurs at times of syzygy each month. Named not for the season of spring but from the German *springen* ("to leap up"), a spring tide also brings a lower low water.

Syzygy: The nearly straight-line configuration that occurs twice a month, when the Sun and the Moon are in conjunction (on the same side of Earth, at the new Moon) and when they are in opposition (on opposite sides of Earth, at the full Moon). In both cases, the gravitational effects of the Sun and the Moon reinforce each other, and tidal range is increased.

Vanishing Tide: A mixed tide of considerable inequality in the two highs and two lows, so that the lower high (or higher low) may appear to vanish. □□

Glossary of Almanac Oddities

■ Many readers have expressed puzzlement over the rather obscure entries that appear on our **Right-Hand Calendar Pages, 121–147.** These "oddities" have long been fixtures in the Almanac, and we are pleased to provide some definitions. (Once explained, they may not seem so odd after all!)

–Beth Krommes

Ember Days: The four periods observed by some Christian denominations for prayer, fasting, and the ordination of clergy are called Ember Days. Specifically, these are the Wednesdays, Fridays, and Saturdays that occur in succession following (1) the First Sunday in Lent; (2) Whitsunday–Pentecost; (3) the Feast of the Holy Cross, September 14; and (4) the Feast of St. Lucia, December 13. The word *ember* is perhaps a corruption of the Latin *quatuor tempora,* "four times."

Folklore has it that the weather on each of the 3 days foretells the weather for the next 3 months; that is, in September, the first Ember Day, Wednesday, forecasts the weather for October; Friday predicts November; and Saturday foretells December.

Distaff Day (January 7): This was the first day after Epiphany (January 6), when women were expected to return to their spinning following the Christmas holiday. A distaff is the staff that women used for holding the flax or wool in spinning.

(Hence the term "distaff" refers to women's work or the maternal side of the family.)

Plough Monday (January): Traditionally, the first Monday after Epiphany was called Plough Monday because it was the day when men returned to their plough, or daily work, following the Christmas holiday. (Every few years, Plough Monday and Distaff Day fall on the same day.) It was customary at this time for farm laborers to draw a plough through the village, soliciting money for a "plough light," which was kept burning in the parish church all year. This traditional verse captures the spirit of it:

> *"Yule is come and Yule is gone,*
> *and we have feasted well;*
> *so Jack must to his flail again*
> *and Jenny to her wheel."*

Three Chilly Saints (May): Mamertus, Pancras, and Gervais were three early Christian saints. Because their feast days, on May 11, 12, and 13, respectively, are traditionally cold, they have come to be known as the Three Chilly Saints. An old French saying translates to: "St. Mamertus, St. Pancras, and St. Gervais do not pass without a frost."

Midsummer Day (June 24): To the farmer, this day is the midpoint of the growing season, halfway between planting and harvest. (Midsummer Eve is an occasion for festivity and celebrates fertility.) The Anglican church considered it a "Quarter Day," one of the four major divisions of the liturgical year. It also marks the feast day of St. John the Baptist.

Cornscateous Air (July): First used by early almanac makers, this term signifies warm, damp air. Though it signals ideal climatic conditions for growing corn, it poses a danger to those affected by asthma and other respiratory problems.

Dog Days (July 3–August 11): These 40 days are traditionally the year's hottest and unhealthiest. They once coincided with the year's heliacal (at sunrise) rising of the Dog Star, Sirius. Ancient folks thought that the "combined heat" of Sirius and the Sun caused summer's swelter.

Lammas Day (August 1): Derived from the Old English *hlaf maesse,* meaning "loaf mass," Lammas Day marked the beginning of the harvest. Traditionally, loaves of bread were baked from the first-ripened grain and brought to the churches to be consecrated. Eventually, "loaf mass" became "Lammas." In Scotland, Lammastide fairs became famous as the time when trial marriages could be made. These marriages could end after a year with no strings attached.

Cat Nights Begin (August 17): This term harks back to the days when people believed in witches. An Irish legend says that a witch could turn into a cat and regain herself eight times, but on the ninth time (August 17), she couldn't change back, hence the saying: "A cat has nine lives." Because August is a "yowly" time for cats, this may have initially prompted the speculation about witches on the prowl.

Harvest Home (September): In Europe and Britain, the conclusion of the harvest each autumn was marked by festivals of fun, feasting, and thanksgiving known as "Harvest Home." It was also a time to hold elections, pay workers, and collect rents. These festivals usually took place around the autumnal equinox.

Certain groups in the United States, particularly the Pennsylvania Dutch, have kept the tradition alive.

St. Luke's Little Summer (October): This is a spell of warm weather that occurs on or near St. Luke's feast day (October 18) and is sometimes called Indian summer.

Indian Summer (November): A period of warm weather following a cold spell or a hard frost, Indian summer can occur between St. Martin's Day (November 11) and November 20. Although there are differing dates for its occurrence, for more than 200 years the Almanac has adhered to the saying "If All Saints' (November 1) brings out winter, St. Martin's brings out Indian summer." The term may have come from early Native Americans, some of whom believed that the condition was caused by a warm wind sent from the court of their southwestern god, Cautantowwit.

Halcyon Days (December): This refers to about 2 weeks of calm weather that often follow the blustery winds of autumn's end. Ancient Greeks and Romans experienced this weather around the time of the winter solstice, when the halcyon, or kingfisher, was brooding in a nest floating on the sea. The bird was said to have charmed the wind and waves so that the waters were especially calm during this period.

Beware the Pogonip (December): The word *pogonip* refers to an uncommon occurrence—frozen fog. The word was coined by Native Americans to describe the frozen fogs of fine ice needles that occur in the mountain valleys of the western United States and Canada. According to their tradition, breathing the fog is injurious to the lungs. □□

Get Ready for the

BEST
COMET
EVER

(Maybe.)

BY BOB BERMAN

What is nature's greatest spectacle? The Grand Canyon at sunrise? A monster tornado? If historical accounts are any guide, it's a great comet. These have inspired awe and terror in civilizations around the world.

Life-altering comets are rare. In most years, a dozen or so faint comets sweep through the inner solar system, unseen by the naked eye and visible only under dark skies through binoculars or a telescope. Many barely develop a tail. Some of these may indeed brighten dramatically, but they fly too close to the Sun to be easily seen. Some, like Comet McNaught, which passed by Earth in 2007 and was clearly visible in the Southern Hemisphere, may be out of our view.

Yet the cosmic deck sometimes deals aces. The world saw and adored Comet Hale-Bopp in 1997. Some of our grandparents gaped at the even-brighter Great Comet of 1910, whose tail swept across half the sky. Then there was the Great Comet of 1680, which made New Yorkers pour into the streets "overcome with terror," according to newspaper reports of the day.

With such a potential for spectacle, astronomers perked up when Vitali Nevski and Artyom Novichonok of the International Scientific Optical Network (ISON), in Russia, discovered a dim speck of a comet on September 21, 2012. The facility's modest 16-inch telescope revealed the faint iceball just beyond Jupiter, flying toward Earth, and the observers quickly named it for the observatory that had found it: Comet ISON.

This celestial Icarus may be completely wrecked before it even reaches perihelion. That is the great unknown.

Numerous astronomers calculated an orbit that will prove to be amazing: In early November 2013, Comet ISON will be visible to the naked eye about half an hour before sunrise, low in the southeastern sky. It heads almost straight toward the Sun, where, in late November 2013, its ices will turn to

–NASA

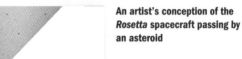

An artist's conception of the *Rosetta* spacecraft passing by an asteroid

vapor at a frantic rate and release thousands of tons of embedded pebbles and dust, which will be blown outward by the solar wind into a tail at least a million miles long.

ISON will zoom northward at breakneck speed (100 times faster than a rifle bullet!), passing over Earth's Northern Hemisphere—perfect for observers throughout the United States and Canada. At this time, ISON will be 34 million miles from Earth, nearly as close as Mars.

On November 28, the comet will streak a mere 750,000 miles above the Sun's white-hot gaseous surface, while being whipped by gravity violently around it and flung back into space. This dramatic passage—less than one Sun-width above its 10,000°F photosphere (gaseous visible surface)—may destroy the comet. Indeed, this celestial Icarus may be completely wrecked before it even reaches perihelion. That is the great unknown in this magical event.

However, the consensus among astronomers is that ISON will emerge from its solar ordeal with an even longer tail and a dazzling brilliance

> The consensus among astronomers is that ISON will emerge with a dazzling brilliance that will outshine the full Moon.

Mission Almost Accomplished

We are about to learn much more about comets, thanks to the *Rosetta* spacecraft, an international mission spearheaded by the European Space Agency, with assistance from NASA, which was launched on March 2, 2004. It will rendezvous with dim, distant comet 67P/Churyumov-Gerasimenko (aka C-G) in May 2014 and map its nucleus in great detail in August. The spacecraft will send a probe to land on the comet's surface in November and take a complete inventory of the comet's chemical and mineralogical composition.

2014   THE OLD FARMER'S ALMANAC   155

that will outshine the full Moon.

Assuming that it survives its trial by fire, ISON becomes a dazzling spectacle in the predawn eastern sky in early December 2013. In fact, ISON should shine at its very brightest from November 23 to December 6, when it will mostly be around 8 degrees high in the east, 30 minutes before sunrise, with the tail pointing straight up and possibly spreading across a sizable chunk of the sky.

In ensuing weeks, as it does a slow fade, ISON flies higher and higher, passing closest to Earth on Christmas day as a heaven-sent holiday gift. By early January 2014, fading but still obvious, it will be shifting leftward into the north before hovering on January 8 a mere 2 degrees from the North Star, which is out all night long.

The Comet–Cat Caveat

Astronomers can always predict *where* a comet will be located on any given night; predicting its *appearance* is more challenging. In 1973, a comet named Kohoutek was expected to dazzle the world. *Time* magazine even put it on its cover. However, because it was ultimately visible only from perfectly dark rural sites, it proved to be the dud of the century. Two years later, when astronomers discovered Comet West, the by-then gun-shy news media paid almost no attention—unfortunately. West proved to be one of the best comets of our lives, with a double tail that stretched as long as 20 full Moons in a row.

All of Comet ISON's orbital and brightness parameters seem to promise a genuine spectacle. Yet, when contacted

to give an ISON prediction for this article, renowned comet hunter David Levy repeated his famous observation: "Comets are like cats; they both have tails, and they both do precisely what they want."

A depiction of Augsburg, Germany, with the comets of 1680, 1682, and 1683 in the sky

ISON's orbit suggests that it is fresh from the Oort cloud, a distant halo of icy objects that surrounds our solar system. Veteran comet experts warn that new comets with orbits that skim the Sun are notoriously unpredictable. Results can range from spectacular to zero. Comet ISON's orbit closely resembles that of the Great Comet of 1682. Some astronomers have speculated that they could be twins—pieces of the same parent object. If so, that historically dramatic event portends a truly exceptional spectacle this time around.

It's an exciting time to be a comet investigator or observer. □□

Bob Berman is the author of six books, including *The Sun's Heartbeat* (Little, Brown and Company, 2011). He is also the director of astronomy for SLOOH, the global online observatory.

Now New & Improved

The Jacuzzi® Walk-In Hot Tub...
your own personal fountain of youth.

The world's leader in hydrotherapy and relaxation makes bathing safe, comfortable and affordable.

The moment you step into your New Jacuzzi® Walk-In Hot Tub you'll see the superior design and the quality of the craftsmanship. The new entry step is low, so it is easy and safe to get in and out. The new double-sealing door is 100% guaranteed not to leak. The high 17" seat enables you to sit comfortably while you bathe and to access the easy-to-reach controls. Best of all, your tub comes with the patented Jacuzzi® PointPro® jet system with a new jet pattern– which gives you a perfectly balanced water-to-air ratio to massage you thoroughly but gently. These high-volume, low-pressure pumps are arranged in a pattern that creates swirls and spirals that provide both a total body massage and targeted treatment of specific pressure points. There is even an in-line heater to maintain the water temperature. The tub features a high gloss acrylic coating which is more durable, scratch resistant and easier to clean than traditional gel-coat surfaces. It's American made with full metal frame construction and comes with a limited lifetime warranty on both the tub and the operating system.

Why Jacuzzi is the Best

✓ **Maximum Pain Relief** - Therapeutic water AND air jets to help you feel your best.

✓ **Personalized Massage** - New adjustable jet placement for pinpoint control.

✓ **Easy and Safe Entry** - Low entry, double-sealing leakproof door that is easy to open and close.

✓ **Comfortable Seating** - Convenient 17 inch raised seat.

✓ **Durable and Easy to Clean** - State of the art acrylic surface.

✓ **Worry Free Enjoyment** - Thanks to Jacuzzi Inc.'s Limited Lifetime Warranty.

✓ **No Hassle Installation** - Designed to fit in your existing tub space.

Isn't it time you rediscovered the comfort and luxury of a soothing therapeutic hot tub experience again? Call now and knowledgeable product experts will answer any questions and you can have one in your home next week. Don't wait, call now.

New & Improved! Jacuzzi®

Walk-In Hot Tub

For information call:

1-888-228-5574

Call now Toll-Free and mention your special promotion code 50227.

Third-party financing available with approved credit. Aging in the Home Remodelers Inc. is neither a broker nor a lender. Not available in Hawaii and Alaska

© 2013 Aging in the Home Remodelers Inc.

80743

A FLIGHT OF FANCY

BY HENRY WALTERS

. . . coming soon to the sky near you

If you climb a hill with a view on a September day when a northerly breeze has a shiver in it, keep an eye cocked skyward for one of the natural world's most thrilling pageants. Each fall, all across North America, millions of diurnal raptors, including eagles, falcons, harriers, hawks, kites, and ospreys, make their way southward, some species to wintering grounds as distant as the Pampas of central Argentina, where they will spend a second summer. While most of our backyard songbirds migrate by night, birds of prey (owls excepted) travel primarily by day, when warm, rising air acts as a cushion to hold them aloft.

In summer, we tend to get only a few glimpses of raptors: a red-tailed hawk perched along the verge of an interstate; an osprey fishing over a pond; a tiny, mouse-hunting American kestrel atop a telephone pole. Even a knowledgeable biologist might be proud to find just one sharp-shinned hawk nest after a whole summer spent walking the woods. But come autumn, these secretive birds appear overhead in droves, a ragged parade of powerful soarers, heading south a few weeks ahead of the first winter snows.

Raptors evoke such awe partly because of their sheer massiveness. The osprey, for example, has a wingspan of 5½ feet; the bald eagle spans 7 feet and can weigh up to 14 pounds. Seeing such an animal aloft, rising effortlessly, elicits oohs, aahs, and expressions of disbelief. Yet despite their size and unparalleled grace, hawks and their relatives lead difficult lives. Data from bird-banding suggest that fewer than 5 of every 10 fledgling raptors survive until their

A male osprey from John James Audubon's Birds of America

A red-tailed hawk glides over Hawk Mountain Sanctuary.

first birthday. Starvation, even for these birds at the top of the food chain, claims all but the fittest—and luckiest. Twice a year, they make a journey of thousands of miles, with little to eat along the way.

Humans have not made these trips less perilous. Until the middle of the 20th century, hawk shooting was a common practice, allowed and even encouraged by some state and local officials, who put bounties on the wings of the "chicken hawk" (northern goshawk) and "duck hawk" (peregrine falcon), among others. Often the shooting was indiscriminate. In 1932, Richard Pough, an early conservationist, reported from rural Pennsylvania:

On top of Blue Mountain, above Drehersville, Schuylkill County, an appalling slaughter was going on . . . . When 100 or 150 men armed with pump guns, automatics, double-barreled shotguns, are sitting on top of the mountain looking for a target . . . no bird is safe . . . . Wounded hawks were strung up in trees as decoys . . . .

Ostensibly carried out to reduce "pest" species, these annual shoots existed mostly for sport. (Until the advent of quality field glasses, or binoculars, even serious ornithology had required the use of a shotgun: Often a fast-flying bird in the treetops could not be identified, let alone studied, without first bringing it down to earth.) As our relationship to the natural world began to change and stewardship of its fauna took

Seeing such an animal aloft, rising effortlessly, elicits oohs, aahs, and expressions of disbelief.

on greater importance, descriptions such as Pough's became a call to arms—or rather, a call to lay them aside.

By 1935, Blue Mountain would be transformed into the Hawk Mountain Sanctuary, a 1,400-acre preserve (now 2,600 acres) that was the world's first refuge for birds of prey. The gunners on its slopes would be replaced by hawk watchers—scientists, bird enthusiasts, and casual observers, such as hikers who happened to glimpse the vast movement taking place each fall.

The tidal rhythm of this silent, airborne current dates back at least as far as the last glaciation. Each fall at Hawk Mountain, more than 18,000 raptors, on average, are counted and identified; around 7,000 of these appear over a few days in mid-September. Attuned to the diminishing length of the day, broad-winged hawks, smaller cousins of the more familiar red-tailed, abandon their solitary lifestyle and move en masse in huge, loose flocks. To save precious energy for the flight southward over Central America to Brazil, these hawks rely on thermals, pockets of rapidly rising warm air, to launch them skyward without needing to flap their wings. Thermals are invisible, but the birds use each other to find them, crisscrossing the landscape in search of a naturally occurring elevator ride.

Observed from a mountaintop, the sight is staggering: Dozens,

Watching the migration at Hawk Mountain Sanctuary

—Tom Raub/Hawk Mountain Sanctuary

For sheer wonder, few spectacles can so mesmerize an audience as a silent ribbon of hawks overhead.

hundreds, sometimes thousands of birds, swirl as if in a tight cylinder, rising like steam from a tea kettle. (Hawk watchers call such a group a "kettle.") At the top of the draft, where the warm air dissipates, the birds peel off southward, one by one, in a swift glide, in search of the next warm current. They can be counted as they stream off the top of the thermal, a long river of raptors whose source lies somewhere in the Canadian north woods, a river that increases in strength as the geography of the continent funnels them together. In 2004, more than 520,000 broad-wings, most in homogeneous flocks, were counted in a single day over Corpus Christi, Texas.

While counting individual birds might seem like a distraction from the pleasure of the jaw-dropping spectacle, it serves an important purpose. Keeping an eye—indeed, many eyes—on the skies can help us to keep watch on our environment; the raptors' place at the top of the food chain makes them *indicator species;* they reflect the health of the entire ecosystem. For example, precipitous declines in the peregrine falcon population in the 1950s alerted the conservation community to the disastrous effects of DDT. Rachel Carson's

Silent Spring brought national attention to the issue and, after a nationwide ban on the pesticide was enacted in 1972, birds began to recover.

Since then, bald eagles and ospreys have returned to their former breeding grounds, and the peregrine falcon, which had been eradicated from the eastern half of the United States, has been reintroduced to the region with slow but steady success.

From almost anywhere in North America, one pair of binoculars and a hill with good northern exposure are all that you need to witness the migration. Clear days in September and October, following the passage of a cold front, often bring a large "push," or sustained movement, of raptors. While identifying birds in flight, even large ones, can be difficult, a good field guide and friendly advice from other hawk watchers make the challenge far less daunting. For sheer wonder, few spectacles can so mesmerize an audience as a silent ribbon of hawks overhead, making a pilgrimage that few of us can fathom.

Henry Walters is a naturalist, teacher, falconer, and official counter at the Pack Monadnock Raptor Migration Observatory in Peterborough, New Hampshire, one of the premier hawk-watch sites in New England. Read his blog at **Almanac.com/Blogs.**

(continued)

Fr e Heirloom Se ds!
Small Seed Company Offering $20.00 In Free Heirloom Seeds Just To Get The Word Out About How Delicious Old Time Varieties Taste!

By Mike Walters
Staff Writer

If you want to grow better tasting vegetables, this will be the most important message you will read this year. Here's why:

Heirloom Solutions in Thomson, Illinois is celebrating the 2014 gardening season by actually giving away $20.00 in free heirloom seeds to readers of the Old Farmer's Almanac. Why would they do that?

The answer is simple. To prove to the world that old time heirloom varieties just plain taste better! The world's become a pretty crazy place these days, but there's one thing you can depend on year after year... and that's the extraordinary taste of the old time varieties.

You know the ones I'm talking about... the ones Grandma and Grandpa used to grow.

The folks at Heirloom Solutions are so confident that you'll love the old time heirloom vegetable varieties that they are willing to "go the extra mile" to convince Old Farmer's Almanac readers with this unusual offer.

Here's how to get your free seeds:

If you have a computer you can go watch a special video about this free heirloom seeds offer by going to:

www.FreeHeirloomSeeds.com

If you don't have a computer, you can simply send $2.00 to cover some of the shipping and handling for the new 2014 catalog. Be sure to include your address so we'll know where to send your catalog as well as your phone number so one of the guys can call and tell you how to get the seeds you want.

Don't worry, no one will pressure you into ordering anything you don't want. They simply don't allow that.

To get your new 2014 catalog and $20.00 in free heirloom seeds, please send $2.00 to:

**Heirloom Solutions
2200 Illinois Route 84
P.O. Box 487
Thomson, IL 61285**

Nature

A bald eagle (right) *and an American kestrel* (below) *amaze raptor migration enthusiasts.*

TAKING COUNT

Spring and fall migrations present ideal opportunities for taking a raptor census. Trained hawk counters station themselves at more than 100 locations across the United States and Canada each season.

On busy days, no single counter can monitor the entire sky; instead, multiple counters partition the sky into sections, or assign themselves separate streams of birds to count. *How* do they count?

One by one by one. Handheld clickers help to keep track of the total.

The counter must be sure to distinguish migrant raptors from locals that may not be moving yet—otherwise, how do you know that you're not counting the same bird twice? (This is the most commonly asked question among those first arriving at a hawk watch.)

As the pace increases, hawk watchers sometimes refer to birds by nickname: "sharpie" (sharp-shinned hawk), "T-V" (turkey vulture), "chocolate falcon" (merlin), and "gray ghost" (male northern harrier), among others.

With each new migrant-spotting, a landmark on the horizon is named to help other watchers locate the bird themselves. At each watch site, a secret language emerges: "Here's a bird, a glass up [i.e., one binocular field] above the camel's hump, moving left above the poodle-tail spruce, under a porcupine cumulus, it's an 'os'

–photos, Bill Moses/Hawk Mountain Sanctuary

[osprey] on a peel . . . ."

Counters relay their sightings quickly and accurately to a coordinating counter, who both verifies the identification of the birds and keeps a running tally as they streak south.

Friendly banter and camaraderie are never lacking among hawk enthusiasts and for good reason: To produce accurate data, year after year, a hawk watch needs a group of dedicated volunteers. If you are interested in finding a hawk watch site near you, visit www.hawkcount.org.

Often, the most important function of such a site is the opportunity that it provides for environmental education among students, naturalists, and even unsuspecting passers-by. The spectacle speaks to one and all. *–H. W.* □□

Best Fishing Days and Times

The best times to fish are when the fish are naturally most active. The Sun, Moon, tides, and weather all influence fish activity. For example, fish tend to feed more at sunrise and sunset, and also during a full Moon (when tides are higher than average). However, most of us go fishing when we can get the time off, not because it is the best time. But there *are* best times, according to fishing lore:

The Best Fishing Days for 2014, when the Moon is between new and full:

January 1–15

January 30–February 14

March 1–16

March 30–April 15

April 29–May 14

May 28–June 13

June 27–July 12

July 26–August 10

August 25–September 8

September 24–October 8

October 23–November 6

November 22–December 6

December 21–31

- One hour before and one hour after high tides, and one hour before and one hour after low tides. (The times of high tides for Boston are given on pages 120–146; also see pages 250–251. Inland, the times for high tides correspond with the times when the Moon is due south. Low tides are halfway between high tides.)

- During the "morning rise" (after sunup for a spell) and the "evening rise" (just before sundown and the hour or so after).

- During the rise and set of the Moon.

- When the barometer is steady or on the rise. (But even during stormy periods, the fish aren't going to give up feeding. The smart fisherman will find just the right bait.)

- When there is a hatch of flies—caddis flies or mayflies, commonly.

- When the breeze is from a westerly quarter, rather than from the north or east.

- When the water is still or slightly rippled, rather than during a wind.

How to Estimate the Weight of a Fish

Measure the fish from the tip of its nose to the tip of its tail. Then measure its girth at the thickest portion of its midsection.

The weight of a fat-bodied fish (bass, salmon) = (length x girth x girth)/800

The weight of a slender fish (trout, northern pike) = (length x girth x girth)/900

Example: If a fish is 20 inches long and has a 12-inch girth, its estimated weight is (20 x 12 x 12)/900 = 2,880/900 = 3.2 pounds

salmon

trout

catfish

What are the three most important

ROTATION, ROTA

very year, working on the soil pays off in unexpected pounds of produce. Often, it's while consuming, canning, or just contemplating the harvest that visions of next season's plot dance through our heads. We are already planning our rotations.

Many beginning gardeners do not realize that repeating a plot plan over consecutive years by growing annual

compiled by Almanac editors

168

words for vegetable gardeners?

..ON, ROTATION

vegetables in the same place results in plants that fail to thrive and a harvest that declines from one year to the next. Often, blame falls on bugs, diseases, bad weather, bad timing, bad soil, even bad karma.

While these factors may be at play, many times the culprit is bad habit: Failure to rotate crops. If this sounds like you, here's what to do.

Draw a plot plan of your most recent vegetable garden. Write in the types of vegetables that grew in each area.

This written record is critical. Where you plant in one growing season dictates where you plant in the next. The core principle of crop rotation is planting annual vegetables based on their botanical family. Plants in the same family are genetically related and thus share similar characteristics (leaf appearance, tendrils for climbing, for example).

When performed properly, crop rotation brings many benefits . . .

- **FEWER INSECT PESTS AND SOIL-BORNE DISEASES:** Plants with family ties are vulnerable to the same pests and diseases. When overwintering insects that live in the soil come looking for last year's host vegetables, they won't find any members of the plant family.

- **IMPROVED SOIL NUTRITION:** Some plants add nutrients to the soil, while some extract nutrients.

- **BETTER SOIL STRUCTURE:** Deep-rooted plants penetrate and break up the subsoil, allowing air and water in. They also draw up trace minerals and needed nutrients.

In the accompanying chart, you'll find annual vegetables and some herbs sorted by family name (both common and Latin).

(continued)

Selected Annual Vegetables and Herbs

FAMILY	MEMBERS
Carrot, aka Parsley (*Apiacaeae* or *Umbelliferae*)	caraway, carrot*, celeriac, celery, chervil, cilantro, dill, fennel, lovage, parsley, parsnip
Goosefoot, aka Chard (*Chenopodiaceae*)	beet*, orache, quinoa, spinach, Swiss chard
Gourd, aka Squash (*Cucurbitaceae*)	cucumber, gourd, melon, pumpkin, squash (summer and winter), watermelon
Grass (*Poaceae*, aka *Gramineae*)	sweet corn
Mallow (*Malvaceae*)	okra
Mint (*Lamiaceae*, aka *Labiatae*)	anise hyssop, basil, Chinese artichoke, lavender, mint, oregano, rosemary, sage, summer savory, sweet marjoram, thyme
Morning Glory (*Convolvulaceae*)	sweet potato
Mustard, aka Cabbage (*Brassicaceae*, aka *Cruciferae*)	arugula, bok choi, broccoli, brussels sprouts, cabbage, cauliflower, collard, kale, kohlrabi, komatsuna, mizuna, mustard greens, radish*, rutabaga, turnip, watercress
Nightshade (*Solanaceae*)	eggplant, pepper, potato, tomatillo, tomato
Onion (*Alliaceae**)	chives, garlic, leek, onion, shallot
Pea, aka Legume (*Fabaceae*, aka *Leguminosae*)	bush, kidney, lima, pole, and soy beans; lentil; pea; peanut
Sunflower, aka Aster (*Asteraceae*, aka *Compositae*)	artichoke (globe and Jerusalem), calendula, chamomile, dandelion, endive, escarole, lettuce, radicchio, salsify, sunflower, tarragon

*These can be planted among any family.

–Dorling Kindersly/Getty Images

ROTATION BASICS

The practice of crop rotation requires that vegetable crops in the same family not be planted in the same place/s (or same soil, if you're using pots) every year. The vegetable family must rotate together. However, it is not necessary to grow every family or every plant in each family.

Rotation schedules vary in complexity. A few sources advise putting 2 years between same-site plantings; most recommend at least 3, ideally 4, or, depending on the size of your garden and desired harvest, even more years, adding cover crops (annual rye, buckwheat, or crimson clover) to the cycle.

Consider the size of your plot and the plants you want. For a very small garden, try a 3-year plot, where you could grow legumes (pea family) in the first year; tomatoes and other nightshade plants in the next year, and gourds in the third year. The fourth year brings you back to legumes to repeat the cycle. Alternatively, these three families could also be planted in three separate plots in the first year and rotated in this order in ensuing years.

4 PLOTS, 4 YEARS

A 4-year rotation could be four plots, rows, or pie shapes in a circle, with a different plant family in each one. For example, in plot or row one, the mustard family; in the next plot or row, the nightshade or gourd family; in the third, the carrot or onion family; and in the fourth, the pea family. Every year, the plant families would move to the next plot, always in that order.

(continued)

8 PLOTS, 8 YEARS

The 8-year rotation practiced by Maine market farmer Eliot Coleman on his Four Season Farm and recommended in his book *The New Organic Grower* (Chelsea Green, 1995) has been cited extensively. His pattern, briefly, is potatoes after sweet corn; sweet corn after cabbage; cabbage after peas; peas after tomatoes; tomatoes after beans; beans after root crops (e.g., carrots, beets); root crops after squashes; and squashes after potatoes. Plus, he advises planting green manure cover crops between some families.

PEAS, PLEASE

Members of the pea family (legumes) add nitrogen to the soil.

PLAN YOUR NEXT GARDEN

Make a list of the vegetables that you want to grow, keeping the family members together based on the chart on page 170. Develop a garden plan based on the family groups and the multiyear rotation examples above.

If this is a new garden, designate an area for each plant family. Keep the design simple.

If you are introducing crop rotation into an existing garden, identify the plant families in your garden. With luck, some family members will be clustered. However, if your last garden was a riotous arrangement of scattered plants, you have a few options: You could begin a new garden; amend the soil of the existing plot with a cover crop and grow vegetables next season; or choose a limited

number of plant families that you want to grow again, note where they grew last year, and plan to grow and rotate families more or less within those spaces.

COMBINE LONG AND SHORT ROTATIONS

In areas with long growing seasons (see the Frost and Growing Seasons chart, page 242), it is possible to harvest three crops from the same plot in one season; this is **succession planting.** For best results, the three crops should follow the rules of rotation. For example, radishes and others in the mustard family would be planted in early spring; tomatoes and other nightshades in summer; and beets, spinach, and chard—the goosefoot family—in late summer.

Another technique for increasing your yield is **intercropping:** growing two or more vegetables in the same garden space within the same garden season. Ideally, one is a crop that matures quickly and the other/s are slower growing. For best results, intercrop members of the same family. For example, set radishes between cabbages or other members of the mustard family. Or grow lettuce between endive and escarole. Remember to space plants in a way that allows all of them to get plenty of sunlight.

Crop rotation may sound complicated and a bit of work. But if you spend a little time considering past and future plot plans now, it will begin to make sense and save you a lot of time and cents later.

□□

Plant a perfect garden with our Garden Planner; see page 226.

TRY A DR® FIELD AND BRUSH MOWER WITH OUR
6-MONTH TRIAL!

CLEAR meadows, trails, underbrush from woodlots, pastures.

CUT 8-foot field grass, saplings 3" thick, tough brush.

CHOP everything into small pieces.

Tow-Behind Model

NEW PRO MODELS!

Self-Propelled Model

79593X © 2013

Call for a FREE DVD and Catalog!

TOLL FREE **800-731-0493**

DRfieldbrush.com

STUMP REMOVAL
FAST & EASY!

ELIMINATE Landscape Eyesores with a DR® STUMP GRINDER.

- EXPAND lawn areas.
- OPEN UP fields and meadows.
- BLAZE new trails.
- REMOVE mowing hazards.

The DR® STUMP GRINDER uses carbide-tipped cutting teeth that take over 360 "bites" per second, to pulverize stumps into a pile of woodchips. Quickly and easily, you can grind any size tree stump below ground level. Gone forever!

79594X © 2013

Call for a FREE DVD and Catalog!

TOLL FREE **800-731-0493**

DRstumpgrinder.com

Soil Matters

All vegetables need nutrients to thrive and produce the results that we like to eat.

■ Test your soil. Results will reveal its pH, phosphorus, lime, potassium, soluble salts, soil texture, and more. However, a general test will not reveal insects, diseases, or chemical residues.

■ Achieve the proper soil pH. A very high or very low soil pH may result in plant nutrient deficiency or toxicity. A pH value of 7 is neutral; microbial activity is greatest and plant roots absorb/access nutrients best when the pH is in the 5.5 to 7 range.

■ Add organic matter to your soil. It improves structure, slowly releases nutrients, and increases beneficial microbial activity. (Note: It is virtually impossible to know the nutrient content of aged manure.)

KNOW YOUR N–P–K

Plants' primary nutrients are nitrogen (N), phosphorus (P), and potassium (K). These are available in chemical/synthetic (nonorganic) fertilizers (on the package, the numbers of each nutrient indicate the percentage of net weight contained) or as organic additives suggested here.

■ Nitrogen (N) promotes strong leaf and stem growth and dark green color, such as desired in broccoli, cabbage, greens and lettuce, and herbs. Add aged manure to the soil and apply alfalfa meal or fish or blood meal to increase available nitrogen.

■ Phosphorus (P) promotes root and early plant growth, including setting blossoms and developing fruit, and seed formation; it's important for cucumbers, peppers, squash, tomatoes–any edible that develops after a flower has been pollinated. Add (fast-acting) bonemeal or (slow-release) rock phosphate to increase phosphorus.

■ Potassium (K) promotes plant root vigor and disease and stress resistance and enhances flavor; it's vital for carrots, radishes, turnips, and onions and garlic. Add green sand, wood ashes, gypsum, or kelp to increase potassium.

Avoid applying excess chemical/synthetic fertilizer. It can damage roots and/or reduce the availability of other elements. It is virtually impossible to overdo organic fertilizers. Plants can not distinguish between synthetic and organic fertilizers.

□□

NATURE'S

AVENGERS

Superheroes and villains aren't just in the movies. They're all around us— in our backyards, gardens, even our houses.

by Sally Roth

T he world is literally crawling with insects—about 10 quintillion (that's 10,000,000,000,000,000,000) creeping, crawling, flying, burrowing bugs, according to scientists at the Smithsonian Institution. (This is only a guess because it's impossible to count that many bugs.) Every one of them has superpowers of some sort. Sometimes, like those comic-book characters in skintight suits, they work for the good of humanity:

■ **Leap tall objects in a single bound? Child's play for a grasshopper.**

■ **Lift objects a hundred times heavier than itself? Nice work, itty-bitty ant.**

■ **Emit poison gas that makes bad guys back off in a hurry? Stinkbug at your service.**

Sometimes, these heroes show a darker side—if not to us, to each other.

–photo composite above, Life on White/Getty Images; opposite page, James Hager/Getty Images

SPIDERS ● Were it not for spiders, we'd be up to our necks in insects. (Sorry, arachnophobes, but those creepy spiders that make you cower should be your very best friends.) Hunters one and all, spiders stalk with infinite patience, chase with incredible speed, and snatch prey with lightning quickness. They use more tricks than any human hunter can conceive.

Let's start with that web. Whether it's a messy, dust-collecting cobweb in the corner of the ceiling or a classic beauty stretched across branches in the garden, web silk is miraculous—better than steel in tensile strength and tougher than Kevlar at resisting fracture.

All spiders make silk, but not all make webs. Some, like wolf spiders, depend on their terrific vision (four pairs of eyes help a lot) and speed (eight synchronized legs) to run down their prey.

The crab spider clan performs some of the sneakiest tricks. Being often white or yellow, crab spiders blend perfectly with the center of an aster or the snowy petals of a Shasta daisy, where they lie in wait, ready to pounce on any visiting pollinators.

The camouflage doesn't stop there. The backs of some species,

A goldenrod crab spider ambushes an unsuspecting bumblebee. including the lovely and common white crab spider, glow under ultraviolet light. (It's even better than a cloak of invisibility!) Wasps, whose eyes detect the ultraviolet spectrum, find the glow irresistible. When they arrive on the flower, it's breakfast time— for the spider, not the wasp.

Arachnophobia is no joke, of course. Certain spiders can cause serious harm when they sink their venomous fangs into our flesh. However, unless you're poking around in the secretive haunts of brown recluses and black widows or tickling a tarantula whose irritating hairs can be worse than a bite, serious injuries from spiders seldom occur.

Still, all spiders have venom and fangs with which to inject it. In the wild world, the poison liquefies prey (stinkbugs are a favorite), so the spider can suck it up or munch it more easily. In laboratories, researchers are investigating the possibilities of spider venom for pesticides as well as for medicine.

WASPS ● Unfortunately for spiders, even the heroes are fair game. Birds gladly gobble up spiders, but wasps are an even bigger menace. Although adult wasps don't eat spiders (nectar and pollen keep them going), baby wasps crave arachnids. The larvae that hatch inside that big gray paper ball or mud tube (or whatever sort of architectural wonder a wasp makes for its home) are voracious eaters, and they want fresh, living meat. This is why we often see wasps coasting or creeping over plant foliage: They're on the hunt. One quick sting and the spider is paralyzed but not dead; sadly for the spider, it's not even close to dead.

The mother wasp carries the immobilized spider to her home, stuffs it into a cell with a wasp egg, and then goes back for more, until each wasp-to-be has a well-stocked larder. When the larvae hatch, they dine on helpless, living spiders.

Nightmarish, you say? It gets worse.

Some wasps are parasites that lay their eggs inside the bug that's going to serve as the food supply. The larval wasps eat the hapless host alive, bit by bit, getting their nourishment from the inside while the host slowly shrivels but remains alive.

For many species of parasitic wasps, including teeny-tiny braconids, the target is a juicy caterpillar. Other species have other favorite happy meals: Aphid wasps, only ⅛ of an inch long, lay a single egg inside an aphid, which serves as exactly enough living food to nourish the larval wasp until it pupates. Then the aphid host (usually there are many of them in an aphid colony) turns into an "aphid mummy," a bloated carcass that serves as a safe place where the new wasp can transform before eventually emerging.

QUIT BUGGIN' THE BUGS AND BE THEIR HERO

■ Give nature a hand by making your yard more appealing to hero bugs, and you'll have better gardens and more fun watching the heroics.

Set aside the pesticides. They may be a quick fix, but natural controls are better and healthier in the long run.

Include plants with clusters of tiny flowers to nourish the tiny wasps that do such a big job of preying on pests. Plant dill, fennel, parsley, yarrow, sedums, and native asters. Allow your arugula, radishes, and broccoli to go into bloom; nurture wild mustards, clover, dandelions, and goldenrod in a wilder, undisturbed corner.

Wasps that visit flowers when looking for pollen or nectar will explore to find the caterpillars, aphids, and other insects they use as larval hosts, reducing your populations of cabbageworms, codling moths, cutworms, tomato and tobacco hornworms, corn borers, and a host of other destructive caterpillars.

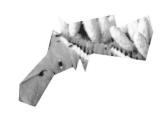

This tomato hornworm is host to tiny white wasp cocoons.

Unsavory habits aside, wasps are just as much heroes as the insects they kidnap. Without wasps, our garden pests would zoom to plague proportions.

CATERPILLARS ● The heroics of all caterpillars fall into the self-sacrificing category. Their main role is to be food.

It's hard to admire a 4-inch-long tomato hornworm when it defoliates your precious 'Brandywine' plant overnight—unless you're a hungry house wren, for whom the caterpillar is a lovely lunch, or a tiny braconid wasp, which sees the hornworm as a living larder for its children. The larvae's tiny white cocoons will decorate the outside of the shriveling, dying caterpillar host like grains of rice in a tidy, crowded row. (If you love tomatoes and hate hornworms, don't pluck off that cocoon-dotted caterpillar. Let the wasps emerge for more allies in the fight against pests.)

LADYBUGS ● Sometimes, deciding which bugs are heroes and which are villains can be difficult. At other times, the champions are unmistakable.

Ladybugs lead the list of champs. Cute as a button, sure, but beneath that happy little exterior is a voracious killer that scuttles over, under, and around stems and leaves in search of prey. What's their target? Aphids. Only aphids. Miss Ladybug's kids are even fiercer than wasp babies. They are eating machines. Mama ladybugs lay their eggs in the midst of aphid colonies. When the tiger-striped larvae hatch, it's Armageddon for the aphids.

LACEWINGS ● Poor aphids. They enjoy the attentions of green lacewings, too. These lovely, diaphanous-wing

BUG BITES

■ Just about every critter under the Sun—at least those that are not strict vegetarians—eats bugs.

■ There are more bugs in 10 square feet of rain forest than people in Manhattan.

■ There are about 1.5 billion bugs for every man, woman, and child on Earth.

Above: **Ladybugs clean up an invasion of aphids.** *Below:* **An assassin bug enjoys a cockroach for lunch.**

–Nature Picture Library/Getty Images

–Stephen Dalton/Getty Images

insects are supreme aphid killers, although they'll grab any other insects that sit still long enough. The lacewing's youngsters, hatched from a beautiful arrangement of eggs held on long stalks, bear the nickname "aphid lions," although they are not above eating small caterpillars or other juicy meals. Aphids—food that can't get away or doesn't even try—are their mainstay.

ASSASSIN BUGS ● Assassin bugs eat aphids, too, but they also go after bigger game: Leafhoppers. Boll weevils. Beetles. Spiders. Caterpillars. Stinkbugs. Anything they can get in their embrace long enough to pierce its body and suck out the juices. Sometimes assassins take up residence in houses, where they dine on cockroaches, bedbugs, and other yummy bites. Most of us never notice the killers or we kill them, not realizing they are unsung heroes.

PRAYING MANTISES ● The biggest hero of all—sizewise—is the praying mantis. (Yes, "praying," not "preying," although insects that venture too near those fierce claws would probably disagree.) Maybe it's the 360-degree field of vision (more than an owl's 270-degree view), with those alert eyes, or the mantis habit of staying in one spot (they're fiercely territorial) that makes this insect seem like a superhero if you're lucky enough to host one. Unfortunately, compared to other hero bugs, praying mantises are few in number. Like hawks, grizzly bears, and other top predators, every mantis needs a big territory to support its eating habits.

Mantises eat plenty of garden pests, but they don't ask "Friend or foe?" before those razor legs zap out and latch on. They eat anything that they can get their claws

The Invention of the Year is Great News for your Ears

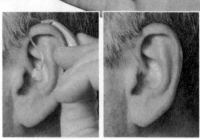

NEW Batteries for Life! ask for details

Perfect Choice HD™ is simple to use, hard to see and easy to afford... it's like reading glasses for your ears™!

New Personal Sound Amplification Product is an affordable way to "turn up the volume!"

Over the years, technology has made the way we live easier, safer and more convenient. In many cases, it's even made many products more affordable... (remember how much the first VCR used to cost?). Now, if you need some help in turning up the volume on the world around you, a new solution has been invented... it's called Perfect Choice HD™.

Perfect Choice HD is NOT a hearing aid. Hearing aids can only be sold by an audiologist or a licensed hearing instrument specialist following hearing tests and fitting appointments. Once they have you tested and fitted, you could pay as much as $5000 for the product.

Reading glasses for your ears. While some people need hearing aids, many just need the extra boost in volume that a PSAP gives them. Now, thanks to the efforts of the doctor who leads a renowned hearing institute, there is Perfect Choice HD. It's a PSAP designed to accurately amplify sounds and deliver them to your ear. Because we've developed an efficient production process, we can make a great product at an affordable price. The unit has been designed to have an easily accessible battery, but it is small and lightweight enough to hide behind your ear... only you'll know you have it on. It's comfortable and won't make you feel like you have something stuck in your ear. It

Affordable, Simple to use, Virtually impossible to see

provides high quality audio so sounds and conversations will be easier to hear and understand.

We want you to be happy with Perfect Choice HD, so we are offering to let you try it for yourself with our exclusive home trial. . If you are not totally satisfied with this product, simply return it within 60 days for a refund of the full product purchase price. Don't wait... and miss out on another conversation... call now!

Perfect Choice HD™

Call now and find out how you can get Batteries for Life!

Please mention promotional code 46793.

1-888-827-9415

1998 Ruffin Mill Road • Colonial Heights, VA 23834

80398

Perfect Choice HD is not a hearing aid. If you believe you need a hearing aid, please consult a physician.

–Christian Prandl/Getty Images

A fly is no match for a hungry praying mantis.

third mantis will stalk the mating pair and try to nab either or both for lunch while they're otherwise occupied.

A FEW MORE ● All insects work to make life livable by keeping nature in balance. Ants may be annoying in the kitchen, but they're major caretakers of trees and plants: They eat pest insects, clean up debris, loosen the soil with the tunnels of their super societies, and harvest and store seeds. Grasshoppers chomp through the garden, but they're a vital food source for birds, rodents, and people in many places. Even those hordes of mosquitoes have a good side. Their wiggling aquatic larvae feed many a predatory water creature. The belief that purple martins, swallows, and bats control mosquitoes is also a myth. Nothing eats adult mosquitoes in significant quantities except possibly toads, when the bugs are rising from foliage at dusk. Even flies are heroic: They're the sanitary engineers, working to remove carrion by eating it. In turn, their fat, buzzing bodies feed many a bird, bat, and dragonfly.

on, including butterflies, frogs, and mice, plus a plethora of insects, including their own kin but not their mates, at least not during "the act." The belief that the female usually eats the male after mating is a myth that got started when mantis couples were observed in captivity. In the wild, the male makes his getaway 7 times out of 10. Sometimes, though, a

The web of life is much more complicated than even the most beautiful spider silk, and every bug is both a hero and a villain. □□

Sally Roth's latest book is *Attracting Songbirds to Your Backyard* (Rodale, 2012). She spends hours every day getting to know the helpful, heroic bugs in her gardens in the Colorado Rockies.

Health & Wellness

Farm gal gets into three car accidents!

Discovers how to soothe-away her pain even when it hurts really bad.

Hello, my name is Judy Mueller, and I want to tell you about the "wonder rub" that soothes my pain every time it flares up! It changed my life and I pray it will change yours. Here's my story…

It started when my friend Kim was in a tractor accident that left him with excruciating pain. But one day I visited and he was smiling. He said he found a pain relief rub called **PAIN BUST-R II®** at our supermarket. He was thrilled to finally get some relief! I was happy for him, but back then, pain wasn't something I had to deal with often. But then everything changed for me…

The Day My Pain Started

I was in 3 separate car accidents, one after another. I was in extreme pain from my knees, neck and back. And when my arthritis kicked in, it was like a nightmare!

I Couldn't Sleep Comfortably!

My pain used to wake me up at night. I had to do something for relief. I tried all sorts of ointments, liniments and creams but they didn't work. Then Kim insisted I try **PAIN BUST-R II**. I listened!

Starts Working on Contact!

When I applied **PAIN BUST-R II** to my to my back, neck and knees, something amazing happened…RELIEF! Now I rub it in where it

hurts every day! It feels great! My pain calms down and I feel much better! That's why I'm writing to you today!

Just Rub It In and You're Good to Go!

At the end of the day, I take my shower, rub **PAIN BUST-R II** on again and comfortably settle in for the evening!

Now My Whole Family Uses It!

I turned others onto **PAIN BUST-R II**. My son uses it on his bad knees. My daughter broke her tailbone and uses it constantly. My mom really suffered with joint pain and **PAIN BUST-R II** really helps her too!

"Like a Vacation from Arthritis PAIN!"

Listen, I have chronic pain and know nothing will take it away completely. But **PAIN BUST-R II** takes it away for a time. So I can do my work or rest without arthritis pain getting in the way!

If you suffer from Arthritis or any other kind of pain, you really should try **PAIN BUST-R II**. It helps me get through the day. I don't know what I'd do without it!

All my best,

Judy Mueller

*IMAGE DOES NOT DEPICT ACTUAL CORRESPONDENT. MODELS ARE USED TO PROTECT PRIVACY.

REDUCE ARTHRITIS PAIN…ON CONTACT! SATISFACTION GUARANTEED!

TO ORDER PAIN BUST-R II: If you would like to purchase **PAIN BUST-R II** as part of this special promotion, please send a check or money order written out to "**PAIN BUST-R II**" for either $9.90 for 1 tube, $16.80 for 2 tubes, or $21.90 for 3 tubes to: CCA Industries, Inc., Dept. OFA-14, PO Box 7486, E. Rutherford, NJ 07073. Please neatly print your name, address and phone number with your payment. All prices include shipping and

handling in the US as part of this special offer.

If you prefer to order by phone using your credit or debit card, please call **1-800-451-5773 and ask for offer OFA-14.**

We are so confident that Pain Bust-R II will help relieve your arthritis pain that we stand behind it with our **Money Back Guarantee!**

Act quickly – this offer may not be repeated.

©2013 CCA Industries, Inc

On the 220th anniversary of the birth of America's first prominent health food advocate, Sylvester Graham, we present . . .

–illustration, Renée Quintal Daily; portrait insert, Emma Silverman/Sylvester's restaurant

THE
Wholly Grail
OF
WHOLE GRAINS

HEALTH ADVOCATES HAVE URGED US TO EAT MORE "WHOLE" grains at least since the days of Sylvester Graham, the "poet of bran." Many people have gotten the message, and whole grain consumption is on the rise. Yet less than 5 percent of us get the recommended three 16-gram servings per day, and whole grains constitute only 11 percent of the grains we eat.

This may be because consumers find it challenging to make sense of the proliferating array of "whole grain" products in the marketplace—many of which may only be masquerading as whole grains. Confused? Read on. We've separated the wheat from the chaff.

(continued)

Opposite page: *This portrait of Sylvester Graham, the "poet of bran," hangs in Sylvester's restaurant in Northampton, Massachusetts.*

by Margaret Boyles

Meet the "POET OF BRAN AND PUMPKINS"

–a reference to Sylvester Graham by Ralph Waldo Emerson, New England essayist and poet (1803–82)

—Emma Silverman

For his role in culinary history, Sylvester Graham deserves more than a place on your pantry shelf. He was born in West Suffield, Connecticut, in 1794, the 17th child of a depressed woman and a colonial preacher who died soon after Sylvester's birth.

Before long, the grieving mother was determined by the court to be "the subject of a melancholy derangement" (Graham's words), and the child was put into the care of family members. They variously "acted like a father" and "treated [him] like a laborer" on a farm.

By age 14, after a stint at a boarding school, Graham returned to his mother's home. His imagination and powers of verbal persuasion, as well as a philosophical bent, suggested maturity beyond his years and made him a subject of both attention and derision. He held several jobs—at a paper mill and as a farmhand, clerk, and teacher—for brief periods. Restlessness and bouts of consumption plagued him.

At age 29, he enrolled at Amherst College to prepare for the ministry, only to succumb to "dreary feelings and dark despondency" and become "much emaciated." Yet his ability to move and compel an audience through oratory grew stronger.

Graham's enthusiasm for good health through temperance in *everything* probably

A local newspaper once referred to Graham as "Dr. Bran, the philosopher of sawdust pudding."

grew out of concern for his own weak constitution. He lectured on the Graham System, a vegetarian diet that included whole wheat flour and no white sugar and alcohol. He published pamphlets on topics from chastity to bread-baking, as well as his core treatise, *Lectures on the Science of Human Life.* He encouraged strictly scheduled mealtimes, cheerfulness at the dining table, open windows, and hard mattresses. A local newspaper once referred to Graham as "Dr. Bran, the philosopher of sawdust pudding."

Graham died in 1851 and was buried in the Bridge Street Cemetery in Northampton, Massachusetts.

Details about the creation of the first Graham cracker are not known, but historians are certain that it bore no resemblance to the eponymous and tasty rectangles that we consume today.

(continued)

GRIT

Celebrating Rural America Since 1882

Get the Most Out of Country Living

In every issue:

- Gardening projects & plans
- Recipes – All kinds!
- Practical articles & advice
- Country wisdom
- Tips from experienced readers
- and much more ...

6 issues $10

SUBSCRIBE TODAY!
www.Grit.com/EGRADDZE
(866) 803-7096

ALSO
Visit us online for:

- **GRIT eNews**

- **Wiser Living Apps**

- **GRIT Country**

www.Grit.com/Almanac

True grains are edible seeds from the grass family of plants, the Poaceae. These include barley, corn, oats, rice, rye, and wheat, as well as millet, sorghum, and teff (seeds of a species of "lovegrass" native to the northern Ethiopian highlands). Foods based on corn, rice, and wheat provide nearly half of the calories for the world's human population.

Other seeds not part of Poaceae but sometimes classified as whole grains because they have similar uses and nutritional profiles include amaranth, buckwheat, flax, and quinoa. Plant scientists and nutritionists call this group of plants pseudograins or pseudocereals.

Although the various food grains and pseudograins originated in different geographic regions and differ widely in their soil and environmental requirements, all of them are grown commercially somewhere in North America.

The "Whole" Story

There is currently no legal definition of a whole grain. However, health and nutrition experts coalesce around a 2006 FDA "guidance" document for whole grain labels. This states that a whole grain should contain all three parts of the seed—bran, germ, and endosperm—in the relative proportions present in the original seed.

Refining typically removes the bran (fiber-rich outer coating) and the germ (the part of the seed that grows into a new plant), leaving only the starchy endosperm that supplies food to the young plant before it sets down roots. Removing the bran and germ eliminates most of

the fiber, 25 percent of the protein, and at least 17 nutrients present in the unrefined grain.

Beware of promotional or package-label terms such as "multigrain," "100 percent wheat," and "contains whole grains." Ditto for "natural," "organic," and "stone-ground." These products may contain only a small fraction of whole grain or none at all. Similarly, the terms "enriched," "degerminated," and "polished" always refer to refined grains.

A label that promotes a product as "100 percent whole [name of grain/s]" ensures that the product contains no refined grains. Otherwise, check the ingredient list on the nutrition label: A whole grain should be listed as the first ingredient.

Remember, too, that the more ingredients a product contains, the more its whole grain fraction will be diluted and the more calories in the form of added sugars, fats, and refined grains you'll likely have to consume to get your whole grain serving. *(continued)*

IS YOUR MEMORY SLIPPING AWAY?

Are you tired of feeling "foggy"... absent-minded... or confused? Find out how some people stay sharp and mentally focused - even at age 90!

By Steven Wuzubia, Health Correspondent;

Clearwater, Florida: Nothing's more frustrating than when you forget names... misplace your keys... or just feel "a little confused". And even though your foggy memory gets laughed off as just another "senior moment", it's not very funny when it keeps happening to you.

Like gray hair and reading glasses... some people accept their memory loss as just a part of getting older. But it doesn't have to be that way.

Today, people in their 70's, 80's even their 90's... are staying mentally fit, focused and "fog-free". So what do they know that you don't? Well, the secret may be as easy as taking a tiny pill called Lipogen PS Plus.

UNBLOCK YOUR BRAIN

Made exclusively in Israel, this incredible supplement feeds your brain the nutrients it needs to stay healthy. It was developed by Dr. Meir Shinitzky, Ph.D., former visiting professor at Duke University, and recipient of the prestigious J.F. Kennedy Prize.

Dr. Shinitzky explains: "Science has shown, when your brain nutrient levels drop, you can start to experience memory problems. Your ability to concentrate and stay focused becomes compromised. And gradually, a "mental fog" sets in. It can damage every aspect of your life".

In recent years, researchers identified the importance of a remarkable compound called phosphatidylserine (PS). It's the key ingredient in *Lipogen PS Plus*. And crucial to your ability to learn and remember things as you age.

YOUR MEMORY UNLEASHED!

Lipogen PS Plus is an impressive fusion of the most powerful, natural memory compounds on Earth.

It produces amazing results, especially for people

 Officially Reviewed by the U.S. Food and Drug Administration:

Lipogen PS Plus safety has been reviewed by the FDA (FDA GRAS Notice No. GRN 000186) PS is the ONLY health supplement with a FDA "qualified health claim" for BOTH, COGNITIVE DYSFUNCTION AND Dementia.

who have tried everything to improve their memory before, but failed. *Lipogen PS Plus* gives your brain the vital boost it needs to jump-start your focus and mental clarity. "It truly is a godsend!" says Shinitzky.

 ### MY MEMORY WAS STARTING TO FAIL ME.

I would forget all kinds of things and I've noticed my memory seemed to be getting pretty unreliable. Something I just said would completely slip my mind and I was worried about it. I read about *Lipogen* and wanted to try it. I began to notice I wasn't forgetting things anymore. It's great. I have actual recall, which is super. Thanks *Lipogen* for giving me my memory back.

- Ethel Macagnoney

SIGNIFICANT IMPROVEMENTS

In 1992, doctors tested phosphatidylserine on a select group of people aged 60-80 years old. Their test scores showed impressive memory improvement. Test subjects could remember more and were more mentally alert. But doctors noticed something else.

The group taking phosphatidylserine, not only enjoyed sharper memory, but were also more upbeat and remarkably happy. In contrast, the moods of the individuals who took the placebo remained unaffected.

SPECIAL "SEE FOR YOURSELF" RISK-FREE SUPPLY

We've made arrangements with the distributor of *Lipogen PS Plus* to offer you a special "Readers Only Discount". This trial is 100% risk-free.

It's a terrific deal. If *Lipogen PS Plus* doesn't help you think better, remember more... and improve your mind, clarity and mood – you won't pay a penny! (Except S&H).

So don't wait. Now you can join the thousands of people who think better, remember more—and enjoy clear, "fog-free" memory. Think of it as making a "wake-up call" to your brain.

CALL NOW, TOLL FREE! SIMPLY DIAL...

1-800-609-3558

THESE STATEMENTS HAVE NOT BEEN EVALUATED BY THE FDA. THESE PRODUCTS ARE NOT INTENDED TO DIAGNOSE, TREAT, CURE OR PREVENT ANY DISEASE. RESULTS MAY VARY.

Food

The surest way to know that you're eating whole grains is to cook a dish containing the unadulterated whole grain yourself: an entrée made with brown rice, a side of hulled barley, a bowl of oatmeal. Or bake your own bread using only whole grain flours.

To help you better understand and identify grains, consult these definitions.

True Grits

Berries (wheat, rye), **groats** (oats, buckwheat), and **kernels** (corn) are all terms for grains in whole-seed form (minus the hull).

Grits are any coarsely ground whole or refined grain. (Cracked wheat and polenta are grits.)

Meals and **flours** are grains that have been ground; meal is generally considered the coarser one. "Refined" or "degerminated" means that part or all of the bran and germ have been removed.

Rolled or **flaked** grains are whole grains that have been cooked, rolled flat, and baked, losing minimal amounts of nutrients and fiber in the process. They are considered whole grains. Do not confuse them with dry-cereal flakes, which may or may not be 100 percent whole grain.

Wheat 14 Ways

Bulgur is whole wheat berries that have been steamed, roasted, and crushed. It qualifies as a whole grain.

Couscous, not a grain but a form of wheat pasta, is available in both refined and whole grain forms.

Cracked wheat is simply coarsely crushed whole wheat berries. It qualifies as a whole grain but beware of products with "cracked wheat" as part of their name ("cracked-wheat bread"), which may contain only a small amount of cracked wheat, with the rest refined flour.

Cream of wheat, farina, and **semolina** are refined wheat products. **Wheatena,** a hot cereal product developed in 1879, is considered a whole grain.

Einkorn, emmer, farro, kamut, and **spelt** are ancient strains of wheat finding their way into modern specialty markets because of their unusual (and, some say, superior) cooking, flavor, or nutritional characteristics.

Triticale is a whole grain hybrid of wheat and rye.

Whole white wheat sounds like a contradiction, but it is a true whole grain. White wheats are albino species that lack the genes that give other wheats their brown color. White wheat has a milder flavor a bit closer to refined white flours.

–illustrations, Renée Quintal Daily

Kernels of Truth

Corn is the only native American grain. **Corn on the cob** is the only true whole grain that's eaten fresh.

Cornmeal, corn flour, and **corn grits** can be made from either whole or degerminated corn kernels.

Hominy refers to whole corn that's been soaked in a strong alkaline solution (usually lye), a process known as nixtamalization. Although the process makes B vitamins and amino acids more available and may increase hominy's calcium content, it generally removes most of the bran, so hominy can't be considered a whole grain.

Polenta is coarsely ground kernels of special varieties of hard flint corn that take on a creamy, gelatinous texture when cooked.

The special varieties of corn called **popcorn** "pop" when steam builds up inside their hard, moisture-resistant hulls. All grains "pop" to a certain degree, but popcorn produces the most spectacular explosion.

Barley: 1, 2, 3

Barley malt is an ingredient used in making beer, whiskey, malt vinegar, and Ovaltine. It also appears in many baked goods. Malting is the process of soaking a whole grain (typically barley, but also other grains) in water until it sprouts and then heat-drying the sprouted grain to prevent further germination.

Pearled barley has had its outer coating (which contains the bran) removed; the remaining seed has been polished. It is not considered a whole grain.

Whole barley is called hulled barley (also brown barley, pot barley, and scotch barley). It retains the bran that pearling removes.

Gluten, Good and Bad

Gluten is a protein found in barley, rye, triticale, and wheat, as well as products made from these grains. It gives bread dough its elasticity and capacity to rise. Extracted from wheat, gluten appears in meat substitutes and as a flavoring, stabilizing, or thickening agent in many prepared foods. You've probably noticed the explosion of products advertised as "gluten-free." A gluten-free diet is the only medically accepted treatment for the autoimmune condition called *celiac disease* and other gluten-intolerance conditions.

(continued)

How Much Is Enough?

Sylvester Graham had a good idea. Research shows that eating whole grains can reduce the risk of cardiovascular diseases, type II diabetes, some cancers, gum disease, asthma, and obesity. The research suggests that three or four 16-gram servings a day can improve and maintain health. Here's what 16 grams looks like:

½ cup cooked, 100 percent plain, whole grain (brown rice, hulled barley, whole millet); or

½ cup cooked oatmeal (1 ounce dry); or

½ cup 100 percent whole grain pasta; or

1 slice 100 percent whole grain bread; or

5 small whole wheat crackers; or

2 rye crisps; or

1 6-inch-diameter, 100 percent whole wheat flour tortilla or corn tortilla; or

3 cups plain, air-popped popcorn; or

1 cup 100 percent whole grain cereal flakes (dry, boxed)

Prepared foods containing whole grain flour, such as crackers, chips, pretzels, waffles, and others, may count as a serving, if you eat enough of them to get a full 16 grams (just over ½ ounce) of whole grain.

21st-Century Stamp Act

To promote truth in whole grain labeling, the Whole Grains Council, a nonprofit trade organization, has developed a Whole Grain Stamp program, which quantifies a product's whole grain content.

Margaret Boyles lives in a wood-heated house in central New Hampshire, where she grows vegetables, eats weeds, and keeps chickens.

NO-PAIN GRAINS

A good way to get your recommended grains is to cook them yourself. Here, from **Almanac.com,** *are a few easy and delicious recipes, chosen specifically for their whole grain ingredients.*

Tabbouleh

1 cup bulgur
boiling water
1½ cups chopped fresh parsley
½ cup finely chopped fresh mint
1 cup finely chopped onions or scallions
¾ cup chopped tomatoes
¾ cup extra-virgin olive oil
½ cup lemon juice
salt and freshly ground black pepper, to taste
parsley sprig, for garnish

Place the bulgur in a mixing bowl and add boiling water to cover. Let stand until all of the liquid is absorbed, about 1 to 2 hours. Let cool. Combine with the remaining ingredients and garnish with a sprig of parsley. **Makes 6 servings.**

–Renée Quintal Daily

Farro Salad

In place of farro, you may use barley or spelt.

1½ cups farro
4 to 5 dried tomatoes, roughly chopped
⅓ cup crumbled feta cheese
6 to 8 basil leaves, roughly chopped
2 to 3 scallions, finely chopped
¼ cup olive oil
1 tablespoon red-wine or balsamic
    vinegar

Cover the farro with water and soak overnight, then boil for 15 to 20 minutes, or until tender. Or cover with water, cover the pot, and cook on medium low until the water is absorbed.

In a medium bowl, combine all of the ingredients and mix well. **Makes 6 servings.**

MIX IN'S

■ Add nuts (walnuts, pine nuts, slivered almonds–toasted, if desired), dried fruit (cranberries, blueberries), and/or grated cheese to any finished grain salad.

Chicken Salad With Grains

Use wheat berries, farro, brown rice, buckwheat groats, quinoa, or a combination in this versatile dish.

5 scallions, white and green parts,
    finely chopped
1 small fennel bulb, core removed and
    thinly sliced
1 Granny Smith or other firm tart apple,
    peeled and cored, thinly sliced
2 cups cooked grains
roasted chicken meat, roughly chopped
1 cup toasted pine nuts
3 tablespoons fresh lemon juice
4 tablespoons extra-virgin olive oil
⅓ cup chopped flat-leaf parsley
kosher or sea salt
freshly ground black pepper

In a large mixing bowl, combine all of the ingredients except the salt and pepper, then toss well to coat. Season to taste. **Makes 8 servings.**

□□

Table of Measures

APOTHECARIES'
1 scruple = 20 grains
1 dram = 3 scruples
1 ounce = 8 drams
1 pound = 12 ounces

AVOIRDUPOIS
1 ounce = 16 drams
1 pound = 16 ounces
1 hundredweight = 100 pounds
1 ton = 2,000 pounds
1 long ton = 2,240 pounds

LIQUID
4 gills = 1 pint
63 gallons = 1 hogshead
2 hogsheads = 1 pipe or butt
2 pipes = 1 tun

DRY
2 pints = 1 quart
4 quarts = 1 gallon
2 gallons = 1 peck
4 pecks = 1 bushel

LINEAR
1 hand = 4 inches
1 link = 7.92 inches

1 span = 9 inches
1 foot = 12 inches
1 yard = 3 feet
1 rod = 5½ yards
1 mile = 320 rods = 1,760 yards = 5,280 feet
1 international nautical mile = 6,076.1155 feet
1 knot = 1 nautical mile per hour
1 fathom = 2 yards = 6 feet
1 furlong = ⅛ mile = 660 feet = 220 yards
1 league = 3 miles = 24 furlongs
1 chain = 100 links = 22 yards

SQUARE
1 square foot = 144 square inches
1 square yard = 9 square feet
1 square rod = 30¼ square yards = 272¼ square feet
1 acre = 160 square rods = 43,560 square feet
1 square mile = 640 acres = 102,400 square rods
1 square rod = 625 square links

1 square chain = 16 square rods
1 acre = 10 square chains

CUBIC
1 cubic foot = 1,728 cubic inches
1 cubic yard = 27 cubic feet
1 cord = 128 cubic feet
1 U.S. liquid gallon = 4 quarts = 231 cubic inches
1 imperial gallon = 1.20 U.S. gallons = 0.16 cubic foot
1 board foot = 144 cubic inches

KITCHEN
3 teaspoons = 1 tablespoon
16 tablespoons = 1 cup
1 cup = 8 ounces
2 cups = 1 pint
2 pints = 1 quart
4 quarts = 1 gallon

TO CONVERT CELSIUS AND FAHRENHEIT:

$°C = (°F − 32)/1.8$
$°F = (°C × 1.8) + 32$

Metric Conversions

LINEAR
1 inch = 2.54 centimeters
1 centimeter = 0.39 inch
1 meter = 39.37 inches
1 yard = 0.914 meter
1 mile = 1.61 kilometers
1 kilometer = 0.62 mile

SQUARE
1 square inch = 6.45 square centimeters
1 square yard = 0.84 square meter

1 square mile = 2.59 square kilometers
1 square kilometer = 0.386 square mile
1 acre = 0.40 hectare
1 hectare = 2.47 acres

CUBIC
1 cubic yard = 0.76 cubic meter
1 cubic meter = 1.31 cubic yards

HOUSEHOLD
½ teaspoon = 2 mL
1 teaspoon = 5 mL
1 tablespoon = 15 mL

¼ cup = 60 mL
⅓ cup = 75 mL
½ cup = 125 mL
⅔ cup = 150 mL
¾ cup = 175 mL
1 cup = 250 mL
1 liter = 1.057 U.S. liquid quarts
1 U.S. liquid quart = 0.946 liter
1 U.S. liquid gallon = 3.78 liters
1 gram = 0.035 ounce
1 ounce = 28.349 grams
1 kilogram = 2.2 pounds
1 pound = 0.45 kilogram

WHEN INSPIRATION STRIKES, TAKE NOTES

• • • • •

ON WHATEVER SCRAP PAPER IS AT HAND.

• • • • •

Those JOTS *could change your life.*

by Martie Majoros

This year marks the **200th anniversary** of "The Star-Spangled Banner," the lyrics for which took shape on a letter, as explained here. This got us thinking: What other **remarkable accomplishments** originated as notes on **envelopes, napkins,** and the like?

The KEY MOMENT

During the War of 1812, on the evening of September 13, 1814, Francis Scott Key, a lawyer and poet, was negotiating the release of an American prisoner with British Navy officers in Baltimore's inner harbor. Key watched as the British

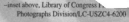

Volumes OF VERSE

Upon her death in 1886, Emily Dickinson left hundreds of unpublished snippets of verse scribbled on bits of paper and stored in boxes in her attic. Her sister, Lavinia, discovered 40 unpublished booklets, nearly 400 poems, and drafts of poems written on scrap paper. She and other relatives subsequently published the poems. Although Dickinson is now regarded as a prolific American poet, only 10 of her poems are known to have been published during her lifetime.

• • • • •

attacked Fort McHenry in an attempt to capture the city of Baltimore. Early the next morning, Key saw the tattered United States flag flying over the fort, indicating victory. Inspired, he wrote a poem on the back of a letter, describing the battle and his relief at seeing the flag. When he returned to Baltimore a few days later, Key revised the poem, which he titled "Defence of Fort McHenry." The poem was soon published, along with Key's instructions that it be sung to the tune of an 18th-century melody, "To Anacreon in Heaven." Later that same year, a music store republished the song, this time with a different name: "The Star-Spangled Banner."

• • • • •

FITTING THE BILL

In 1940, nearing the end of his career and in need of money, actor and writer W. C. Fields wrote the plot outline for *Never Give a Sucker an Even Break* on the only paper he had on hand—a grocery bill. The plot, a movie-within-a-movie, features Fields as himself trying to sell an outrageous script to the fictional Esoteric Film Studio. He sold the idea to Universal Studios for $25,000. The film was released in 1941, and, as he often did, Fields used a pseudonym—in this case, Otis Criblecoblis—to denote his screenplay credit.

c o n t i n u e d

197

FIRST ACT FILLERS

Aaron Sorkin, who won an Oscar for Best Writing for an Adapted Screenplay for *The Social Network* in 2011, wrote his first Broadway play, *A Few Good Men,* while tending bar at a Broadway theater in New York City. He served patrons before the curtain went up and then again at intermission, leaving him time during the whole first act(s) to pen his play—on cocktail napkins. Several years later, he was asked to write the screenplay for the movie, and the film success of *A Few Good Men* in 1992 launched his career.

Giving CREDIT

David H. Shepard created the first machine designed to read credit card receipts. His 1953 invention required a simplified font, and Shepard sketched the block-shape design for the numbers on a cocktail napkin in New York City's Waldorf Astoria hotel. Initially, the credit card machines were used primarily at gas stations, where the unadorned design of Shepard's numbers made them easier to read, even if they had become smudged with grease and oil. The same font is still used today, although the numbers are now contained in a magnetic strip on the card.

• • • • •

NOTHING to LAUGH AT

In 1974, Arthur Laffer, a professor of business economics at the University of Chicago, was dining at a Washington, D.C., restaurant with friends Donald Rumsfeld, Dick Cheney, and Jude Wanniski, a reporter for the *Wall Street Journal.* The conversation turned to the economy, recession, and President Ford's "Whip Inflation Now" (WIN) proposal to increase taxes. To illustrate that increased taxes result in decreased revenues, Laffer reached for a cocktail napkin and drew a simple graph. In a *Wall Street Journal* article several years later, Wanniski dubbed the illustration the "Laffer Curve." The concept became the basis for President Reagan's "trickle-down theory" of economics.

—AP Photos

LASER-SHARP

In 1951, physicist Charles Townes, developer of the maser (precursor to the laser), was in Washington, D.C., meeting with a group of scientists who were attempting to create a more powerful maser. Townes awoke early and, while waiting for breakfast at his hotel to be served, he wandered into nearby Franklin Park. Sitting on a park bench in the quiet morning, Townes conceived a way to create shorter wavelengths, a necessary component of today's laser. Many years later, Townes recalled, "I pulled out an envelope from my pocket and wrote down the equation. . . .

–NASA/JPL-Caltech

Hydrogen maser

I went home, and I worked it out some more and wrote down in a notebook just how to do it." In 1964, Townes and fellow scientists Alexander Prokhorov and Nikolay Basov shared a Nobel Prize for their contributions to the development of lasers.

Concrete THINKING

Structural engineer Tung-Yen Lin often conceived designs as he was flying home from technical meetings, and he would record them on the backs of envelopes. In the mid–20th century, he gained recognition for promoting the use of one idea created in such a way –prestressed concrete, a combination of compressed concrete and steel tendons, which has changed the landscape of industrial design. It is now a common component

–UC Berkeley

in construction projects worldwide and is used in high-rise buildings, bridges, and overpasses.

• • • • •

NOTEWORTHY OBSERVATION

If something can't be explained off the back of an envelope, it's rubbish.

–Richard Branson, English business magnate
and founder of Virgin Atlantic Airlines (b. 1950)

c o n t i n u e d

NOTEWORTHY OBSERVATIONS

Any worthwhile
expedition
can be planned
on the back of an
envelope.

*–attributed to H. W. Tilman,
20th-century English explorer
and author of numerous
mountaineering and
sailing books*

• • • • •

Well, my husband
does that on the back
of an old envelope.

*–Elsa Einstein, wife of Albert,
to astronomer Edwin Hubble
during a visit to the Mount
Wilson Observatory in southern
California, when told that
the giant reflector was used to
determine the shape of the
universe, 1931*

The POWER of TWO

Engineers Charles Chapman and Frank Perkins were facing unemployment during the Great Depression of the 1930s, when they joined forces to found the manufacturing company F. Perkins Limited. Their goal was to produce high-speed diesel engines to improve upon the diesels then being used and rival the power of gasoline engines. During one of Perkins's visits to Chapman's home in North Kent, England, the two sketched out a design. Later, Chapman recalled, "As we sat there and made suggestions, using the arm of my chair as a desk, I made rough thumbnail sketches, illustrating them on the back of one of my envelopes." Their diesel design is widely used today in buses, fire engines, and ships.

**Sectional view of a
four-cylinder Perkins
engine**

TAKE NOTE

The University of Alabama at Birmingham School of Public Health sponsors an annual back-of-the-envelope contest that awards seed money for health research grants. The awards are rated on their creativity and innovation. One key requirement for all applicants: All entries must be submitted on the back of a standard #10 envelope.   □□

Martie Majoros, a frequent contributor to Almanac publications, writes from the shores of Lake Champlain in Burlington, Vermont.

How We Predict the Weather

We derive our weather forecasts from a secret formula that was devised by the founder of this Almanac, Robert B. Thomas, in 1792. Thomas believed that weather on Earth was influenced by sunspots, which are magnetic storms on the surface of the Sun.

Over the years, we have refined and enhanced that formula with state-of-the-art technology and modern scientific calculations. We employ three scientific disciplines to make our long-range predictions: solar science, the study of sunspots and other solar activity; climatology, the study of prevailing weather patterns; and meteorology, the study of the atmosphere. We predict weather trends and events by comparing solar patterns and historical weather conditions with current solar activity.

Our forecasts emphasize temperature and precipitation deviations from averages, or normals. These are based on 30-year statistical averages prepared by government meteorological agencies and updated every 10 years. The most-recent tabulations span the period 1981 through 2010.

We believe that nothing in the universe happens haphazardly, that there is a cause-and-effect pattern to all phenomena. However, although neither we nor any other forecasters have as yet gained sufficient insight into the mysteries of the universe to predict the weather with total accuracy, our results are almost always very close to our traditional claim of 80 percent.

How Accurate Was Our Forecast for Winter 2012–13?

■ Our forecast for this past winter's temperatures was nearly perfect. We were correct in our forecast temperature change from the previous winter in 15 of the 16 regions—yielding an accuracy rate greater than 94%—as every region east of the line from the Dakotas to Texas was colder than the previous winter, while every region west of that line, except for the Desert Southwest, was warmer.

Our snowfall forecast was not as accurate. It read: "Snowfall will be above normal near the Great Salt Lake and in the areas from El Paso to Detroit to Virginia Beach, but below normal in most other locations that typically have snow." We were correct about above-normal snowfall near the Great Salt Lake. In fact, of the 22 cities we show on the regional maps in the western state regions, Salt Lake City was the only one with above-normal

snowfall. As for the other area for which we predicted above-normal snowfall (from El Paso to Detroit to Virginia Beach), it occurred near where we predicted, but a few hundred miles north of our forecast. We did not forecast the above-normal snowfall that fell in portions of New England, although we did predict four snowy periods in this area's winter season.

Our winter precipitation forecast—"Most of the areas suffering from drought will receive sufficient winter precipitation to bring improvement"—was correct. While drought remained an issue in parts of the country, the extent and intensity of the drought declined substantially from its peak in August 2012.

The accuracy of our winter season temperature forecasts is shown in the table below, using a city selected from each region. On average, our forecasts differed from actual conditions by 0.99 degree F.

Region/ City	Nov.–Mar. Temp. Variations From Normal (degrees F)		Region/ City	Nov.–Mar. Temp. Variations From Normal (degrees F)	
	PREDICTED	ACTUAL		PREDICTED	ACTUAL
1/Concord, NH	−2.3	+0.9	9/Green Bay, WI	+1.7	+1.4
2/Atlantic City, NJ	−1.5	−0.3	10/Kansas City, MO	+0.8	+0.8
3/Harrisburg, PA	−1.1	+0.3	11/Oklahoma City, OK	−0.4	+0.8
4/Raleigh, NC	−1.4	−0.9	12/Billings, MT	+1.9	+1.3
5/Orlando, FL	−1.0	+0.1	13/Reno, NV	+0.3	+0.2
6/Cleveland, OH	−0.3	−0.5	14/Albuquerque, NM	−1.0	+0.4
7/Charleston, SC	−1.8	−0.8	15/Eugene, OR	+2.2	+0.6
8/Tupelo, MS	−1.6	0.0	16/Los Angeles, CA	+0.7	+0.3

Get your local forecast at Almanac.com/Weather.

Weather Regions

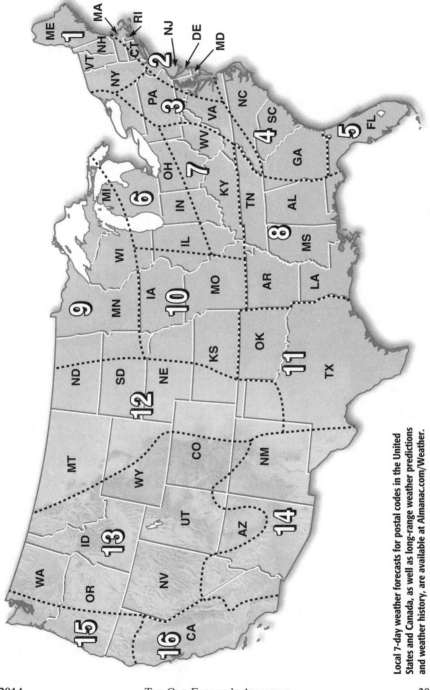

Local 7-day weather forecasts for postal codes in the United States and Canada, as well as long-range weather predictions and weather history, are available at Almanac.com/Weather.

Northeast

SUMMARY: Winter will be milder than normal across the north but colder in the south, with precipitation and snowfall both slightly above normal. The coldest periods will be in early and mid-December, late January, and late February. The snowiest periods will be in early November, early to mid-December, late December, and early February.

April and May will be slightly cooler than normal, with near-normal rainfall.

Summer will be hotter than normal, with slightly below-normal rainfall. The hottest periods will occur in early to mid-July, late July, and mid-August.

September and October will be warmer than normal, with rainfall slightly above normal in the north and a bit below in the south.

NOV. 2013: Temp. 38° (1° below avg.); precip. 5" (1.5" above avg.). 1–4 Rain and snow showers, chilly. 5–10 Snowstorm, then flurries, cold. 11–15 Rain, then snow showers, cold. 16–18 Showers, mild. 19–24 Snow showers, cold. 25–30 Periods of rain and snow, mild.

DEC. 2013: Temp. 26.5° (1° above avg. north, 4° below south); precip. 4" (1" above avg.). 1–4 Flurries, very cold. 5–6 Sunny, mild. 7–11 Rain to snowstorm, then sunny, cold. 12–16 Rain and snow showers, mild. 17–20 Sunny, very cold. 21–30 Rain and snow, then flurries, cold. 31 Snowstorm.

JAN. 2014: Temp. 26° (3° above avg.); precip. 2.5" (0.5" below avg.). 1–5 Snow showers, cold. 6–8 Sunny, mild. 9–10 Flurries, cold. 11–15 Sunny, mild. 16–18 Rainy, mild. 19–22 Snow showers, cold. 23–27 Periods of rain and snow, mild. 28–31 Sunny, cold.

FEB. 2014: Temp. 22° (1° below avg.); precip. 1.5" (1" below avg.). 1–6 Snowstorm, then flurries, seasonable. 7–16 Sunny; cold, then mild. 17–23 Snow, then sunny, cold. 24–28 Snow, then sunny, very cold.

MAR. 2014: Temp. 34.5° (2° above avg. north, 1° below south); precip. 2.5" (0.5" below avg.). 1–5 Snow to rain, turning mild north; flurries, cold south. 6–16 Occasional flurries and sprinkles, seasonable. 17–25 Rain to snow, then snow showers, cold. 26–28 Rain and snow showers, cold. 29–31 Rainy, mild.

APR. 2014: Temp. 46° (avg.); precip. 2.5" (0.5" below avg.). 1–3 Showers, mild. 4–8 Showers, then sunny, nice. 9–11 Showers, warm. 12–14 Rain to snow, then sunny, cool. 15–19 Rainstorm, then sunny, cool. 20–25 Rain to snow north, t-storms south, then sunny; warm, then cool. 26–30 Showers, then sunny, cool.

MAY 2014: Temp. 55° (1° below avg.); precip. 4" (0.5" above avg.). 1–7 A few showers, cool. 8–10 Sunny, very warm. 11–16 T-storms, then sunny, cool. 17–20 Showers, cool. 21–27 Scattered t-storms, warm. 28–31 Showers, cool.

JUNE 2014: Temp. 65° (avg.); precip. 3.5" (avg.). 1–5 Sunny, turning warm. 6–11 T-storms, then sunny, cool. 12–19 A few showers, cool. 20–22 T-storms, warm. 23–28 Scattered showers, cool. 29–30 Sunny, cool.

JULY 2014: Temp. 71° (1° above avg.); precip. 4.5" (0.5" above avg.). 1–2 Sunny, cool. 3–6 T-storms, seasonable. 7–11 Sunny, hot. 12–20 Scattered t-storms, cool. 21–31 A few t-storms, very warm and humid.

AUG. 2014: Temp. 69° (3° above avg.); precip. 3" (1" below avg.). 1–8 T-storms, then sunny, warm. 9–12 Scattered t-storms, warm. 13–17 Sunny; cool, then hot. 18–20 T-storms, then sunny, cool. 21–25 Sunny, turning hot. 26–31 Scattered t-storms; cool, then warm.

SEPT. 2014: Temp. 60° (1° above avg.); precip. 4" (1" above avg. north, 1" below south). 1–4 Showers, then sunny, cool. 5–9 Showers north, sunny south; turning warm. 10–16 Showers, then sunny, cool. 17–26 Scattered showers, seasonable. 27–30 Sunny, warm.

OCT. 2014: Temp. 49° (1° above avg.); precip. 3.5" (avg.). 1–6 Sunny, nice. 7–12 Showers, then sunny, cool. 13–18 Rain to snow, then sunny, cold. 19–24 Rain, then sunny, chilly. 25–31 Rainy periods, mild.

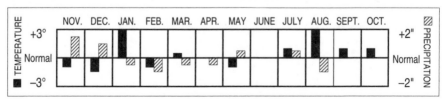

Atlantic Corridor

SUMMARY: Winter will be colder and drier than normal, although snowfall will be above normal in most of the region. The coldest periods will be in early and mid-December and in early to mid-February. The snowiest periods will be in early and mid-December, and in early and mid-February.

April and May will be drier and much warmer than normal.

Summer will be hotter and rainier than normal, with the hottest periods in early June, early to mid-July, and early to mid-August.

September and October will be warmer and drier than normal, with a hurricane threat in early to mid-September.

NOV. 2013: Temp. 47.5° (0.5° above avg.); precip. 5.5" (2" above avg.). 1–5 Stormy, rainy, cool. 6–11 Misty, cool north; sunny, then rain, warm south. 12–16 Misty north, sunny south; cool. 17–22 Showers, mild. 23–24 Sunny, cool. 25–30 Rain, then sunny, cold.

DEC. 2013: Temp. 35° (4° below avg.); precip. 2" (1" below avg.). 1–5 Sunny, very cold. 6–11 Rain to snow, then sunny, cold. 12–16 Rain and snow north, rainy periods south. 17–19 Sunny, very cold. 20–23 Snow to rain, then sunny, cold. 24–29 Rain and snow, then sunny, cold. 30–31 Rain and snow north; sunny, cold south.

JAN. 2014: Temp. 37° (2° above avg.); precip. 2" (1.5" below avg.). 1–2 Showers and flurries. 3–9 Sunny, cold. 10–15 Sunny north, rain south; mild. 16–18 Rainy, mild. 19–21 Sunny, cold. 22–27 Rainy periods, mild. 28–31 Sunny, cold.

FEB. 2014: Temp. 32° (2° below avg.); precip. 3" (avg.). 1–3 Stormy, heavy rain and snow. 4–10 Sunny, cold. 11–15 Rain and snow, then flurries, cold. 16–20 Heavy rain to snow, then sunny, cold. 21–26 Rain to snow, then sunny, cold. 27–28 Rain and snow.

MAR. 2014: Temp. 43° (1° below avg.); precip. 3" (1" below avg.). 1–8 Snow showers, cold. 9–14 Sunny, then showers, turning warm. 15–16 Sunny, cool. 17–21 Heavy rain, then sunny, cool. 22–25 Rain, then sunny, cool. 26–31 Sunny, then rainy, warm.

APR. 2014: Temp. 56° (4° above avg.); precip. 2.5" (1" below avg.). 1–2 Sunny, warm. 3–7 T-storms, then sunny, pleasant. 8–12 A few t-storms, warm. 13–17 Sunny, then showers, cool. 18–21

Sunny, turning very warm. 22–25 T-storms, then sunny, cool. 26–30 Scattered showers, cool.

MAY 2014: Temp. 65° (3° above avg.); precip. 2" (1" below avg.). 1–7 T-storms, then scattered showers, cool. 8–11 Sunny, nice. 12–16 Heavy rain, then sunny, cool. 17–20 Showers, then sunny, cool. 21–25 Sunny, warm. 26–31 Showers, then sunny, warm.

JUNE 2014: Temp. 74° (3° above avg.); precip. 3.5" (avg.). 1–6 Showers, then sunny, hot. 7–11 A few t-storms, turning cool. 12–16 Rainy periods, cool north; sunny, warm south. 17–23 T-storms, then sunny, hot. 24–30 Scattered showers, cool north; t-storms, hot south.

JULY 2014: Temp. 76° (avg.); precip. 6" (2" above avg.). 1–7 Scattered t-storms, cool. 8–11 Sunny, hot. 12–15 Showers, cool north; heavy t-storms, warm south. 16–19 T-storms, then sunny, cool. 20–28 T-storms, very warm and humid. 29–31 Sunny, warm.

AUG. 2014: Temp. 76° (2° above avg.); precip. 4" (avg.). 1–6 T-storms, then sunny, pleasant. 7–12 Scattered t-storms, hot and humid. 13–16 Sunny, cool. 17–21 T-storms, then sunny, cool. 22–25 Sunny, hot. 26–31 Scattered t-storms, warm.

SEPT. 2014: Temp. 67° (avg.); precip. 3" (0.5" below avg.). 1–11 T-storms, then sunny, pleasant. 12–15 Hurricane threat. 16–17 Sunny, cool. 18–23 T-storms, then sunny, cool. 24–26 T-storms, warm. 27–30 Sunny, cool.

OCT. 2014: Temp. 57° (1° above avg.); precip. 2.5" (1" below avg.). 1–7 Showers north, sunny south; warm. 8–11 Sunny, cool. 12–18 Rain, then sunny, cool. 19–24 Showers, then sunny, cool. 25–31 Rainy, mild north; rain, then sunny, cool south.

Boston
Hartford
Providence
New York
Philadelphia
Baltimore
Atlantic City
Washington
Richmond

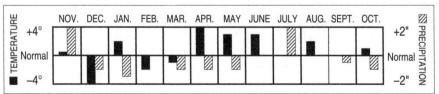

Appalachians

SUMMARY: Winter will be colder and drier than normal, with the coldest periods in early and late December, early January, and early February. Snowfall will be near normal in the north and above normal in the south, with the snowiest periods in early November and in mid- and late February.

April and May will be drier and much warmer than normal.

Summer will be hotter and rainier than normal, with the hottest periods in mid- to late June and in early to mid-July.

September and October will be a bit drier than normal, with near-normal temperatures.

NOV. 2013: Temp. 44° (avg.); precip. 3.5" (avg.). 1–5 Rain and snow, chilly. 6–8 Sunny, cool. 9–14 Rain, then snow showers, cool. 15–22 Sunny, then showers, mild. 23–27 Rainy periods, cool. 28–30 Flurries, cool.

DEC. 2013: Temp. 30° (6° below avg.); precip. 1.5" (1.5" below avg.). 1–5 Snow showers, cold. 6–11 Rain and snow, then sunny, cold. 12–19 Rain and snow, then sunny, cold. 20–21 Snow to rain. 22–31 Snow showers, very cold.

JAN. 2014: Temp. 33° (3° above avg.); precip. 2.5" (0.5" below avg.). 1–9 Flurries, cold. 10–17 Rainy periods, mild. 18–21 Snow showers, cold. 22–26 Rainy periods, mild. 27–31 Snow showers, cold north; rain showers, mild south.

FEB. 2014: Temp. 28° (2° below avg.); precip. 1.5" (1" below avg.). 1–11 Rain to snow, then flurries, cold. 12–16 Snowy periods, seasonable. 17–20 Flurries, cold. 21–26 Snowstorm, then flurries, cold. 27–28 Rain to snow.

MAR. 2014: Temp. 38° (2° below avg.); precip. 3" (avg.). 1–9 Flurries, cold. 10–15 A few showers, mild. 16–21 Rain, then sunny, cold. 22–25 Snow showers, then sunny, cold. 26–31 Rain, then sunny, mild.

APR. 2014: Temp. 53° (3° above avg.); precip. 2.5" (1" below avg.). 1–2 Sunny, warm. 3–6 Rain, then sunny, cool. 7–11 Rainy periods, warm. 12–17 Showers, cool. 18–21 Sunny, then

t-storms, warm. 22–25 Sunny, cool. 26–30 Scattered showers, warm.

MAY 2014: Temp. 62° (2° above avg.); precip. 3" (1" below avg.). 1–7 Rainy periods, cool. 8–11 Sunny, warm. 12–16 T-storms, then sunny, cool. 17–25 Sunny, turning hot. 26–31 Scattered t-storms, warm.

JUNE 2014: Temp. 70° (2° above avg.); precip. 5" (1" above avg.). 1–5 T-storms, then sunny, warm. 6–12 T-storms, then sunny, cool. 13–19 Scattered t-storms, warm. 20–23 Sunny, hot. 24–30 A couple of t-storms; cool north, hot south.

JULY 2014: Temp. 73.5° (0.5° above avg.); precip. 5" (1.5" above avg.). 1–5 Rainy periods, cool. 6–9 Sunny, nice. 10–13 T-storms; hot, then cool. 14–21 Scattered t-storms, then sunny, cool. 22–31 A few t-storms, hot, then sunny, cool.

AUG. 2014: Temp. 73° (2° above avg.); precip. 4" (0.5" above avg.). 1–6 T-storms, then sunny, nice. 7–11 Heavy t-storms, warm and humid. 12–21 T-storms, then sunny, cool. 22–25 Sunny, warm. 26–31 Scattered t-storms, warm.

SEPT. 2014: Temp. 64° (avg.); precip. 3.5" (avg.). 1–5 Rain, then sunny, cool. 6–9 Sunny, warm. 10–18 Rainy periods, then sunny, cool. 19–23 Showers, cool. 24–30 Rain, then sunny, cool.

OCT. 2014: Temp. 53° (avg.); precip. 2" (1" below avg.). 1–6 Showers, then sunny, warm. 7–12 Showers, then sunny, cool. 13–23 Showers, then sunny, cool. 24–28 Rainy periods, mild. 29–31 Showers and flurries, cool.

Elmira
Scranton
Harrisburg
Frederick
Roanoke
Asheville

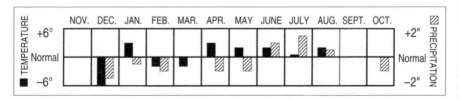

Southeast

SUMMARY: Winter will be colder and drier than normal, but with above-normal snowfall in much of the region. The coldest periods will be in early and late December, early to mid-January, and early February. The snowiest periods will be in early to mid-February and in late February.

April and May will be a bit warmer than normal, with near-normal rainfall.

Summer will be hotter than normal, with above-normal rainfall, especially near the coast. The hottest periods will occur in mid- and late June and in mid-July.

September and October will be slightly cooler than normal, with near-normal rainfall. Expect a hurricane threat in mid-September.

NOV. 2013: Temp. 53° (2° below avg.); precip. 4.5" (1.5" above avg.). 1–8 Heavy rain, then sunny, cold. 9–19 Rain, then sunny, cool. 20–22 Showers, warm. 23–30 Rain, then sunny, cool.

DEC. 2013: Temp. 43° (4° below avg.); precip. 2.5" (1" below avg.). 1–5 Sunny, cold. 6–11 Rain and snow showers, then sunny, cold. 12–16 Rainy periods, mild. 17–20 Sunny, cold. 21–25 Rainy periods; warm, then cool. 26–31 Sunny, cold.

JAN. 2014: Temp. 45° (2° above avg.); precip. 3" (1.5" below avg.). 1–9 Showers, then sunny, cold. 10–18 Rainy periods, mild. 19–22 Rain and snow showers, cold. 23–31 Rainy periods, mild.

FEB. 2014: Temp. 41° (5° below avg.); precip. 4" (avg.). 1–6 Rain, then sunny, cold. 7–14 Periods of rain and snow, then sunny, cold. 15–20 Rain, then sunny, cold. 21–26 Rain to snow, then sunny, cold. 27–28 Rainy, cool.

MAR. 2014: Temp. 52° (3° below avg.); precip. 3.5" (1" below avg.). 1–8 Showers, then sunny, cold. 9–14 Rain, then sunny, warm. 15–21 Rain, then sunny, cool. 22–27 Sunny, turning warm. 28–31 Rainy periods, turning cool.

APR. 2014: Temp. 64° (1° above avg.); precip. 3" (1" below avg. north, 1" above south). 1–2 Sunny, warm. 3–11 A few t-storms, warm. 12–21 Sunny; cool, then warm. 22–26 Showers, then sunny, cool. 27–30 Sunny, warm.

MAY 2014: Temp. 71° (avg.); precip. 3.5" (avg.). 1–12 Scattered t-storms, cool. 13–16 Sunny, nice. 17–21 T-storms, then sunny, cool. 22–26 Scattered t-storms, warm. 27–31 Sunny, warm.

JUNE 2014: Temp. 81° (3° above avg.); precip. 5" (0.5" above avg.). 1–4 Scattered t-storms, cool. 5–8 T-storms, warm. 9–13 Scattered t-storms, cool. 14–23 Isolated t-storms, hot and humid. 24–30 Scattered t-storms, hot.

JULY 2014: Temp. 82° (avg.); precip. 5.5" (3" above avg. east, 1" below west). 1–5 Scattered t-storms, cool. 6–13 Sunny, warm. 14–23 Scattered P.M. t-storms, warm. 24–31 Heavy t-storms, cool.

AUG. 2014: Temp. 79° (1° below avg.); precip. 6" (1" above avg.). 1–8 A few t-storms, cool. 9–13 Isolated t-storms, warm. 14–22 Sunny, cool. 23–31 Scattered t-storms, very warm.

SEPT. 2014: Temp. 73° (1° below avg.); precip. 4.5" (1" above avg. north, 1" below south). 1–7 T-storms, then sunny, cool. 8–10 Scattered t-storms, warm. 11–15 Hurricane threat. 16–23 Sunny, nice. 24–30 T-storms, warm.

OCT. 2014: Temp. 64° (avg.); precip. 4" (1" below avg. north, 1" above south). 1–7 T-storms, then sunny, warm. 8–12 Showers, then sunny, cool. 13–15 T-storms, warm. 16–18 Sunny, cool. 19–23 Showers, then sunny, cool. 24–31 Heavy rain, then sunny, cool.

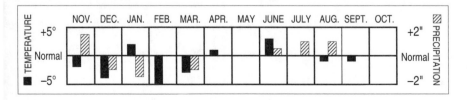

Florida

SUMMARY: Winter will be colder than normal, with rainfall below normal in northern and central counties and above normal in the south. The coldest temperatures will occur in early November, early to mid-December, and in late January.

April and May will be hotter and rainier than normal, especially in the south.

Summer will be hotter than normal, with the hottest periods in mid-June, from late June through early July, and in early August. Rainfall will be much above normal in the north but a bit below normal in the south.

September and October will be warmer and rainier than normal, with several hurricane threats in September.

NOV. 2013: Temp. 67° (2° below avg.); precip. 1.5" (1" below avg.). 1–8 T-storms, then sunny, quite cool. 9–16 Showers, then sunny, cool. 17–23 Showers, then sunny, turning warm. 24–30 A few showers; warm, then cool.

DEC. 2013: Temp. 61° (2° below avg.); precip. 1.5" (1" below avg.). 1–5 Sunny, cool. 6–11 T-storms, then sunny, cold. 12–16 Scattered t-storms, warm. 17–20 Sunny, cool. 21–24 Scattered showers, warm. 25–31 Showers, cool.

JAN. 2014: Temp. 63° (3° above avg.); precip. 2.5" (2" below avg. north, 2" above south). 1–9 T-storms, then sunny, cool. 10–20 Scattered t-storms, warm. 21–26 Sunny, warm. 27–30 T-storms, then sunny, cool. 31 Sunny, warm.

FEB. 2014: Temp. 66° (5° below avg.); precip. 3.5" (1" above avg.). 1–6 T-storms, then sunny, cool. 7–14 Heavy t-storms, then sunny, cool. 15–20 Showers, then sunny, cool. 21–28 Showers, cool.

MAR. 2014: Temp. 66° (1° below avg.); precip. 3" (avg.). 1–8 A few showers, cool. 9–15 T-storms, then sunny, seasonable. 16–18 T-storms, warm. 19–22 Sunny north, t-storms south; cool. 23–31 Sunny north, t-storms south; warm.

APR. 2014: Temp. 73° (2° above avg.); precip. 2.5" (2" below avg. north, 2" above south). 1–6 Sunny north, t-storms south; warm. 7–12 Scattered t-storms, warm. 13–21 Sunny, nice north and central; scattered t-storms south. 22–30 A couple of t-storms, warm.

MAY 2014: Temp. 79° (2° above avg.); precip. 7" (3" above avg.). 1–5 Sunny, seasonable. 6–13

A few t-storms, warm. 14–19 Sunny, warm. 20–22 T-storms, seasonable. 23–28 Sunny, hot north; a few t-storms south. 29–31 Heavy t-storms.

JUNE 2014: Temp. 84° (2° above avg.); precip. 6.5" (avg.). 1–8 Scattered t-storms; hot north, seasonable south. 9–14 A few t-storms, warm. 15–22 Sunny north, a few t-storms south; hot. 23–30 Occasional t-storms; hot north, seasonable south.

JULY 2014: Temp. 85° (2° above avg.); precip. 8.5" (2" above avg.). 1–10 Isolated t-storms, hot. 11–17 Daily t-storms, seasonable. 18–23 A few t-storms, warm. 24–31 Several t-storms, seasonable.

AUG. 2014: Temp. 83° (1° above avg.); precip. 7.5" (4" above avg. north, 4" below south). 1–11 Daily t-storms, hot and humid. 12–21 Scattered t-storms; turning cooler north, very warm and humid south. 22–27 Daily t-storms, seasonable north; isolated t-storms, hot south. 28–31 A couple of t-storms, seasonable.

SEPT. 2014: Temp. 82° (2° above avg.); precip. 7.5" (2" above avg.). 1–2 Hurricane threat. 3–12 A few t-storms; cool, then warm. 13–16 Hurricane threat. 17–21 Sunny north, scattered t-storms south; warm. 22–27 Hurricane threat. 28–30 T-storms, warm.

OCT. 2014: Temp. 77° (2° above avg.); precip. 8" (4" above avg.). 1–4 Showers, warm. 5–9 Sunny, warm. 10–15 Scattered t-storms, warm. 16–25 Heavy t-storms, warm. 26–31 T-storms, then sunny, cool.

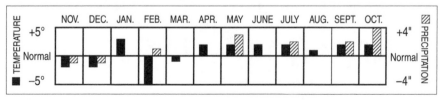

Lower Lakes

SUMMARY: Winter will be slightly milder than normal, with near-normal precipitation and below-normal snowfall in most of the region. The coldest periods will be in mid- to late December, early and mid-January, and in early to mid-February. The snowiest periods will be in mid- and late December and in late January.

April and May will be warmer and a bit rainier than normal.

Summer will be hotter than normal, with rainfall slightly below normal despite a tropical rainstorm threat in mid-July. The hottest periods will be in mid-June, early to mid-July, and late August.

September and October will be warmer and drier than normal in the east but slightly cooler and rainier than normal in the west.

NOV. 2013: Temp. 42° (1° above avg.); precip. 3" (0.5" above avg.). 1–6 Rain, then snow showers, cold. 7–11 Rainy periods, mild. 12–14 Snow showers, cold. 15–20 A few showers, mild. 21–24 Rain, then snow showers, cold. 25–27 Rainy, mild. 28–30 Snow showers, cold.

DEC. 2013: Temp. 29° (3° below avg.); precip. 3.5" (0.5" above avg.). 1–4 Lake snows, cold. 5–6 Rainy, mild. 7–10 Lake snows, cold. 11–15 Rain and wet snow, mild. 16–19 Lake snows, cold. 20–28 Rain to snow, then lake snows, very cold. 29–31 Snowy, not as cold.

JAN. 2014: Temp. 30.5° (3.5° above avg.); precip. 3" (0.5" above avg.). 1–5 Snow showers, cold. 6–11 Flurries, then rain and wet snow, mild. 12–16 Showers, mild. 17–20 Snow showers, cold. 21–24 Rainy, mild. 25–31 Snowy periods, cold.

FEB. 2014: Temp. 29° (2° above avg.); precip. 0.5" (1.5" below avg.). 1–4 Snow showers, mild. 5–8 Lake snows, cold. 9–18 Sunny, then sprinkles and flurries, turning mild. 19–25 Snow, then sunny, seasonable. 26–28 Snow showers, cold.

MAR. 2014: Temp. 37° (1° below avg.); precip. 3" (avg.). 1–7 Snow showers, cold. 8–11 Sunny, turning warm. 12–15 Rainy periods, cooler. 16–19 Rain, then wet snow, colder. 20–24 Snow showers, cold. 25–31 Rainy periods, mild.

APR. 2014: Temp. 52.5° (4.5° above avg.); precip. 3" (0.5" below avg.). 1–6 T-storms, then sunny, mild. 7–10 Scattered t-storms, warm. 11–17 Rain, then showers, cool. 18–20 Sunny, turning

warm. 21–24 T-storms, then sunny, cool. 25–30 Sunny, then t-storms, warm.

MAY 2014: Temp. 57° (1° below avg.); precip. 4.5" (1" above avg.). 1–7 A few showers and t-storms, cool. 8–10 Sunny, then t-storms, warm. 11–18 T-storms, then showers, cool. 19–23 Sunny, very warm. 24–31 A few t-storms, cool.

JUNE 2014: Temp. 66° (avg.); precip. 4.5" (1" above avg.). 1–5 Sunny, turning hot. 6–10 T-storms, then sunny, cool. 11–17 A few t-storms, cool. 18–20 Sunny, hot. 21–26 T-storms, then sunny, cool. 27–30 Heavy t-storms, then sunny, cool.

JULY 2014: Temp. 73° (2° above avg.); precip. 3.5" (avg.). 1–5 Scattered t-storms, warm. 6–10 Sunny, hot. 11–16 Tropical rains, then sunny, warm. 17–22 Scattered t-storms, warm. 23–31 Sunny, nice.

AUG. 2014: Temp. 73° (4° above avg.); precip. 2" (2" below avg.). 1–7 T-storms, then sunny, nice. 8–12 Scattered t-storms, warm. 13–24 Sunny; cool, then hot. 25–31 A few t-storms, warm.

SEPT. 2014: Temp. 63.5° (1.5° above avg.); precip. 3" (0.5" below avg.). 1–7 T-storms, then sunny; cool, then warm. 8–15 T-storms, then sunny, cool. 16–22 Scattered t-storms, then sunny, cool. 23–30 A couple of t-storms, warm.

OCT. 2014: Temp. 51.5° (1° above avg. east, 2° below west); precip. 2" (0.5" below avg. east, 1" above west). 1–2 Sunny, warm. 3–8 T-storms, then sunny, cool. 9–17 Scattered showers, chilly. 18–23 Rain and snow showers, then sunny, cool. 24–27 Rainy, mild. 28–31 Showers, mild.

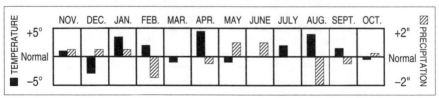

Ohio Valley

SUMMARY: Winter will be colder and drier than normal, with below-normal snowfall. The coldest periods will be in December, early January, and early February, with the snowiest periods in early December and early March.

April and May will be warmer and drier than normal.

Summer will be hotter and rainier than normal, with the hottest periods in mid- to late June and early to mid-July. Watch for a tropical rain threat in mid-July.

September and October will be slightly cooler and drier than normal.

NOV. 2013: Temp. 45° (1° below avg.); precip. 3" (0.5" below avg.). 1–4 Showers, then flurries, chilly. 5–7 Snow, then sunny, cool. 8–11 Rainy, mild. 12–14 Snow showers, cold. 15–20 A few showers, mild. 21–23 T-storms, then sunny, cool. 24–27 Rainy periods, mild. 28–30 Snow showers, cold.

DEC. 2013: Temp. 33° (4° below avg.); precip. 2.5" (0.5" below avg.). 1–4 Snow, then sunny, cold. 5–10 Rain to snow, then flurries, cold. 11–14 Snow to rain, then sunny, cold. 15–16 Rainy, mild. 17–19 Snow showers, cold. 20–31 Rain, then snow showers, cold.

JAN. 2014: Temp. 38° (5° above avg.); precip. 3" (avg.). 1–8 Snow showers, cold. 9–11 Rainy, mild. 12–17 Showers, quite cold. 18–20 Flurries, cold. 21–26 Rainy periods, mild. 27–31 Rain and snow showers; cold, then mild.

FEB. 2014: Temp. 32° (2° below avg.); precip. 1" (2" below avg.). 1–9 Rain, then snow showers, cold. 10–15 Sunny, mild. 16–23 Snow showers, cold. 24–28 Sunny, cold.

MAR. 2014: Temp. 42° (3° below avg.); precip. 2.5" (1.5" below avg.). 1–9 Rain to snow, then sunny, cold. 10–12 Sunny, warm. 13–15 Showers, then sunny, cool. 16–21 T-storms, then sunny, cool. 22–24 Showers, then flurries, cold. 25–31 A couple of showers, mild.

APR. 2014: Temp. 59° (4° above avg.); precip. 2.5" (1" below avg.). 1–2 Sunny, warm. 3–5 T-storms, then sunny, cool. 6–11 Scattered t-storms, warm. 12–18 Showers, then sunny, cool. 19–20

Sunny, warm. 21–24 T-storms, then sunny, cool. 25–30 Sunny, turning very warm.

MAY 2014: Temp. 64° (1° above avg.); precip. 3.5" (1" below avg.). 1–8 Rain, then showers, cool. 9–13 Scattered t-storms, warm. 14–20 Sunny, cool. 21–25 Sunny, very warm. 26–31 A couple of t-storms; cool, then warm.

JUNE 2014: Temp. 74° (3° above avg.); precip. 5" (1" above avg.). 1–4 T-storms, then sunny, nice. 5–8 Scattered t-storms, warm. 9–14 Sunny, cool. 15–23 Scattered t-storms, turning hot and humid. 24–26 Sunny, cool. 27–30 T-storms, warm.

JULY 2014: Temp. 77° (2° above avg.); precip. 3.5" (0.5" below avg.). 1–5 Scattered t-storms, warm. 6–10 Sunny, turning hot. 11–14 Tropical rains. 15–19 Sunny, warm. 20–26 A few showers, warm. 27–31 Sunny, cool.

AUG. 2014: Temp. 75° (2° above avg.); precip. 6" (2" above avg.). 1–7 Heavy t-storms, then sunny, nice. 8–12 A few t-storms, warm. 13–24 Sunny; cool, then warm. 25–31 Scattered t-storms, warm.

SEPT. 2014: Temp. 66° (1° below avg.); precip. 2" (1" below avg.). 1–6 Showers, then sunny, cool. 7–9 Sunny, warm. 10–14 T-storms, then sunny, cool. 15–23 Scattered showers, cool. 24–28 Showers, then sunny, warm. 29–30 Rainy, cool.

OCT. 2014: Temp. 57° (avg.); precip. 2" (0.5" below avg.). 1–6 Sunny, then scattered t-storms, warm. 7–11 Sunny, chilly. 12–14 Showers, warm. 15–23 Showers, then sunny, cool. 24–31 Showers, then sunny, cool.

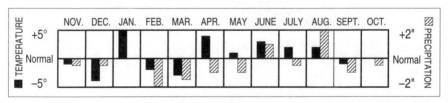

Deep South

SUMMARY: Winter will be colder than normal, with below-normal precipitation and snowfall in all but the northernmost part of the region. The coldest periods will occur in early to mid- and late December and in early to mid- and late February. The snowiest periods across the north will be in late December, mid- to late January, and in early to mid- and late February.

April and May will be slightly rainier than normal, with above-normal temperatures, especially in the north.

Summer will be much hotter than normal, with near-normal rainfall despite a hurricane threat in early to mid-July. The hottest periods will occur from mid-June through early July and in early August.

September and October will be drier than normal, with near-normal temperatures.

NOV. 2013: Temp. 53° (2° below avg.); precip. 6" (1" above avg.). 1–7 Rainy, then sunny, cold. 8–14 Rain, then sunny, cold. 15–19 Sunny, then showers, mild. 20–27 Rainy periods, cool. 28–30 Sunny, cool.

DEC. 2013: Temp. 46° (2° below avg.); precip. 4" (1" below avg.). 1–4 Sunny, cool. 5–10 T-storms, then sunny, cold. 11–15 Rainy periods, mild. 16–18 Sunny, cold. 19–24 Rainy periods, mild. 25–31 Rain and snow showers north, showers south; cold.

JAN. 2014: Temp. 51° (6° above avg.); precip. 5.5" (3" above avg. north, 2" below south). 1–7 Showers, then sunny, cool. 8–12 Rainy, mild. 13–16 Showers, mild. 17–19 Sunny, cool. 20–26 Snow to rain north, rainy periods elsewhere; turning warm. 27–31 T-storms, mild.

FEB. 2014: Temp. 43° (4° below avg.); precip. 4" (1" below avg.). 1–6 Rain, then sunny, cold. 7–11 Snow north, rain south, then sunny, cold. 12–19 Rain, then sunny, cool. 20–25 Rain, then sunny north; rainy periods south; cool. 26–28 Snow north, rain south; cold.

MAR. 2014: Temp. 53° (3° below avg.); precip. 5" (1" below avg.). 1–7 Showers, cold. 8–11 Rainy, cool. 12–15 Sunny, nice. 16–21 Rain, then sunny, cool. 22–25 Showers, then sunny, cool. 26–31 Scattered t-storms, warm.

APR. 2014: Temp. 65° (2° above avg.); precip. 5.5" (1" above avg.). 1–3 T-storms, warm. 4–6 Sunny, nice. 7–11 A few t-storms, warm. 12–15 Sunny, cool. 16–20 Sunny north, t-storms south;

turning warm. 21–26 Showers, then sunny, nice. 27–30 T-storms, warm.

MAY 2014: Temp. 71.5° (2° above avg. north, 1° below south); precip. 4.5" (0.5" below avg.). 1–6 Scattered t-storms, cool. 7–9 Sunny, warm north; t-storms, cool south. 10–18 A few t-storms, warm. 19–24 Sunny, warm. 25–31 T-storms, then sunny, hot north; t-storms, cool south.

JUNE 2014: Temp. 82° (4° above avg.); precip. 3" (2" below avg.). 1–7 Scattered t-storms, warm. 8–10 Sunny, cool. 11–17 Scattered t-storms north, sunny south; hot. 18–21 Sunny, hot. 22–30 Scattered t-storms, hot.

JULY 2014: Temp. 82.5° (3° above avg. north, avg. south); precip. 5.5" (1" above avg.). 1–10 Isolated t-storms, hot north; daily t-storms, seasonable south. 11–14 Hurricane threat. 15–20 A few t-storms, warm and humid. 21–31 Sunny, cool north; a few t-storms south.

AUG. 2014: Temp. 80.5° (0.5° above avg.); precip. 5.5" (1" above avg.). 1–6 Scattered t-storms; hot, then cool. 7–15 Daily t-storms, very warm and humid. 16–22 Sunny, nice. 23–31 Daily t-storms north, isolated t-storms south; warm and humid.

SEPT. 2014: Temp. 76° (avg.); precip. 3.5" (1" below avg.). 1–8 Sunny, cool. 9–17 Scattered t-storms, warm. 18–22 Sunny, cool. 23–30 Scattered t-storms, warm.

OCT. 2014: Temp. 65° (avg.); precip. 1" (2" below avg.). 1–5 Sunny, warm. 6–12 T-storms, then sunny, cool. 13–18 Scattered t-storms, cool. 19–22 Sunny, cool. 23–25 T-storms, warm. 26–31 Sunny, cool.

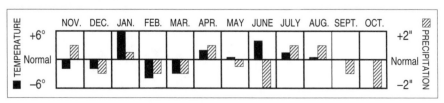

Upper Midwest

SUMMARY: Winter temperatures will be above normal in the east and below normal in the western parts of the region, with above-normal precipitation and snowfall. The coldest periods will be in mid- and late December, in early January, and from late February into early March. The snowiest periods will occur in mid- and late December, early January, and early February.

April and May will be warmer than normal, with near-normal precipitation.

Summer will be hotter and drier than normal, with drought a possibility. The hottest periods will occur in early July and early and mid-August.

September and October will be slightly warmer and drier than normal, on average, despite snow in mid- to late October.

NOV. 2013: Temp. 32° (3° above avg.); precip. 2" (avg.). 1–5 Snow showers, then sunny, cold. 6–8 Sunny, mild. 9–13 Snow, then flurries, cold. 14–19 Rain and snow showers, mild. 20–24 Sunny, mild. 25–30 Snow, then flurries, cold.

DEC. 2013: Temp. 14.5° (1° above avg. east, 4° below west); precip. 2" (1" above avg.). 1–4 Sunny, turning mild. 5–9 Snow, then sunny, cold. 10–15 Snowstorms, mild. 16–19 Snow showers, very cold. 20–28 Snow showers; mild, then very cold. 29–31 Snowy, cold.

JAN. 2014: Temp. 14.5° (7° above avg. east, 4° below west); precip. 1.5" (0.5" above avg.). 1–5 Snowstorm, then flurries east; snow showers, then sunny, frigid west. 6–9 Rain and snow east, snow west; quite mild. 10–17 Periods of rain and snow, quite mild east; snow showers, very cold west. 18–23 Snow showers; cold, then mild east; cold west. 24–26 Flurries, mild east; sunny, frigid west. 27–31 Snow showers, cold.

FEB. 2014: Temp. 16° (3° above avg.); precip. 0.7" (0.3" below avg.). 1–3 Flurries, turning mild. 4–7 Heavy snow east; flurries, cold west. 8–19 Flurries, mild. 20–25 Snow, then sunny, cold. 26–28 Snowy periods, cold.

MAR. 2014: Temp. 23° (5° below avg.); precip. 1" (0.5" below avg.). 1–9 Snow showers, then sunny, cold. 10–11 Sunny, mild. 12–15 Snow, then sunny, cold. 16–24 Rain to snow, then sunny, cold. 25–31 Flurries, then sunny, turning warm.

APR. 2014: Temp. 48° (6° above avg.); precip. 2.5" (0.5" above avg.). 1–7 Rain, then sunny, warm. 8–12 Showers, then sunny, seasonable.

13–18 Rain to snow, then sunny, warm. 19–22 Rain, then sunny, cool. 23–30 Showers, warm.

MAY 2014: Temp. 54° (1° below avg.); precip. 2.5" (0.5" below avg.). 1–5 Rain to wet snow, then sunny, cool. 6–8 Sunny, warm. 9–18 T-storms, then a few showers, cool. 19–21 Sunny, hot. 22–31 T-storms, then a few showers, turning cool.

JUNE 2014: Temp. 59° (4° below avg.); precip. 3" (1" below avg.). 1–3 Sunny, cool. 4–9 Showers east, sunny west; cool. 10–17 A few showers, cool. 18–26 Rain, then a couple of showers, cool. 27–30 Sunny, cool.

JULY 2014: Temp. 70° (2° above avg.); precip. 3.5" (avg.). 1–6 T-storms, then sunny, hot. 7–11 Heavy t-storms, then sunny, cooler. 12–20 Scattered t-storms, cool. 21–26 Sunny; cool east, warm west. 27–31 A couple of t-storms, warm.

AUG. 2014: Temp. 71° (5° above avg.); precip. 2.5" (1" below avg.). 1–9 Sunny, turning hot. 10–12 T-storms. 13–20 Sunny, turning hot. 21–28 T-storms, then sunny, warm. 29–31 T-storms, turning cool.

SEPT. 2014: Temp. 60° (2° above avg.); precip. 2.5" (0.5" below avg.). 1–3 Scattered t-storms, cool. 4–7 Sunny, warm. 8–11 Showers, cool. 12–14 Sunny, warm. 15–22 Showers, then sunny, cool. 23–30 A few t-storms, turning warm.

OCT. 2014: Temp. 46° (1° below avg.); precip. 2.5" (avg.). 1–4 Showers, turning cool. 5–10 Rain to snow, then sunny, cool. 11–17 Rain and snow showers, cool. 18–21 Snow, then sunny, cold. 22–31 Rainy periods, then sunny, mild.

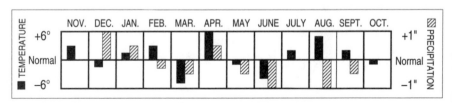

Heartland

SUMMARY: Winter temperatures will be colder than normal, especially in the north, with the coldest periods in mid- and late December, early January, mid-January, and early March. Precipitation will be slightly below normal in the north and above in the south, while snowfall will be below normal in the central portion of the region, but above normal in the north and south. The snowiest periods will be in early November, late December, mid-January, early to mid-February, and late February.

April and May will be warmer and drier than normal.

Summer will be hotter and rainier than normal, with the hottest periods in early and late July and in mid- to late August.

September and October will be slightly rainier than normal, with near-normal temperatures.

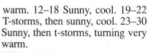

NOV. 2013: Temp. 42° (1° below avg.); precip. 2.5" (avg.). 1–6 Rain and wet snow, then sunny, cold. 7–13 Rain, then flurries, cold. 14–19 Sunny north, showers south; mild. 20–23 Sunny north; rain, then sunny south. 24–30 Rain, then sunny, turning cold.

DEC. 2013: Temp. 30° (2° below avg.); precip. 1.5" (avg.). 1–4 Sunny, turning mild. 5–9 Rain to snow, then sunny, cold. 10–18 Rain, then snow showers, cold. 19–28 Rain to snow, then sunny, very cold. 29–31 Snow, then sunny, cold.

JAN. 2014: Temp. 31.5° (avg. north, 5° above south); precip. 2" (avg. north, 1.5" above south). 1–5 Sunny, cold. 6–9 Rainy periods, mild. 10–15 Rain and snow showers, mild. 16–19 Rain to snow, cold. 20–24 Snow showers north; rainy, mild south. 25–29 Sunny, turning mild. 30–31 Rain and snow showers, mild.

FEB. 2014: Temp. 31° (avg.); precip. 1" (0.5" below avg.). 1–6 Snow north, rain south, then sunny, cold. 7–13 Snow, then sunny, cold. 14–19 Snow north, rain south, then sunny, mild. 20–26 Rain to snow, then sunny, cold. 27–28 Rain and snow, cold.

MAR. 2014: Temp. 40° (4° below avg.); precip. 2" (0.5" below avg.). 1–11 Flurries, then sunny; cold, then warm. 12–21 Rain and wet snow north, rainy periods south; cool. 22–24 Sunny, cold. 25–31 Showers, warm.

APR. 2014: Temp. 58° (4° above avg.); precip. 3.5" (1" above avg. north, 1" below south). 1–5 Rain, then sunny, warm. 6–11 A few t-storms,

warm. 12–18 Sunny, cool. 19–22 T-storms, then sunny, cool. 23–30 Sunny, then t-storms, turning very warm.

MAY 2014: Temp. 64° (avg.); precip. 3" (1.5" below avg.). 1–5 Showers, cool. 6–9 Sunny, warm. 10–16 A few t-storms, cool. 17–22 Sunny, turning warm. 23–27 T-storms, then sunny, cool. 28–31 Sunny, warm.

JUNE 2014: Temp. 72° (avg.); precip. 7.5" (3" above avg.). 1–3 Showers, cool. 4–13 T-storms, then sunny, cool. 14–19 A couple of t-storms, turning warm. 20–30 Several t-storms; turning cool north, hot south.

JULY 2014: Temp. 78° (1° above avg.); precip. 3.5" (0.5" below avg.). 1–8 T-storms, then sunny, hot. 9–15 Scattered t-storms, then sunny, cool. 16–28 T-storms, then sunny, cool. 29–31 T-storms, hot.

AUG. 2014: Temp. 78° (3° above avg.); precip. 3" (0.5" below avg.). 1–5 T-storms, then sunny, cool. 6–14 Scattered t-storms, warm. 15–23 Sunny; cool, then hot. 24–31 A few t-storms, warm.

SEPT. 2014: Temp. 69° (2° above avg.); precip. 3" (0.5" below avg.). 1–4 Showers, cool. 5–7 Sunny, warm. 8–13 T-storms, then sunny, cool. 14–18 A couple of t-storms, cool. 19–27 T-storms, then sunny, warm. 28–30 T-storms, turning cool.

OCT. 2014: Temp. 54° (2° below avg.); precip. 4" (1" above avg.). 1–3 Rainy periods, warm. 4–10 Heavy t-storms, then sunny, chilly. 11–21 Showers, then sunny, cool. 22–28 Rain, then sunny, cool. 29–31 Sunny, warm.

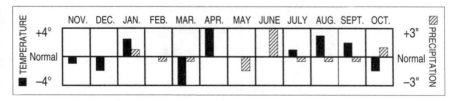

Texas–Oklahoma

SUMMARY: Winter temperatures will be slightly colder than normal, on average, with precipitation and snowfall a bit above normal in Oklahoma and north of The Metroplex. Elsewhere across Texas, temperatures will be above normal, with below-normal rainfall and snowfall. The coldest periods will be in mid- to late December, early January, and early to mid-February, while the snowiest periods across the north will occur in mid- to late December and mid-February.

April and May will be slightly warmer and rainier than normal, on average.

Summer will be hotter and slightly drier than normal, with pockets of major drought likely. The hottest periods will be in early July, mid- to late July, and early to mid-August. Hurricanes should stay east and south of Texas.

September and October will be drier than normal, with temperatures above normal in Texas and below normal in Oklahoma.

NOV. 2013: Temp. 55° (2° below avg.); precip. 3.5" (2" above avg. north, 1" below south). 1–5 Rain, then sunny, cool. 6–13 Rain, then sunny, cool. 14–18 Sunny, warm. 19–24 Rainy periods, cool. 25–30 Sunny, cool.

DEC. 2013: Temp. 51.5° (1° below avg. north, 4° above south); precip. 1.5" (1" below avg.). 1–4 Sunny, turning warm. 5–8 Showers, then sunny, cool. 9–14 Rainy periods, warm. 15–19 Sunny; cool, then warm. 20–25 Snow north, rain south, then sunny, cold. 26–31 Sunny north, showers south; turning bright.

JAN. 2014: Temp. 56° (7° above avg.); precip. 1" (1" below avg.). 1–7 Sunny; cold, then mild. 8–15 Rain, then sunny, warm. 16–18 Showers, then sunny, cool. 19–26 Occasional rain; warm, then cool. 27–31 Sunny, turning warm.

FEB. 2014: Temp. 48° (2° below avg.); precip. 3.5" (1.5" above avg.). 1–5 Sunny, mild. 6–10 Rain and wet snow north, heavy rain south, then sunny, cold. 11–18 Rain, then sunny, turning mild. 19–22 Sunny, cold north; drizzle south. 23–28 Snow, then showers north, rainy periods south; cool.

MAR. 2014: Temp. 56° (3° below avg.); precip. 2" (0.5" below avg.). 1–9 Periods of rain and snow north, rain south; chilly. 10–14 Sunny, cool. 15–20 Rain, then sunny, cool. 21–24 Showers, cool. 25–31 Sunny, then showers, warm.

APR. 2014: Temp. 67.5° (1.5° above avg.); precip. 4" (2" above avg. north, avg. south). 1–3 Sunny, warm. 4–10 Rainy periods, seasonable.

Oklahoma City ⊙
Dallas ⊙
Houston ⊙
San Antonio ⊙

11–15 Sunny, warm. 16–18 Showers, cool. 19–25 T-storms, then sunny, cool. 26–30 Rain and heavy t-storms north and central; sunny, hot south.

MAY 2014: Temp. 72° (1° below avg.); precip. 4.5" (2" below avg. north, 1" above south). 1–11 A few t-storms, cool. 12–17 Sunny, nice. 18–25 Scattered t-storms, warm. 26–31 T-storms, then sunny, cool.

JUNE 2014: Temp. 82° (3° above avg.); precip. 2" (2" below avg.). 1–3 Sunny, nice. 4–11 A few t-storms, cool north; sunny, warm south. 12–30 Sunny, hot, isolated t-storms.

JULY 2014: Temp. 84° (3° above avg.); precip. 3" (avg.). 1–12 Sunny, hot, Gulf t-storms. 13–19 Scattered t-storms; cooler north, hot south. 20–23 Sunny; cool north, hot south. 24–31 Scattered t-storms; hot south, warm north.

AUG. 2014: Temp. 83° (2° above avg.); precip. 3.5" (1" above avg.). 1–6 Sunny, hot. 7–15 Scattered t-storms, hot. 16–27 A few t-storms, turning cooler. 28–31 Sunny, warm.

SEPT. 2014: Temp. 77.5° (1.5° above avg.); precip. 3" (0.5" below avg.). 1–6 Scattered t-storms; cool north, hot south. 7–13 T-storms; cool north, warm south. 14–26 T-storms, then sunny, warm. 27–30 T-storms, then sunny, cool north; a few t-storms, warm south.

OCT. 2014: Temp. 66° (4° below avg. north, 2° above south); precip. 3.5" (0.5" below avg.). 1–3 Sunny north, t-storms south; warm. 4–9 T-storms, then sunny, cool. 10–19 Scattered t-storms, cool north; sunny, warm south. 20–31 T-storms, then sunny, cool.

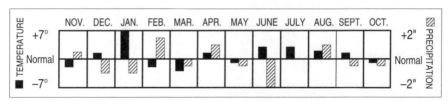

High Plains

SUMMARY: Winter temperatures will be much colder than normal across the north, but milder than normal in the south, with the coldest periods in mid- and late December, early to mid-January, late February, and early March. Precipitation and snowfall will be below normal, with the snowiest periods in mid-December and mid- to late February.

April and May will be much warmer and slightly drier than normal.

Summer temperatures will be about one degree hotter than normal, on average, with rainfall slightly above normal in the north and slightly below in the south. The hottest periods will be in early July, mid- to late July, and early and mid-August.

September will be warmer than normal, followed by a cooler-than-normal October. Precipitation will be above normal in the south, below in the north.

NOV. 2013: Temp. 40.5° (6° above avg. north, 1° above south); precip. 1" (avg.). 1–3 Rain to snow. 4–5 Sunny, mild. 6–12 Rain and snow, then sunny, cold. 13–17 Sunny, mild. 18–27 Rain and snow showers; mild north, cold south. 28–30 Sunny, cold.

DEC. 2013: Temp. 27.5° (4° below avg. north, 3° above south); precip. 0.5" (avg.). 1–3 Sunny, mild. 4–7 Rain to snow, then sunny, cold. 8–11 Snow showers, mild. 12–16 Snowy periods, cold. 17–20 Snow showers, cold north; showers, mild south. 21–24 Snow showers, very cold. 25–31 Snowy periods, turning mild.

JAN. 2014: Temp. 28° (7° below avg. north, 7° above south); precip. 0.2" (0.3" below avg.). 1–4 Snow showers, very cold. 5–15 Snow showers, very cold north; sunny, warm south. 16–22 Snow showers, very cold north; sunny, cold, then warm south. 23–28 Sunny; cold, then mild. 29–31 Snow showers, cold north; sunny, warm south.

FEB. 2014: Temp. 26° (2° below avg.); precip. 1" (0.5" above avg.). 1–5 Sunny; cold north, seasonable south. 6–14 Snow showers, cold. 15–21 Sunny, cold north; snowy periods central; showers, warm south. 22–28 Snowy periods, cold.

MAR. 2014: Temp. 37° (2° below avg.); precip. 0.5" (0.5" below avg.). 1–6 Snow showers, cold. 7–10 Sunny, mild north; snowy periods south. 11–14 Sunny, warm. 15–22 Snow showers, cold. 23–31 Sunny, turning warm.

APR. 2014: Temp. 53° (5° above avg.); precip. 2" (avg.). 1–3 Showers, then sunny, warm. 4–9 Showers, mild. 10–17 Sunny, turning warm. 18–21 Rain and snow, then sunny, cool. 22–25 Showers, mild.

26–30 Sunny, nice north; t-storms south.

MAY 2014: Temp. 61° (3° above avg.); precip. 2" (0.5" below avg.). 1–7 Showers, then sunny, warm. 8–14 Rainy periods, cool north; sunny, turning hot south. 15–22 Showers, then sunny, warm. 23–31 Scattered t-storms; cool, then hot.

JUNE 2014: Temp. 64° (3° below avg.); precip. 4" (1" above avg.). 1–5 Rainy, chilly north; sunny, warm south. 6–12 Sunny north, t-storms south; cool. 13–22 Rainy periods, cool north; sunny, hot south. 23–26 Sunny; cool north, hot south. 27–30 T-storms, cool.

JULY 2014: Temp. 74° (2° above avg.); precip. 2" (1" above avg. north, 1" below south) 1–6 Sunny, turning hot. 7–13 T-storms, then sunny, cooler. 14–23 Scattered t-storms; cool north, hot south. 24–28 A couple of t-storms, hot. 29–31 Sunny, cool north; t-storms south.

AUG. 2014: Temp. 75° (4° above avg.); precip. 1.5" (0.5" below avg.). 1–3 Sunny, hot. 4–11 T-storms, then sunny, warm. 12–14 Sunny, hot. 15–20 Sunny, hot north; t-storms, cool south. 21–31 Isolated t-storms; cool, then warm.

SEPT. 2014: Temp. 64° (3° above avg.); precip. 1.7" (0.5" below avg. north, 1" above south). 1–5 Sunny, warm north; rainy periods, cool south. 6–9 T-storms, then sunny, cool. 10–15 Scattered t-storms; warm, then cool. 16–24 Sunny, warm. 25–30 Rain to wet snow, then sunny, cool.

OCT. 2014: Temp. 46° (3° below avg.); precip. 1.5" (avg. north, 1" above south). 1–10 Rain to snow, then sunny, cold. 11–16 Showers, mild. 17–22 Snow showers north, rainy periods south; chilly. 23–31 Rain and snow, then sunny, mild.

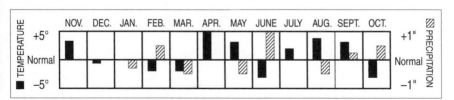

Intermountain

SUMMARY: Winter will be much snowier than normal, with near-normal rainfall. The snowiest periods will be in late November, early and mid-December, mid- and late January, mid-February, and early March. Temperatures will be below normal in the north and near normal in the south, with the coldest periods in mid-December, mid- and late January, and in early to mid-February.

April and May will be drier and much warmer than normal.

Summer will be cooler than normal in the north and warmer in the south, with the hottest periods in mid-July and early to mid-August. Rainfall will be close to normal.

September and October will be slightly cooler than normal, on average, with near-normal rainfall.

NOV. 2013: Temp. 41° (3° above avg. north, 1° below south); precip. 1.5" (avg.). 1–4 Showers north, sunny south; cool. 5–10 Rain and snow showers, chilly. 11–16 Showers north, sunny south; mild. 17–23 Showers, mild north; sunny, turning cold south. 24–30 Snow, then sunny, cool.

DEC. 2013: Temp. 31° (2° below avg.); precip. 2" (0.5" above avg.). 1–6 Snow, then sunny, cool. 7–9 Showers north, mild. 10–15 Snow, then sunny, cold. 16–22 Rain and snow showers, then sunny, cold. 23–31 Periods of snow, then rain north; sunny south; turning mild.

JAN. 2014: Temp. 33.5° (2° below avg. north, 5° above south); precip. 3" (1.5" above avg.). 1–6 Rain and snow showers north, sunny south; mild. 7–11 Rain, then snow showers north; rain, then sunny south; turning cold. 12–17 Flurries, very cold north; rain, then snowy periods south. 18–28 Snow, then sunny, cold. 29–31 Snow showers north, snowstorm south.

FEB. 2014: Temp. 33° (1° below avg.); precip. 2" (avg. north, 1" above south). 1–5 Rain and wet snow, mild north; sunny, cool south. 6–16 Snow showers, cold. 17–28 Snow showers north; periods of rain and snow south; chilly.

MAR. 2014: Temp. 42° (1° below avg.); precip. 1" (0.5" below avg.). 1–7 Sunny north, snowstorms south; cold. 8–14 Sunny, cool. 15–23 Snow showers, then sunny, mild. 24–31 A few showers; mild, then cool.

APR. 2014: Temp. 51° (2° above avg.); precip. 0.5" (0.5" below avg.). 1–9 A couple of showers, seasonable. 10–16 Showers north, sunny south; turning warm. 17–20 Sunny, cool. 21–25

Showers north, sunny south; cool. 26–30 Sunny, warm north; periods of rain and snow south.

MAY 2014: Temp. 63° (6° above avg.); precip. 0.5" (0.5" below avg.). 1–8 Isolated showers; warm, then cooler. 9–16 Sunny, warm. 17–23 Showers north; sunny, warm south. 24–31 Sunny, warm.

JUNE 2014: Temp. 64° (2° below avg.); precip. 1" (0.5" above avg.). 1–7 Scattered showers, turning cooler. 8–13 Sunny, hot north; scattered showers south. 14–22 A couple of t-storms, cool. 23–30 Sunny, cool.

JULY 2014: Temp. 74.5° (avg. north, 3° above south); precip. 0.5" (avg.). 1–10 Sunny north, a few t-storms south; cool. 11–21 Isolated t-storms, hot. 22–31 Sunny, turning cool north; scattered t-storms, warm south.

AUG. 2014: Temp. 73.5° (avg. north, 3° above south); precip. 0.5" (0.5" below avg.). 1–13 Sunny north, scattered t-storms south; warm. 14–18 Sunny, hot north; t-storms south. 19–24 Sunny, cool. 25–31 Isolated t-storms; cool, then warm.

SEPT. 2014: Temp. 62° (avg.); precip. 0.5" (0.5" below avg.). 1–5 Sunny north, a few t-storms south; warm. 6–19 Scattered showers, cool north; sunny, warm, then cool south. 20–30 Scattered t-storms, cool.

OCT. 2014: Temp. 50° (1° below avg.); precip. 1.5" (0.5" above avg.). 1–6 Rain to wet snow, then sunny, cool. 7–13 Sunny north, rainy periods south; cool. 14–19 Sunny; warm, then cool. 20–27 Showers, then sunny, mild. 28–31 Rain to snow.

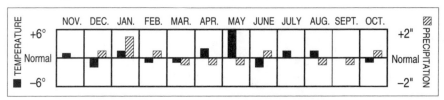

Get your local forecast at Almanac.com/Weather. **2014**

Desert Southwest

SUMMARY: Winter will be colder than normal, with the coldest periods in early and mid-December and in late January. Precipitation will be below normal in the east and above normal in the west, with snowfall below normal in most places that normally receive snow.

April and May will be warmer and rainier than normal.

Summer will be hotter than normal, with below-normal rainfall. The hottest periods will be in late June, late July, and early to mid-August.

September and October will be slightly drier than normal, with temperatures above normal in the east and below in the west.

NOV. 2013: Temp. 54° (2° below avg.); precip. 1.3" (0.3" above avg.). 1–5 Showers, then sunny, cool. 6–11 T-storms, then sunny, cool. 12–17 Sunny, mild. 18–23 Periods of rain and snow east, sunny west; cool. 24–30 Showers, then sunny, cool.

DEC. 2013: Temp. 45° (3° below avg.); precip. 0.3" (0.2" below avg.). 1–9 Sunny; cold, then mild. 10–17 Rain and snow showers, cold. 18–24 Rain and snow, then sunny, cold. 25–31 Sunny, turning mild.

JAN. 2014: Temp. 50° (5° above avg. east, 1° below west); precip. 0.8" (0.3" below avg. east, 1" above west). 1–5 Sunny, cool. 6–10 Showers, then sunny, mild. 11–21 Sunny east, showers west; mild. 22–28 Sunny, cool. 29–31 Showers, chilly.

FEB. 2014: Temp. 48° (3° below avg.); precip. 0.5" (avg.). 1–4 Sunny, cool. 5–10 Scattered showers, seasonable. 11–18 Showers, cool. 19–24 Sunny, cool. 25–28 Rain and snow showers, chilly.

MAR. 2014: Temp. 56° (2° below avg.); precip. 0.5" (avg.). 1–6 Sunny east, rainy periods west; chilly. 7–14 Sunny; cool, then warmer. 15–19 Showers, then sunny, cool. 20–31 Sunny, warm.

APR. 2014: Temp. 64° (1° below avg.); precip. 1.5" (1" above avg.). 1–5 Scattered t-storms, cool. 6–16 Sunny, seasonable. 17–25 Sunny; cool, then warm. 26–30 Rainy periods, cool.

MAY 2014: Temp. 77° (3° above avg.); precip. 0.4" (0.1" below avg.). 1–4 Sunny, warm. 5–16 Isolated t-storms, warm. 17–31 Sunny, hot.

JUNE 2014: Temp. 83° (2° above avg. east, 2° below west); precip. 0.4" (0.1" below avg.). 1–10 Scattered t-storms, cool. 11–22 Sunny, nice. 23–30 Isolated t-storms, hot.

JULY 2014: Temp. 89° (2° above avg.); precip. 1.3" (0.2" below avg.). 1–3 T-storms, cool east; sunny west. 4–8 Isolated t-storms, hot. 9–14 Scattered t-storms, not as hot. 15–24 Isolated t-storms, hot. 25–31 Scattered t-storms, hot and humid.

AUG. 2014: Temp. 87° (2° above avg.); precip. 1" (0.5" below avg.). 1–6 Isolated t-storms, hot and humid. 7–16 Scattered t-storms, hot and humid. 17–21 Sunny, hot. 22–25 T-storms, cool east; sunny, warm west. 26–31 Sunny, hot.

SEPT. 2014: Temp. 80° (3° above avg. east, 1° below west); precip. 0.7" (0.3" below avg.). 1–3 Sunny, hot. 4–12 A few t-storms, turning cool. 13–25 Sunny; cool, then hot. 26–30 Sunny, cool.

OCT. 2014: Temp. 67° (1° below avg.); precip. 1.2" (0.2" above avg.). 1–4 Sunny; warm east, cool west. 5–10 T-storms, then sunny, cool. 11–17 T-storms, then sunny, cool. 18–21 A couple of showers, warm. 22–28 Sunny, cool. 29–31 Showers, mild.

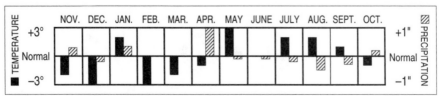

Pacific Northwest

SUMMARY: Winter will be much snowier than normal, with frequent snows from mid-December through the first three weeks of January. Rainfall will be near normal, with temperatures below normal, on average, in the north and above in the south. The coldest periods will occur in mid- to late December, early to mid-January, and mid- to late January.

April and May will be much warmer and slightly drier than normal.

Summer will be warmer than normal, with the hottest periods in early to mid-June and mid-July. Rainfall will be below normal in the north, above in the south.

September and October will be warmer and rainier than normal.

NOV. 2013: Temp. 49° (2° above avg.); precip. 7.5" (2" above avg. north, avg. south). 1–5 Rainy, mild. 6–9 Showers, cool. 10–19 Rainy periods, mild. 20–21 Sunny, mild. 22–25 Rain, turning cool. 26–30 Stormy, heavy rain.

DEC. 2013: Temp. 44° (2° below avg. north, 4° above south); precip. 9.5" (3" above avg.). 1–4 Heavy rain, mild. 5–11 Rainy periods, turning cool. 12–13 Sunny, cold. 14–18 Snow to rain, turning mild. 19–22 Snowy periods north, rain south; turning cold. 23–25 Snowstorm, very cold. 26–31 Rainy, turning mild.

JAN. 2014: Temp. 38° (5° below avg.); precip. 7.5" (avg. north, 3" above south). 1–4 Rain, heavy south; cool. 5–11 Snow and rain, then flurries, cold. 12–17 Snow, then sunny, very cold. 18–24 Snowstorm, then sunny, cool. 25–31 Rainy periods, cool.

FEB. 2014: Temp. 44° (avg.); precip. 3.5" (1.5" below avg.). 1–4 Rain, some heavy, seasonable. 5–9 Showers, turning mild. 10–15 Sunny, cool. 16–23 A few showers; cool, then mild. 24–28 Rainy periods, cool.

MAR. 2014: Temp. 49° (2° above avg.); precip. 2.5" (1.5" below avg.). 1–7 Sunny, cool. 8–15 Rainy periods; mild, then cool. 16–21 Sunny, warm. 22–31 Rainy periods, turning cool.

APR. 2014: Temp. 51° (1° above avg.); precip. 2.5" (0.5" below avg.). 1–5 Showers, mild. 6–8 Sunny, seasonable. 9–16 Occasional rain, cool. 17–19 Sunny, cool. 20–26 Rain and drizzle, cool. 27–30 Sunny, turning warm.

MAY 2014: Temp. 61° (6° above avg.); precip. 2" (0.5" above avg. north, 0.5" below south). 1–5 Sunny, warm. 6–10 Showers, then sunny, warm. 11–16 Showers, then sunny, hot. 17–23 Rainy periods, turning cool. 24–28 Sunny, very warm. 29–31 Showers.

JUNE 2014: Temp. 63° (3° above avg.); precip. 2" (avg. north, 1" above south). 1–11 Showers, then sunny, hot. 12–14 Misty, mild. 15–21 Showers, turning cool. 22–30 Scattered showers, seasonable.

JULY 2014: Temp. 65° (avg.); precip. 0.2" (0.3" below avg.). 1–8 Showers, then sunny, cool. 9–14 Isolated t-storms, warm. 15–17 Sunny, hot. 18–25 Scattered showers, then sunny, cool. 26–31 Showers, then sunny, cool.

AUG. 2014: Temp. 66° (avg.); precip. 0.5" (0.5" below avg.). 1–7 Sunny, turning warm. 8–16 Scattered showers, then sunny, warm. 17–23 Showers, then sunny, cool. 24–31 Scattered showers, then sunny, warm.

SEPT. 2014: Temp. 61.5° (0.5° above avg.); precip. 4" (2.5" above avg.). 1–4 Sunny, very warm. 5–18 Heavy rain, then rainy periods, seasonable. 19–25 Showers, cool. 26–29 Sunny, turning warm. 30 Rain.

OCT. 2014: Temp. 56° (2° above avg.); precip. 3" (avg.). 1–7 Rain, then sunny, cool. 8–12 Rain, then sunny, cool. 13–14 Sunny, warm. 15–23 Rainy periods; cool, then mild. 24–27 Showers, mild. 28–31 Rainy, mild.

Seattle
Portland
Eugene
Eureka

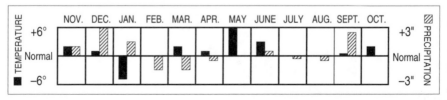

Pacific Southwest

SUMMARY: Winter will be much rainier and cooler than normal, with mountain snowfall much greater than normal. Most of the rain, snow, and storminess will come in January and February, when storm damage will be a concern. The coldest periods will be in mid-December and mid- to late January.

April and May will be warmer and drier than normal.

Summer will be warmer than normal, with near-normal rainfall. The hottest periods will be in the latter half of July and mid- to late August.

September and October will bring near-normal temperatures, on average, with rainfall above normal in the north and below in the south.

NOV. 2013: Temp. 58° (1° below avg. north, 1° above south); precip. 1" (0.5" below avg.). 1–3 Sunny, warm. 4–6 Showers north, sunny south. 7–10 T-storms, then sunny, cool. 11–18 A few showers north, sunny south; seasonable. 19–21 Sunny, cool. 22–30 Showers, then sunny, cool.

DEC. 2013: Temp. 54° (avg.); precip. 2" (1" above avg. north, 0.5" below south). 1–5 Rain, then sunny, cool. 6–10 Heavy rain north, showers south; cool. 11–15 Rainy periods, cold. 16–21 Rainy periods, some heavy; cool. 22–31 Clouds and drizzle, cool north; sunny, turning warm south.

JAN. 2014: Temp. 53° (1° below avg.); precip. 8" (5" above avg.). 1–3 Clouds and occasional drizzle, cool. 4–10 Heavy rain, then sunny, chilly. 11–14 Heavy rain, mild. 15–16 Showers. 17–19 Heavy rain, mild. 20–24 Rainy periods, cold. 25–27 Sunny, cool. 28–31 Rainy, cool.

FEB. 2014: Temp. 52.5° (2.5° below avg.); precip. 5" (2" above avg.). 1–3 Sunny, mild. 4–8 Heavy rain north, showers south; cool. 9–15 Rainy periods, cool. 16–21 Rain, some heavy, cool. 22–28 Showers, then sunny, cool.

MAR. 2014: Temp. 56° (1° below avg.); precip. 2.5" (0.5" above avg. east, 1" below west). 1–4 Sunny north, rainy periods south; cool. 5–8 Rain, then sunny, cool. 9–12 Showers north, sunny south; cool. 13–20 Showers, then sunny, turning warm. 21–25 Scattered showers, cooler. 26–31 Rainy periods, cool.

APR. 2014: Temp. 60° (avg.); precip. 0.7" (0.3" below avg.). 1–8 Showers, then sunny, cool. 9–14 Sunny, turning warm north; A.M. clouds, P.M. sun, south. 15–20 Showers, then sunny, warm. 21–25

Sunny, cool. 26–30 Sunny, warm north; showers, cool south.

MAY 2014: Temp. 66° (2° above avg.); precip. 0.4" (0.1" below avg.). 1–5 Sunny, hot inland; A.M. clouds and sprinkles, P.M. sun coast. 6–10 Sunny, warm north; A.M. clouds and sprinkles, P.M. sun south. 11–19 Sunny, warm inland; A.M. clouds and sprinkles, P.M. sun coast. 20–27 Sunny; warm north, cool south. 28–31 Sunny, warm inland; A.M. clouds and sprinkles, P.M. sun coast.

JUNE 2014: Temp. 68° (avg.); precip. 0.1" (avg.). 1–3 Scattered showers, cool. 4–8 Sunny, warm inland; fog and drizzle coast. 9–12 Sunny, warm. 13–17 Sunny inland; A.M. clouds and sprinkles, P.M. sun coast; cool. 18–21 Sunny, cool. 22–30 Sunny; warm, then cool.

JULY 2014: Temp. 72° (1° above avg.); precip. 0.03" (0.03" above avg.). 1–6 Scattered showers, seasonable. 7–16 Sunny; turning hot inland, warm coast. 17–25 Sunny, nice. 26–31 Sunny, warm.

AUG. 2014: Temp. 72° (1° above avg.); precip. 0.1" (avg.). 1–7 Isolated showers, warm. 8–12 Sunny, turning cool. 13–22 Sunny; warm, then cool. 23–29 Sunny; hot inland, cool coast. 30–31 Scattered showers, warm.

SEPT. 2014: Temp. 70° (avg.); precip. 0.1" (0.1" below avg.). 1–6 Sunny; warm inland, cool coast. 7–14 A.M. clouds, mist coast; sunny inland; cool. 15–23 Sunny, turning warm. 24–30 Scattered showers, then sunny, cool.

OCT. 2014: Temp. 65° (avg.); precip. 1" (1" above avg. north, avg. south). 1–6 A few showers north, sunny south; cool. 7–13 T-storms north, showers south; then sunny, cool. 14–26 Sunny; cool, then warm. 27–31 Rainy periods, cool.

San Francisco ⊙

⊙ Fresno

Los Angeles ⊙

San Diego ⊙

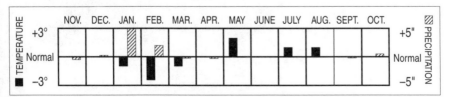

In honor of fitness expert Jack LaLanne . . .

100 YEARS OF WEIGHT LOSS

by Alice Cary

To me, this one thing—

physical culture and

nutrition—is the

salvation of America.

–Jack LaLanne
(1914–2011)

The next time you go to a gym, thank Jack LaLanne's mother. She gave birth to Jack on September 26, 1914. One day, 15 years later, she got fed up with her short, scrawny son, a junk-food junkie and high school dropout, and hauled him from their San Francisco home to a nutrition lecture. The talk inspired the boy to begin studying *Gray's Anatomy* and start bodybuilding by working out with weights. People thought that he was crazy. Even doctors believed that this sort of exertion would likely lead to a heart attack.

By the time he was 21, LaLanne had opened a health studio (the first of many), complete with a gym, juice bar, and health food store—and people thought that he was nuttier still.

To retain his svelte 5-foot 6-inch, 150-pound shape, LaLanne ate two healthy, low-fat meals a day: breakfast, often egg whites, oatmeal, soy milk, and fruit; and dinner, usually fish, salad, and more egg whites. He did not snack. Daily workouts included 2 hours of swimming and weightlifting. (He designed the first leg extension machine, as well as several other pieces of fitness equipment.)

Beginning in 1951, LaLanne brought his fitness message to the masses with *The Jack LaLanne Show* on television. The program went nationwide in 1959 and continued into the 1980s, airing over 3,000 shows. On the show, he preached the virtues of drinking fruit and vegetable juices and popularized the then-revolutionary notion that it was important for women, the disabled, and the elderly to build strength. In fact, women in the 1950s weren't encouraged to exercise.

Many experts warned that such efforts might damage their reproductive health.

Throughout his life, LaLanne completed a variety of feats to bring attention to his message, including . . .

- **AT AGE 40, he swam the length of the Golden Gate Bridge underwater, towing 140 pounds of equipment, including air tanks.**

- **AT 45, he did 1,000 push-ups and 1,000 chin-ups in 1 hour, 22 minutes.**

- **AT 60, he swam from Alcatraz to San Francisco's Fisherman's Wharf while handcuffed, shackled, and towing a 1,000-lb. boat.**

–www.jacklalanne.com

- **AT 70 *(above)*, handcuffed and shackled again, towing 70 boats carrying a total of 70 people, he swam a mile and a half through California's Long Beach Harbor.**

(continued)

SOUND BITES

LaLanne's on-air adages became slogans for viewers of his TV program everywhere:

- ■ Exercise is king, nutrition is queen—put them together and you've got a kingdom.
- ■ Don't exceed the feed limit.
- ■ Ten seconds on the lips and a lifetime on the hips.
- ■ Better to wear out than to rust out.

HISTORICAL
AND OCCASIONALLY
H Y S T E R I C A L
FITNESS ATTEMPTS

Through the years, a parade of personalities has promoted a variety of methods and gizmos to lose weight, some more successful than others.

MUSCLE FLEXERS

A Prussian named Eugen Sandow, purveyor of a system of exercises with dumbbells, is regarded as the father of bodybuilding. Said to have the perfect male body, he created

Bodybuilder Eugen Sandow

quite a Victorian stir with his stage shows, at which he flexed his muscles while wearing a fig leaf and gladiator sandals, emulating the poses of ancient Greek statues. In 1911, he earned the title of "Special Instructor of Physical Culture to the King of England."

Before his death in 1925, Sandow inspired many, including a feeble Ellis Island immigrant youngster named Charles Atlas, who lived in Brooklyn and kept a photograph of Sandow on his bureau. After watching a lion stretch in the Bronx Zoo, Atlas was inspired to begin flexing his muscles, using the principles of isometric opposition, a type of resistance training that forgoes equipment such as barbells. Atlas's simple "Dynamic-Tension" mail-order course was inexpensive and appealed to the masses, but it also had its celebrity adherents,

A 1941 ad promoting Charles Atlas's "Dynamic-Tension" bodybuilding system

including King George VI of England, Mahatma Gandhi, and Franklin Roosevelt, whose birthday Atlas helped to celebrate. By the 1950s, he boasted nearly a million customers around the world.

PEDAL PUSHERS

A 1930s contraption called the Wonder Cycle Exercisulator required riders to push pedals in an effort to simulate horseback riding. A more modern invention called the iGallop looks much sleeker but works on a similar premise. The Lifecycle, a stationary bike invented by an American chemist named Keene Dimick, came along in 1968.

Dimick built it in an attempt to relieve his chronic back pain. Today, stationary cyclists gather for spin classes, in which they pedal to pop music and sometimes watch videos that simulate scenery in motion.

WALKERS

Borrowing an idea from

Teddy Roosevelt, President John F. Kennedy challenged the

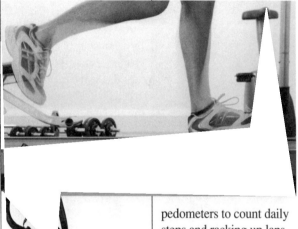

military and his staff to attempt a 50-mile hike in a day. Press Secretary Pierre Salinger firmly refused, but Attorney General Robert F. Kennedy accepted his brother's challenge, hiking through snow and slush along the C&O Canal towpath while wearing leather oxfords!

Today, with a wide assortment of shoes from which to choose, people walk everywhere, wearing pedometers to count daily steps and racking up laps on tracks and in malls. Many prefer treadmills, which has encouraged a few inventors to try to ease the monotony by coming up with treadmill apparatuses that actually travel themselves as someone walks or runs on them.

(continued)

SHAKERS

After Jack LaLanne helped to pave the way for women to exercise, women's gyms, aka "figure salons," began to open in the 1960s. Many of the machines offered only passive exercise, such as vibrating belts that were supposed to shake pounds away from thighs and other "problem areas." These belt

—Everett/SuperStock

exercisers were inspired by machines developed in the 1850s by Swedish Dr. Gustav Zander, who used them to rehabilitate injured or disabled workers. The Zander Institutes (first in Stockholm and later around the world) contained 27 custom machines to help women, the elderly, and others who were excluded from gymnasiums of the day. Zander's mechanical horse, in fact, is an early version of the Stairmaster.

Now for a shaking exercise guaranteed to burn calories, folks grab a Hula Hoop.

NO SWEAT

Some spas advocate body wraps for health and cleansing. Wrestlers sometimes wear thermal suits for losing weight to reach their weight-class limit, and baseball relief pitchers wear them to warm up quickly. However, weight loss that results from wearing suits that cause sweating is temporary. It results in little real change (except, perhaps, dehydration) because instead of eliminating fat, this method simply rids the

body of water weight. Those pounds return as soon as enthusiasts start chugging water.

COUNTERS

Americans started counting their calories after the concept was popularized in 1918 by Dr. Lulu Hunt Peters, a Los Angeles physician who struggled with weight and published what may be the first modern diet book, *Diet and Health, With Key to the Calories.* Dr. Lulu's newfangled system helped her to lose 70 pounds.

SHOCKERS

Some weight watchers have tried to burn calories by wearing an electrically stimulating abdominal belt that "shocks" abs into shape. Supposedly, wearing such a belt for from 10 to 60 minutes a day will cause your muscles to contract, thus avoiding the need for an actual workout. Scientists say that while they tone muscles, they don't burn fat. What's more, most people's abdominal muscles are hidden by fat, so no one will notice the toning. The units can also cause burns and interfere with pacemakers and defibrillators.

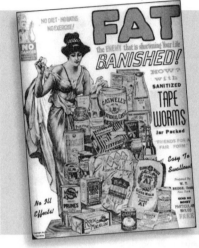

A DUBIOUS DIET

■ The Tapeworm Diet was billed as a "natural enemy" to overeating in the early 1900s, although pills offered for sale may not have contained an actual tapeworm. Rumors spread about opera singer Maria Callas, who shed 66 pounds in 2 years. The source of her weight loss has been heatedly debated; she may have consumed a tapeworm after eating raw meat.

ALTERNATIVES
TO EXERCISE

STANDING

Experts say that people who simply stand for 2 minutes for every 20 of sitting can reap significant rewards, such as reducing the risk of Type 2 diabetes. Prolonged sitting slows metabolism, causing an accumulation of fat in livers, hearts, and brains. One approach: Stand every time you answer the phone or eat lunch. An increasing number of workers are using stand-up desks, adjustable desks that allow both standing and sitting, and even desks with built-in treadmills.

SITTING

Many office chairs have evolved into "workout" chairs that offer a variety of workout options, such as resistance pulleys. For another spin on this theme, "Hawaii" or "hula" chairs come equipped with a gyrating seat.

PHONE TONING

Turn phone calls into workout sessions by standing, squatting, or lifting weights while you talk. One Japanese inventor designed a "dumbbell phone," consisting of a weight that attaches to a landline. □□

Alice Cary, a frequent contributor to the Almanac, has fond memories of watching *The Jack LaLanne Show* as a child.

The Old Farmer's Almanac
GARDEN PLANNER

An Easy Garden Planner for Vegetables, Herbs, & Fruit

The Old Farmer's Almanac Garden Planner—completely FREE for 30 days!

The Old Farmer's Almanac Garden Planner makes it simple to plan your vegetable beds, as well as add plants and move them around to achieve your perfect layout. Our planner will work with nearly any size or shape of garden, whether you wish to plant in traditional rows, raised beds, or square-foot gardens. The **Garden Planner** will help you to achieve the ideal plan for the space you have available.

With the **Garden Planner**'s detailed growing information—specific to your very own location—you can produce the perfect garden plan!

- Choose from among 130 vegetable, herbs, and fruit
- Add or remove plants and varieties
- Allow for the proper amount of space
- Learn how to group plants for maximum success
- Get frost dates and planting reminders
- Start next year's plan and incorporate crop rotation
- Learn about successful succession planting
- Include notes about your plants and how they grow
- Keep track of your garden plans

The **Garden Planner** works like software with which you are familiar and includes features such as copy, paste, and undo! It also includes built-in tutorial videos to make sure that you are getting the most out of the **Garden Planner**.

The Old Farmer's Almanac Garden Planner is completely FREE for 30 days—more than ample time to try it out! Getting started is easy: No credit card details are required, and there is no obligation to subscribe. If you find it useful (as we expect you will!), try it FREE for 30 days; if you like it, pay just $25/year.

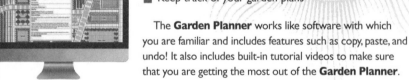

Why wait? Start planning now!
Visit **Almanac.com/GardenPlanner14** today!

Mother Nature's Insect Control

MOSQUITO DUNKS®
MOSQUITO BITS®

Kills mosquitoes before they're old enough to bite!®

- #1 biological mosquito killer—100% natural, biodegradable, works for 30 days or more.
- Use in bird baths, planters, potted plants—in any standing water.
- Controls larvae within 24 hours—will not harm animals, fish, birds, honey bees or plants.
- Mosquito Bits®—a versatile granular application with a spice shaker top — easily broadcasts over treatment area.

Caterpillar & Webworm Control

- 100% natural alternative. Contains no synthetic toxins.
- Controls caterpillars and worms on fruit trees, vegetables, ornamentals, and shade trees in and around the home and garden.
- *USE UP TO THE DAY OF HARVEST.*

Year-Round® Spray Oil

- Apply early in the growing season to prevent insect and fungal damage.
- Protection for your garden, vegetables, house plants, fruit trees, and ornamentals—both indoors and out.
- Recommended by top growers and agricultural experts — *USE UP TO THE DAY OF HARVEST.*

FOR ORGANIC PRODUCTION

OMRI®
Listed

Summit *...responsible solutions.*
800.227.8664   SummitResponsibleSolutions.com

Summit ... *responsible solutions®*, Year Round® Spray Oil, Mosquito Dunks®, and Mosquito Bits® are registered trademarks of Summit Chemical Company.

WINNERS
in the 2013 Essay Contest

My Funniest Family Moment

FIRST PRIZE: $250

When I met the family of my boyfriend Barry, they made me feel right at home. As we helped his mother to clean a closet, we found an old Polaroid camera with one picture left in it. Having never liked being photographed but with no way to get out of it gracefully, I stood in front of the wood cookstove in their country kitchen. Picture taken, we waited the one minute for it to develop. I was not especially excited to see the result. Mama Rosie peeled the paper and immediately burst into hysterical laughter. Surprised, Barry went over to look and he, too, burst out laughing. It was all I could do not to cry, and I just stood there helplessly for what seemed an eternity. Finally, they brought the picture to me and I, too, could only laugh. The picture had been exposed the year before, and it was of their prized Duroc boar hog!

–Christine Finneyfrock, Lignum, Virginia

faucet over the water trough running when he arrived. This became almost a daily discovery. Unbeknownst to him, his father had been dealing with the same issue every evening. By Saturday, the barnyard was a flooded, muddy mess when the two arrived. With frustration and anger, the yelling began. Accusations of irresponsibility and hurtful assessments of getting old and forgetful flew back and forth between them. The heated exchange stopped when one of them noticed the bull heading over to get a drink. Both men stared in disbelief as the animal stuck out its tongue and carefully used it to turn the spigot handle. The fresh, cool water spurted up from the well and he lapped happily. After getting his fill, the big beast lumbered away, presumably forgetting to turn off the flow. Father and son laughed heartily, and so has every other farmer who has heard this story.

–Stacey Pauley, Mooresville, Indiana

SECOND PRIZE: $150

Back when my husband and father-in-law were in the cattle business, they took turns caring for the herd. My husband took the morning shift. His dad looked after the herd in the evening. One summer, my husband began finding the

THIRD PRIZE: $100

In 1951, my brother, Bill, left Tennessee for Flint, Michigan, to take a job in an automobile plant. There, he met and married Rosie Butcher, a dyed-in-the-wool city girl. Shortly after the wedding, Mom went to visit her new daughter-in-law. The two quickly developed a warm relationship. Rosie, however, had heard a lot of misinformation about Tennessee people from comic strips, and she enjoyed poking fun at Mom about her hillbilly ways. Mom had a good sense of humor, and she took Rosie's ribbing with stoical good grace. Mom's brain, though, was not idle; she was waiting to get even. Later, Bill and Rosie came to visit us for Thanksgiving. While Mom was preparing dinner, Bill and Rosie went out for a walk. Mom took the turkey out of the oven, removed the stuffing, and inserted a stuffed Cornish game hen. Then she restuffed the turkey and placed it back in the oven. At dinnertime, Mom proceeded to remove the stuffing from the turkey. Then, she started to carve the bird. Suddenly, she gasped in horror as she reached in and pulled out the hen. Looking shocked, she exclaimed, "Oh, what am I going to do? I've cooked a pregnant turkey!" Rosie started to cry. It took us two hours to console her and convince her that turkeys lay eggs.

–*Lucy A. Tharp, Crossville, Tennessee*

HONORABLE MENTION

It was 1957. I was in grade 2 and the youngest of a French Roman Catholic family that never ate meat on Friday. That Friday, I could not decide what I wanted in my lunch box. I loved my mother's homemade bread, and I thought her sliced pickled beets would be just the right taste with it. So the beet sandwich was made and wrapped with care. At lunchtime, all of my classmates were amazed at my pink bread. Where did I get it? Quickly, I had to come up with an answer, so I said, "My parents told me that they love me so much and that I am so special that they make me pink bread to show their love." That night, the telephone kept ringing while my mother was trying to make our supper. The neighbors wanted to get her "pink bread recipe." It took a few days for Mother to realize that the beets were the cause of the pink bread that everyone was talking about. I still find myself making tiny beet sandwiches that I toast in the oven for party snacks.

–*Andrew Pearson, Coweta, Oklahoma*

□□

ANNOUNCING THE 2014 ESSAY CONTEST TOPIC: MY MOST UNUSUAL COINCIDENCE

In 200 words or less, please tell us about your coincidence. See below for details.

ESSAY AND RECIPE CONTEST RULES

Cash prizes (first, $250; second, $150; third, $100) will be awarded for the best essay on the subject "My Most Unusual Coincidence" and the best recipe using carrots (see page 50). All entries become the property of Yankee Publishing, which reserves all rights to the material. The deadline for entries is Friday, January 24, 2014. Label "Essay Contest" or "Recipe Contest" and mail to The Old Farmer's Almanac, P.O. Box 520, Dublin, NH 03444. You can also enter at Almanac.com/EssayContest or Almanac.com/RecipeContest. Include your name, mailing address, and email address. Winners will appear in *The 2015 Old Farmer's Almanac* and on our Web site, Almanac.com.

by Heidi Stonehill

Crack These Cryptogram Codes

A cryptogram is a communication in code. Here, cipher letters are substituted for "true" letters. To decipher these messages, determine the true letter that each code letter represents. (Hint: Look at the short words first; these might be familiar words such as "a," "of," "and," or "the.") Each cryptogram here uses a different code.

Answers on page 235.

1 The Old Farmer Says

This 19th-century Almanac advice still rings true today. **Hint: B = A, K = S**

B EICEJI BZCOAM CL KOAKPRAJ RK QJIW AJFJKKBIW MC

_ _____ _____ __ _____ __ ____ _____ __

NCCH PJBXMP. SJ AJJH MPJ KOAKPRAJ LICZ COMKRHJ

____ _____. __ ____ ___ _____ ____ _____

BAH MPJ KOAKPRAJ CL XCQJ RA COI PJBIMK BAH PCZJK

___ ___ _____ __ ____ __ ___ _____ ___ _____

MC ZBVJ OK PBEEW.

__ ____ __ _____.

2 Culinary Clue

To learn a secret for making great pies, solve this cipher. **Hint: F = A, P = G**

JKC F JTFNS, ODEXDC QBDRCAIO,

___ _ _____, _____ _____,

AID RKTX AODEIBTI FEX BEPCDXBDEOI.

___ ____ _____ ___ _____.

3 The Saying Goes

The following proverb sums up this exercise. **Hint: T = G, U = F**

GSRMP LM GSV VMW YVULIV BLF YVTRM.

_____ __ ___ ___ _____ ___ _____.

□□

Heidi Stonehill, senior editor at *The Old Farmer's Almanac*, plays puzzles until the cows come home.

Gestation and Mating Tables

	Proper Age or Weight for First Mating	Period of Fertility (yrs.)	Number of Females for One Male	Period of Gestation (days)	
				AVERAGE	RANGE
Ewe	1 yr. or 90 lbs.	6		147 / 151[1]	142–154
Ram	12–14 mos., well matured	7	50–75[2] / 35–40[3]		
Mare	3 yrs.	10–12		336	310–370
Stallion	3 yrs.	12–15	40–45[4] / record 252[5]		
Cow	15–18 mos.[6]	10–14		283	279–290[7] 262–300[8]
Bull	1 yr., well matured	10–12	50[4] / thousands[5]		
Sow	5–6 mos. or 250 lbs.	6		115	110–120
Boar	250–300 lbs.	6	50[2] / 35–40[3]		
Doe goat	10 mos. or 85–90 lbs.	6		150	145–155
Buck goat	well matured	5	30		
Bitch	16–18 mos.	8		63	58–67
Male dog	12–16 mos.	8	8–10		
Queen cat	12 mos.	6		63	60–68
Tom cat	12 mos.	6	6–8		
Doe rabbit	6 mos.	5–6		31	30–32
Buck rabbit	6 mos.	5–6	30		

[1]For fine wool breeds. [2]Hand-mated. [3]Pasture. [4]Natural. [5]Artificial. [6]Holstein and beef: 750 lbs.; Jersey: 500 lbs. [7]Beef; 8–10 days shorter for Angus. [8]Dairy.

Incubation Period of Poultry (days)	
Chicken	21
Duck	26–32
Goose	30–34
Guinea	26–28

Average Life Span of Animals in Captivity (years)			
Cat (domestic)	14	Goat (domestic)	14
Chicken (domestic)	8	Goose (domestic)	20
Dog (domestic)	13	Horse	22
Duck (domestic)	10	Rabbit (domestic)	6

	Estral/Estrous Cycle (including heat period)		Length of Estrus (heat)		Usual Time of Ovulation	When Cycle Recurs If Not Bred
	AVERAGE	RANGE	AVERAGE	RANGE		
Mare	21 days	10–37 days	5–6 days	2–11 days	24–48 hours before end of estrus	21 days
Sow	21 days	18–24 days	2–3 days	1–5 days	30–36 hours after start of estrus	21 days
Ewe	16½ days	14–19 days	30 hours	24–32 hours	12–24 hours before end of estrus	16½ days
Doe goat	21 days	18–24 days	2–3 days	1–4 days	Near end of estrus	21 days
Cow	21 days	18–24 days	18 hours	10–24 hours	10–12 hours after end of estrus	21 days
Bitch	24 days	16–30 days	7 days	5–9 days	1–3 days after first acceptance	Pseudo-pregnancy
Queen cat		15–21 days	3–4 days, if mated	9–10 days, in absence of male	24–56 hours after coitus	Pseudo-pregnancy

PUTTING THE WORLD RIGHT

with
old-fashioned
ways

• • • • • • • • • • • •

by Tim Clark

Sure, old-time farming beliefs and sayings seem crazy today—but some of them are based on thousands of years of practical experience.

When this publication began in 1792, the founder, Robert B. Thomas, called it a *Farmer's Almanac*. He did so because farmers had a special interest in knowing certain information, particularly the phases of the Moon and the location of the Sun and Moon in the zodiac on any given day. Farmers believed then—as many do today—that certain crops should be planted only under a waxing Moon and others only under a waning Moon (see "Planting by the Moon's Phase" on page 244 or at

Almanac.com), and that other agricultural chores should be performed only when the stars and planets were in a favorable alignment (see "Secrets of the Zodiac" on page 246).

Such beliefs may seem dubious or unscientific. We may call them folklore, superstition, or "old wives' tales."

Timing planting by careful observation of natural signs, such as the blooming of other plants or the behavior of animals—phenology, as it's called today—is now seen as a sophisticated way to improve a crop's chances of success. Illinois farmers know to plant tomatoes when the peach trees blossom, and Alabama farmers wait to hear the first whippoorwill before planting corn.

Some old sayings that tie planting to holy days or certain-numbered days clearly have less to do with nature and more to do with the farmer's frame of mind. There's no scientific evidence that planting potatoes on St. Patrick's Day, for example, will improve the yield. But who's to say that it will not make for a more confident—and efficient—farmer?

Some farm folklore has ancient roots. For example, many sayings about the power of iron objects—rusty nails scattered around crops or horseshoes hung in the boughs of barren fruit trees—may be relics of the Iron Age, when weapons forged from the new metal seemed to make their wielders invincible.

Consider that when there is a death in the family of a Pennsylvania Dutch farmer, he goes out to tell his bees right away. Folklorists trace the belief back to the times when bees were considered messengers to the gods. The tradition may persist because it permits a grieving farmer a moment of privacy when he needs it most.

The following beliefs—some strange, some funny, some even disgusting—are all examples of what former folklorist and editor of Funk and Wagnalls' *Standard Dictionary of Folklore, Mythology, and Legend* Maria Leach (1892–1977) called "the inextinguishable hope that all that is wrong in the world can somehow be put right."

(continued)

Planting

Manure spread in the light of the Moon (from the day the Moon is new to the day it is full) will dry up and blow away; in the dark of the Moon (from the day after it is full to the day before it is new), it will sink into the earth.

To make a plant grow, spit into the hole you have dug for it.

Anything planted by a pregnant woman will flourish.

Never thank a person for giving you a plant, or it will die; in fact, the best way to ensure that plant slips will thrive is to steal them.

Crops that ripen above ground should be planted in the morning; plant crops that ripen underground after noon.

Never plant anything on the 31st of the month.

Anything planted on Good Friday will grow well.

Never plant until the frogs have croaked three times, because there will be a killing frost before then.

Plant clover on the day of the new Moon.

Peppers should be planted only by a violent-tempered person, a red-haired person, or a person in a bad mood.

Never plant onions near potatoes, or the eyes of the potatoes will weep. Likewise, all plants with eyes must be underground by Good Friday, or they will weep for the Crucifixion.

Plant corn after the first woodpecker appears.

Plant beans when the horns of the Moon point upward.

Always begin sowing on a Friday and end on a Friday. If you finish earlier, hang your seed bag on the fence and leave it there until Friday.

Unless you sit on thyme after sowing it, it will not grow.

Corn must not be planted on a date ending in zero.

Flax will grow tall if you show it your buttocks.

Plant watermelons a week after apple blossom time.

It's time to plant corn when your wife comes to bed naked.

Pest Control

Scatter elder leaves over your cabbage to keep the bugs away.

Put a horseshoe in the fire, and as long as it glows red-hot, hawks will not bother your chickens.

To make a scarecrow more effective, make its arms from hickory wood.

Plant cucumbers while you are wearing your pajamas, on the first day of May, before sunrise, and no bugs will eat them.

Husbandry

A new cow won't be homesick if you bring a stone from the place you got her and put it in the manger.

To cure founder in a horse, cut three locks of hair from your private parts, place them between the halves of an apple or potato, and feed it to the horse.

A billy goat kept in the barn will prevent cows from miscarrying.

Don't talk about hens at mealtime, or their eggs won't hatch.

If a cow has indigestion, feed her an onion sandwich, stolen bread, or bread taken in silence from a neighbor.

After weaning, feed the cow a tuft of hair from her calf's head to prevent lowing.

If you want a hen to hatch only pullets, put a girl's bonnet under her eggs.

Predicting the Crops

Water dripping from your eaves on New Year's Day means a good year.

If the smoke goes straight up on the first day of February, it will be a good crop year.

Sleet in February portends a good apple crop.

March snow is as good as manure.

If you can wet a handkerchief with rain on Easter, it will be a good year for farmers.

Early thunder brings fine crops.

If locust trees are heavy with blossoms, it will be a good corn year.

A white Christmas means a good year for fruit.

In a year when plums flourish, all else fails. □□

Pets

HOW TO GET BITTEN BY A PET

It can happen—

and be avoided—

more easily than

you think.

by Sophia Yin

When I was about 8 years old and at the park with my parents, a gopher popped its head out of a hole.

As an animal lover, I had to investigate. I offered food to the gopher and, when it wouldn't come out, reached into the hole to pet it.

Chomp! It bit my index finger and ducked back into its hole.

Since then, I've learned that the gopher was afraid and reacted normally to an unfamiliar being invading its space.

People get bitten all the time by doing things to or around pets and wildlife that are predictably unsafe. Here are five situations that can lead to animal bites, based on true tales from our Facebook fans. (To avoid injury, I tell you how to **play it safe**.)

Expect to get bitten if you try to grab or rescue a scared pet or wild animal.

➡ Animals often do not know that you are trying to help them. Paula L. recalls, "I was bitten twice by squirrels: once when picking up an injured baby and once when rescuing one trapped in a swimming pool. Even though I used a piece of lumber as an escape bridge for the one in the pool, he nipped me as he flew past me."

A stray cat bit Borin M. when he tried to help it. "I had it by the scruff of the neck, but it swirled around and got my thumb all the way in the back of its mouth and sawed away on it."

PLAY IT SAFE:

When animals, even pets, are scared, especially if they are in emergency escape mode, they will defend themselves. (This is one reason that animal control officers advise people not to attempt the rescue of wildlife and stray animals.) If you have to grab a *small* scared, struggling pet, try to cover it with a towel; use a thick blanket if it's a *large* animal. The cover will help to protect you while you try to handle or move it.

Expect to get bitten if you handle animals, especially pocket pets (small animals, often rodents), that don't know you well or have not been trained to accept or enjoy handling.

➡ Consider what happened to Cha'kwaian E.: "When I was a kid, my guinea pig bit me when I was trying to get him out of the cage to pet him. It was the first time he had been taken out of it."

Die H.'s experience was similar: "My friend's hamster bit nearly every time he was touched."

PLAY IT SAFE:

Pocket pets need to be trained to like their humans and to enjoy handling. Give treats whenever you enter the room or approach the cage and when you're handling the animal. The animal will learn to like you and no longer fear being handled.

continued ➡

Expect to get bitten if you get in the middle of an ongoing fight or one that's about to begin between animals.

➡ As a child, Tanya A. got in between two fighting male rabbits. "Happy was not so happy when I tried to separate him from the other rabbit. He sunk his teeth into my hand! When I pulled my hand back, he was dangling from it and wouldn't let go."

Sometimes animals fear members of their own species and take this out on a different target entirely. "I was at our shelter," writes Miranda W., "introducing to each other three ferrets that had been housed separately, since adopters were interested in taking all three. One ferret was very unhappy with the other two. When a happy one got close to the unhappy one, it redirected onto my left arm and gave me some amazing puncture wounds."

PLAY IT SAFE:

Why would a pet turn and bite *you* when the enemy is another animal? Think of the "two-guys-in-a-bar syndrome." If two guys who have had too much to drink start a heated argument, you avoid prodding them verbally. Doing so would only agitate them more and cause them to redirect that agitation toward you. Once they are in a full-blown fight, they may swing at anything, including you.

When an animal fight is about to break out, divert your pet's attention. Startle it with a loud sound or spray it with water. Call it to do something it likes, such as get a treat, jump into the car, or chase its favorite toy. These techniques may also work if a fight is under way.

If you need to physically break up a fight, grab your pet's rear end and quickly pull, keeping your hands away from its head and teeth. If a small animal is involved, throw a thick towel or blanket over it to protect your hands and then move it. You can also try to place a board, pillow, or large object in between the fighters.

Expect to get bitten if you harass or pester pets, especially if they are preoccupied.

➡ One day, when my dog training assistant Melissa was at the dog park, an unruly child kept running at her dog Niko and waving his arms. "Niko barked at first, then ran after the child and nipped his shorts," says Melissa. "This is how Niko plays with dogs or people that he is nervous around but still wants to play with." Melissa called Niko and kept him away from the child. Later, the child was bitten by a larger dog after running at it and pushing a tennis ball in its face.

Gwen C. describes one incident when she was young: "I was bitten by my dog for messing with her tail while she was eating."

continued ➡

by butting me with his head. All is good and there is lots of purring until he abruptly gets sick of me and will lash out."

Milena D. learned her pet's signal: "My hedgehog bites to communicate when he's had enough petting and wants to go back in his home to eat or sleep."

PLAY IT SAFE:

While dogs should tolerate some inappropriate or unexpected human behavior, they are—well—animals. In general, avoid bothering animals in the same situations where you wouldn't want to be bothered, such as when eating, drinking, resting, or whenever the pet indicates that it doesn't want to interact. Usually, the pet will signal this by moving away. More subtle signs of uneasiness include lowering the head, pulling the ears back, looking away, becoming tense, raising the lip, and growling.

When this happens, avoid yelling or diving at, hugging, or kissing a pet or otherwise violating its personal space. Parents, in particular, should watch how their child interacts with a pet—especially one that they do not know well.

Expect to get bitten if a pet loses patience or wants to be left alone.

➡ "I have a slightly unpredictable cat," writes Leah E. "He will ask me to pet him

PLAY IT SAFE:

Recognize the signs or situations that indicate when a pet needs a break. Pets that haven't been rewarded enough for tolerating handling, especially by kids, are more likely to react sooner to bad human etiquette. Practice pairing treats with handling so that the pet learns that being handled is a positive experience. ☐☐

Sophia Yin, a veterinarian and applied animal behaviorist based in San Francisco, is the author of numerous books on animal behavior. Her Web site, www.drsophiayin.com, and Facebook page provide free articles and videos.

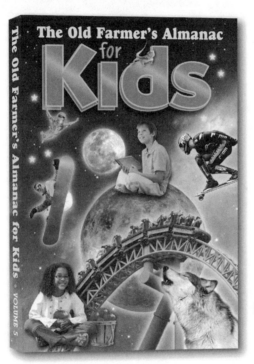

Frosts and Growing Seasons

■ Dates given are normal averages for a light freeze; local weather and topography may cause considerable variations. The possibility of frost occurring after the spring dates and before the fall dates is 50 percent. The classification of freeze temperatures is usually based on their effect on plants. **Light freeze:** 29° to 32°F—tender plants killed. **Moderate freeze:** 25° to 28°F—widely destructive to most vegetation. **Severe freeze:** 24°F and colder—heavy damage to most plants.   *–courtesy of National Climatic Data Center*

State	City	Growing Season (days)	Last Spring Frost	First Fall Frost	State	City	Growing Season (days)	Last Spring Frost	First Fall Frost
AK	Juneau	148	May 8	Oct. 4	ND	Bismarck	129	May 14	Sept. 21
AL	Mobile	273	Feb. 28	Nov. 29	NE	Blair	167	Apr. 25	Oct. 10
AR	Pine Bluff	240	Mar. 16	Nov. 12	NE	North Platte	137	May 9	Sept. 24
AZ	Phoenix	*	*	*	NH	Concord	123	May 20	Sept. 21
AZ	Tucson	332	Jan. 19	Dec. 18	NJ	Newark	217	Apr. 3	Nov. 7
CA	Eureka	322	Jan. 27	Dec. 16	NM	Carlsbad	215	Mar. 31	Nov. 2
CA	Sacramento	296	Feb. 10	Dec. 4	NM	Los Alamos	149	May 11	Oct. 8
CA	San Francisco	*	*	*	NV	Las Vegas	283	Feb. 16	Nov. 27
CO	Denver	156	Apr. 30	Oct. 4	NY	Albany	153	May 2	Oct. 3
CT	Hartford	165	Apr. 26	Oct. 9	NY	Syracuse	167	Apr. 28	Oct. 13
DE	Wilmington	202	Apr. 10	Oct. 30	OH	Akron	192	Apr. 18	Oct. 28
FL	Miami	*	*	*	OH	Cincinnati	192	Apr. 13	Oct. 23
FL	Tallahassee	239	Mar. 22	Nov. 17	OK	Lawton	222	Mar. 29	Nov. 7
GA	Athens	227	Mar. 24	Nov. 7	OK	Tulsa	224	Mar. 27	Nov. 7
GA	Savannah	268	Mar. 1	Nov. 25	OR	Pendleton	187	Apr. 13	Oct. 18
IA	Atlantic	148	May 2	Sept. 28	OR	Portland	236	Mar. 23	Nov. 15
IA	Cedar Rapids	163	Apr. 25	Oct. 6	PA	Franklin	163	May 6	Oct. 17
ID	Boise	148	May 10	Oct. 6	PA	Williamsport	167	Apr. 30	Oct. 15
IL	Chicago	186	Apr. 20	Oct. 24	RI	Kingston	147	May 8	Oct. 3
IL	Springfield	182	Apr. 13	Oct. 13	SC	Charleston	260	Mar. 9	Nov. 25
IN	Indianapolis	181	Apr. 17	Oct. 16	SC	Columbia	213	Apr. 1	Nov. 1
IN	South Bend	175	Apr. 26	Oct. 19	SD	Rapid City	140	May 9	Sept. 27
KS	Topeka	174	Apr. 19	Oct. 11	TN	Memphis	235	Mar. 22	Nov. 13
KY	Lexington	192	Apr. 15	Oct. 25	TN	Nashville	204	Apr. 6	Oct. 28
LA	Monroe	256	Mar. 3	Nov. 15	TX	Amarillo	184	Apr. 18	Oct. 20
LA	New Orleans	301	Feb. 12	Dec. 11	TX	Denton	242	Mar. 18	Nov. 16
MA	Worcester	170	Apr. 26	Oct. 14	TX	San Antonio	269	Feb. 28	Nov. 25
MD	Baltimore	200	Apr. 11	Oct. 29	UT	Cedar City	132	May 21	Oct. 1
ME	Portland	156	May 2	Oct. 6	UT	Spanish Fork	167	May 1	Oct. 16
MI	Lansing	145	May 10	Oct. 3	VA	Norfolk	247	Mar. 20	Nov. 23
MI	Marquette	154	May 11	Oct. 13	VA	Richmond	206	Apr. 6	Oct. 30
MN	Duluth	124	May 21	Sept. 23	VT	Burlington	147	May 8	Oct. 3
MN	Willmar	153	Apr. 30	Oct. 1	WA	Seattle	251	Mar. 10	Nov. 17
MO	Jefferson City	187	Apr. 13	Oct. 18	WA	Spokane	153	May 2	Oct. 3
MS	Columbia	247	Mar. 13	Nov. 16	WI	Green Bay	150	May 6	Oct. 4
MS	Vicksburg	240	Mar. 20	Nov. 16	WI	Sparta	133	May 13	Sept. 24
MT	Fort Peck	140	May 8	Sept. 26	WV	Parkersburg	183	Apr. 21	Oct. 22
MT	Helena	121	May 19	Sept. 18	WY	Casper	119	May 22	Sept. 19
NC	Fayetteville	221	Mar. 28	Nov. 5					

Frosts do not occur every year.

Planting by the Moon's Phase

According to this age-old practice,
cycles of the Moon affect plant growth.

■ Plant flowers and vegetables that bear crops above ground during the light, or waxing, of the Moon: from the day the Moon is new to the day it is full.

■ Plant flowering bulbs and vegetables that bear crops below ground during the dark, or waning, of the Moon: from the day after it is full to the day before it is new again.

The Moon Favorable columns give the best planting days based on the Moon's phases for 2014. (See the **Left-Hand Calendar Pages, 120–146,** for the exact days of the new and full Moons.) The Planting Dates columns give the safe periods for planting in areas that receive frost. See **Frosts and Growing Seasons, page 242,** for first/last frost dates and the average length of the growing season in your area.

Get local seed-sowing dates at Almanac.com/PlantingTable.

■ Aboveground crops are marked *.
■ (E) means early; (L) means late.
■ Map shades correspond to shades of date columns.

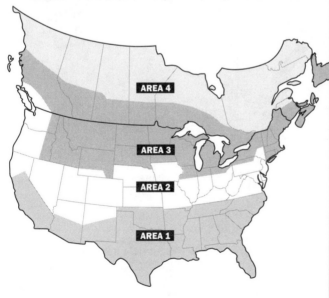

* Barley	
* Beans	(E)
	(L)
Beets	(E)
	(L)
* Broccoli plants	(E)
	(L)
* Brussels sprouts	
* Cabbage plants	
Carrots	(E)
	(L)
* Cauliflower plants	(E)
	(L)
* Celery plants	(E)
	(L)
* Collards	(E)
	(L)
* Corn, sweet	(E)
	(L)
* Cucumbers	
* Eggplant plants	
* Endive	(E)
	(L)
* Kale	(E)
	(L)
Leek plants	
* Lettuce	
* Muskmelons	
* Okra	
Onion sets	
* Parsley	
Parsnips	
* Peas	(E)
	(L)
* Pepper plants	
Potatoes	
* Pumpkins	
Radishes	(E)
	(L)
* Spinach	(E)
	(L)
* Squashes	
Sweet potatoes	
* Swiss chard	
* Tomato plants	
Turnips	(E)
	(L)
* Watermelons	
* Wheat, spring	
* Wheat, winter	

Planting Dates	Moon Favorable	Planting Dates	Moon Favorable	Planting Dates	Moon Favorable	Planting Dates	Moon Favorable
/15–3/7	3/1–7	3/15–4/7	3/15–16, 3/30–4/7	5/15–6/21	5/28–6/13	6/1–30	6/1–13, 6/27–30
/15–4/7	3/15–16, 3/30–4/7	4/15–30	4/15, 4/29–30	5/7–6/21	5/7–14, 5/28–6/13	5/30–6/15	5/30–6/13
/7–31	8/7–10, 8/25–31	7/1–21	7/1–12	6/15–7/15	6/27–7/12	—	—
/7–28	2/15–28	3/15–4/3	3/17–29	5/1–15	5/15	5/25–6/10	5/25–27
/1–30	9/9–23	8/15–31	8/15–24	7/15–8/15	7/15–25, 8/11–15	6/15–7/8	6/15–26
/15–3/15	3/1–15	3/7–31	3/7–16, 3/30–31	5/15–31	5/28–31	6/1–25	6/1–13
/7–30	9/7–8, 9/24–30	8/1–20	8/1–10	6/15–7/7	6/27–7/7	—	—
/11–3/20	2/11–14, 3/1–16	3/7–4/15	3/7–16, 3/30–4/15	5/15–31	5/28–31	6/1–25	6/1–13
/11–3/20	2/11–14, 3/1–16	3/7–4/15	3/7–16, 3/30–4/15	5/15–31	5/28–31	6/1–25	6/1–13
/15–3/7	2/15–28	3/7–31	3/17–29	5/15–31	5/15–27	5/25–6/10	5/25–27
/1–9/7	8/11–24	7/7–31	7/13–25	6/15–7/21	6/15–26, 7/13–21	6/15–7/8	6/15–26
/15–3/7	3/1–7	3/15–4/7	3/15–16, 3/30–4/7	5/15–31	5/28–31	6/1–25	6/1–13
/7–31	8/7–10, 8/25–31	7/1–8/7	7/1–12, 7/26–8/7	6/15–7/21	6/27–7/12	—	—
/15–28	—	3/7–31	3/7–16, 3/30–31	5/15–6/30	5/28–6/13, 6/27–30	6/1–30	6/1–13, 6/27–30
/15–30	9/24–30	8/15–9/7	8/25–9/7	7/15–8/15	7/26–8/10	—	—
/11–3/20	2/11–14, 3/1–16	3/7–4/7	3/7–16, 3/30–4/7	5/15–31	5/28–31	6/1–25	6/1–13
/7–30	9/7–8, 9/24–30	8/15–31	8/25–31	7/1–8/7	7/1–12, 7/26–8/7	—	—
/15–31	3/15–16, 3/30–31	4/1–17	4/1–15	5/10–6/15	5/10–14, 5/28–6/13	5/30–6/20	5/30–6/13
/7–31	8/7–10, 8/25–31	7/7–21	7/7–12	6/15–30	6/27–30	—	—
/7–4/15	3/7–16, 3/30–4/15	4/7–5/15	4/7–15, 4/29–5/14	5/7–6/20	5/7–14, 5/28–6/13	5/30–6/15	5/30–6/13
/7–4/15	3/7–16, 3/30–4/15	4/7–5/15	4/7–15, 4/29–5/14	6/1–30	6/1–13, 6/27–30	6/15–30	6/27–30
/15–3/20	3/1–16	4/7–5/15	4/7–15, 4/29–5/14	5/15–31	5/28–31	6/1–25	6/1–13
/15–9/7	8/25–9/7	7/15–8/15	7/26–8/10	6/7–30	6/7–13, 6/27–30	—	—
/11–3/20	2/11–14, 3/1–16	3/7–4/7	3/7–16, 3/30–4/7	5/15–31	5/28–31	6/1–15	6/1–13
/7–30	9/7–8, 9/24–30	8/15–31	8/25–31	7/1–8/7	7/1–12, 7/26–8/7	6/25–7/15	6/27–7/12
/15–4/15	2/15–28, 3/17–29	3/7–4/7	3/17–29	5/15–31	5/15–27	6/1–25	6/14–25
/15–3/7	3/1–7	3/1–31	3/1–16, 3/30–31	5/15–6/30	5/28–6/13, 6/27–30	6/1–30	6/1–13, 6/27–30
/15–4/7	3/15–16, 3/30–4/7	4/15–5/7	4/15, 4/29–5/7	5/15–6/30	5/28–6/13, 6/27–30	6/1–30	6/1–13, 6/27–30
/15–6/1	4/15, 4/29–5/14, 5/28–6/1	5/25–6/15	5/28–6/13	6/15–7/10	6/27–7/10	6/25–7/7	6/27–7/7
/1–28	2/15–28	3/1–31	3/17–29	5/15–6/7	5/15–27	6/1–25	6/14–25
/20–3/15	3/1–15	3/1–31	3/1–16, 3/30–31	5/15–31	5/28–31	6/1–15	6/1–13
/15–2/4	1/16–29	3/7–31	3/17–29	4/1–30	4/16–28	5/10–31	5/15–27
/15–2/7	1/15, 1/30–2/7	3/7–31	3/7–16, 3/30–31	4/15–5/7	4/15, 4/29–5/7	5/15–31	5/28–31
/15–30	9/24–30	8/7–31	8/7–10, 8/25–31	7/15–31	7/26–31	7/10–25	7/10–12
/1–20	3/1–16	4/1–30	4/1–15, 4/29–30	5/15–6/30	5/28–6/13, 6/27–30	6/1–30	6/1–13, 6/27–30
/10–28	2/15–28	4/1–30	4/16–28	5/1–31	5/15–27	6/1–25	6/14–25
/7–20	3/7–16	4/23–5/15	4/29–5/14	5/15–31	5/28–31	6/1–30	6/1–13, 6/27–30
/21–3/1	1/21–29, 2/15–28	3/7–31	3/17–29	4/15–30	4/16–28	5/15–6/5	5/15–27
9/1–21	10/9–21	9/7–30	9/9–23	8/15–31	8/15–24	7/10–31	7/13–25
/7–3/15	2/7–14, 3/1–15	3/15–4/20	3/15–16, 3/30–4/15	5/15–31	5/28–31	6/1–25	6/1–13
0/1–21	10/1–8	8/1–9/15	8/1–10, 8/25–9/8	7/17–9/7	7/26–8/10, 8/25–9/7	7/20–8/5	7/26–8/5
/15–4/15	3/15–16, 3/30–4/15	4/15–30	4/15, 4/29–30	5/15–6/15	5/28–6/13	6/1–30	6/1–13, 6/27–30
/23–4/6	3/23–29	4/21–5/9	4/21–28	5/15–6/15	5/15–27, 6/14–15	6/1–30	6/14–26
/7–3/15	2/7–14, 3/1–15	3/15–4/15	3/15–16, 3/30–4/15	5/1–31	5/1–14, 5/28–31	5/15–31	5/28–31
/7–20	3/7–16	4/7–30	4/7–15, 4/29–30	5/15–31	5/28–31	6/1–15	6/1–13
/20–2/15	1/20–29, 2/15	3/15–31	3/17–29	4/7–30	4/16–28	5/10–31	5/15–27
/1–10/15	9/9–23, 10/9–15	8/1–20	8/11–20	7/1–8/15	7/13–25, 8/11–15	—	—
/15–4/7	3/15–16, 3/30–4/7	4/15–5/7	4/15, 4/29–5/7	5/15–6/30	5/28–6/13, 6/27–30	6/1–30	6/1–13, 6/27–30
/15–28	—	3/1–20	3/1–16	4/7–30	4/7–15, 4/29–30	5/15–6/10	5/28–6/10
0/15–12/7	10/23–11/6, 11/22–12/6	9/15–10/20	9/24–10/8	8/11–9/15	8/25–9/8	8/5–30	8/5–10, 8/25–30

Secrets of the Zodiac

The Man of the Signs

Ancient astrologers believed that each astrological sign influenced a specific part of the body. The first sign of the zodiac—Aries—was attributed to the head, with the rest of the signs moving down the body, ending with Pisces at the feet.

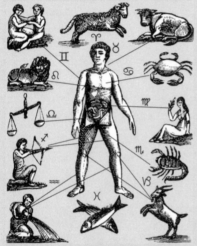

♈ Aries, head . . . . . . **ARI**   *Mar. 21–Apr. 20*
♉ Taurus, neck . . . . . **TAU**   *Apr. 21–May 20*
♊ Gemini, arms . . . **GEM**   *May 21–June 20*
♋ Cancer, breast . . . **CAN**   *June 21–July 22*
♌ Leo, heart . . . . **LEO**   *July 23–Aug. 22*
♍ Virgo, belly . . . . . **VIR**   *Aug. 23–Sept. 22*
♎ Libra, reins . . . . . . **LIB**   *Sept. 23–Oct. 22*
♏ Scorpio, secrets . . **SCO**   *Oct. 23–Nov. 22*
♐ Sagittarius, thighs .**SAG**   *Nov. 23–Dec. 21*
♑ Capricorn, knees .**CAP**   *Dec. 22–Jan. 19*
♒ Aquarius, legs . . **AQU**   *Jan. 20–Feb. 19*
♓ Pisces, feet . . . . . . **PSC**   *Feb. 20–Mar. 20*

Astrology vs. Astronomy

■ **Astrology** is a tool we use to plan events according to the placements of the Sun, the Moon, and the planets in the 12 signs of the zodiac. In astrology, the planetary movements do not cause events; rather, they explain the path, or "flow," that events tend to follow. **Astronomy** is the study of the actual placement of the known planets and constellations. *(The placement of the planets in the signs of the zodiac is not the same astrologically and astronomically.)* The Moon's astrological place is given on **page 247**; its astronomical place is given in the **Left-Hand Calendar Pages, 120–146.**

The dates in the **Best Days** table, **page 248**, are based on the astrological passage of the Moon. However, consider all indicators before making any major decisions.

When Mercury Is Retrograde

■ Sometimes the other planets appear to be traveling backward through the zodiac; this is an illusion. We call this illusion *retrograde motion.*

Mercury's retrograde periods can cause our plans to go awry. However, this is an excellent time to reflect on the past. Intuition is high during these periods, and coincidences can be extraordinary.

When Mercury is retrograde, remain flexible, allow extra time for travel, and avoid signing contracts. Review projects and plans at these times, but wait until Mercury is direct again to make any final decisions.

In 2014, Mercury will be retrograde during February 6–28, June 7–July 2, and October 4–25.

–Celeste Longacre

Gardening by the Moon's Sign

Use the chart on the next page to find the best dates for the following garden tasks:

■ **Plant, transplant, and graft:** Cancer, Scorpio, or Pisces.

■ **Harvest:** Aries, Leo, Sagittarius, Gemini, or Aquarius.

■ **Build/fix fences or garden beds:** Capricorn.

■ **Control insect pests, plow, and weed:** Aries, Gemini, Leo, Sagittarius, or Aquarius.

■ **Prune:** Aries, Leo, or Sagittarius. During a waxing Moon, pruning encourages growth; during a waning Moon, it discourages growth.

Setting Eggs by the Moon's Sign

■ Chicks take about 21 days to hatch. Those born under a waxing Moon, in the fruitful signs of Cancer, Scorpio, and Pisces, are healthier and mature faster. To ensure that chicks are born during these times, determine the best days to "set eggs" (to place eggs in an incubator or under a hen). To calculate, find the three fruitful birth signs on the chart below. Use the **Left-Hand Calendar Pages, 120–146,** to find the dates of the new and full Moons.

Using only the fruitful dates between the new and full Moons, count back 21 days to find the best days to set eggs.

E X A M P L E :

The Moon is new on May 28 and full on June 13. Between these dates, on June 9 and 10, the Moon is in the sign of Scorpio. To have chicks born on June 9, count back 21 days; set eggs on May 19.

The Moon's Astrological Place, 2013–14

	Nov.	Dec.	Jan.	Feb.	Mar.	Apr.	May	June	July	Aug.	Sept.	Oct.	Nov.	Dec.
1	LIB	SCO	CAP	PSC	PSC	TAU	GEM	CAN	LEO	LIB	SAG	CAP	PSC	ARI
2	LIB	SAG	CAP	PSC	ARI	TAU	GEM	LEO	VIR	LIB	SAG	CAP	PSC	ARI
3	SCO	SAG	AQU	ARI	ARI	GEM	CAN	LEO	VIR	SCO	SAG	AQU	PSC	TAU
4	SCO	CAP	AQU	ARI	ARI	GEM	CAN	VIR	LIB	SCO	CAP	AQU	ARI	TAU
5	SAG	CAP	PSC	TAU	TAU	GEM	LEO	VIR	LIB	SAG	CAP	PSC	ARI	GEM
6	SAG	AQU	PSC	TAU	TAU	CAN	LEO	VIR	LIB	SAG	AQU	PSC	TAU	GEM
7	CAP	AQU	ARI	TAU	GEM	CAN	LEO	LIB	SCO	CAP	AQU	ARI	TAU	CAN
8	CAP	PSC	ARI	GEM	GEM	LEO	VIR	LIB	SCO	CAP	PSC	ARI	GEM	CAN
9	AQU	PSC	TAU	GEM	CAN	LEO	VIR	SCO	SAG	AQU	PSC	TAU	GEM	CAN
10	AQU	ARI	TAU	CAN	CAN	LEO	LIB	SCO	SAG	AQU	ARI	TAU	CAN	LEO
11	PSC	ARI	GEM	CAN	CAN	VIR	LIB	SAG	CAP	PSC	ARI	GEM	CAN	LEO
12	PSC	ARI	GEM	CAN	LEO	VIR	LIB	SAG	CAP	PSC	TAU	GEM	CAN	VIR
13	ARI	TAU	GEM	LEO	LEO	LIB	SCO	SAG	AQU	ARI	TAU	GEM	LEO	VIR
14	ARI	TAU	CAN	LEO	VIR	LIB	SCO	CAP	AQU	ARI	GEM	CAN	LEO	VIR
15	TAU	GEM	CAN	VIR	VIR	SCO	SAG	CAP	PSC	TAU	GEM	CAN	VIR	LIB
16	TAU	GEM	LEO	VIR	VIR	SCO	SAG	AQU	PSC	TAU	CAN	LEO	VIR	LIB
17	TAU	GEM	LEO	VIR	LIB	SCO	CAP	AQU	ARI	TAU	CAN	LEO	VIR	SCO
18	GEM	CAN	LEO	LIB	LIB	SAG	CAP	PSC	ARI	GEM	CAN	LEO	LIB	SCO
19	GEM	CAN	VIR	LIB	SCO	SAG	AQU	PSC	TAU	GEM	LEO	VIR	LIB	SCO
20	CAN	LEO	VIR	SCO	SCO	CAP	AQU	ARI	TAU	CAN	LEO	VIR	SCO	SAG
21	CAN	LEO	LIB	SCO	SAG	CAP	PSC	ARI	GEM	CAN	VIR	LIB	SCO	SAG
22	CAN	LEO	LIB	SAG	SAG	AQU	PSC	TAU	GEM	CAN	VIR	LIB	SAG	CAP
23	LEO	VIR	LIB	SAG	SAG	AQU	ARI	TAU	GEM	LEO	VIR	LIB	SAG	CAP
24	LEO	VIR	SCO	CAP	CAP	PSC	ARI	GEM	CAN	LEO	LIB	SCO	CAP	AQU
25	VIR	LIB	SCO	CAP	CAP	PSC	ARI	GEM	CAN	VIR	LIB	SCO	CAP	AQU
26	VIR	LIB	SAG	AQU	AQU	ARI	TAU	GEM	LEO	VIR	SCO	SAG	CAP	PSC
27	VIR	SCO	SAG	AQU	AQU	ARI	TAU	CAN	LEO	VIR	SCO	SAG	AQU	PSC
28	LIB	SCO	CAP	PSC	PSC	TAU	GEM	CAN	LEO	LIB	SCO	CAP	AQU	ARI
29	LIB	SCO	CAP	—	PSC	TAU	GEM	LEO	VIR	LIB	SAG	CAP	PSC	ARI
30	SCO	SAG	AQU	—	ARI	TAU	CAN	LEO	VIR	SCO	SAG	AQU	PSC	TAU
31	—	SAG	AQU	—	ARI	—	CAN	—	LIB	SCO	—	AQU	—	TAU

Best Days for 2014

This chart is based on the Moon's sign and shows the best days each month for certain activities.

—Celeste Longacre

	JAN.	FEB.	MAR.	APR.	MAY	JUNE	JULY	AUG.	SEPT.	OCT.	NOV.	DEC.
Quit smoking	19, 24	16, 21	20, 28	25	22, 26	18, 23	15, 20	12, 16	12, 22	10, 19	15, 16	13, 18
Begin diet to lose weight	19, 24	16, 21	20, 28	25	22, 26	18, 23	15, 20	12, 16	12, 22	10, 19	15, 16	13, 18
Begin diet to gain weight	5, 9, 14	1, 6	5, 15	2, 11	4, 9	5, 10	2, 7	3, 30	8, 27	6, 24	2, 29	4, 31
Cut hair to encourage growth	4, 5, 9, 10	1, 2, 5, 6	1, 5, 6	1, 2, 13, 14	11, 12	7, 8	4, 5, 6	1, 2, 28, 29	8, 25	5, 6	1, 2, 29	3, 4, 30, 31
Cut hair to discourage growth	22, 23	17, 18	17, 18	24, 25	21, 22	17, 18, 19	15, 16	11, 12	12, 13	21, 22	17, 18	15, 16
Have dental care	19, 20	15, 16	15, 16	11, 12	8, 9	4, 5, 6	2, 3, 29, 30	25, 26, 27	21, 22, 23	19, 20	15, 16	13, 14
Start projects	2, 3	1, 2	31	30	29, 30	28, 29	27, 28	26, 27	25, 26	24, 25	23, 24	23, 24
End projects	29, 30	27, 28	28, 29	27, 28	26, 27	25, 26	24, 25	23, 24	22, 23	21, 22	20, 21	20, 21
Go camping	26, 27	22, 23	21, 22	18, 19	15, 16	11, 12	9, 10	5, 6	1, 2, 3, 29, 30	26, 27	22, 23	20, 21
Plant aboveground crops	5, 6, 14, 15	1, 2, 10, 11	1, 10, 11	6, 7	3, 4, 13	1, 9, 10	7, 8	3, 4, 30, 31	8, 26, 27, 28	5, 6, 24, 25	1, 2, 29, 30	26, 27
Plant belowground crops	24, 25	20, 21	19, 20, 28, 29	16, 17, 24, 25	21, 22	18, 19	15, 16, 24, 25	20, 21	17, 18	14, 15	20, 21	18, 19
Destroy pests and weeds	7, 8	3, 4	3, 4, 30, 31	26, 27	24, 25	20, 21	17, 18	13, 14	10, 11	7, 8	4, 5	1, 2, 28, 29
Graft or pollinate	14, 15	10, 11, 12	10, 11	6, 7	3, 4, 31	1, 27, 28	24, 25	20, 21, 22	16, 17, 18	14, 15	10, 11	8, 9
Prune to encourage growth	7, 8	3, 4	2, 3	8, 9, 10	6, 7	2, 3, 29, 30	9, 10	5, 6	2, 3, 30, 31	7, 8, 26, 27	4, 5, 23	1, 2, 28, 29
Prune to discourage growth	26, 27	22, 23	21, 22, 23	18, 19	23, 24, 25	20, 21	17, 18	23, 24	19, 20	16, 17, 18	13, 14	20, 21
Harvest aboveground crops	9, 10	5, 6	5, 6	1, 2, 11, 12	8, 9	5, 6	2, 3	7, 8	4, 5	1, 2, 29	24, 25, 26	3, 4, 30, 31
Harvest belowground crops	19, 20	16, 24, 25	24, 25	20, 21	26, 27	22, 23	19, 20	15, 16, 17	12, 13	19, 20	15, 16, 17	13, 14
Can, pickle, or make sauerkraut	24, 25	20, 21	19, 20	16, 17, 24, 25	21, 22	18, 19	15, 16	20, 21	16, 17, 18	14, 15	10, 11	18, 19
Cut hay	7, 8	3, 4	3, 4, 30, 31	26, 27	24, 25	20, 21	17, 18	13, 14	10, 11	7, 8	4, 5	1, 2, 28, 29
Begin logging	1, 28, 29	24, 25	24, 25	20, 21	17, 18	14, 15	11, 12	7, 8	4, 5	1, 2, 28, 29	24, 25	22, 23
Set posts or pour concrete	1, 28, 29	24, 25	24, 25	20, 21	17, 18	14, 15	11, 12	7, 8	4, 5	1, 2, 28, 29	24, 25	22, 23
Breed animals	24, 25	20, 21	19, 20	16, 17	13, 14	9, 10	7, 8	3, 4, 30, 31	26, 27, 28	24, 25	20, 21	18, 19
Wean animals or children	19, 24	16, 21	20, 28	25	22, 26	18, 23	15, 20	12, 16	12, 22	10, 19	15, 16	13, 18
Castrate animals	3, 4, 30, 31	26, 27	26, 27	22, 23	19, 20	16, 17	13, 14	9, 10	6, 7	3, 4, 30, 31	27, 28	24, 25
Slaughter livestock	24, 25	20, 21	19, 20	16, 17	13, 14	9, 10	7, 8	3, 4, 30, 31	26, 27, 28	24, 25	20, 21	18, 19

Plants That Repel Pests

■ Some plants repel insects. By planting specific herbs and flowering plants among your vegetables and berries, you can shoo away unwanted pests. This avoids the need for insecticides and/or the time that would have been spent picking off bugs, while adding beauty to the bed and edibles to your harvest.

PLANT THESE PLANTS ...	TO REPEL ...
Basil	flies, hornworms, mosquitoes
Borage	tomato worms
Catnip	aphids, flea beetles
Dead nettle	potato bugs
Flax	potato bugs
Garlic	Japanese beetles
Horseradish	potato bugs
Hyssop	cabbage moths
Leek	carrot flies
Marigold	Mexican bean beetles, nematodes
Mint	cabbage moths, mosquitoes
Nasturtium	squash bugs, striped pumpkin beetles
Rosemary	cabbage moths, carrot flies, Mexican bean beetles
Rue	Japanese beetles
Sage	cabbage moths, carrot flies
Summer savory	bean beetles
Tansy	ants, Japanese beetles, squash bugs, striped cucumber beetles
Thyme	cabbage worms

Plants That Attract Insects

■ A variety of plants attract beneficial insects that dine on garden pests. Carrots, dill, parsley, and parsnip, for instance, attract praying mantises, ladybugs, and spiders.

■ Trap crops grown in or around garden beds lure insects and other pests away from plants that you want to protect. Once these trap plants become infested, destroy the pests or pull up the plants and discard them. Here are a few trap crops and the pests that find them irresistible:

Chervil	slugs	**Mustard**	aphids, flea hoppers, cabbage webworms
Collard	diamondback moths		
Dill	tomato hornworms	**Nasturtium**	aphids, flea beetles
Lovage	tomato hornworms	**Radish**	flea beetles, root maggots
Marigold	slugs, spider mites, thrips	**Thyme**	slugs

Tide Corrections

Many factors affect the times and heights of the tides: the shoreline, the time of the Moon's southing (crossing the meridian), and the Moon's phase. The High Tide column on the **Left-Hand Calendar Pages, 120–146,** lists the times of high tide at Commonwealth Pier in Boston Harbor. The heights of some of these tides, reckoned from Mean Lower Low Water, are given on the **Right-Hand Calendar Pages, 121–147.** Use the table below to calculate the approximate times and heights of high tide at the places shown. Apply the time difference to the times of high tide at Boston and the height difference to the heights at Boston. A tide calculator can be found at **Almanac.com/Tides.**

E X A M P L E :

The conversion of the times and heights of the tides at Boston to those at Cape Fear, North Carolina, is given below:

High tide at Boston	11:45 A.M.
Correction for Cape Fear	– 3 55
High tide at Cape Fear	7:50 A.M.
Tide height at Boston	11.6 ft.
Correction for Cape Fear	– 5.0 ft.
Tide height at Cape Fear	6.6 ft.

Estimations derived from this table are *not* meant to be used for navigation. *The Old Farmer's Almanac* accepts no responsibility for errors or any consequences ensuing from the use of this table.

Tidal Site Difference:	Time (h. m.)	Height (ft.)
Canada		
Alberton, PE	*–5 45	–7.5
Charlottetown, PE	*–0 45	–3.5
Halifax, NS.	–3 23	–4.5
North Sydney, NS	–3 15	–6.5
Saint John, NB	+0 30	+15.0
St. John's, NL	–4 00	–6.5
Yarmouth, NS	–0 40	+3.0
Maine		
Bar Harbor	–0 34	+0.9
Belfast.	–0 20	+0.4
Boothbay Harbor.	–0 18	–0.8
Chebeague Island	–0 16	–0.6
Eastport.	–0 28	+8.4
Kennebunkport	+0 04	–1.0
Machias.	–0 28	+2.8
Monhegan Island.	–0 25	–0.8
Old Orchard	0 00	–0.8
Portland.	–0 12	–0.6
Rockland.	–0 28	+0.1
Stonington.	–0 30	+0.1
York	–0 09	–1.0
New Hampshire		
Hampton	+0 02	–1.3
Portsmouth	+0 11	–1.5
Rye Beach.	–0 09	–0.9
Massachusetts		
Annisquam	–0 02	–1.1
Beverly Farms.	0 00	–0.5
Boston.	0 00	0.0

Tidal Site Difference:	Time (h. m.)	Height (ft.)
Cape Cod Canal		
East Entrance	–0 01	–0.8
West Entrance.	–2 16	–5.9
Chatham Outer Coast . .	+0 30	–2.8
Inside	+1 54	**0.4
Cohasset	+0 02	–0.07
Cotuit Highlands	+1 15	**0.3
Dennis Port	+1 01	**0.4
Duxbury–Gurnet Point. . .	+0 02	–0.3
Fall River.	–3 03	–5.0
Gloucester	–0 03	–0.8
Hingham	+0 07	0.0
Hull.	+0 03	–0.2
Hyannis Port	+1 01	**0.3
Magnolia–Manchester . .	–0 02	–0.7
Marblehead	–0 02	–0.4
Marion.	–3 22	–5.4
Monument Beach	–3 08	–5.4
Nahant.	–0 01	–0.5
Nantasket.	+0 04	–0.1
Nantucket	+0 56	**0.3
Nauset Beach.	+0 30	**0.6
New Bedford	–3 24	–5.7
Newburyport	+0 19	–1.8
Oak Bluffs	+0 30	**0.2
Onset–R.R. Bridge	–2 16	–5.9
Plymouth.	+0 05	0.0
Provincetown.	+0 14	–0.4
Revere Beach	–0 01	–0.3
Rockport	–0 08	–1.0
Salem.	0 00	–0.5
Scituate	–0 05	–0.7

Tidal Site	Difference:	Time (h. m.)	Height (ft.)
Wareham		−3 09	−5.3
Wellfleet		+0 12	+0.5
West Falmouth.		−3 10	−5.4
Westport Harbor		−3 22	−6.4
Woods Hole			
Little Harbor		−2 50	**0.2
Oceanographic			
Institute		−3 07	**0.2
Rhode Island			
Bristol		−3 24	−5.3
Narragansett Pier		−3 42	−6.2
Newport.		−3 34	−5.9
Point Judith		−3 41	−6.3
Providence.		−3 20	−4.8
Sakonnet		−3 44	−5.6
Watch Hill		−2 50	−6.8
Connecticut			
Bridgeport		+0 01	−2.6
Madison.		−0 22	−2.3
New Haven		−0 11	−3.2
New London		−1 54	−6.7
Norwalk.		+0 01	−2.2
Old Lyme			
Highway Bridge		−0 30	−6.2
Stamford		+0 01	−2.2
Stonington		−2 27	−6.6
New York			
Coney Island		−3 33	−4.9
Fire Island Light		−2 43	**0.1
Long Beach		−3 11	−5.7
Montauk Harbor		−2 19	−7.4
New York City–Battery . .		−2 43	−5.0
Oyster Bay.		+0 04	−1.8
Port Chester		−0 09	−2.2
Port Washington		−0 01	−2.1
Sag Harbor.		−0 55	−6.8
Southampton			
Shinnecock Inlet		−4 20	**0.2
Willets Point		0 00	−2.3
New Jersey			
Asbury Park.		−4 04	−5.3
Atlantic City		−3 56	−5.5
Bay Head–Sea Girt		−4 04	−5.3
Beach Haven		−1 43	**0.24
Cape May		−3 28	−5.3
Ocean City		−3 06	−5.9
Sandy Hook		−3 30	−5.0
Seaside Park		−4 03	−5.4
Pennsylvania			
Philadelphia.		+2 40	−3.5
Delaware			
Cape Henlopen		−2 48	−5.3

Tidal Site	Difference:	Time (h. m.)	Height (ft.)
Rehoboth Beach.		−3 37	−5.7
Wilmington		+1 56	−3.8
Maryland			
Annapolis		+6 23	−8.5
Baltimore.		+7 59	−8.3
Cambridge.		+5 05	−7.8
Havre de Grace		+11 21	−7.7
Point No Point		+2 28	−8.1
Prince Frederick			
Plum Point		+4 25	−8.5
Virginia			
Cape Charles		−2 20	−7.0
Hampton Roads		−2 02	−6.9
Norfolk		−2 06	−6.6
Virginia Beach.		−4 00	−6.0
Yorktown.		−2 13	−7.0
North Carolina			
Cape Fear.		−3 55	−5.0
Cape Lookout		−4 28	−5.7
Currituck		−4 10	−5.8
Hatteras			
Inlet.		−4 03	−7.4
Kitty Hawk		−4 14	−6.2
Ocean		−4 26	−6.0
South Carolina			
Charleston		−3 22	−4.3
Georgetown		−1 48	**0.36
Hilton Head		−3 22	−2.9
Myrtle Beach		−3 49	−4.4
St. Helena			
Harbor Entrance		−3 15	−3.4
Georgia			
Jekyll Island.		−3 46	−2.9
St. Simon's Island		−2 50	−2.9
Savannah Beach			
River Entrance		−3 14	−5.5
Tybee Light.		−3 22	−2.7
Florida			
Cape Canaveral		−3 59	−6.0
Daytona Beach.		−3 28	−5.3
Fort Lauderdale		−2 50	−7.2
Fort Pierce Inlet.		−3 32	−6.9
Jacksonville			
Railroad Bridge.		−6 55	**0.1
Miami Harbor Entrance . .		−3 18	−7.0
St. Augustine		−2 55	−4.9

Varies widely; accurate only to within 1½ hours. Consult local tide tables for precise times and heights.

**Where the difference in the Height column is so marked, the height at Boston should be multiplied by this ratio.*

Time Corrections

■ Astronomical data for Boston is given on **pages 104, 108–109,** and **120–146.** Use the Key Letter shown to the right of each time on those pages with this table to find the number of minutes that you must add to or subtract from Boston time to get the correct time for your city. (Because of complex calculations for different locales, times are approximate.) For more information on the use of Key Letters and this table, **see How to Use This Almanac, page 116.**

Get times simply and specifically: Download astronomical times calculated for your zip code and presented like a Left-Hand Calendar Page at **Almanac.com/Access.**

TIME ZONES: Codes represent *standard time.* Atlantic is −1, Eastern is 0, Central is 1, Mountain is 2, Pacific is 3, Alaska is 4, and Hawaii-Aleutian is 5.

State	City	North Latitude °	North Latitude '	West Longitude °	West Longitude '	Time Zone Code	A (min.)	B (min.)	C (min.)	D (min.)	E (min.)
AK	Anchorage	61	10	149	59	4	−46	+27	+71	+122	+171
AK	Cordova	60	33	145	45	4	−55	+13	+55	+103	+149
AK	Fairbanks	64	48	147	51	4	−127	+2	+61	+131	+205
AK	Juneau	58	18	134	25	4	−76	−23	+10	+49	+86
AK	Ketchikan	55	21	131	39	4	−62	−25	0	+29	+56
AK	Kodiak	57	47	152	24	4	0	+49	+82	+120	+154
AL	Birmingham	33	31	86	49	1	+30	+15	+3	−10	−20
AL	Decatur	34	36	86	59	1	+27	+14	+4	−7	−17
AL	Mobile	30	42	88	3	1	+42	+23	+8	−8	−22
AL	Montgomery	32	23	86	19	1	+31	+14	+1	−13	−25
AR	Fort Smith	35	23	94	25	1	+55	+43	+33	+22	+14
AR	Little Rock	34	45	92	17	1	+48	+35	+25	+13	+4
AR	Texarkana	33	26	94	3	1	+59	+44	+32	+18	+8
AZ	Flagstaff	35	12	111	39	2	+64	+52	+42	+31	+22
AZ	Phoenix	33	27	112	4	2	+71	+56	+44	+30	+20
AZ	Tucson	32	13	110	58	2	+70	+53	+40	+24	+12
AZ	Yuma	32	43	114	37	2	+83	+67	+54	+40	+28
CA	Bakersfield	35	23	119	1	3	+33	+21	+12	+1	−7
CA	Barstow	34	54	117	1	3	+27	+14	+4	−7	−16
CA	Fresno	36	44	119	47	3	+32	+22	+15	+6	0
CA	Los Angeles–Pasadena–Santa Monica	34	3	118	14	3	+34	+20	+9	−3	−13
CA	Palm Springs	33	49	116	32	3	+28	+13	+1	−12	−22
CA	Redding	40	35	122	24	3	+31	+27	+25	+22	+19
CA	Sacramento	38	35	121	30	3	+34	+27	+21	+15	+10
CA	San Diego	32	43	117	9	3	+33	+17	+4	−9	−21
CA	San Francisco–Oakland–San Jose	37	47	122	25	3	+40	+31	+25	+18	+12
CO	Craig	40	31	107	33	2	+32	+28	+25	+22	+20
CO	Denver–Boulder	39	44	104	59	2	+24	+19	+15	+11	+7
CO	Grand Junction	39	4	108	33	2	+40	+34	+29	+24	+20
CO	Pueblo	38	16	104	37	2	+27	+20	+14	+7	+2
CO	Trinidad	37	10	104	31	2	+30	+21	+13	+5	0
CT	Bridgeport	41	11	73	11	0	+12	+10	+8	+6	+4
CT	Hartford–New Britain	41	46	72	41	0	+8	+7	+6	+5	+4
CT	New Haven	41	18	72	56	0	+11	+8	+7	+5	+4
CT	New London	41	22	72	6	0	+7	+5	+4	+2	+1
CT	Norwalk–Stamford	41	7	73	22	0	+13	+10	+9	+7	+5
CT	Waterbury–Meriden	41	33	73	3	0	+10	+9	+7	+6	+5
DC	Washington	38	54	77	1	0	+35	+28	+23	+18	+13
DE	Wilmington	39	45	75	33	0	+26	+21	+18	+13	+10

State	City	North Latitude °	North Latitude '	West Longitude °	West Longitude '	Time Zone Code	Key Letters A (min.)	B (min.)	C (min.)	D (min.)	E (min.)
FL	Fort Myers	26	38	81	52	0	+87	+63	+44	+21	+4
FL	Jacksonville	30	20	81	40	0	+77	+58	+43	+25	+11
FL	Miami	25	47	80	12	0	+88	+57	+37	+14	−3
FL	Orlando	28	32	81	22	0	+80	+59	+42	+22	+6
FL	Pensacola	30	25	87	13	1	+39	+20	+5	−12	−26
FL	St. Petersburg	27	46	82	39	0	+87	+65	+47	+26	+10
FL	Tallahassee	30	27	84	17	0	+87	+68	+53	+35	+22
FL	Tampa	27	57	82	27	0	+86	+64	+46	+25	+9
FL	West Palm Beach	26	43	80	3	0	+79	+55	+36	+14	−2
GA	Atlanta	33	45	84	24	0	+79	+65	+53	+40	+30
GA	Augusta	33	28	81	58	0	+70	+55	+44	+30	+19
GA	Macon	32	50	83	38	0	+79	+63	+50	+36	+24
GA	Savannah	32	5	81	6	0	+70	+54	+40	+25	+13
HI	Hilo	19	44	155	5	5	+94	+62	+37	+7	−15
HI	Honolulu	21	18	157	52	5	+102	+72	+48	+19	−1
HI	Lanai City	20	50	156	55	5	+99	+69	+44	+15	−6
HI	Lihue	21	59	159	23	5	+107	+77	+54	+26	+5
IA	Davenport	41	32	90	35	1	+20	+19	+17	+16	+15
IA	Des Moines	41	35	93	37	1	+32	+31	+30	+28	+27
IA	Dubuque	42	30	90	41	1	+17	+18	+18	+18	+18
IA	Waterloo	42	30	92	20	1	+24	+24	+24	+25	+25
ID	Boise	43	37	116	12	2	+55	+58	+60	+62	+64
ID	Lewiston	46	25	117	1	3	−12	−3	+2	+10	+17
ID	Pocatello	42	52	112	27	2	+43	+44	+45	+46	+46
IL	Cairo	37	0	89	11	1	+29	+20	+12	+4	−2
IL	Chicago–Oak Park	41	52	87	38	1	+7	+6	+6	+5	+4
IL	Danville	40	8	87	37	1	+13	+9	+6	+2	0
IL	Decatur	39	51	88	57	1	+19	+15	+11	+7	+4
IL	Peoria	40	42	89	36	1	+19	+16	+14	+11	+9
IL	Springfield	39	48	89	39	1	+22	+18	+14	+10	+6
IN	Fort Wayne	41	4	85	9	0	+60	+58	+56	+54	+52
IN	Gary	41	36	87	20	1	+7	+6	+4	+3	+2
IN	Indianapolis	39	46	86	10	0	+69	+64	+60	+56	+52
IN	Muncie	40	12	85	23	0	+64	+60	+57	+53	+50
IN	South Bend	41	41	86	15	0	+62	+61	+60	+59	+58
IN	Terre Haute	39	28	87	24	0	+74	+69	+65	+60	+56
KS	Fort Scott	37	50	94	42	1	+49	+41	+34	+27	+21
KS	Liberal	37	3	100	55	1	+76	+66	+59	+51	+44
KS	Oakley	39	8	100	51	1	+69	+63	+59	+53	+49
KS	Salina	38	50	97	37	1	+57	+51	+46	+40	+35
KS	Topeka	39	3	95	40	1	+49	+43	+38	+32	+28
KS	Wichita	37	42	97	20	1	+60	+51	+45	+37	+31
KY	Lexington–Frankfort	38	3	84	30	0	+67	+59	+53	+46	+41
KY	Louisville	38	15	85	46	0	+72	+64	+58	+52	+46
LA	Alexandria	31	18	92	27	1	+58	+40	+26	+9	−3
LA	Baton Rouge	30	27	91	11	1	+55	+36	+21	+3	−10
LA	Lake Charles	30	14	93	13	1	+64	+44	+29	+11	−2
LA	Monroe	32	30	92	7	1	+53	+37	+24	+9	−1
LA	New Orleans	29	57	90	4	1	+52	+32	+16	−1	−15
LA	Shreveport	32	31	93	45	1	+60	+44	+31	+16	+4
MA	Brockton	42	5	71	1	0	0	0	0	0	−1
MA	Fall River–New Bedford	41	42	71	9	0	+2	+1	0	0	−1
MA	Lawrence–Lowell	42	42	71	10	0	0	0	0	0	+1
MA	Pittsfield	42	27	73	15	0	+8	+8	+8	+8	+8
MA	Springfield–Holyoke	42	6	72	36	0	+6	+6	+6	+5	+5
MA	Worcester	42	16	71	48	0	+3	+2	+2	+2	+2

(continued)

Time Corrections

State	City	North Latitude °	'	West Longitude °	'	Time Zone Code	A (min.)	B (min.)	C (min.)	D (min.)	E (min.)
MD	Baltimore	39	17	76	37	0	+32	+26	+22	+17	+13
MD	Hagerstown	39	39	77	43	0	+35	+30	+26	+22	+18
MD	Salisbury	38	22	75	36	0	+31	+23	+18	+11	+6
ME	Augusta	44	19	69	46	0	−12	−8	−5	−1	0
ME	Bangor	44	48	68	46	0	−18	−13	−9	−5	−1
ME	Eastport	44	54	67	0	0	−26	−20	−16	−11	−8
ME	Ellsworth	44	33	68	25	0	−18	−14	−10	−6	−3
ME	Portland	43	40	70	15	0	−8	−5	−3	−1	0
ME	Presque Isle	46	41	68	1	0	−29	−19	−12	−4	+2
MI	Cheboygan	45	39	84	29	0	+40	+47	+53	+59	+64
MI	Detroit–Dearborn	42	20	83	3	0	+47	+47	+47	+47	+47
MI	Flint	43	1	83	41	0	+47	+49	+50	+51	+52
MI	Ironwood	46	27	90	9	1	0	+9	+15	+23	+29
MI	Jackson	42	15	84	24	0	+53	+53	+53	+52	+52
MI	Kalamazoo	42	17	85	35	0	+58	+57	+57	+57	+57
MI	Lansing	42	44	84	33	0	+52	+53	+53	+54	+54
MI	St. Joseph	42	5	86	26	0	+61	+61	+60	+60	+59
MI	Traverse City	44	46	85	38	0	+49	+54	+57	+62	+65
MN	Albert Lea	43	39	93	22	1	+24	+26	+28	+31	+33
MN	Bemidji	47	28	94	53	1	+14	+26	+34	+44	+52
MN	Duluth	46	47	92	6	1	+6	+16	+23	+31	+38
MN	Minneapolis–St. Paul	44	59	93	16	1	+18	+24	+28	+33	+37
MN	Ortonville	45	19	96	27	1	+30	+36	+40	+46	+51
MO	Jefferson City	38	34	92	10	1	+36	+29	+24	+18	+13
MO	Joplin	37	6	94	30	1	+50	+41	+33	+25	+18
MO	Kansas City	39	1	94	20	1	+44	+37	+33	+27	+23
MO	Poplar Bluff	36	46	90	24	1	+35	+25	+17	+8	+1
MO	St. Joseph	39	46	94	50	1	+43	+38	+35	+30	+27
MO	St. Louis	38	37	90	12	1	+28	+21	+16	+10	+5
MO	Springfield	37	13	93	18	1	+45	+36	+29	+20	+14
MS	Biloxi	30	24	88	53	1	+46	+27	+11	−5	−19
MS	Jackson	32	18	90	11	1	+46	+30	+17	+1	−10
MS	Meridian	32	22	88	42	1	+40	+24	+11	−4	−15
MS	Tupelo	34	16	88	34	1	+35	+21	+10	−2	−11
MT	Billings	45	47	108	30	2	+16	+23	+29	+35	+40
MT	Butte	46	1	112	32	2	+31	+39	+45	+52	+57
MT	Glasgow	48	12	106	38	2	−1	+11	+21	+32	+42
MT	Great Falls	47	30	111	17	2	+20	+31	+39	+49	+58
MT	Helena	46	36	112	2	2	+27	+36	+43	+51	+57
MT	Miles City	46	25	105	51	2	+3	+11	+18	+26	+32
NC	Asheville	35	36	82	33	0	+67	+55	+46	+35	+27
NC	Charlotte	35	14	80	51	0	+61	+49	+39	+28	+19
NC	Durham	36	0	78	55	0	+51	+40	+31	+21	+13
NC	Greensboro	36	4	79	47	0	+54	+43	+35	+25	+17
NC	Raleigh	35	47	78	38	0	+51	+39	+30	+20	+12
NC	Wilmington	34	14	77	55	0	+52	+38	+27	+15	+5
ND	Bismarck	46	48	100	47	1	+41	+50	+58	+66	+73
ND	Fargo	46	53	96	47	1	+24	+34	+42	+50	+57
ND	Grand Forks	47	55	97	3	1	+21	+33	+43	+53	+62
ND	Minot	48	14	101	18	1	+36	+50	+59	+71	+81
ND	Williston	48	9	103	37	1	+46	+59	+69	+80	+90
NE	Grand Island	40	55	98	21	1	+53	+51	+49	+46	+44
NE	Lincoln	40	49	96	41	1	+47	+44	+42	+39	+37
NE	North Platte	41	8	100	46	1	+62	+60	+58	+56	+54
NE	Omaha	41	16	95	56	1	+43	+40	+39	+37	+36
NH	Berlin	44	28	71	11	0	−7	−3	0	+3	+7
NH	Keene	42	56	72	17	0	+2	+3	+4	+5	+6

Get local rise, set, and tide times at Almanac.com/Astronomy.

State	City	North Latitude °	'	West Longitude °	'	Time Zone Code	Key Letters A (min.)	B (min.)	C (min.)	D (min.)	E (min.)
NH	Manchester–Concord........	42	59	71	28	0	0	0	+1	+2	+3
NH	Portsmouth................	43	5	70	45	0	–4	–2	–1	0	0
NJ	Atlantic City..............	39	22	74	26	0	+23	+17	+13	+8	+4
NJ	Camden	39	57	75	7	0	+24	+19	+16	+12	+9
NJ	Cape May................	38	56	74	56	0	+26	+20	+15	+9	+5
NJ	Newark–East Orange	40	44	74	10	0	+17	+14	+12	+9	+7
NJ	Paterson.................	40	55	74	10	0	+17	+14	+12	+9	+7
NJ	Trenton..................	40	13	74	46	0	+21	+17	+14	+11	+8
NM	Albuquerque	35	5	106	39	2	+45	+32	+22	+11	+2
NM	Gallup	35	32	108	45	2	+52	+40	+31	+20	+11
NM	Las Cruces	32	19	106	47	2	+53	+36	+23	+8	–3
NM	Roswell	33	24	104	32	2	+41	+26	+14	0	–10
NM	Santa Fe.................	35	41	105	56	2	+40	+28	+19	+9	0
NV	Carson City–Reno	39	10	119	46	3	+25	+19	+14	+9	+5
NV	Elko	40	50	115	46	3	+3	0	–1	–3	–5
NV	Las Vegas................	36	10	115	9	3	+16	+4	–3	–13	–20
NY	Albany..................	42	39	73	45	0	+9	+10	+10	+11	+11
NY	Binghamton	42	6	75	55	0	+20	+19	+19	+18	+18
NY	Buffalo..................	42	53	78	52	0	+29	+30	+30	+31	+32
NY	New York	40	45	74	0	0	+17	+14	+11	+9	+6
NY	Ogdensburg	44	42	75	30	0	+8	+13	+17	+21	+25
NY	Syracuse.................	43	3	76	9	0	+17	+19	+20	+21	+22
OH	Akron...................	41	5	81	31	0	+46	+43	+41	+39	+37
OH	Canton..................	40	48	81	23	0	+46	+43	+41	+38	+36
OH	Cincinnati–Hamilton	39	6	84	31	0	+64	+58	+53	+48	+44
OH	Cleveland–Lakewood	41	30	81	42	0	+45	+43	+42	+40	+39
OH	Columbus................	39	57	83	1	0	+55	+51	+47	+43	+40
OH	Dayton..................	39	45	84	10	0	+61	+56	+52	+48	+44
OH	Toledo..................	41	39	83	33	0	+52	+50	+49	+48	+47
OH	Youngstown..............	41	6	80	39	0	+42	+40	+38	+36	+34
OK	Oklahoma City............	35	28	97	31	1	+67	+55	+46	+35	+26
OK	Tulsa	36	9	95	60	1	+59	+48	+40	+30	+22
OR	Eugene.................	44	3	123	6	3	+21	+24	+27	+30	+33
OR	Pendleton................	45	40	118	47	3	–1	+4	+10	+16	+21
OR	Portland	45	31	122	41	3	+14	+20	+25	+31	+36
OR	Salem...................	44	57	123	1	3	+17	+23	+27	+31	+35
PA	Allentown–Bethlehem	40	36	75	28	0	+23	+20	+17	+14	+12
PA	Erie	42	7	80	5	0	+36	+36	+35	+35	+35
PA	Harrisburg	40	16	76	53	0	+30	+26	+23	+19	+16
PA	Lancaster	40	2	76	18	0	+28	+24	+20	+17	+13
PA	Philadelphia–Chester	39	57	75	9	0	+24	+19	+16	+12	+9
PA	Pittsburgh–McKeesport	40	26	80	0	0	+42	+38	+35	+32	+29
PA	Reading	40	20	75	56	0	+26	+22	+19	+16	+13
PA	Scranton–Wilkes-Barre	41	25	75	40	0	+21	+19	+18	+16	+15
PA	York	39	58	76	43	0	+30	+26	+22	+18	+15
RI	Providence...............	41	50	71	25	0	+3	+2	+1	0	0
SC	Charleston	32	47	79	56	0	+64	+48	+36	+21	+10
SC	Columbia................	34	0	81	2	0	+65	+51	+40	+27	+17
SC	Spartanburg	34	56	81	57	0	+66	+53	+43	+32	+23
SD	Aberdeen	45	28	98	29	1	+37	+44	+49	+54	+59
SD	Pierre	44	22	100	21	1	+49	+53	+56	+60	+63
SD	Rapid City	44	5	103	14	2	+2	+5	+8	+11	+13
SD	Sioux Falls...............	43	33	96	44	1	+38	+40	+42	+44	+46
TN	Chattanooga..............	35	3	85	19	0	+79	+67	+57	+45	+36
TN	Knoxville................	35	58	83	55	0	+71	+60	+51	+41	+33
TN	Memphis	35	9	90	3	1	+38	+26	+16	+5	–3
TN	Nashville	36	10	86	47	1	+22	+11	+3	–6	–14

(continued)

Time Corrections

State/ Province	City	North Latitude °	North Latitude '	West Longitude °	West Longitude '	Time Zone Code	A (min.)	B (min.)	C (min.)	D (min.)	E (min.)
TX	Amarillo	35	12	101	50	1	+85	+73	+63	+52	+43
TX	Austin	30	16	97	45	1	+82	+62	+47	+29	+15
TX	Beaumont	30	5	94	6	1	+67	+48	+32	+14	0
TX	Brownsville	25	54	97	30	1	+91	+66	+46	+23	+5
TX	Corpus Christi	27	48	97	24	1	+86	+64	+46	+25	+9
TX	Dallas–Fort Worth	32	47	96	48	1	+71	+55	+43	+28	+17
TX	El Paso	31	45	106	29	2	+53	+35	+22	+6	–6
TX	Galveston	29	18	94	48	1	+72	+52	+35	+16	+1
TX	Houston	29	45	95	22	1	+73	+53	+37	+19	+5
TX	McAllen	26	12	98	14	1	+93	+69	+49	+26	+9
TX	San Antonio	29	25	98	30	1	+87	+66	+50	+31	+16
UT	Kanab	37	3	112	32	2	+62	+53	+46	+37	+30
UT	Moab	38	35	109	33	2	+46	+39	+33	+27	+22
UT	Ogden	41	13	111	58	2	+47	+45	+43	+41	+40
UT	Salt Lake City	40	45	111	53	2	+48	+45	+43	+40	+38
UT	Vernal	40	27	109	32	2	+40	+36	+33	+30	+28
VA	Charlottesville	38	2	78	30	0	+43	+35	+29	+22	+17
VA	Danville	36	36	79	23	0	+51	+41	+33	+24	+17
VA	Norfolk	36	51	76	17	0	+38	+28	+21	+12	+5
VA	Richmond	37	32	77	26	0	+41	+32	+25	+17	+11
VA	Roanoke	37	16	79	57	0	+51	+42	+35	+27	+21
VA	Winchester	39	11	78	10	0	+38	+33	+28	+23	+19
VT	Brattleboro	42	51	72	34	0	+4	+5	+5	+6	+7
VT	Burlington	44	29	73	13	0	0	+4	+8	+12	+15
VT	Rutland	43	37	72	58	0	+2	+5	+7	+9	+11
VT	St. Johnsbury	44	25	72	1	0	–4	0	+3	+7	+10
WA	Bellingham	48	45	122	29	3	0	+13	+24	+37	+47
WA	Seattle–Tacoma–Olympia	47	37	122	20	3	+3	+15	+24	+34	+42
WA	Spokane	47	40	117	24	3	–16	–4	+4	+14	+23
WA	Walla Walla	46	4	118	20	3	–5	+2	+8	+15	+21
WI	Eau Claire	44	49	91	30	1	+12	+17	+21	+25	+29
WI	Green Bay	44	31	88	0	1	0	+3	+7	+11	+14
WI	La Crosse	43	48	91	15	1	+15	+18	+20	+22	+25
WI	Madison	43	4	89	23	1	+10	+11	+12	+14	+15
WI	Milwaukee	43	2	87	54	1	+4	+6	+7	+8	+9
WI	Oshkosh	44	1	88	33	1	+3	+6	+9	+12	+15
WI	Wausau	44	58	89	38	1	+4	+9	+13	+18	+22
WV	Charleston	38	21	81	38	0	+55	+48	+42	+35	+30
WV	Parkersburg	39	16	81	34	0	+52	+46	+42	+36	+32
WY	Casper	42	51	106	19	2	+19	+19	+20	+21	+22
WY	Cheyenne	41	8	104	49	2	+19	+16	+14	+12	+11
WY	Sheridan	44	48	106	58	2	+14	+19	+23	+27	+31
CANADA											
AB	Calgary	51	5	114	5	2	+13	+35	+50	+68	+84
AB	Edmonton	53	34	113	25	2	–3	+26	+47	+72	+93
BC	Vancouver	49	13	123	6	3	0	+15	+26	+40	+52
MB	Winnipeg	49	53	97	10	1	+12	+30	+43	+58	+71
NB	Saint John	45	16	66	3	–1	+28	+34	+39	+44	+49
NS	Halifax	44	38	63	35	–1	+21	+26	+29	+33	+37
NS	Sydney	46	10	60	10	–1	+1	+9	+15	+23	+28
ON	Ottawa	45	25	75	43	0	+6	+13	+18	+23	+28
ON	Peterborough	44	18	78	19	0	+21	+25	+28	+32	+35
ON	Thunder Bay	48	27	89	12	0	+47	+61	+71	+83	+93
ON	Toronto	43	39	79	23	0	+28	+30	+32	+35	+37
QC	Montreal	45	28	73	39	0	–1	+4	+9	+15	+20
SK	Saskatoon	52	10	106	40	1	+37	+63	+80	+101	+119

The Old Farmer's
General Store

There's more of everything at Almanac.com.

2014   THE OLD FARMER'S ALMANAC

Index to Advertisers

Index to Advertisers

General Store Classifieds

For advertising information, contact Bernie Gallagher, 203-263-7171.

Classifieds

CATALOGS/BOOKS/PUBLICATIONS

FREE BOOKLET: Pro-and-con assessment of Jehovah's Witnesses teachings. Bible Standard (OFA), 1156 St. Matthews Rd., Chester Springs PA 19425. www.biblestandard.com

FREE BOOKLETS: Life, immortality, soul, pollution crisis, Judgment Day, restitution. Sample magazine. Bible Standard (OF), 1156 St. Matthews Rd., Chester Springs PA 19425. www.biblestandard.com

CIDER PRESS

CIDER PRESSES
4 models — Made in USA
Old-fashioned style — Hardwood
New Polymer Drum
Free catalog: happyvalleyranch.com
or call: **913-849-3103**

CRAFTS

TANDY LEATHER
We have a free 172-page Buyers' Guide
full of supplies for the leather craftsman.
Saddle and tack hardware,
leather, tools, and more
farm and ranch essentials.
Tandy Leather Factory,
Dept. 14FA, 1900 SE Loop 820,
Ft. Worth TX 76140
www.tandyleatherfactory.com

FARM & GARDEN

OPEN-POLLINATED CORN SEED. Silage, grain, wildlife. Available certified organic, 75-85-87-90-120-day. Open-pollinated Cinderella pumpkin seed. Green Haven, 607-566-9253. Web site: www.openpollinated.com

FERTILIZER

NEPTUNE'S HARVEST
ORGANIC FERTILIZERS:
Extremely effective. Commercially proven.
Outperform chemicals. Wholesale/retail/farm.
Catalog. 800-259-4769.
www.neptunesharvest.com

FINANCIAL

FREE MONEY! Any purpose! Anyone eligible! Apply today: Director, 402 West Mt. Vernon, 250, Nixa MO 65714. Application processing fee: $3.

FOOD & RECIPES

FRESH, HEALTHY NUTS
Kettle-cooked, honey-roasted, raw redskin
peanuts, and more. Make your own holiday gifts
& treats. Free recipes with order.
Call Farmer Dave, 252-232-3324,
or visit **FarmerDavesMKT.com**

FRUIT TREES

ANTIQUE APPLE TREES. 100+ varieties! Catalog, $3. Urban Homestead, 818-B Cumberland St., Bristol VA 24201. www.OldVaApples.com

GREENHOUSES

EXTEND YOUR GROWING SEASON 3–4 months! Easy-to-assemble greenhouse kits starting at $349. Free brochure or see everything online. Hoop House, Mashpee, MA. Phone: 800-760-5192. www.hoophouse.com

HOME PRODUCTS

LAUNDRY BALLS. Since 1997. Physics, no chemicals. Woman-based business in Iowa. Many green and health products. Free newsletter. 888-452-4968. www.mysticwondersinc.com

HEALTH

LOW-T? LOW ENERGY & LIBIDO?
Get More Energy and Vitality, Stronger Libido.
All-Natural. FREE Offer!
www.testovex.com

HEALTH AIDS

COLLOIDAL SILVER WATER,
8-oz. spray bottle: $12.95.
Colloidal silver cream,
8-oz. spray bottle: $12.95.
www.ColloidalResearch.com

WHO'S SLEEPING WITH
YOU TONIGHT?
Nontoxic Kleen Green stops bed bugs, scabies,
lice, and mites fast! Safe for children and pets.
Fast, confidential shipping.
800-807-9350
www.kleengreen.com

Classifieds

REVEREND GRACE, healer. Removes bad luck, evil spells, crossed conditions. Reunites loved ones. Guaranteed! In the name of Jesus, call now. 602-430-1762.

BROTHER ROY. Spiritual root worker. Healing oils, health, luck. Success guaranteed. Phone: 912-262-6897 or 912-264-3259.

SPIRITUALISTS

INTERNATIONAL ADVISOR PSYCHIC HEALER JOHN

Helps you with all immediate problems. Helps where other readers have failed! Honest, caring, and understanding of your needs. Call once, be convinced! Visa/MC. Call: **707-579-5123**

HOLYLAND CRYSTALS

Can change your life overnight.
Help in love, health, and all matters.
Send $25 and emergency prayer request to:
PO Box 911, Nashville TN 37076.
Toll-free: **800-399-0604**

BROTHER DANIEL, LOUISIANA BAYOU

Master spiritualist ends your confusion and problems today for good! 100% results in love, money, luck, health, employment success.
Free lucky lotto numbers!
772-971-2830

PROPHET R works with spirits, roots, herbs, candles, lucky hands, and can remove unnatural conditions. Lucky Mojo's. 919-813-8787.

PSYCHIC www.Card-Reading.com. 36 years' experience. Need clarity about love? Career? Marriage? Reunites lovers. Spiritual balancing. 512-385-5803.

SISTER BENNETT. Second-generation intuitive Tarot card reader and healer. Knowledgeable about candle magic. Call 904-486-6381.

MISS ANGELA. Spiritual healer can help relieve life's problems. Reunites lost love. Restores health and happiness. Removes bad luck of all kinds. Never fails. 601-717-0025.

NEED HELP FAST?! Spiritualist Leza cures all evil spells. Reunites lovers; potions; luck. Valdosta, GA. 229-630-5386 or 229-244-1306.

FAMOUS NEW ORLEANS spiritual healer helps with life's difficulties. Love, relationships, business, family, health, and more! Let me guide you where others have failed. 504-975-3112.

MISS JESSICA removes evil, bad luck, and spells. Will help where other readers have failed. POB 396, Eufaula AL 36072. Call: 334-695-7306.

MISS GEORGIA ROSE, spiritualist. Removes bad luck. Reunites loved ones. Solves all problems. One free reading. 815-970-5683.

MISS JANET, spiritual reader and advisor. Will tell your love past, present, and future. Answers all questions in life! 256-727-5550.

MADISON, spiritual reader, healer, & advisor. Solves your problems. Guaranteed results in love, marriage, business. 516-308-4443.

MRS. KING, spiritual reader, advisor, helps in matters of life where others have failed. Call 912-283-0635.

MRS. RUTH, Southern-born spiritualist. Removes evil, bad luck. Helps all problems. Free sample reading. 3938 Hwy. 431 South, Eufaula AL 36027. 334-616-6363.

SPIRITUAL WORKER SOPHIA

Can remove and cast away spells.
Fixes all problems and answers all questions.
Spiritual work, $25.
Call now: **601-264-0908**

BEWARE OF IMITATORS AND DECEIVERS

Sister Margaret's vision and power
can wipe away tears, reunite lovers.
Removes evil and spells!
Make your dreams reality.
Get help now! **209-200-3679**

DOCTOR CROSS, LOVE SPECIALIST

Never lose your lover. Give me one day,
and your lover will commit to you for life!
Removes hexes, spells, and bad luck.
Guaranteed.
800-615-4868

LOVE AND RELATIONSHIP SPECIALIST Leslee. 40-year psychic. I can help. Amazing insight! Phone: 800-541-6999. Web site: www.accurate-leslee.com

BRING BACK lover, guaranteed. Destroys evil, solves all problems permanently. Free reading: 214-799-9435.

SISTER CHEROKEE, gifted Indian reader. Gives good luck, blessings, guidance, winning hits. Originally from Egypt. 404-325-7336.

There's more of everything at Almanac.com.

ATTENTION: SISTER LIGHT, Spartanburg, South Carolina. One free reading when you call. I will help in all problems. 864-576-9397.

FREE READING. Sister Cindy, psychic. Call now: 229-376-7994.

MOTHER THOMPSON
Healing spiritualist.
Born with a veil, has the spiritual power.
Reunites lovers; helps in health, business, marriage. One call will achieve your life goals.
Call: **323-383-8857**

RETURNS STOLEN LOVERS
forever in 24 hours.
I perform 2 Love Miracles.
100% Guaranteed! Never Failed.
310-962-7187 or **702-885-4716**

ARE YOU LONELY?
Confused, Depressed? Need Answers?
Call Psychic Jennifer.
Reunites Lover.
Free Readings. 310-438-8868
www.psychicjenn.com

DR. SAMUEL
CHARLESTON, SC
Solves impossible problems.
Love, lost nature, sickness, bad luck, court cases, evil spells, lucky bags.
Toll-free: **866-954-7256**

INDIAN SPIRITUAL WOMAN
Your Soul Mate Specialist.
Helps you with all kinds of problems. Immediately!
424-200-1511

RESULTS IN AN HOUR. Spiritualist solves all problems. Breaks curses. Reunites lovers. Free reading: 817-823-9963.

AMAZINGLY GIFTED PSYCHIC. Removes all evil blockages. Returns lovers forever. Complimentary reading. 214-632-5181.

HOLY RELIGIOUS GOD-GIFTED PSYCHIC
Love Specialist
Specializing; Reuniting Lovers Permanently!
Returns: Love, Passion, Romance, Sex, Commitment!
Guaranteed Amazing Results!
FREE 15-MINUTE READING!
888-420-3015

SARAH DAVIS. Helps in all problems. Removes curses, evil, voodoo, bad luck. Returns loved ones. Marriage, business, health, money. Call for lucky numbers: 512-586-3696.

FREE LIFE, LOVE READING. Destroys Evil Negativity, Solves Problems Completely, Fulfilling Unconditional Love Forevermore 100%. Phone: 817-282-3144.

STEAM MODEL TOYS

WORKING STEAM ENGINES! Stationary engines, steam tractors, rollers, trains, and accessories. Great discounts! Catalog: $6.95, refundable. Yesteryear Toys & Books Inc., Box 537, Alexandria Bay NY 13607. 800-481-1353. Web site: www.yesteryeartoys.com

WANTED TO BUY

BUYING VINTAGE RADIOS, vacuum tubes, microphones, Western Electric items, audio amplifiers, turntables, old movie equipment. 203-272-6030. Larry2942@cox.net

CASH FOR 78-RPM RECORDS! Send $2 (refundable) for illustrated booklet identifying collectible labels, numbers, with actual prices I pay. Docks, Box 780218(FA), San Antonio TX 78278-0218.

The Old Farmer's Almanac consistently reaches a proven, responsive audience and is known for delivering readers who are active buyers. The 2015 edition closes on May 2, 2014. Ad opportunities are also available in the All-Seasons Garden Guide, which closes on January 10, 2014. For ad rates or ad information, please contact Bernie Gallagher by email at OFAads@aol.com, by phone at 203-263-7171, by fax at 203-263-7174, or by mail at The Old Farmer's Almanac, PO Box 959, Woodbury CT 06798.

Advertisements and statements contained herein are the sole responsibility of the persons or entities that post the advertisement, and The Old Farmer's Almanac does not make any warranty as to the accuracy, completeness, truthfulness, or reliability of such advertisements. The Old Farmer's Almanac has no liability whatsoever for any third-party claims arising in connection with such advertisements or any products or services mentioned therein.

A sampling from the hundreds of letters, clippings, articles, and emails sent to us by Almanac readers from all over the United States and Canada during the past year.

Who Invented Blue Jeans?

Haven't you always wanted to know?

–courtesy of F.L.M., St. Louis, Missouri, who sent us Stuff Every American Should Know *by Denise Kiernan and Joseph D'Agnese. Copyright © 2012 by Denise Kiernan and Joseph D'Agnese. Reprinted with permission of Quirk Books.*

The answer, surprisingly, is not Levi Strauss, although he certainly helped to popularize them in the United States. Before this all-American garment became popular in the Wild West, variations were being sold in other parts of the world. In the 16th century, merchants in Bombay, India, sold a hard-wearing blue fabric out of the Dungri Fort that was dubbed "dungaree." In the port town of Genoa, Italy, sailors used a similar fabric to make sails, tarps, and clothing. And the city of Nîmes, France—about 300 miles from Genoa, along the French-Italian Riviera—was home to a factory that produced *serge de Nîmes,* from which comes the English word "denim." The French spoke of the Italian fabric as the "blue of Genoa" *(bleu de Gênes),* hence "blue jeans" in English.

Denim was an ideal choice for working-class clothing. It was remarkably durable, concealed stains, and became more comfortable with use.

In 1853, at the time of the California gold rush, a German dry-goods merchant named Levi Strauss opened a business in San Francisco, intending to sell supplies to miners. Strauss teamed up with a Nevada tailor, Jacob Davis, to create pants that stood up to the punishing grind of mining work. When customers complained that the pockets and other parts of the pants tore too easily, Strauss and Davis strengthened the stress points of the garment with copper rivets. They received a U.S. patent for this design in 1873. A rivet placed in the crotch was dropped from the design during World War II to save copper.

Amusement

Instructions for the Assembly of Just About Anything

You can try this in the privacy of your own home.

–courtesy of A. K. and T. C., Dublin, New Hampshire

Grasp gizmo in your left hand. With your right hand, insert the doohickey into the little whoosie just below the bright red thingamajig and gently–gently!–turn it in a clockwise direction until you hear a click. Attach the long thingamabob to the whatchamacallit. Do not under any circumstances allow the metal whatsit on the end to come in contact with the black plastic thingummy. Failure to follow these instructions will result in damage to the doodad.

How "Hail to the Chief" Became the Presidential Song

–courtesy of V.M.P., Tulsa, Oklahoma

Well. First of all, the origin of the song dates back to an epic poem by Sir Walter Scott called *The Lady of the Lake*. Published in 1810, it refers to a Scottish chieftain. Because the poem became extremely popular, it was turned into an English musical by British composer James Sanderson. Using a line from *The Lady of the Lake*—"Hail to the Chief who in triumph advances!"—Sanderson set it to music in 1812.

The song made its way to America with new wording and was first used to honor the late George Washington for a celebration of his birthday in 1815.

A few years later, in 1828, the song was first played for a living president—John Quincy Adams—when he arrived for a ground-breaking ceremony for the Chesapeake and Ohio Canal. As President Adams approached, the U.S. Marine Band played "Hail to the Chief."

It would become officially linked to presidential appearances because of Sarah Polk, wife of the 11th president, James K. Polk (1845–49). According to historian William Seal, Sarah Polk was protective of her husband's image and concerned that he "was not an impressive figure, so some announcement was necessary to avoid the embarrassment of his entering a crowded room unnoticed." Gradually, from that point on, "Hail to the Chief" came to be played at various presidential events.

By 1954, the U.S. Dept. of Defense had made "Hail to the Chief" the official musical announcement of and tribute to the president of the United States.

(continued)

Some Folks Are Fond of Puns

Others hate 'em. How do you feel about these?

—courtesy of S. P., Scottsdale, Arizona

The fattest knight at King Arthur's round table was **Sir Cumference.** He acquired his size from too much pi.

• • • • •

No matter how much you push the envelope, it'll still be **stationery.**

• • • • •

A hole has been found in the wall of a nudist camp. The police are **looking into it.**

• • • • •

Two silkworms had a race. They ended up **in a tie.**

• • • • •

The short fortune-teller who escaped from prison was a **small medium at large.**

• • • • •

A vulture boards an airplane carrying two dead raccoons. The stewardess looks at him and says, "I'm sorry, sir, **only one carrion allowed** per passenger."

• • • • •

Did you hear about the patient who refused Novocain during a root canal? He wanted to **transcend dental medication.**

• • • • •

A **backward poet** writes inverse.

• • • • •

Don't Mess With Senior Citizens

They didn't get to be old by being fools.

—courtesy of C. M., Biddeford Pool, Maine

A senior citizen couple is traveling by car from Victoria to Prince George, British Columbia.

After almost 11 hours on the road, they are too tired to continue and decide to take a room. But they plan to sleep for only 4 hours and then get back on the road. When they check out 4 hours later, the desk clerk hands them a bill for $350. The husband explodes and demands to know why the charge is so high. He tells the clerk that although it's a nice hotel, the rooms certainly aren't worth $350 for 4 hours. Then the clerk tells him that $350 is the standard rate.

The husband then insists on speaking to the manager.

The manager appears, listens to him, and then explains that the hotel has an Olympic-size swimming pool and a huge conference center that were available for the couple to use.

"But we didn't use them," the husband says.

"Well, they are here and you could have," explains the manager.

The manager then goes on to explain that the couple could also have taken in one of the shows for which the hotel is famous. "We have the best entertainers from New York, Hollywood, and Las Vegas perform here," the manager says.

"But we didn't go to any of those shows," the husband says.

"Well, they were here and you could have," the manager replies.

No matter what amenity the manager mentions, the husband replies, "But we didn't use it!"

The manager is unmoved, and eventually the husband gives up and agrees to pay. As he didn't have the checkbook, he asks his wife to write the check. She does and gives it to the manager.

The manager is surprised when he looks at the check. "But, ma'am, this is only made out for $50."

"That's correct," she responds. "I charged you $300 for sleeping with me."

"But I didn't," exclaims the manager.

"Well, too bad. I was here and you could have," she says.

Eight Things That Fingernails Can Tell You

Do you suppose that these are all true?
–courtesy of S. N., Montreal, Quebec

1. A white mark on the nail denotes misfortune ahead.

2. **Pale or lead-color nails indicate sadness or melancholy.**

3. Broad nails indicate a gentle, timid, and rather bashful nature.

4. **Lovers of knowledge have round nails.**

5. People with narrow nails are ambitious and somewhat quarrelsome.

6. **Small nails indicate littleness of the mind and a quarrelsome disposition.**

7. Men who rejoice in war and violence often have red and spotted nails.

8. **Nails growing into the flesh at the side indicate luxurious tastes.**

And Finally . . .
–courtesy of R.D.H., Danforth, Maine

Don't worry about the future,
The present is all thou hast.
The future will soon be present,
And the present will soon be past.

Send your contribution for *The 2015 Old Farmer's Almanac* by January 24, 2014, to "A & P," The Old Farmer's Almanac, P.O. Box 520, Dublin, NH 03444, or email it to almanac@ypi.com (subject: A & P).

□□

Vinegar Can Be Used For WHAT?

CANTON (Special)- Research from the U.S. to Asia reports that VINEGAR-- *Mother Nature's Liquid Gold*-- is one of the most powerful aids for a healthier, longer life.

Each golden drop is a natural storehouse of vitamins and minerals to help fight ailments and extend life. In fact:
- Studies show it helps boost the immune system to help prevent cancer, ease arthritic pain, and fight cholesterol build-up in arteries.

And that's not all!

Want to control Your weight?

Since ancient times a teaspoon of apple cider vinegar in water at meals has been the answer. Try it.

Worried about age spots? Troubled by headaches? Aches and pain?

You'll find a vinegar home remedy for your problem among the 308 researched and available for the first time in the exclusive *"The Vinegar Book,"* by natural health author Emily Thacker.

As *The Wall Street Journal* wrote in a vinegar article: "Have a Problem?

Chances are Vinegar can help solve it."

This fascinating book shows you step by step how to mix *inexpensive* vinegar with kitchen staples to help:
- Lower blood pressure
- Speed up your metabolism
- Fight pesky coughs, colds
- Relieve painful leg cramps
- Soothe aching muscles
- Fade away headaches
- Gain soft, radiant skin
- Help lower cholesterol
- Boost immune system in its prevention of cancer
- Fight liver spots
- Natural arthritis reliever
- Use for eye and ear problems
- Destroy bacteria in foods
- Relieve itches, insect bites
- Skin rashes, athlete's foot
- Heart and circulatory care, and so much more

You'll learn it's easy to combine vinegar and herbs to create tenderizers, mild laxatives, tension relievers.

Enjoy bottling your own original and delicious vinegars. And tasty pickles and pickling treats that win raves!

You'll discover vinegar's amazing history through the ages *PLUS easy-to-make cleaning formulas that save you hundreds of dollars every year.*

"The Vinegar Book" is so amazing that you're invited to use and enjoy its wisdom on a **90 day No-Risk Trial basis. If not delighted simply tear off and return** *the cover only* **for a prompt refund.** To order right from the publisher at the introductory low price of $12.95 plus $3.98 postage & handling (total of $16.93, OH residents please add 6.25% sales tax) do this now:

Write "Vinegar Preview" on a piece of paper and mail it along with your check or money order payable to: James Direct Inc., Dept. V1290, 500 S. Prospect Ave., Box 980, Hartville, Ohio 44632.

You can charge to your VISA, MasterCard, Discover or American Express by mail. Be sure to include your card number, expiration date and signature.

Want to save even more? Do a favor for a relative or friend and order 2 books for only $20 postpaid. It's such a thoughtful gift.

Remember: It's not available in book stores at this time. And you're protected by the publisher's 90-Day Money Back Guarantee.

SPECIAL BONUS - Act promptly and you'll also receive Brain & Health Power Foods booklet absolutely FREE. It's yours to keep just for previewing *"The Vinegar Book."* Supplies are limited. Order today.

©2013 JDI V0122S02

http://www.jamesdirect.com

A Reference Compendium

PHASES OF THE MOON

New

WAXING

First Quarter

Full

Last Quarter

WANING

New

The Origin of Full-Moon Names

■ Historically, the Native Americans who lived in the area that is now the northern and eastern United States kept track of the seasons by giving a distinctive name to each recurring full Moon. This name was applied to the entire month in which it occurred. These names, and some variations, were used by the Algonquin tribes from New England to Lake Superior.

Name	Month	Variations
Full Wolf Moon	**January**	Full Old Moon
Full Snow Moon	**February**	Full Hunger Moon
Full Worm Moon	**March**	Full Crow Moon Full Crust Moon Full Sugar Moon Full Sap Moon
Full Pink Moon	**April**	Full Sprouting Grass Moon Full Egg Moon Full Fish Moon
Full Flower Moon	**May**	Full Corn Planting Moon Full Milk Moon
Full Strawberry Moon	**June**	Full Rose Moon Full Hot Moon
Full Buck Moon	**July**	Full Thunder Moon Full Hay Moon
Full Sturgeon Moon	**August**	Full Red Moon Full Green Corn Moon
Full Harvest Moon*	**September**	Full Corn Moon Full Barley Moon
Full Hunter's Moon	**October**	Full Travel Moon Full Dying Grass Moon
Full Beaver Moon	**November**	Full Frost Moon
Full Cold Moon	**December**	Full Long Nights Moon

The Harvest Moon is always the full Moon closest to the autumnal equinox. If the Harvest Moon occurs in October, the September full Moon is usually called the Corn Moon.

When Will the Moon Rise Today?

■ A lunar puzzle involves the timing of moonrise. If you enjoy the out-of-doors and the wonders of nature, you may wish to commit to memory the following gem:

 The new Moon always rises near sunrise;

 The first quarter near noon;

 The full Moon always rises near sunset;

 The last quarter near midnight.

Moonrise occurs about 50 minutes later each day.

Meanings of Full-Moon Names

January's full Moon was called the **Wolf Moon** because it appeared when wolves howled in hunger outside the villages.

February's full Moon was called the **Snow Moon** because it was a time of heavy snow. It was also called the **Hunger Moon** because hunting was difficult and hunger often resulted.

March's full Moon was called the **Worm Moon** because, as the Sun increasingly warmed the soil, earthworms became active and their castings (excrement) began to appear.

April's full Moon was called the **Pink Moon** because it heralded the appearance of the moss pink, or wild ground phlox— one of the first spring flowers.

May's full Moon was called the **Flower Moon** because blossoms were abundant everywhere at this time.

June's full Moon was called the **Strawberry Moon** because it appeared when the strawberry harvest took place.

July's full Moon was called the **Buck Moon** because it arrived when male deer started growing new antlers.

August's full Moon was called the **Sturgeon Moon** because this large fish, which is found in the Great Lakes and Lake Champlain, was caught easily at this time.

September's full Moon was called the **Corn Moon** because this was the time to harvest corn.

The **Harvest Moon** is the full Moon that occurs closest to the autumnal equinox. It can occur in either **September** or **October.** At this time, crops such as corn, pumpkins, squash, and wild rice are ready for gathering.

October's full Moon was called the **Hunter's Moon** because this was the time to hunt in preparation for winter.

November's full Moon was called the **Beaver Moon** because it was the time to set beaver traps, before the waters froze over.

December's full Moon was called the **Cold Moon.** It was also called the **Long Nights Moon** because nights at this time of year were the longest.

The Origin of Month Names

January. For the Roman god Janus, protector of gates and doorways. Janus is depicted with two faces, one looking into the past, the other into the future.

February. From the Latin *februa,* "to cleanse." The Roman Februalia was a month of purification and atonement.

March. For the Roman god of war, Mars. This was the time of year to resume military campaigns that had been interrupted by winter.

April. From the Latin *aperio,* "to open (bud)," because plants begin to grow now.

May. For the Roman goddess Maia, who oversaw the growth of plants. Also from the Latin *maiores,* "elders," who were celebrated now.

June. For the Roman goddess Juno, patroness of marriage and the well-being of women. Also from the Latin *juvenis,* "young people."

July. To honor Roman dictator Julius Caesar (100 B.C.–44 B.C.). In 46 B.C., with the help of Sosigenes, he developed the Julian calendar, the precursor to the Gregorian calendar we use today.

August. To honor the first Roman emperor (and grandnephew of Julius Caesar), Augustus Caesar (63 B.C.–A.D. 14).

September. From the Latin *septem,* "seven," because this was the seventh month of the early Roman calendar.

October. From the Latin *octo,* "eight," because this was the eighth month of the early Roman calendar.

November. From the Latin *novem,* "nine," because this was the ninth month of the early Roman calendar.

December. From the Latin *decem,* "ten," because this was the tenth month of the early Roman calendar.

Easter Dates (2014–17)

■ Christian churches that follow the Gregorian calendar celebrate Easter on the first Sunday after the paschal full Moon on or just after the vernal equinox.

YEAR	EASTER
2014	April 20
2015	April 5
2016	March 27
2017	April 16

■ The Julian calendar is used by some churches, including many Eastern Orthodox. The dates below are Julian calendar dates for Easter converted to Gregorian dates.

YEAR	EASTER
2014	April 20
2015	April 12
2016	May 1
2017	April 16

Friggatriskaidekaphobia Trivia

Here are a few facts about Friday the 13th:

■ In the 14 possible configurations for the annual calendar (see any perpetual calendar), the occurrence of Friday the 13th is this:

6 of 14 years have one Friday the 13th.
6 of 14 years have two Fridays the 13th.
2 of 14 years have three Fridays the 13th.

■ No year is without one Friday the 13th, and no year has more than three.

■ 2014 has one Friday the 13th, in June.

■ Months that have a Friday the 13th begin on a Sunday.

The Origin of Day Names

■ The days of the week were named by ancient Romans with the Latin words for the Sun, the Moon, and the five known planets. These names have survived in European languages, but English names also reflect Anglo-Saxon and Norse influences.

English	Latin	French	Italian	Spanish	Anglo-Saxon and Norse
SUNDAY	dies Solis (Sol's day)	dimanche	domenica	domingo	Sunnandaeg (Sun's day)
		from the Latin for "Lord's day"			
MONDAY	dies Lunae (Luna's day)	lundi	lunedì	lunes	Monandaeg (Moon's day)
TUESDAY	dies Martis (Mars's day)	mardi	martedì	martes	Tiwesdaeg (Tiw's day)
WEDNESDAY	dies Mercurii (Mercury's day)	mercredi	mercoledì	miércoles	Wodnesdaeg (Woden's day)
THURSDAY	dies Jovis (Jupiter's day)	jeudi	giovedì	jueves	Thursdaeg (Thor's day)
FRIDAY	dies Veneris (Venus's day)	vendredi	venerdì	viernes	Frigedaeg (Frigga's day)
SATURDAY	dies Saturni (Saturn's day)	samedi	sabato	sábado	Saeterndaeg (Saturn's day)
		from the Latin for "Sabbath"			

How to Find the Day of the Week for Any Given Date

To compute the day of the week for any given date as far back as the mid–18th century, proceed as follows:

■ Add the last two digits of the year to one-quarter of the last two digits (discard any remainder), the day of the month, and the month key from the key box below. Divide the sum by 7; the remainder is the day of the week (1 is Sunday, 2 is Monday, and so on). If there is no remainder, the day is Saturday. If you're searching for a weekday prior to 1900, add 2 to the sum before dividing; prior to 1800, add 4. The formula doesn't work for days prior to 1753. From 2000 through 2099, subtract 1 from the sum before dividing.

Example:

The Dayton Flood was on March 25, 1913.

Last two digits of year:	13
One-quarter of these two digits:	3
Given day of month:	25
Key number for March:	4
Sum:	45

45 ÷ 7 = 6, with a remainder of 3. The flood took place on Tuesday, the third day of the week.

KEY	
January	1
leap year	0
February..............	4
leap year	3
March	4
April..................	0
May	2
June	5
July	0
August	3
September.............	6
October	1
November..............	4
December	6

Animal Signs of the Chinese Zodiac

■ The animal designations of the Chinese zodiac follow a 12-year cycle and are always used in the same sequence. The Chinese year of 354 days begins 3 to 7 weeks into the western 365-day year, so the animal designation changes at that time, rather than on January 1. **See page 119** for the exact date of the start of the Chinese New Year.

Rat

Ambitious and sincere, you can be generous with your money. Compatible with the dragon and the monkey. Your opposite is the horse.

1924	**1936**	**1948**
1960	**1972**	**1984**
1996	**2008**	**2020**

Dragon

Robust and passionate, your life is filled with complexity. Compatible with the monkey and the rat. Your opposite is the dog.

1928	**1940**	**1952**
1964	**1976**	**1988**
2000	**2012**	**2024**

Monkey

Persuasive, skillful, and intelligent, you strive to excel. Compatible with the dragon and the rat. Your opposite is the tiger.

1932	**1944**	**1956**
1968	**1980**	**1992**
2004	**2016**	**2028**

Ox or Buffalo

A leader, you are bright, patient, and cheerful. Compatible with the snake and the rooster. Your opposite is the sheep.

1925	**1937**	**1949**
1961	**1973**	**1985**
1997	**2009**	**2021**

Snake

Strong-willed and intense, you display great wisdom. Compatible with the rooster and the ox. Your opposite is the pig.

1929	**1941**	**1953**
1965	**1977**	**1989**
2001	**2013**	**2025**

Rooster or Cock

Seeking wisdom and truth, you have a pioneering spirit. Compatible with the snake and the ox. Your opposite is the rabbit.

1933	**1945**	**1957**
1969	**1981**	**1993**
2005	**2017**	**2029**

Tiger

Forthright and sensitive, you possess great courage. Compatible with the horse and the dog. Your opposite is the monkey.

1926	**1938**	**1950**
1962	**1974**	**1986**
1998	**2010**	**2022**

Horse

Physically attractive and popular, you like the company of others. Compatible with the tiger and the dog. Your opposite is the rat.

1930	**1942**	**1954**
1966	**1978**	**1990**
2002	**2014**	**2026**

Dog

Generous and loyal, you have the ability to work well with others. Compatible with the horse and the tiger. Your opposite is the dragon.

1934	**1946**	**1958**
1970	**1982**	**1994**
2006	**2018**	**2030**

Rabbit or Hare

Talented and affectionate, you are a seeker of tranquility. Compatible with the sheep and the pig. Your opposite is the rooster.

1927	**1939**	**1951**
1963	**1975**	**1987**
1999	**2011**	**2023**

Sheep or Goat

Aesthetic and stylish, you enjoy being a private person. Compatible with the pig and the rabbit. Your opposite is the ox.

1931	**1943**	**1955**
1967	**1979**	**1991**
2003	**2015**	**2027**

Pig or Boar

Gallant and noble, your friends will remain at your side. Compatible with the rabbit and the sheep. Your opposite is the snake.

1935	**1947**	**1959**
1971	**1983**	**1995**
2007	**2019**	**2031**

A Table Foretelling the Weather Through All the Lunations of Each Year, or Forever

■ This table is the result of many years of actual observation and shows what sort of weather will probably follow the Moon's entrance into any of its quarters. For example, the table shows that the week following January 7, 2014, will be fair and frosty, because the Moon enters the first quarter that day at 10:39 P.M. EST. (See the **Left-Hand Calendar Pages, 120–146,** for 2014 Moon phases.)

Editor's note: Although the data in this table is taken into consideration in the yearlong process of compiling the annual long-range weather forecasts for *The Old Farmer's Almanac,* we rely far more on our projections of solar activity.

Time of Change	Summer	Winter
Midnight to 2 A.M.	Fair	Hard frost, unless wind is south or west
2 A.M. to 4 A.M.	Cold, with frequent showers	Snow and stormy
4 A.M. to 6 A.M.	Rain	Rain
6 A.M. to 8 A.M.	Wind and rain	Stormy
8 A.M. to 10 A.M.	Changeable	Cold rain if wind is west; snow, if east
10 A.M. to noon	Frequent showers	Cold with high winds
Noon to 2 P.M.	Very rainy	Snow or rain
2 P.M. to 4 P.M.	Changeable	Fair and mild
4 P.M. to 6 P.M.	Fair	Fair
6 P.M. to 10 P.M.	Fair if wind is northwest; rain if wind is south or southwest	Fair and frosty if wind is north or northeast; rain or snow if wind is south or southwest
10 P.M. to midnight	Fair	Fair and frosty

This table was created more than 180 years ago by Dr. Herschell for the Boston Courier; *it first appeared in* The Old Farmer's Almanac *in 1834.*

Safe Ice Thickness*

Ice Thickness	Permissible Load	Ice Thickness	Permissible Load
3 inches	Single person on foot	12 inches	Heavy truck (8-ton gross)
4 inches	Group in single file	15 inches	10 tons
7½ inches	Passenger car (2-ton gross)	20 inches	25 tons
8 inches	Light truck (2½-ton gross)	30 inches	70 tons
10 inches	Medium truck (3½-ton gross)	36 inches	110 tons

*Solid, clear, blue/black pond and lake ice

Slush ice has only half the strength of blue ice. The strength value of river ice is 15 percent less.

Heat Index °F (°C)

Temp. °F (°C)	RELATIVE HUMIDITY (%)								
	40	45	50	55	60	65	70	75	80
100 (38)	109 (43)	114 (46)	118 (48)	124 (51)	129 (54)	136 (58)			
98 (37)	105 (41)	109 (43)	113 (45)	117 (47)	123 (51)	128 (53)	134 (57)		
96 (36)	101 (38)	104 (40)	108 (42)	112 (44)	116 (47)	121 (49)	126 (52)	132 (56)	
94 (34)	97 (36)	100 (38)	103 (39)	106 (41)	110 (43)	114 (46)	119 (48)	124 (51)	129 (54)
92 (33)	94 (34)	96 (36)	99 (37)	101 (38)	105 (41)	108 (42)	112 (44)	116 (47)	121 (49)
90 (32)	91 (33)	93 (34)	95 (35)	97 (36)	100 (38)	103 (39)	106 (41)	109 (43)	113 (45)
88 (31)	88 (31)	89 (32)	91 (33)	93 (34)	95 (35)	98 (37)	100 (38)	103 (39)	106 (41)
86 (30)	85 (29)	87 (31)	88 (31)	89 (32)	91 (33)	93 (34)	95 (35)	97 (36)	100 (38)
84 (29)	83 (28)	84 (29)	85 (29)	86 (30)	88 (31)	89 (32)	90 (32)	92 (33)	94 (34)
82 (28)	81 (27)	82 (28)	83 (28)	84 (29)	84 (29)	85 (29)	86 (30)	88 (31)	89 (32)
80 (27)	80 (27)	80 (27)	81 (27)	81 (27)	82 (28)	82 (28)	83 (28)	84 (29)	84 (29)

EXAMPLE: *When the temperature is 88°F (31°C) and the relative humidity is 60 percent, the heat index,*

The UV Index for Measuring Ultraviolet Radiation Risk

The U.S. National Weather Service's daily forecasts of ultraviolet levels use these numbers for various exposure levels:

UV Index Number	Exposure Level	Time to Burn	Actions to Take
0, 1, 2	Minimal	60 minutes	Apply SPF 15 sunscreen
3, 4	Low	45 minutes	Apply SPF 15 sunscreen; wear a hat
5, 6	Moderate	30 minutes	Apply SPF 15 sunscreen; wear a hat
7, 8, 9	High	15–25 minutes	Apply SPF 15 to 30 sunscreen; wear a hat and sunglasses; limit midday exposure
10 or higher	Very high	10 minutes	Apply SPF 30 sunscreen; wear a hat, sunglasses, and protective clothing; limit midday exposure

"Time to Burn" and "Actions to Take" apply to people with fair skin that sometimes tans but usually burns. People with lighter skin need to be more cautious. People with darker skin may be able to tolerate more exposure.

85	90	95	100
135 (57)			
126 (52)	131 (55)		
117 (47)	122 (50)	127 (53)	132 (56)
110 (43)	113 (45)	117 (47)	121 (49)
102 (39)	105 (41)	108 (42)	112 (44)
96 (36)	98 (37)	100 (38)	103 (39)
90 (32)	91 (33)	93 (34)	95 (35)
85 (29)	86 (30)	86 (30)	87 (31)

or how hot it feels, is 95°F (35°C).

What Are Cooling/Heating Degree Days?

■ Each degree of a day's average temperature above 65°F is considered one cooling degree day, an attempt to measure the need for air-conditioning. If the average of the day's high and low temperatures is 75°, that's ten cooling degree days.

Similarly, each degree of a day's average temperature below 65° is considered one heating degree and is an attempt to measure the need for fuel consumption. For example, a day with temperatures ranging from 60° to 40° results in an average of 50°, or 15 degrees less than 65°. Hence, that day would be credited as 15 heating degree days.

How to Measure Hail

■ The **Torro Hailstorm Intensity Scale** was introduced by Jonathan Webb of Oxford, England, in 1986 as a means of categorizing hailstorms. The name derives from the private and mostly British research body named the TORnado and storm Research Organisation.

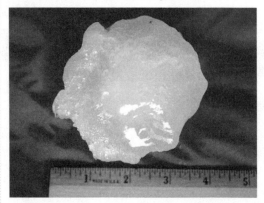

H0 True hail of pea size causes no damage

H1 Leaves and flower petals are punctured and torn

H2 Leaves are stripped from trees and plants

H3 Panes of glass are broken; auto bodies are dented

H4 Some house windows are broken; small tree branches are broken off; birds are killed

H5 Many windows are smashed; small animals are injured; large tree branches are broken off

H6 Shingle roofs are breached; metal roofs are scored; wooden window frames are broken away

H7 Roofs are shattered to expose rafters; autos are seriously damaged

H8 Shingle and tile roofs are destroyed; small tree trunks are split; people are seriously injured

H9 Concrete roofs are broken; large tree trunks are split and knocked down; people are at risk of fatal injuries

H10 Brick houses are damaged; people are at risk of fatal injuries

How to Measure Wind Speed

■ The **Beaufort Wind Force Scale** is a common way of estimating wind speed. It was developed in 1805 by Admiral Sir Francis Beaufort of the British Navy to measure wind at sea. We can also use it to measure wind on land.

Admiral Beaufort arranged the numbers 0 to 12 to indicate the strength of the wind from calm, force 0, to hurricane, force 12. Here's a scale adapted to land.

"Used Mostly at Sea but of Help to All Who Are Interested in the Weather"

Beaufort Force	Description	When You See or Feel This Effect	Wind Speed (mph)	(km/h)
0	Calm	Smoke goes straight up	less than 1	less than 2
1	Light air	Wind direction is shown by smoke drift but not by wind vane	1–3	2–5
2	Light breeze	Wind is felt on the face; leaves rustle; wind vanes move	4–7	6–11
3	Gentle breeze	Leaves and small twigs move steadily; wind extends small flags straight out	8–12	12–19
4	Moderate breeze	Wind raises dust and loose paper; small branches move	13–18	20–29
5	Fresh breeze	Small trees sway; waves form on lakes	19–24	30–39
6	Strong breeze	Large branches move; wires whistle; umbrellas are difficult to use	25–31	40–50
7	Moderate gale	Whole trees are in motion; walking against the wind is difficult	32–38	51–61
8	Fresh gale	Twigs break from trees; walking against the wind is very difficult	39–46	62–74
9	Strong gale	Buildings suffer minimal damage; roof shingles are removed	47–54	75–87
10	Whole gale	Trees are uprooted	55–63	88–101
11	Violent storm	Widespread damage	64–72	102–116
12	Hurricane	Widespread destruction	73+	117+

Retired Atlantic Hurricane Names

These storms have been some of the most destructive and costly.

NAME	YEAR	NAME	YEAR	NAME	YEAR
Dennis	2005	Dean	2007	Paloma	2008
Katrina	2005	Felix	2007	Igor	2010
Rita	2005	Noel	2007	Tomas	2010
Stan	2005	Gustav	2008	Irene	2011
Wilma	2005	Ike	2008	Sandy	2012

Atlantic Tropical (and Subtropical) Storm Names for 2014		
Arthur	Isaias	Rene
Bertha	Josephine	Sally
Cristobal	Kyle	Teddy
Dolly	Laura	Vicky
Edouard	Marco	Wilfred
Fay	Nana	
Gonzalo	Omar	
Hanna	Paulette	

Eastern North-Pacific Tropical (and Subtropical) Storm Names for 2014		
Amanda	Iselle	Rachel
Boris	Julio	Simon
Cristina	Karina	Trudy
Douglas	Lowell	Vance
Elida	Marie	Winnie
Fausto	Norbert	Xavier
Genevieve	Odile	Yolanda
Hernan	Polo	Zeke

How to Measure Hurricane Strength

■ The **Saffir-Simpson Hurricane Wind Scale** assigns a rating from 1 to 5 based on a hurricane's intensity. It is used to give an estimate of the potential property damage from a hurricane landfall. Wind speed is the determining factor in the scale, as storm surge values are highly dependent on the slope of the continental shelf in the landfall region. Wind speeds are measured at a height of 33 feet (10 meters) using a 1-minute average.

CATEGORY ONE. Average wind: 74–95 mph. Significant damage to mobile homes. Some damage to roofing and siding of well-built frame homes. Large tree branches snap and shallow-rooted trees may topple. Power outages may last a few to several days.

CATEGORY TWO. Average wind: 96–110 mph. Mobile homes may be destroyed. Major roof and siding damage to frame homes. Many shallow-rooted trees snap or topple, blocking roads. Widespread power outages could last from several days to weeks. Potable water may be scarce.

CATEGORY THREE. Average wind: 111–129 mph. Most mobile homes destroyed. Frame homes may sustain major roof damage. Many trees snap or topple, blocking numerous roads. Electricity and water may be unavailable for several days to weeks.

CATEGORY FOUR. Average wind: 130–156 mph. Mobile homes destroyed. Frame homes severely damaged or destroyed. Windborne debris may penetrate protected windows. Most trees snap or topple. Residential areas isolated by fallen trees and power poles. Most of the area uninhabitable for weeks to months.

CATEGORY FIVE. Average wind: 157+ mph. Most homes destroyed. Nearly all windows blown out of high-rises. Most of the area uninhabitable for weeks to months.

How to Measure a Tornado

■ The original **Fujita Scale** (or F Scale) was developed by Dr. Theodore Fujita to classify tornadoes based on wind damage. All tornadoes, and other severe local windstorms, were assigned a number according to the most intense damage caused by the storm. An enhanced F (EF) scale was implemented in the United States on February 1, 2007. The EF scale uses 3-second gust estimates based on a more detailed system for assessing damage, taking into account different building materials.

F SCALE		EF SCALE (U.S.)
F0 • 40–72 mph (64–116 km/h)	light damage	EF0 • 65–85 mph (105–137 km/h)
F1 • 73–112 mph (117–180 km/h)	moderate damage	EF1 • 86–110 mph (138–178 km/h)
F2 • 113–157 mph (181–253 km/h)	considerable damage	EF2 • 111–135 mph (179–218 km/h)
F3 • 158–207 mph (254–332 km/h)	severe damage	EF3 • 136–165 mph (219–266 km/h)
F4 • 208–260 mph (333–419 km/h)	devastating damage	EF4 • 166–200 mph (267–322 km/h)
F5 • 261–318 mph (420–512 km/h)	incredible damage	EF5 • over 200 mph (over 322 km/h)

Wind/Barometer Table

Barometer (Reduced to Sea Level)	Wind Direction	Character of Weather Indicated
30.00 to 30.20, and steady	westerly	Fair, with slight changes in temperature, for one to two days
30.00 to 30.20, and rising rapidly	westerly	Fair, followed within two days by warmer and rain
30.00 to 30.20, and falling rapidly	south to east	Warmer, and rain within 24 hours
30.20 or above, and falling rapidly	south to east	Warmer, and rain within 36 hours
30.20 or above, and falling rapidly	west to north	Cold and clear, quickly followed by warmer and rain
30.20 or above, and steady	variable	No early change
30.00 or below, and falling slowly	south to east	Rain within 18 hours that will continue a day or two
30.00 or below, and falling rapidly	southeast to northeast	Rain, with high wind, followed within two days by clearing, colder
30.00 or below, and rising	south to west	Clearing and colder within 12 hours
29.80 or below, and falling rapidly	south to east	Severe storm of wind and rain imminent; in winter, snow or cold wave within 24 hours
29.80 or below, and falling rapidly	east to north	Severe northeast gales and heavy rain or snow, followed in winter by cold wave
29.80 or below, and rising rapidly	going to west	Clearing and colder

Note: *A barometer should be adjusted to show equivalent sea-level pressure for the altitude at which it is to be used. A change of 100 feet in elevation will cause a decrease of ¹/₁₀ inch in the reading.*

Windchill Table

■ As wind speed increases, your body loses heat more rapidly, making the air feel colder than it really is. The combination of cold temperature and high wind can create a cooling effect so severe that exposed flesh can freeze.

TEMPERATURE (°F)

Frostbite occurs in   30 minutes   10 minutes   5 minutes

EXAMPLE: When the temperature is 15°F and the wind speed is 30 miles per hour, the windchill, or how cold it feels, is −5°F. For a Celsius version of this table, visit Almanac.com/WindchillCelsius.

–courtesy National Weather Service

How to Measure Earthquakes

■ In 1979, seismologists developed a measurement of earthquake size called **Moment Magnitude.** It is more accurate than the previously used Richter scale, which is precise only for earthquakes of a certain size and at a certain distance from a seismometer. All earthquakes can now be compared on the same scale.

Magnitude	Effect
Less than 3	Micro
3–3.9	Minor
4–4.9	Light
5–5.9	Moderate
6–6.9	Strong
7–7.9	Major
8 or more	Great

A Gardener's Worst Phobias

Name of Fear	Object Feared
Alliumphobia	Garlic
Anthophobia	Flowers
Apiphobia	Bees
Arachnophobia	Spiders
Batonophobia	Plants
Bufonophobia	Toads
Dendrophobia	Trees
Entomophobia	Insects
Lachanophobia	Vegetables
Melissophobia	Bees
Mottephobia	Moths
Myrmecophobia	Ants
Ornithophobia	Birds
Ranidaphobia	Frogs
Rupophobia	Dirt
Scoleciphobia	Worms
Spheksophobia	Wasps

Herbs to Plant in Lawns

Choose plants that suit your soil and your climate. All of these can withstand mowing and considerable foot traffic.

Ajuga or bugleweed *(Ajuga reptans)*
Corsican mint *(Mentha requienii)*
Dwarf cinquefoil *(Potentilla tabernaemontani)*
English pennyroyal *(Mentha pulegium)*
Green Irish moss *(Sagina subulata)*
Pearly everlasting *(Anaphalis margaritacea)*
Roman chamomile *(Chamaemelum nobile)*
Rupturewort *(Herniaria glabra)*
Speedwell *(Veronica officinalis)*
Stonecrop *(Sedum ternatum)*
Sweet violets (*Viola odorata* or *V. tricolor*)
Thyme *(Thymus serpyllum)*
White clover *(Trifolium repens)*
Wild strawberries *(Fragaria virginiana)*
Wintergreen or partridgeberry *(Mitchella repens)*

Lawn-Growing Tips

■ Test your soil: The pH balance should be 7.0 or more; 6.2 to 6.7 puts your lawn at risk for fungal diseases. If the pH is too low, correct it with liming, best done in the fall.

■ The best time to apply fertilizer is just before it rains.

■ If you put lime and fertilizer on your lawn, spread half of it as you walk north to south, the other half as you walk east to west to cut down on missed areas.

■ Any feeding of lawns in the fall should be done with a low-nitrogen, slow-acting fertilizer.

■ In areas of your lawn where tree roots compete with the grass, apply some extra fertilizer to benefit both.

■ Moss and sorrel in lawns usually means poor soil, poor aeration or drainage, or excessive acidity.

■ Control weeds by promoting healthy lawn growth with natural fertilizers in spring and early fall.

■ Raise the level of your lawn-mower blades during the hot summer days. Taller grass resists drought better than short.

■ You can reduce mowing time by redesigning your lawn, reducing sharp corners and adding sweeping curves.

■ During a drought, let the grass grow longer between mowings and reduce fertilizer.

■ Water your lawn early in the morning or in the evening.

Flowers and Herbs That Attract Butterflies

Allium .... *Allium*
Aster........................ *Aster*
Bee balm .... *Monarda*
Butterfly bush.............. *Buddleia*
Catmint.................... *Nepeta*
Clove pink .... *Dianthus*
Cornflower.............. *Centaurea*
Creeping thyme ...... *Thymus serpyllum*
Daylily .... *Hemerocallis*
Dill .... *Anethum graveolens*
False indigo .... *Baptisia*
Fleabane................... *Erigeron*
Floss flower .... *Ageratum*
Globe thistle............. *Echinops*
Goldenrod .... *Solidago*
Helen's flower .... *Helenium*
Hollyhock................... *Alcea*
Honeysuckle............... *Lonicera*
Lavender .... *Lavandula*
Lilac........................ *Syringa*
Lupine .... *Lupinus*
Lychnis.................... *Lychnis*

Mallow..................... *Malva*
Mealycup sage .... *Salvia farinacea*
Milkweed .... *Asclepias*
Mint .... *Mentha*
Oregano .... *Origanum vulgare*
Pansy .... *Viola*
Parsley .... *Petroselinum crispum*
Phlox .... *Phlox*
Privet .... *Ligustrum*
Purple coneflower ...*Echinacea purpurea*
Rock cress .... *Arabis*
Sea holly.................. *Eryngium*
Shasta daisy ....*Chrysanthemum*
Snapdragon .... *Antirrhinum*
Stonecrop................... *Sedum*
Sweet alyssum .... *Lobularia*
Sweet marjoram.... *Origanum majorana*
Sweet rocket.............. *Hesperis*
Tickseed................ *Coreopsis*
Verbena .... *Verbena*
Zinnia..................... *Zinnia*

Flowers* That Attract Hummingbirds

Beard tongue .... *Penstemon*
Bee balm .... *Monarda*
Butterfly bush.............. *Buddleia*
Catmint.................... *Nepeta*
Clove pink .... *Dianthus*
Columbine .... *Aquilegia*
Coral bells .... *Heuchera*
Daylily .... *Hemerocallis*
Desert candle .... *Yucca*
Flag iris .... *Iris*
Flowering tobacco ...... *Nicotiana alata*
Foxglove .... *Digitalis*
Larkspur.............. *Delphinium*
Lily........................ *Lilium*
Lupine .... *Lupinus*
Petunia .... *Petunia*
Pincushion flower .... *Scabiosa*
Red-hot poker.............. *Kniphofia*
Scarlet sage .... *Salvia splendens*

Soapwort .... *Saponaria*
Summer phlox .... *Phlox paniculata*
Trumpet honeysuckle......... *Lonicera sempervirens*
Verbena .... *Verbena*
Weigela .... *Weigela*

*Note: Choose varieties in red and orange shades, if available.

pH Preferences of Trees, Shrubs, Vegetables, and Flowers

■ An accurate soil test will indicate your soil pH and will specify the amount of lime or sulfur that is needed to bring it up or down to the appropriate level. A pH of 6.5 is just about right for most home gardens, since most plants thrive in the 6.0 to 7.0 (slightly acidic to neutral) range. Some plants (azaleas, blueberries) prefer more strongly acidic soil in the 4.0 to 6.0 range, while a few (asparagus, plums) do best in soil that is neutral to slightly alkaline. Acidic, or sour, soil (below 7.0) is counteracted by applying finely ground limestone, and alkaline, or sweet, soil (above 7.0) is treated with ground sulfur.

Common Name	Optimum pH Range	Common Name	Optimum pH Range	Common Name	Optimum pH Range
Trees and Shrubs		Walnut, black	6.0–8.0	Carnation	6.0–7.0
Apple	5.0–6.5	Willow	6.0–8.0	Chrysanthemum	6.0–7.5
Ash	6.0–7.5			Clematis	5.5–7.0
Azalea	4.5–6.0	**Vegetables**		Coleus	6.0–7.0
Basswood	6.0–7.5	Asparagus	6.0–8.0	Coneflower, purple	5.0–7.5
Beautybush	6.0–7.5	Bean, pole	6.0–7.5	Cosmos	5.0–8.0
Birch	5.0–6.5	Beet	6.0–7.5	Crocus	6.0–8.0
Blackberry	5.0–6.0	Broccoli	6.0–7.0	Daffodil	6.0–6.5
Blueberry	4.0–5.0	Brussels sprout	6.0–7.5	Dahlia	6.0–7.5
Boxwood	6.0–7.5	Carrot	5.5–7.0	Daisy, Shasta	6.0–8.0
Cherry, sour	6.0–7.0	Cauliflower	5.5–7.5	Daylily	6.0–8.0
Chestnut	5.0–6.5	Celery	5.8–7.0	Delphinium	6.0–7.5
Crab apple	6.0–7.5	Chive	6.0–7.0	Foxglove	6.0–7.5
Dogwood	5.0–7.0	Cucumber	5.5–7.0	Geranium	6.0–8.0
Elder, box	6.0–8.0	Garlic	5.5–8.0	Gladiolus	5.0–7.0
Fir, balsam	5.0–6.0	Kale	6.0–7.5	Hibiscus	6.0–8.0
Fir, Douglas	6.0–7.0	Lettuce	6.0–7.0	Hollyhock	6.0–8.0
Hemlock	5.0–6.0	Pea, sweet	6.0–7.5	Hyacinth	6.5–7.5
Hydrangea, blue-flowered	4.0–5.0	Pepper, sweet	5.5–7.0	Iris, blue flag	5.0–7.5
Hydrangea, pink-flowered	6.0–7.0	Potato	4.8–6.5	Lily-of-the-valley	4.5–6.0
Juniper	5.0–6.0	Pumpkin	5.5–7.5	Lupine	5.0–6.5
Laurel, mountain	4.5–6.0	Radish	6.0–7.0	Marigold	5.5–7.5
Lemon	6.0–7.5	Spinach	6.0–7.5	Morning glory	6.0–7.5
Lilac	6.0–7.5	Squash, crookneck	6.0–7.5	Narcissus, trumpet	5.5–6.5
Maple, sugar	6.0–7.5	Squash, Hubbard	5.5–7.0	Nasturtium	5.5–7.5
Oak, white	5.0–6.5	Tomato	5.5–7.5	Pansy	5.5–6.5
Orange	6.0–7.5			Peony	6.0–7.5
Peach	6.0–7.0	**Flowers**		Petunia	6.0–7.5
Pear	6.0–7.5	Alyssum	6.0–7.5	Phlox, summer	6.0–8.0
Pecan	6.4–8.0	Aster, New England	6.0–8.0	Poppy, oriental	6.0–7.5
Pine, red	5.0–6.0	Baby's breath	6.0–7.0	Rose, hybrid tea	5.5–7.0
Pine, white	4.5–6.0	Bachelor's button	6.0–7.5	Rose, rugosa	6.0–7.0
Plum	6.0–8.0	Bee balm	6.0–7.5	Snapdragon	5.5–7.0
Raspberry, red	5.5–7.0	Begonia	5.5–7.0	Sunflower	6.0–7.5
Rhododendron	4.5–6.0	Black-eyed Susan	5.5–7.0	Tulip	6.0–7.0
Spruce	5.0–6.0	Bleeding heart	6.0–7.5	Zinnia	5.5–7.0
		Canna	6.0–8.0		

Produce Weights and Measures

Vegetables

Asparagus: 1 pound = 3 cups chopped

Beans (string): 1 pound = 4 cups chopped

Beets: 1 pound (5 medium) = 2½ cups chopped

Broccoli: 1 pound = 6 cups chopped

Cabbage: 1 pound = 4½ cups shredded

Carrots: 1 pound = 3½ cups sliced or grated

Celery: 1 pound = 4 cups chopped

Cucumbers: 1 pound (2 medium) = 4 cups sliced

Eggplant: 1 pound = 4 cups chopped = 2 cups cooked

Garlic: 1 clove = 1 teaspoon chopped

Leeks: 1 pound = 4 cups chopped = 2 cups cooked

Mushrooms: 1 pound = 5 to 6 cups sliced = 2 cups cooked

Onions: 1 pound = 4 cups sliced = 2 cups cooked

Parsnips: 1 pound = 1½ cups cooked, puréed

Peas: 1 pound whole = 1 to 1½ cups shelled

Potatoes: 1 pound (3 medium) sliced = 2 cups mashed

Pumpkin: 1 pound = 4 cups chopped = 2 cups cooked and drained

Spinach: 1 pound = ¾ to 1 cup cooked

Squashes (summer): 1 pound = 4 cups grated = 2 cups sliced and cooked

Squashes (winter): 2 pounds = 2½ cups cooked, puréed

Sweet potatoes: 1 pound = 4 cups grated = 1 cup cooked, puréed

Swiss chard: 1 pound = 5 to 6 cups packed leaves = 1 to 1½ cups cooked

Tomatoes: 1 pound (3 or 4 medium) = 1½ cups seeded pulp

Turnips: 1 pound = 4 cups chopped = 2 cups cooked, mashed

Fruit

Apples: 1 pound (3 or 4 medium) = 3 cups sliced

Bananas: 1 pound (3 or 4 medium) = 1¾ cups mashed

Berries: 1 quart = 3½ cups

Dates: 1 pound = 2½ cups pitted

Lemon: 1 whole = 1 to 3 tablespoons juice; 1 to 1½ teaspoons grated rind

Lime: 1 whole = 1½ to 2 tablespoons juice

Orange: 1 medium = 6 to 8 tablespoons juice; 2 to 3 tablespoons grated rind

Peaches: 1 pound (4 medium) = 3 cups sliced

Pears: 1 pound (4 medium) = 2 cups sliced

Rhubarb: 1 pound = 2 cups cooked

Sowing Vegetable Seeds

Sow or plant in cool weather	Beets, broccoli, brussels sprouts, cabbage, lettuce, onions, parsley, peas, radishes, spinach, Swiss chard, turnips
Sow or plant in warm weather	Beans, carrots, corn, cucumbers, eggplant, melons, okra, peppers, squashes, tomatoes
Sow or plant for one crop per season	Corn, eggplant, leeks, melons, peppers, potatoes, spinach (New Zealand), squashes, tomatoes
Resow for additional crops	Beans, beets, cabbage, carrots, kohlrabi, lettuce, radishes, rutabagas, spinach, turnips

A Beginner's Vegetable Garden

■ A good size for a beginner's vegetable garden is 10x16 feet. It should have crops that are easy to grow. A plot this size, planted as suggested below, can feed a family of four for one summer, with a little extra for canning and freezing or giving away.

Make 11 rows, 10 feet long, with 6 inches between them. Ideally, the rows should run north and south to take full advantage of the sunlight. Plant the following:

ROW
1 Zucchini (4 plants)
2 Tomatoes (5 plants, staked)
3 Peppers (6 plants)
4 Cabbage

ROW
5 Bush beans
6 Lettuce
7 Beets
8 Carrots
9 Chard
10 Radishes
11 Marigolds (to discourage rabbits!)

Traditional Planting Times

■ Plant **corn** when elm leaves are the size of a squirrel's ear, when oak leaves are the size of a mouse's ear, when apple blossoms begin to fall, or when the dogwoods are in full bloom.

■ Plant **lettuce, spinach, peas,** and other cool-weather vegetables when the lilacs show their first leaves or when daffodils begin to bloom.

■ Plant **tomatoes, early corn,** and **peppers** when dogwoods are in peak bloom or when daylilies start to bloom.

■ Plant **cucumbers** and **squashes** when lilac flowers fade.

■ Plant **perennials** when maple leaves begin to unfurl.

■ Plant **morning glories** when maple trees have full-size leaves.

■ Plant **pansies, snapdragons,** and other hardy annuals after the aspen and chokecherry trees leaf out.

■ Plant **beets** and **carrots** when dandelions are blooming.

In the Garden

When to . . .

	. . . FERTILIZE	**. . . WATER**
Beans	After heavy bloom and set of pods	Regularly, from start of pod to set
Beets	At time of planting	Only during drought conditions
Broccoli	3 weeks after transplanting	Only during drought conditions
Brussels sprouts	3 weeks after transplanting	At transplanting
Cabbage	3 weeks after transplanting	2 to 3 weeks before harvest
Carrots	In the fall for the following spring	Only during drought conditions
Cauliflower	3 weeks after transplanting	Once, 3 weeks before harvest
Celery	At time of transplanting	Once a week
Corn	When 8 to 10 inches tall, and when first silk appears	When tassels appear and cobs start to swell
Cucumbers	1 week after bloom, and 3 weeks later	Frequently, especially when fruits form
Lettuce	2 to 3 weeks after transplanting	Once a week
Melons	1 week after bloom, and again 3 weeks later	Once a week
Onion sets	When bulbs begin to swell, and when plants are 1 foot tall	Only during drought conditions
Parsnips	1 year before planting	Only during drought conditions
Peas	After heavy bloom and set of pods	Regularly, from start of pod to set
Peppers	After first fruit-set	Once a week
Potato tubers	At bloom time or time of second hilling	Regularly, when tubers start to form
Pumpkins	Just before vines start to run, when plants are about 1 foot tall	Only during drought conditions
Radishes	Before spring planting	Once a week
Spinach	When plants are one-third grown	Once a week
Squashes, summer	Just before vines start to run, when plants are about 1 foot tall	Only during drought conditions
Squashes, winter	Just before vines start to run, when plants are about 1 foot tall	Only during drought conditions
Tomatoes	2 weeks before, and after first picking	Twice a week

How to Grow Herbs

HERB	START SEEDS INDOORS (weeks before last spring frost)	START SEEDS OUTDOORS (weeks before/after last spring frost)	HEIGHT/SPREAD (inches)	SOIL	LIGHT**
Basil*	6–8	Anytime after	12–24/12	Rich, moist	○
Borage*	Not recommended	Anytime after	12–36/12	Rich, well-drained, dry	○
Chervil	Not recommended	3–4 before	12–24/8	Rich, moist	◑
Chives	8–10	3–4 before	12–18/18	Rich, moist	○
Cilantro/ coriander	Not recommended	Anytime after	12–36/6	Light	○◑
Dill	Not recommended	4–5 before	36–48/12	Rich	○
Fennel	4–6	Anytime after	48–80/18	Rich	○
Lavender, English*	8–12	1–2 before	18–36/24	Moderately fertile, well-drained	○
Lavender, French	Not recommended	Not recommended	18–36/24	Moderately fertile, well-drained	○
Lemon balm*	6–10	2–3 before	12–24/18	Rich, well-drained	○◑
Lovage*	6–8	2–3 before	36–72/36	Fertile, sandy	○◑
Mint	Not recommended	Not recommended	12–24/18	Rich, moist	◑
Oregano*	6–10	Anytime after	12–24/18	Poor	○
Parsley*	10–12	3–4 before	18–24/6–8	Medium-rich	◑
Rosemary*	8–10	Anytime after	48–72/48	Not too acid	○
Sage	6–10	1–2 before	12–48/30	Well-drained	○
Sorrel	6–10	2–3 after	20–48/12–14	Rich, organic	○
Summer savory	4–6	Anytime after	4–15/6	Medium rich	○
Sweet cicely	6–8	2–3 after	36–72/36	Moderately fertile, well-drained	○◑
Tarragon, French	Not recommended	Not recommended	24–36/12	Well-drained	○◑
Thyme, common*	6–10	2–3 before	2–12/7–12	Fertile, well-drained	○◑

*Recommend minimum soil temperature of 70°F to germinate

** ○ full sun   ◑ partial shade

Drying Herbs

Before drying, remove any dead or diseased leaves or stems. Wash under cool water, shake off excess water, and put on a towel to dry completely. Air drying preserves an herb's essential oils; use for sturdy herbs. A microwave dries herbs more quickly, so mold is less likely to develop; use for moist, tender herbs.

■ **Hanging Method:** Gather four to six stems of fresh herbs in a bunch and tie with string, leaving a loop for hanging. Or, use a rubber band with a paper clip attached to it. Hang the herbs in a warm, well-ventilated area, out of direct sunlight, until dry. For herbs that have full seed heads, such as dill or coriander, use a paper bag. Punch holes in the bag for ventilation, label it, and put the herb bunch into the bag before you tie a string around the top of the bag. The average drying time is 1 to 3 weeks.

■ **Microwave Method:** This is better for small quantities, such as a cup or two at a time. Arrange a single layer of herbs between two paper towels and put them in the microwave for 1 to 2 minutes on high power. Let the leaves cool. If they are not dry, reheat for 30 seconds and check again. Repeat as needed. Let cool. Do not overcook, or the herbs will lose their flavor.

Storing Herbs and Spices

■ **Fresh herbs:** Dill and parsley will keep for about 2 weeks with stems immersed in a glass of water tented with a plastic bag. Most other fresh herbs (and greens) will keep for short periods unwashed and refrigerated in tightly sealed plastic bags with just enough moisture to prevent wilting. For longer storage, use moisture- and gas-permeable paper and cellophane. Plastic cuts off oxygen to the plants and promotes spoilage.

■ **Spices and dried herbs:** Store in a cool, dry place.

Cooking With Herbs

■ **Bouquet garni** is usually made with bay leaves, thyme, and parsley tied with string or wrapped in cheesecloth. Use to flavor casseroles and soups. Remove after cooking.

■ **Fines herbes** use equal amounts of fresh parsley, tarragon, chives, and chervil chopped fine. Commonly used in French cooking, they make a fine omelet or add zest to soups and sauces. Add to salads and butter sauces, or sprinkle on noodles, soups, and stews.

How to Grow Bulbs

COMMON NAME	LATIN NAME	HARDINESS ZONE	SOIL	LIGHT*	SPACING (Inches)
Allium	*Allium*	3–10	Well-drained/moist	○	12
Begonia, tuberous	*Begonia*	10–11	Well-drained/moist	◑●	12–15
Blazing star/ gayfeather	*Liatris*	7–10	Well-drained	○	6
		10–11	Well-drained/moist	◑●	8–12
	Zantedeschia	8–10	Well-drained/moist	○◑	8–24
				○	12–24
	Cyclamen	7–9	Well-drained/moist	◑	4
		9–11	Well-drained/fertile	○	12–36
		2–10	Adaptable to most soils	○◑	12–24
		9–11	Well-drained/moist/sandy	○◑	2–4
		4–8	Well-drained/moist	○	12
		4–11	Well-drained/fertile	○◑	4–9
				○	3–6
		5–9	Well-drained	○◑	8–12
	Tigridia	8–10	Well-drained	○	5–6
				○◑	4–6
	Anemone	3–9	Well-drained/moist	○◑	3–6
Bluebell	*Hyacinthoides*	4–9	Well-drained/fertile	○◑	4
Christmas rose/ hellebore	*Helleborus*	4–8	Neutral–alkaline	○◑	18
Crocus	*Crocus*	3–8	Well-drained/moist/fertile	○◑	4
Daffodil	*Narcissus*	3–10	Well-drained/moist/fertile	○◑	6
Fritillary	*Fritillaria*	3–9	Well-drained/sandy	○◑	3
Glory of the snow	*Chionodoxa*	3–9	Well-drained/moist	○◑	3
Grape hyacinth	*Muscari*	4–10	Well-drained/moist/fertile	○◑	3–4
Iris, bearded	*Iris*	3–9	Well-drained	○◑	4
Iris, Siberian	*Iris*	4–9	Well-drained	○◑	4
Ornamental onion	*Allium*	3–10	Well-drained/moist/fertile	○	12
Snowdrop	*Galanthus*	3–9	Well-drained/moist/fertile	○◑	3
Snowflake	*Leucojum*	5–9	Well-drained/moist/sandy	○◑	4
Spring starflower	*Ipheion uniflorum*	6–9	Well-drained loam	○◑	3–6
Star of Bethlehem	*Ornithogalum*	5–10	Well-drained/moist	○◑	2–5
Striped squill	*Puschkinia scilloides*	3–9	Well-drained	○◑	6
Tulip	*Tulipa*	4–8	Well-drained/fertile	○◑	3–6
Winter aconite	*Eranthis*	4–9	Well-drained/moist/fertile	○●	3

FALL-PLANTED BULBS

DEPTH (inches)	BLOOMING SEASON	HEIGHT (inches)	NOTES
3–4	Spring to summer	6–60	Usually pest-free; a great cut flower
1–2	Summer to fall	8–18	North of Zone 10, lift in fall
4	Summer to fall	8–20	An excellent flower for drying; north of Zone 7, plant in spring, lift in fall
2	Summer	8–24	North of Zone 10, plant in spring, lift in fall
1–4	Summer	24–36	Fragrant; north of Zone 8, plant in spring, lift in fall
Level	Summer	18–60	North of Zone 8, plant in spring, lift in fall
1–2	Spring to fall	3–12	Naturalizes well in warm areas; north of Zone 7, lift in fall
4–6	Late summer	12–60	North of Zone 9, lift in fall
2	Summer	12–36	Mulch in winter in Zones 3 to 6
2	Summer	12–24	Fragrant; can be grown outdoors in warm climates
3–4	Summer	6–20	Does well in woodland settings
3–6	Early summer to early fall	12–80	North of Zone 10, lift in fall
4	Spring to late summer	3–72	Divide and replant rhizomes every two to five years
4–6	Early summer	36	Fragrant; self-sows; requires excellent drainage
4	Summer	18–24	North of Zone 8, lift in fall
2	Summer	2–12	Plant in confined area to control
2	Early summer	3–18	North of Zone 6, lift in fall
3–4	Spring	8–20	Excellent for borders, rock gardens and naturalizing
1–2	Spring	12	Hardy, but requires shelter from strong, cold winds
3	Early spring	5	Naturalizes well in grass
6	Early spring	14–24	Plant under shrubs or in a border
3	Midspring	6–30	Different species can be planted in rock gardens, woodland gardens, or borders
3	Spring	4–10	Self-sows easily; plant in rock gardens, raised beds, or under shrubs
2–3	Late winter to spring	6–12	Use as a border plant or in wildflower and rock gardens; self-sows easily
4	Early spring to early summer	3–48	Naturalizes well; a good cut flower
4	Early spring to midsummer	18–48	An excellent cut flower
3–4	Late spring to early summer	6–60	Usually pest-free; a great cut flower
3	Spring	6–12	Best when clustered and planted in an area that will not dry out in summer
4	Spring	6–18	Naturalizes well
3	Spring	4–6	Fragrant; naturalizes easily
4	Spring to summer	6–24	North of Zone 5, plant in spring, lift in fall
3	Spring	4–6	Naturalizes easily; makes an attractive edging
4–6	Early to late spring	8–30	Excellent for borders, rock gardens, and naturalizing
2–3	Late winter to spring	2–4	Self-sows and naturalizes easily

R E F E R E N C E

Substitutions for Common Ingredients

ITEM	QUANTITY	SUBSTITUTION
Baking powder	1 teaspoon	¼ teaspoon baking soda plus ¼ teaspoon cornstarch plus ½ teaspoon cream of tartar
Buttermilk	1 cup	1 tablespoon lemon juice or vinegar plus milk to equal 1 cup; or 1 cup plain yogurt
Chocolate, unsweetened	1 ounce	3 tablespoons cocoa plus 1 tablespoon unsalted butter, shortening, or vegetable oil
Cracker crumbs	¾ cup	1 cup dry bread crumbs; or 1 tablespoon quick-cooking oats (for thickening)
Cream, heavy	1 cup	¾ cup milk plus ⅓ cup melted unsalted butter (this will not whip)
Cream, light	1 cup	⅞ cup milk plus 3 tablespoons melted, unsalted butter
Cream, sour	1 cup	⅞ cup buttermilk or plain yogurt plus 3 tablespoons melted, unsalted butter
Cream, whipping	1 cup	⅔ cup well-chilled evaporated milk, whipped; or 1 cup nonfat dry milk powder whipped with 1 cup ice water
Egg	1 whole	2 yolks plus 1 tablespoon cold water; or 3 tablespoons vegetable oil plus 1 tablespoon water (for baking); or 2 to 3 tablespoons mayonnaise (for cakes)
Egg white	1 white	2 teaspoons meringue powder plus 3 tablespoons water, combined
Flour, all-purpose	1 cup	1 cup plus 3 tablespoons cake flour (not advised for cookies or quick breads); or 1 cup self-rising flour (omit baking powder and salt from recipe)
Flour, cake	1 cup	1 cup minus 3 tablespoons sifted all-purpose flour plus 3 tablespoons cornstarch
Flour, self-rising	1 cup	1 cup all-purpose flour plus 1½ teaspoons baking powder plus ¼ teaspoon salt
Herbs, dried	1 teaspoon	1 tablespoon fresh, minced and packed
Honey	1 cup	1¼ cups sugar plus ½ cup liquid called for in recipe (such as water or oil)
Ketchup	1 cup	1 cup tomato sauce plus ¼ cup sugar plus 3 tablespoons apple-cider vinegar plus ½ teaspoon salt plus pinch of ground cloves combined; or 1 cup chili sauce
Lemon juice	1 teaspoon	½ teaspoon vinegar
Mayonnaise	1 cup	1 cup sour cream or plain yogurt; or 1 cup cottage cheese (puréed)
Milk, skim	1 cup	⅓ cup instant nonfat dry milk plus ¾ cup water

ITEM	QUANTITY	SUBSTITUTION
Milk, to sour	1 cup	1 tablespoon vinegar or lemon juice plus milk to equal 1 cup. Stir and let stand 5 minutes.
Milk, whole	1 cup	½ cup evaporated whole milk plus ½ cup water; or ¾ cup 2 percent milk plus ¼ cup half-and-half
Molasses	1 cup	1 cup honey or dark corn syrup
Mustard, dry	1 teaspoon	1 tablespoon prepared mustard less 1 teaspoon liquid from recipe
Oat bran	1 cup	1 cup wheat bran or rice bran or wheat germ
Oats, old-fashioned (rolled)	1 cup	1 cup steel-cut Irish or Scotch oats
Quinoa	1 cup	1 cup millet or couscous (whole wheat cooks faster) or bulgur
Sugar, dark-brown	1 cup	1 cup light-brown sugar, packed; or 1 cup granulated sugar plus 2 to 3 tablespoons molasses
Sugar, granulated	1 cup	1 cup firmly packed brown sugar; or 1¾ cups confectioners' sugar (makes baked goods less crisp); or 1 cup superfine sugar
Sugar, light-brown	1 cup	1 cup granulated sugar plus 1 to 2 tablespoons molasses; or ½ cup dark-brown sugar plus ½ cup granulated sugar
Sweetened condensed milk	1 can (14 oz.)	1 cup evaporated milk plus 1¼ cups granulated sugar. Combine and heat until sugar dissolves.
Vanilla bean	1-inch bean	1 teaspoon vanilla extract
Vinegar, apple-cider	—	malt, white-wine, or rice vinegar
Vinegar, balsamic	1 tablespoon	1 tablespoon red- or white-wine vinegar plus ½ teaspoon sugar
Vinegar, red-wine	—	white-wine, sherry, champagne, or balsamic vinegar
Vinegar, rice	—	apple-cider, champagne, or white-wine vinegar
Vinegar, white-wine	—	apple-cider, champagne, fruit (raspberry), rice, or red-wine vinegar
Yeast	1 cake (⅗ oz.)	1 package (¼ ounce) or 1 scant tablespoon active dried yeast
Yogurt, plain	1 cup	1 cup sour cream (thicker; less tart) or buttermilk (thinner; use in baking, dressings, sauces)

Types of Fat

■ One way to minimize your total blood cholesterol is to manage the amount and types of fat in your diet. Aim for monounsaturated and polyunsaturated fats; avoid saturated and trans fats.

■ **Monounsaturated fat** lowers LDL (bad cholesterol) and may raise HDL (good cholesterol) or leave it unchanged; found in almonds, avocados, canola oil, cashews, olive oil, peanut oil, and peanuts.

■ **Polyunsaturated fat** lowers LDL and may lower HDL; includes omega-3 and omega-6 fatty acids; found in corn oil, cottonseed oil, fish such as salmon and tuna, safflower oil, sesame seeds, soybeans, and sunflower oil.

■ **Saturated fat** raises both LDL and HDL; found in chocolate, cocoa butter, coconut oil, dairy products (milk, butter, cheese, ice cream), egg yolks, palm oil, and red meat.

■ **Trans fat** raises LDL and lowers HDL; a type of fat common in many processed foods, such as most margarines (especially stick), vegetable shortening, partially hydrogenated vegetable oil, many commercial fried foods (doughnuts, french fries), and commercial baked goods (cookies, crackers, cakes).

Calorie-Burning Comparisons

■ If you hustle through your chores to get to the fitness center, relax. You're getting a great workout already. The left-hand column lists "chore" exercises, the middle column shows the number of calories burned per minute per pound of body weight, and the right-hand column lists comparable "recreational" exercises. For example, a 150-pound person forking straw bales burns 9.45 calories per minute, the same workout he or she would get playing basketball.

Chore	Cal/min/lb	Recreational
Chopping with an ax, fast	**0.135**	Skiing, cross country, uphill
Climbing hills, with 44-pound load	**0.066**	Swimming, crawl, fast
Digging trenches	**0.065**	Skiing, cross country, steady walk
Forking straw bales	**0.063**	Basketball
Chopping down trees	**0.060**	Football
Climbing hills, with 9-pound load	**0.058**	Swimming, crawl, slow
Sawing by hand	**0.055**	Skiing, cross country, moderate
Mowing lawns	**0.051**	Horseback riding, trotting
Scrubbing floors	**0.049**	Tennis
Shoveling coal	**0.049**	Aerobic dance, medium
Hoeing	**0.041**	Weight training, circuit training
Stacking firewood	**0.040**	Weight lifting, free weights
Shoveling grain	**0.038**	Golf
Painting houses	**0.035**	Walking, normal pace, asphalt road
Weeding	**0.033**	Table tennis
Shopping for food	**0.028**	Cycling, 5.5 mph
Mopping floors	**0.028**	Fishing
Washing windows	**0.026**	Croquet
Raking	**0.025**	Dancing, ballroom
Driving a tractor	**0.016**	Drawing, standing position

Freezer Storage Time

(freezer temperature 0°F or colder)

Product	Months in Freezer
Fresh meat	
Beef	6 to 12
Lamb	6 to 9
Veal	6 to 9
Pork	4 to 6
Ground beef, veal, lamb, pork	3 to 4
Frankfurters	1 to 2
Sausage, fresh pork	1 to 2
Ready-to-serve luncheon meats . . . . . Not recommended	
Fresh poultry	
Chicken, turkey (whole). 12	
Chicken, turkey (pieces)	6 to 9
Cornish game hen, game birds	6 to 9
Giblets	3 to 4
Cooked poultry	
Breaded, fried. 4	
Pieces, plain 4	
Pieces covered with broth, gravy 6	
Fresh fruits (prepared for freezing)	
All fruits except those listed below	10 to 12
Avocados, bananas, plantains 3	
Lemons, limes, oranges	4 to 6
Fresh vegetables (prepared for freezing)	
Beans, beets, bok choy, broccoli, brussels sprouts, cabbage, carrots, cauliflower, celery, corn, greens, kohlrabi, leeks, mushrooms, okra, onions, peas, peppers, soybeans, spinach, summer squashes . . . . .10 to 12	
Asparagus, rutabagas, turnips . . .	8 to 10
Artichokes, eggplant	6 to 8
Tomatoes (overripe or sliced) 2	
Bamboo shoots, cucumbers, endive, lettuce, radishes, watercress . . . . Not recommended	
Cheese (except those listed below) 6	
Cottage cheese, cream cheese, feta, goat, fresh mozzarella, Neufchâtel, Parmesan, processed cheese (opened) . . . . Not recommended	

Product	Months in Freezer
Dairy products	
Margarine (not diet) 12	
Butter	6 to 9
Cream, half-and-half 4	
Milk 3	
Ice cream	1 to 2

Freezing Hints

For meals, remember that a quart container holds four servings, and a pint container holds two servings.

To prevent sticking, spread the food to be frozen (berries, hamburgers, cookies, etc.) on a cookie sheet and freeze until solid. Then place in plastic bags and freeze.

Label foods for easy identification. Write the name of the food, number of servings, and date of freezing on containers or bags.

Freeze foods as quickly as possible by placing them directly against the sides of the freezer.

Arrange freezer into sections for each food category.

If power is interrupted, or if the freezer is not operating normally, do not open the freezer door. Food in a loaded freezer will usually stay frozen for 2 days if the freezer door remains closed during that time period.

Plastics

■ In your quest to go green, use this guide to use and sort plastic. The number, usually found with a triangle symbol on a container, indicates the type of resin used to produce the plastic. Call **1-800-CLEANUP** for recycling information in your state.

PETE

Number 1 • *PETE or PET (polyethylene terephthalate)*

IS USED IN . . . . microwavable food trays; salad dressing, soft drink, water, and juice bottles

STATUS . . . . hard to clean; absorbs bacteria and flavors; avoid reusing

IS RECYCLED TO MAKE . . carpet, furniture, new containers, Polar fleece

HDPE

Number 2 • *HDPE (high-density polyethylene)*

IS USED IN . . . . household cleaner and shampoo bottles, milk jugs, yogurt tubs

STATUS . . . . transmits no known chemicals into food

IS RECYCLED TO MAKE . . detergent bottles, fencing, floor tiles, pens

V

Number 3 • *V or PVC (vinyl)*

IS USED IN . . . . cooking oil bottles, clear food packaging, mouthwash bottles

STATUS . . . . is believed to contain phalates that interfere with hormonal development; avoid

IS RECYCLED TO MAKE . . cables, mudflaps, paneling, roadway gutters

LDPE

Number 4 • *LDPE (low-density polyethylene)*

IS USED IN . . . . bread and shopping bags, carpet, clothing, furniture

STATUS . . . . transmits no known chemicals into food

IS RECYCLED TO MAKE . . envelopes, floor tiles, lumber, trash-can liners

PP

Number 5 • *PP (polypropylene)*

IS USED IN . . . . ketchup bottles, medicine and syrup bottles, drinking straws

STATUS . . . . transmits no known chemicals into food

IS RECYCLED TO MAKE . . battery cables, brooms, ice scrapers, rakes

PS

Number 6 • *PS (polystyrene)*

IS USED IN . . . . disposable cups and plates, egg cartons, take-out containers

STATUS . . . . is believed to leach styrene, a possible human carcinogen, into food; avoid

IS RECYCLED TO MAKE . . foam packaging, insulation, light switchplates, rulers

OTHER

Number 7 • *Other (miscellaneous)*

IS USED IN . . . . 3- and 5-gallon water jugs, nylon, some food containers

STATUS . . . . contains bisphenol A, which has been linked to heart disease and obesity; avoid

IS RECYCLED TO MAKE . . custom-made products

Heat Values

Firewood

High Heat Value

1 cord = 200–250 gallons of fuel oil

American beech
Apple
Ironwood
Red oak
Shagbark hickory
Sugar maple
White ash
White oak
Yellow birch

Medium Heat Value

1 cord = 150–200 gallons of fuel oil

American elm
Black cherry
Douglas fir
Red maple
Silver maple
Tamarack
White birch

Low Heat Value

1 cord = 100–150 gallons of fuel oil

Aspen
Cottonwood
Hemlock
Lodgepole pine
Red alder
Redwood
Sitka spruce
Western red cedar
White pine

Fuels

Fuel	BTU (approx.)	Unit of Measure
Oil	141,000	Gallon
Coal	31,000	Pound
Natural gas	1,000	Cubic foot
Steam	1,000	Cubic foot
Electricity	3,413	Kilowatt-hour
Gasoline	124,000	Gallon

How Many Trees in a Cord of Wood?

DIAMETER OF TREE (4½' ABOVE GROUND)	NUMBER OF TREES (PER CORD)
4"	50
6"	20
8"	10
10"	6
12"	4
14"	3

A Few Clues About Cords of Wood

■ A cord of wood is a pile of logs 4 feet wide by 4 feet high by 8 feet long.

■ A cord of wood may contain from 77 to 96 cubic feet of wood.

■ The larger the unsplit logs, the larger the gaps, with fewer cubic feet of wood actually in the cord.

■ A cord of air-dried, dense hardwood weighs about 2 tons (4,000 pounds).

■ From one cord of firewood, you could make 7,500,000 toothpicks, 460,000 personal checks, 30 Boston rockers, or 12 dining room tables with each table seating eight.

Metric Conversion

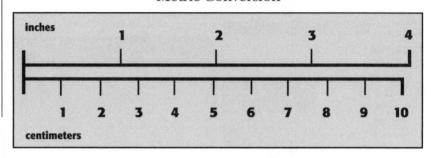

U.S. measure	x this number =	metric equivalent	metric measure	x this number =	U.S. equivalent
inch	2.54	centimeter		0.39	inch
foot	30.48	centimeter		0.033	foot
yard	0.91	meter		1.09	yard
mile	1.61	kilometer		0.62	mile
square inch	6.45	square centimeter		0.15	square inch
square foot	0.09	square meter		10.76	square foot
square yard	0.8	square meter		1.2	square yard
square mile	0.84	square kilometer		0.39	square mile
acre	0.4	hectare		2.47	acre
ounce	28.0	gram		0.035	ounce
pound	0.45	kilogram		2.2	pound
short ton (2,000 pounds)	0.91	metric ton		1.10	short ton
ounce	30.0	milliliter		0.034	ounce
pint	0.47	liter		2.1	pint
quart	0.95	liter		1.06	quart
gallon	3.8	liter		0.26	gallon

■ If you know the U.S. measurement and want to convert it to metric, multiply it by the number in the left shaded column (example: 1 inch equals 2.54 centimeters). If you know the metric measurement, multiply it by the number in the right shaded column (example: 2 meters equals 2.18 yards).

Where Do You Fit in Your Family Tree?

■ Technically it's known as consanguinity; that is, the quality or state of being related by blood or descended from a common ancestor. These relationships are shown below for the genealogy of six generations of one family. *–family tree information courtesy Frederick H. Rohles*

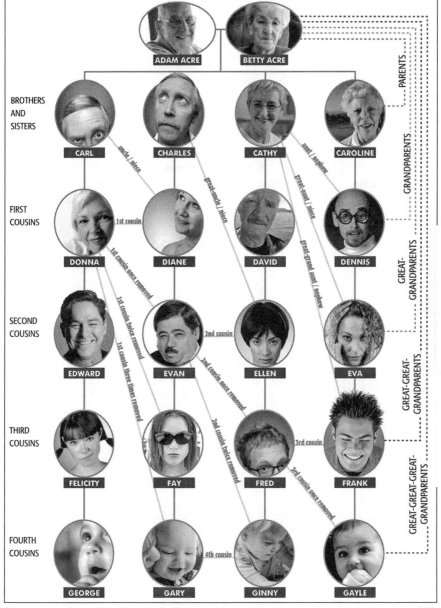

The Golden Rule
(It's true in all faiths.)

Brahmanism:
This is the sum of duty: Do naught unto others which would cause you pain if done to you.
Mahabharata 5:1517

Buddhism:
Hurt not others in ways that you yourself would find hurtful.
Udana-Varga 5:18

Christianity:
All things whatsoever ye would that men should do to you, do ye even so to them; for this is the law and the prophets.
Matthew 7:12

Confucianism:
Surely it is the maxim of loving-kindness: Do not unto others what you would not have them do unto you.
Analects 15:23

Islam:
No one of you is a believer until he desires for his brother that which he desires for himself.
Sunnah

Judaism:
What is hateful to you, do not to your fellowman. That is the entire Law; all the rest is commentary.
Talmud, Shabbat 31a

Taoism:
Regard your neighbor's gain as your own gain and your neighbor's loss as your own loss.
T'ai Shang Kan Ying P'ien

Zoroastrianism:
That nature alone is good which refrains from doing unto another whatsoever is not good for itself.
Dadistan-i-dinik 94:5

–courtesy Elizabeth Pool

Famous Last Words

■ **Waiting, are they? Waiting, are they? Well—let 'em wait.**
(To an attending doctor who attempted to comfort him by saying, "General, I fear the angels are waiting for you.")
–Ethan Allen, American Revolutionary general, d. February 12, 1789

■ **A dying man can do nothing easy.**
–Benjamin Franklin, American statesman, d. April 17, 1790

■ **Now I shall go to sleep. Good night.**
–Lord George Byron, English writer, d. April 19, 1824

■ **Is it the Fourth?**
–Thomas Jefferson, 3rd U.S. president, d. July 4, 1826

■ **Thomas Jefferson—still survives . . .**
(Actually, Jefferson had died earlier that same day.)
–John Adams, 2nd U.S. president, d. July 4, 1826

■ **Friends, applaud. The comedy is finished.**
–Ludwig van Beethoven, German-Austrian composer, d. March 26, 1827

■ **Moose . . . Indian . . .**
–Henry David Thoreau, American writer, d. May 6, 1862

■ **Go on, get out—last words are for fools who haven't said enough.**
(To his housekeeper, who urged him to tell her his last words so she could write them down for posterity.)
–Karl Marx, German political philosopher, d. March 14, 1883

■ **Is it not meningitis?**
–Louisa M. Alcott, American writer, d. March 6, 1888

■ **How were the receipts today at Madison Square Garden?**
–P. T. Barnum, American entrepreneur, d. April 7, 1891

■ **Turn up the lights, I don't want to go home in the dark.**
–O. Henry (William Sidney Porter), American writer, d. June 4, 1910

■ **Get my swan costume ready.**
–Anna Pavlova, Russian ballerina, d. January 23, 1931

■ **Is everybody happy? I want everybody to be happy. I know I'm happy.**
–Ethel Barrymore, American actress, d. June 18, 1959

■ **I'm bored with it all.**
(Before slipping into a coma. He died nine days later.)
–Winston Churchill, English statesman, d. January 24, 1965

■ **You be good. You'll be in tomorrow. I love you.**
–Alex, highly intelligent African Gray parrot, d. September 6, 2007